Social Policy in the Welfare State

George T. Martin, Jr.

Montclair State College
Upper Montclair, New Jersey

Prentice Hall, Englewood Cliffs, New Jersey 07632

Library of Congress Cataloging-in-Publication Data

Martin, George T.
   Social policy in the welfare state/George T. Martin, Jr.
     p.   cm.
   Includes bibliographical references.
   ISBN 0-13-816935-7
   1. Human services—United States. 2. United States—Social
policy—1980– 3. Welfare State. I Title.
HV95.M274   1990
361.6′1′0973—dc20   89–22788
                                                       CIP

Editorial /production supervision
  and interior design: PATRICK WALSH
Page layout: MARK STANFORD
Cover design: BEN SANTORA
Manufacturing buyer: CAROL BYSTROM/ED O'DOUGHERTY

© 1990 by Prentice-Hall, Inc.
A Division of Simon & Schuster
Englewood Cliffs, New Jersey 07632

Printed in the United States of America

10 9 8 7 6 5 4 3 2 1

ISBN 0-13-816935-7

Prentice-Hall International (UK) Limited, *London*
Prentice-Hall of Australia Pty. Limited, *Sydney*
Prentice-Hall Canada Inc., *Toronto*
Prentice-Hall Hispanoamericana, S.A., *Mexico*
Prentice-Hall of India Private Limited, *New Delhi*
Prentice-Hall of Japan, Inc., *Tokyo*
Simon & Schuster Asia Pte. Ltd., *Singapore*
Editora Prentice-Hall do Brasil, Ltda., *Rio de Janeiro*

To Joanna Foley, Tom Martin, and Willodean Martin
for their caring

Contents

List of Abbreviations   ix

Preface   xiii

1 Introduction   1

2 The Contours of Social Policy   7

An Interpretation of Social Policy,   7
   Social Policy and Economics,   10
The Welfare State,   11
Social Science,   14
Social Practice,   15

3 The Historical Development of Social Policy   20

Social Policy in History,   21
Social Practice in History,   25

Social Policy and Social Practice in U.S. History, 26
  Social Practitioner at Work:
  Bertha Capen Reynolds (1885-1978), 28

4 Comparative Perspectives on Social Policy   32
  Rich and Poor Nations, 32
  Welfare States, 35
    Social Welfare Expenditure, 35
    Income Distribution, 36
    Sources of Welfare State Variation, 37
  Welfare States and Socialist Nations, 39

5 Income Security   43
  Income Security and Social Policy, 45
    Income Security Programs, 46
    Changes in Income Security, 48
    The Social Wage, 50
  Income Redistribution, 51
  Poverty, 54
    The Working Poor, 56
    The Feminization of Poverty, 57
  Social Policy Issues, 61
    Family Allowance, 61
    Socialized Child Support, 62
    Workfare, 63
    Full Employment, 65
    Strengthening Current Programs, 66
      The Family Support Act of 1988, 68
  Social Practice, 69
    Social Practitioner at Work: Janet Johnson, 73

6 The Family   82
  The Family in Transition, 84
    Changes in Family Functions, 85
    Changes in Family Composition and Structure, 87
  Social Needs of the Family, 88
  Toward a Family Policy, 90
    Family Allowance, 95
  Social Practice, 96
    Social Practitioner at Work: Michael Vanzetti, 98

7 The School   106

The School in Society, 107
  Allocation and Equality, 108
  Excellence and Universality, 110
The School and Social Policy, 112
  Literacy, 113
  Schools as Child-Care and Health-Care Centers, 114
Social Practice, 117
  Social Practitioner at Work: Terry Murphy, 119

8 Health   123

Rationing, 124
The Medical-Industrial Complex, 128
  Corporatization, 129
  Medicalization, 132
Policy Issues, 135
  AIDS, 136
  Health Security, 140
  An Ecological Strategy, 142
Social Practice, 145
  Social Practitioner at Work: Hannah Engel, 147
Demedicalization, 149
  Holistic Health, 150
  Women and Health, 151
  Work and Health, 155

9 The City   164

Social Science, Social Policy, and the City, 165
Urban Transformation, 167
  The Corporate City, 167
  City and Suburb, 170
  The Fiscal Crisis, 172
Homelessness, 173
  The Homeless Population, 173
  Causes of Homelessness, 174
    Gentrification, 175
    Deinstitutionalization, 176
  Homelessness and Social Policy, 178
    The Conservative Legacy 180
Social Practice, 183
  Social Practitioner at Work: Maureen Howard, 183

Social Policy and the Future of the City,   186
   Public Housing,   187
   Assessing the Quality of City Life,   189
   The Mismatch Problems,   190
The City and Social Change,   192

10   Social Research and Social Policy   202
Applied Sociology,   203
   Identification of Social Need,   205
   Organizational Behavior,   208
   Evaluation,   211
   New Directions for Applied Sociology,   215
Social Practice,   217
   Social Practitioner at Work: Ellen Duane,   218
   Practice, Research, and Policy,   220
      Personal Practice,   221
      Organizational Practice,   222
      Collective Practice,   224

11   Social Change and Social Policy   229
Social Change and Social Policy in the Welfare State,   229
   The Issue of Resources,   232
      Social Welfare Pluralism,   233
Social Planning,   234
Concluding Comments,   238

Name Index   245

Subject Index   248

List of Abbreviations

AA	Alcoholics Anonymous
AAA	Area Agency on Aging
ACORN	Association of Community Organizations for Reform Now
AFDC	Aid to Families with Dependent Children
AIDS	Acquired Immune Deficiency Syndrome
AMA	American Medical Association
ARC	Aids-Related Complex
AZT	Azidothymidine
BLS	Bureau of Labor Statistics
CAD	Coronary Artery Disease
CAT	Computerized Axial Tomography
CBA	Cost Benefit Analysis
CBD	Central Business District
CCC	Civilian Conservation Corps
CCU	Coronary Care Unit

CDC	Center for Disease Control
CETA	Comprehensive Employment and Training Act
CIO	Congress of Industrial Organizations
CMHC	Community Mental Health Center
COS	Charity Organization Society
DHHS	Department of Health and Human Services
DHUD	Department of Housing and Urban Development
DI	Disposable Income
DR	Doctor
DRG	Diagnostic Related Groups
DYFS	Division of Youth and Family Services
EITC	Earned Income Tax Credit
EPA	Environmental Protection Agency
ESEA	Elementary and Secondary Education Act
FHA	Federal Housing Authority
FSA	Family Support Act
GA	General Assistance
GAO	Government Accounting Office
GDP	Gross Domestic Product
GNP	Gross National Product
HIV	Human Immunodeficiency Virus
HMO	Health Maintenance Organization
IRS	Internal Revenue Service
ISR	Institute for Survey Research
IV	Intravenous
LPN	Licensed Practical Nurse
MBD	Minimal Brain Dysfunction
MD	Doctor of Medicine
MIC	Maternal and Infant Clinic
MMPI	Male Marriageable Pool Index
MPH	Miles per Hour
MSW	Master of Social Work
NDEA	National Defense Education Act
NHS	National Health Service
NICU	Neonatal Intensive Care Unit

NIOSH	National Institute of Occupational Safety and Health
NIT	Negative Income Tax
NMU	National Maritime Union
NORC	National Opinion Research Center
OASDI	Old Age, Survivors, and Disability Insurance
OBRA	Omnibus Budget Reconciliation Act
OECD	Organisation for Economic Co-operation and Development
OSHA	Occupational Safety and Health Administration
PhD	Doctor of Philosophy
PPBS	Program Planning and Budgeting System
PQL	Physical Quality of Life
PSID	Panel Study of Income Dynamics
RN	Registered Nurse
SCI	Secondary Consumer Income
SDR	Social Dependency Ratio
SIDS	Sudden Infant Death Syndrome
SIE	Survey of Income and Education
SIPP	Survey of Income and Program Participation
SSI	Supplemental Security Income
STD	Sexually Transmitted Disease
SWE	Social Welfare Expenditure
TOPR	Termination of Parental Rights
UFW	United Farm Workers
UI	Unemployment Insurance
UK	United Kingdom
UN	United Nations
UNESCO	UN Educational, Scientific, and Cultural Organization
US	United States
USSR	Union of Soviet Socialist Republics
WASP	White Anglo-Saxon Protestant
WHO	World Health Organization
YPLL	Years of Potential Life Lost

Preface

This book is a sociological and critical analysis of Welfare State social policy. We give extraordinary attention to the articulation of social policy with social practice. The work of social practitioners, especially social workers, community organizers, teachers, and nurses, is examined in some detail. Face-to-face interviews were conducted with six social practitioners; their various practices are featured in appropriate chapters. With one exception, their true identities and those of their workplaces and cities are concealed in order to protect their privacy and that of the people with whom they work. The exception is Maureen Howard, who chose to allow the use of her real name and that of her agency. Her social practice with homeless people is featured in Chapter 9.

This book is for graduate and undergraduate students of the helping professions and of the social sciences. Our intent is to provide a framework for understanding the current status of Welfare State social policy and social practice. While our focus is on the United States, we include ample consideration of other Welfare States and other types of nations, notably socialist and Third World countries.

We exclude one policy area, criminology, that is often included within the parameters of social policy. We do so because criminology is an established separate subfield of social science and because it is not primarily concerned with the welfare of citizens. The social policy areas that we cover—income security, the family, education, health care, and housing—are the central concerns of the Welfare State. Related policy areas that are covered, although not in separate chapters, include the environment (especially in Chapters 8 and 9), mental health (Chapters 8 and 9), children (Chapters 6, 7, and 8), and transportation (Chapter 9). In our coverage of social policy areas, we highlight contemporary issues and problems, including the feminization of poverty, child care, literacy, AIDS, and homelessness.

The book divides logically into three sections. In the beginning section, Chapters 1-4, we introduce and define social policy and then analyze it from historical and comparative perspectives. In the middle section, Chapters 5-9, we analyze income security, family, education, health, and urban policies. Finally, in the third and last section, Chapters 10 and 11, we return to a general discussion of social policy and focus on the relationships between social research and social policy and between social change and social policy.

The material in this book rests at the intersection of three substantive fields: Social science, social work (or social administration) and social policy. We focus on the connections among research, practice, and policy. We analyze on three levels: The society or nation state (macro), the organization or institution (middle), and the individual (micro) levels. We have integrated the three domains—research, practice, and policy—and the three levels of analysis—societal, organizational, and individual—in each chapter. Our analysis targets a number of auspicious social groups for particular attention: workers, the poor, women, and minority groups. These groups bear the brunt of the failures of Welfare State social policy. They also present the greatest unmet social needs and offer, through their political mobilization, the greatest potential for progressive social change.

There are a number of people who merit acknowledgment for helping me in the process of writing this book. However, because I did not always heed their worthy advice, I alone bear full responsibility for the final product. I include the names of only those people who provided direct and material assistance; first, those who read various drafts and who provided the saving comments that led me to the appropriate voice for the book. As well as providing this essential commentary, these four persons freely extended valued social and emotional support: Joanna Foley, Peter Freund, Jack Hammond, and Laura Kramer. Second, I acknowledge generous bibliographical assistance from the reference librarians at Sprague Library, Montclair State College—especially Eduardo Gil, Kevin Prendergast, Luis Rodriguez, and Patricia Sanders. A third source of material support was Montclair State's Separately Budgeted Research Program, which provided awards of released time for research and writing. Two people at Prentice Hall merit special thanks: Bill Webber for encouraging me to do this book and Nancy Roberts for helping me to bring it to a satisfactory and speedy conclusion. Finally, I acknowledge timely and cooperative help of the following persons in the last stages of work on this book: Patrick Walsh of Prentice Hall's production staff; Jean Margolis of the Sociology Department staff and the librarians at the University of California, Berkeley.

Many other people who helped me in important but indirect ways remain nameless. My perspectives on social policy were sharpened by exchanges with colleagues, especially in the Women's Studies Program, the African American Studies Program, and Local 1904 of the American Federation of Teachers. My students, especially those in my Helping Professions and Institutions classes, continually revitalized me with their inspiring and undaunted idealism. To my study group I acknowledge help in traversing the intellectual history of Marxism and in integrating social practice and theory. To my men's group I acknowledge support in an ongoing effort to reshape my masculine roles within a feminist and socialist framework. To my professional helpers, I acknowledge emotional, spiritual, and physical therapy. It is fitting that this book, which is at heart about mutual caring, was written with the help of the care that I received from all these people.

Finally, it is my hope that this book adds to all the efforts that carry on the struggle to create a more just world, for I do believe that the correct pursuit of social policy is social justice.

1

Introduction

Turn him to any cause of policy the Gordian Knot of it he will unloose.
Shakespeare, *Henry V*, 1599

Social policy is action to influence the course of societal change and to allot societal resources among various groups. Prominent among these resources are the goods and services of the Welfare State. The private sector plays a secondary role in social policy. Its influence is most noticeable in the implementation of social policy—through the operation of private institutions and programs, such as many hospitals, social welfare agencies, and the United Way. These are relevant to any analysis of social policy, but it is our contention that the state dominates social policy in modern societies, even capitalist ones. The very existence of the Welfare State is a manifestation of this dominance.

The state's dominance of social policy is rooted in its command of social welfare expenditure (SWE). SWE comprises four major categories: health, income maintenance, education, and welfare services. In 1972–1985 public SWE averaged 18.2 percent of the gross national product (GNP) in the United States, somewhat more than double private SWE, which averaged 8.8 percent of GNP (Kerns and Glanz, 1988, p. 4). Several qualifications of this data make the preeminence of the public sector even more pronounced. First,

1

the private sector is divided between a nonprofit sphere and a for-profit one, and only the for-profit sphere conforms to the sense of the word *private* that refers to the operations of the capitalist market. Second, some fraction of private-sector expenditure is actually public money (Merriam, 1964, pp. 9–10). The fact that the public sector provides some financing means that it exerts policy influence over the private sector.

The domain of Welfare State social policy is a growing sector of contemporary society. A common measure of its magnitude is public expenditure for social welfare. By this measure, Welfare State social policy expanded considerably in the mid-twentieth century. In 1927 federal, state, and local government SWE represented only about one-fifteenth of all government expenditure and less than 1 percent of GNP (Fox et al., 1981, p. 3). In 1985 public SWE constituted more than half of all public outlays and 18.5 percent of GNP.

Currently, Welfare State social policy is an arena of intensified political conflict among competing classes, ideologies, and interest groups. This is evident in the rising clamor of the debate over what to do about such issues as the escalating costs of health care and increased homelessness. It is also apparent in the proliferation of groups, such as persons with acquired immune deficiency syndrome (AIDS), that place righteous demands on social resources. Finally, the debate is fueled by the emergence of new categories of people, including female householders, who also claim resources from society. The Welfare State has a presumed obligation to meet these claims because by its definition it is responsible for the minimum well-being of all citizens.

At the same time that demands on the Welfare State have increased, it has lost the broad consensual support that was based on its original successes and on the economic growth of 1945–1970. The present crossroads in Welfare State social policy is marked by several instructive signposts:

1. *Economic decline.* Since the early 1970s, the world capitalist economy has been faltering. For example, in the United States, between 1973 and 1986, the average real (corrected for inflation) weekly earnings of workers fell 13.8 percent. This economic decline has not been shared equally. On the one hand, a minority of well-off citizens have gained despite the overall decline. On the other hand, the decline has produced more and greater social needs among the majority of citizens. Thus between 1973 and 1986 the portion of the U.S. population living in poverty rose from 11.1 percent to 13.6 percent.

2. *Fiscal crisis.* Partly because of this economic decline, governments take in relatively less revenue from taxes than they did in the past. At the same time, the decline has raised the costs of government programs for human needs. The expense of providing for growing numbers of poor people when added to the immense burden of defense expenditure has enmeshed some governments in a fiscal crisis: expenses exceed income, creating more debt, greater budgetary competition between warfare and welfare expenditures, and increased pressure for belt tightening.

3. *Demographic change.* The populations of Welfare States are aging. Between 1970 and 1986 the portion of the U.S. population aged sixty-five and over increased from 9.8 percent to 12.1 percent. This demographic change adds to the pressure for expansion of the Welfare State, for the elderly are its principal beneficiaries and they have extraordinary social needs.

Among Welfare States the most common outcome of the political struggles over social policy has been a conservative ascendency. Conservative political parties and leaders have been successful in blaming economic problems on the evils of "big government" (in its welfare, not its warfare function) and the sloth of "welfare recipients." In this way those most harmed by economic stagnation and fiscal crisis—the poor and the working class— have been further victimized by retrenchment in Welfare State social policy from the mid-1970s onward. Between 1960 and 1975 the rate of growth of social expenditure (in real terms) outpaced the rate of growth of gross domestic product (GDP) by 4.6 percent in the United States. In 1975–1981, however, the rate of growth of social expenditure only kept pace with the rate of growth of GDP. Of fifteen Welfare States examined, only five had accelerated social expenditure growth in 1975–1981 over that in 1960–1975 (Dumont, 1987, p. 4). The Welfare State expanded in the post-World War II period of economic growth, which provided a material basis for prowelfare alliances led by organized labor. These alliances weakened in the face of economic stagnation, while the antilabor/antiwelfare coalition gained.

Conservative retrenchment by political leaders such as Ronald Reagan in the United States and Margaret Thatcher in the United Kingdom was facilitated by growing popular distrust of the Welfare State. The new disillusionment comes principally from two sources (Offe, 1988). One is upwardly mobile persons, including a fraction of the working class, who defected from the collectivist ideas of the Welfare State—despite the fact that they have been major beneficiaries of Welfare State social policy. This group may have acted out of a desire to pull up the ladder after they climbed the rungs to a middle-class life, however modest. The other source of disillusionment with the Welfare State is a more general group: those who have come to distrust the power of the state and its abuses in the lives of individuals. It was the desertion of the Welfare State by these former supporters that allowed the conservative retrenchment.

Our analysis of social policy is based in Marxist approaches that stress the dual nature of the Welfare State (Gough, 1979; O'Connor, 1973)—an unstable, contentious convergence of the interest of the capitalist class (owners of the production system) in controlling, training, and stabilizing the working class (wage earners), and the interest of the working class in mitigating economic hardships. Welfare State benefits are partly the fruits of working-class struggle, and they provide unemployed, underemployed, intermittently employed, retired, disabled, and poor workers with subsistence support. We extend Marxist analyses by focusing on the humanistic and social practice aspects of Welfare State social policy. Thus, in addition to the role of class conflict, we give special attention to the following social actors:

1. *Women.* Women play a singular role as the disproportionate majority of constituents and providers of Welfare State social policy.

2. *Organizations.* Processes such as increased societal scale and complexity, bureaucratization, and professionalization are determinant influences on social policy. For example, these processes spurred the creation of the specialized social policy domains of education, health, housing, and welfare. At the same time, these processes make it more difficult to achieve coherent social policy because various bureaucracies and professions strive against one another to gain their parochial objectives.

3. *Practitioners.* Welfare State social policy is realized through a social practice comprising the relationships between Welfare State workers and beneficiaries. Social practice is the sum of these relationships; it is sited at the intersection of the Welfare State and society.

Today, social policy and social practice are at center stage in a political struggle over the future of the Welfare State. The result of this struggle will help to determine the outcome of the Welfare State's main predicament: more people than ever depend on it at a time when its resources are straitened. The right (conservatives) would resolve this predicament by substantially reducing the Welfare State's resources and reach; transferring Welfare State activities to the private sector (privatization) is one means of doing this. Murray's (1984) critique of the War on Poverty represents an intellectual basis for conservative social policy. The middle (liberals) would resolve the predicament by modestly reducing the scope of the Welfare State. Liberals are willing to tolerate Welfare State cutbacks in order to meet the exigencies of the fiscal crisis. They would also make reforms in the Welfare State by introducing more market approaches, such as workfare. Senator Daniel Patrick Moynihan's (1986) ideas are representative of the liberal position on the Welfare State.

The left (socialists) would expand the Welfare State and would pay for it by reductions in defense spending and cuts in subsidies for the well-to-do, including their tax advantages. Socialists defended the Welfare State against Reagan administration cutbacks (Block et al., 1987) in the 1980s, and, in fact, advocated increasing the level of benefits and extending the coverage of programs by implementing policies such as national health insurance. In addition to their charge that the Welfare State does not go far enough in its support of all citizens, socialists criticize it for being authoritarian and impersonal in its interactions with citizens and for being ineffective in redistributing income and wealth.

The social practitioners who work in the Welfare State have a vital interest in the outcome of the current political struggle. These practitioners include social workers and other helping professionals, whether they administrate, consult, organize, counsel, research, study, or teach. For years they have been on the defensive against the dismantling efforts of the Reagan administration and the consolidating activities of liberalism. They find too little support in an impoverished American socialism that is often isolated, divided, and ineffectual. Hence the weariness and apprehension of many social welfare workers, as their caseloads mount and their resources dwindle.

This book assesses the Reagan legacy in various areas of Welfare State social policy. The Reagan administration's conservative policies and practices aimed to unravel the web of programs that constitute the Welfare State and to replace it with nothing, or with scaled-down private programs. Contrary to conventional wisdom, the Reagan administration was not antistate, just anti-Welfare State. The role of the state (and its fiscal crisis) actually expanded under Reagan; it was the nature of, and the beneficiaries of, state intervention that changed. Warfare interests benefited at the expense of welfare interests, and the rich gained at the expense of workers and the poor.

Ultimately, Reagan's attack on the Welfare State was, like many of his other policies, more successful in appearance than in substance. In the words of one Reagan aide, he "only scraped around the edges of the Welfare State, leaving it largely intact" (Weinraub, 1986, p. 16). Indeed, the principal Reagan legacy for the Welfare State may lie in what was not done rather than in what was done. As Heclo (1986, pp. 60–61) noted:

> Reaganism urges Americans to dream dreams but these are necessarily dreams of private advantage, not public accomplishment. Any ideology of negative government is likely to fall prey in the history books to the collective tasks left undone, and an ideology that simultaneously reasserts public moralism is especially vulnerable to charges of both neglect and hypocrisy.

The Reagan legacy of neglect is apparent in the major social problems, including homelessness and poverty, that were allowed to worsen in the 1980s.

The premise of this book is that Welfare State social policy and social practice survived the Reagan years, impaired but largely intact. Although the right is silent about it, the fact is that advanced capitalism is untenable without the Welfare State. Absent Welfare State social policy, capitalist nations would deteriorate into unresolved economic crisis, social conflict, and political anarchy (Offe, 1984, p. 153).

Throughout our analysis various terms are used for the different actors involved in Welfare State social policy and social practice. One term that presents difficulty is *client*, the person for whom Welfare State social policy and social practice are ostensibly organized. Client implies passive consumption and denotes that one is an object of action rather than an actor (Leonard, 1983, p. 80). A better term would be *constituent*, which connotes accountability of the Welfare State to the interests and standards of its beneficiaries (Edmonds, 1984, p. 57). Consistent with our democratic socialist vision, we argue that the Welfare State should maximize empowerment and self-activity on the part of citizens. Thus, although *client* is the generally used term for the recipient of Welfare State programs, we use it reluctantly and prefer alternatives whenever feasible.

Our methodology is critical analysis. Informed judgment is used as a tool to dissect social policy and social practice in the Welfare State. Understanding is the goal of critical analysis, and it is achieved both by examination and by evaluation. This means that definite positions will be taken on the social policy issues analyzed in this book. Our analysis aspires to the standard enunciated about a century and a half ago by Marx (1972, p. 8): "I am speaking of a ruthless criticism of everything existing, ruthless in two senses: The criticism must not be afraid of its own conclusions, nor of conflict with the powers that be."

REFERENCES

Note: Unless otherwise specified, data sources used throughout the book are in the public domain: the *Statistical Abstract of the United States* and other government publications.

Block, Fred, et al., eds. 1987. *The Mean Season: The Attack on the Welfare State.* New York: Pantheon.

Dumont, J. P. 1987. "The Evolution of Social Security During the Recession." *International Labour Review* 126:1–19.

Edmonds, Ronald. 1984. "A Theory and Design of Social Service Reform." *Social Policy* 15:57–64.

Fox, Kenneth, et al. 1981. "Introduction: The Nature of the Public Sector." Pp. 1–9 in *Crisis in the Public Sector: A Reader,* ed. Kenneth Fox et al. New York: Monthly Review Press.

Gough, Ian. 1979. *The Political Economy of the Welfare State.* London: Macmillan.

Heclo, Hugh. 1986. "Reaganism and the Search for a Public Philosophy." Pp. 31–63 in *Perspectives on the Reagan Years,* ed. John L. Palmer. Washington, DC: The Urban Institute Press.

Kerns, Wilmer L., and Milton P. Glanz. 1988. "Private Social Welfare Expenditures, 1972–85." *Social Security Bulletin* 51:3–10.

Leonard, Peter. 1983. "Marxism, the Individual and the Welfare State." Pp. 64–82 in *Approaches to Welfare,* ed. Philip Bean and Stewart MacPherson. London: Routledge & Kegan Paul.

Marx, Karl. 1972 {1844}. "For a Ruthless Criticism of Everything Existing." Letter to Arnold Ruge. Pp. 7–10 in *The Marx-Engels Reader,* ed. Robert C. Tucker. New York: W. W. Norton.

Merriam, Ida C. 1964. "Social Welfare Expenditures, 1963-64." *Social Security Bulletin* 27:3–14.

Moynihan, Daniel Patrick. 1986. *Family and Nation.* New York: Harcourt Brace Jovanovich.

Murray, Charles. 1984. *Losing Ground: American Social Policy 1950–1980.* New York: Basic Books.

O'Connor, James. 1973. *The Fiscal Crisis of the State.* New York: St. Martin's Press.

Offe, Claus. 1984. *Contradictions of the Welfare State,* ed. John Keane. Cambridge, MA: MIT Press.

——. 1988. "Democracy Against the Welfare State? Structural Foundations of Neoconservative Political Opportunities." *Responsibility, Rights, and Welfare: The Theory of the Welfare State.* Boulder, CO: Westview Press.

Weinraub, Bernard. 1986. "The Reagan Legacy." *The New York Times Magazine,* June 22, pp. 12–21.

2

The Contours of Social Policy

*There is no art that hath bin more canker'd in her principles, more soyl'd,
and slubber'd with aphorisming pedantry than the art of policie.*
Milton, *Of Reformation*, 1641

Welfare State social policy is subject to different and ambiguous meanings. It
has been defined variously as the norms of society, the enforcement of its laws,
the administration of its social programs, or the actions of its government. In
this chapter we define social policy and social practice and analyze their
relationships to economics, the Welfare State, and social science. But first we
turn to the question of what social policy is.

AN INTERPRETATION OF SOCIAL POLICY

Welfare State social policy refers to the course of action pursued by the state
to shape society and to allocate its resources. The course of action flows from
a strategy that is based on an idea of how society should be arranged. The
resources allocated through social policy are public goods, to which citizens
have a presumed reasonable claim. The distinctive feature of Welfare State so-

cial policy is that access to its resources depends on political status (being an entitled citizen) rather than on market status (having money to purchase benefits). The major limitation of the market provision of welfare is that access to resources depends on income, which is unequally distributed (Rose, 1986, pp. 34–35).

Our definition of social policy focuses on the public sector for several reasons. One reason, discussed in Chapter 1, is that the state dominates social welfare expenditure—in the United States, by a two-to-one ratio over the private sector. Another is that social policy came of age in the present era of the Welfare State. Although a major Reagan policy initiative was privatization of state functions, social policy remains overwhelmingly dominated by the state. Because of the sheer scale and complexity of modern society, the state alone is capable of effective society-wide policy. Additionally, what Offe (1984, p. 263) has called the state monopoly of social policy grew out of the development of capitalism. Capitalism undermined and atomized traditional institutions, such as the local community, guilds, and religion, that had previously determined social policy.

The private sector, particularly foundations, institutes, and other enclaves of intellectuals, remains an important source of ideas for social policy, but one that is increasingly state funded and state oriented. The nonprofit sphere of the private sector has another role besides generating ideas. Based on a review of research and an in-depth study of three nonprofit organizations, Ostrander (1985) found that they can be a source of reform in the Welfare State. The special innovative role that private, nonprofit agencies can play is to identify local community social needs, thereby contributing to democratizing and decentralizing the Welfare State.

The resources allocated through social policy are intended to meet social needs—to help people. Thus our definition of social policy includes the identification and satisfaction of social needs. Social needs, in turn, have two characteristics: (1) they are basic human needs and include adequate education, income, housing, and health care; and (2) they are relational or collective, expressing connections among individuals, with the Welfare State as intermediary. Social needs became citizen entitlements under the Welfare State. Previously, they were charitable goods dispensed by private parties who usually knew the supplicants. Now, through social policy and social practice in the Welfare State, "help is given to the stranger" (Wilensky and Lebeaux, 1965, p. 141). For example, all citizens have a presumptive entitlement to income security and it is provided through the state; it is not a discretionary and charitable gift delivered in the context of a personal relationship.

Resources are allocated through a number of state activities: (1) income transfers, both direct (benefits) and indirect (tax subsidies); (2) provision of in-kind goods, such as public housing; (3) delivery of services; (4) regulation and enforcement; and (5) socialization, through education and training. The final mechanism of resource allocation is meta-policy, by which policymaking structures are created or altered; the establishment of the U.S. Department of Education in 1979 is an example (MacRae, 1980). The common distinction between policy and program is more semantic than substantive in the Welfare State. Although sometimes useful conceptually, in practice it is difficult to separate policy from program (Hogwood and Peters, 1983, p. 19). The distinction may be necessary for administrative purposes, but it is not fruitful for our purposes.

Social policy's allocative function is contentious: it often means favoring some groups and disfavoring others. Conflict over the allocation of social resources is particularly acute in today's zero-sum economies (Blumberg, 1980; Thurow, 1980), for economic stagnation means that gains made by one group must be balanced by losses for another group. (In the past economic growth meant that different groups could gain at the same time.) Conflict about social policy is rooted in competition over which groups will have their social status or material position enhanced. In an analysis of social policy, one must always ask: Who benefits? Thus Reagan administration social policy favored the white majority over minority groups, men over women, business (capitalists) over labor (workers), and the rich over the poor.

Reagan's support of the New Right's social agenda was a conspicuous example of the allocation of resources. Here the resources were principally heightened status, visibility, and influence for the New Right's agenda. This agenda included opposition to the following: freedom of choice in reproduction (including abortion), the Equal Rights Amendment, homosexuality and gay rights, school busing for integration, sex education in public schools, affirmative action, full employment, national health insurance, the minimum wage, Social Security, and the Occupational Safety and Health Administration. On the other hand, the New Right favored censorship of school texts, classroom prayer, deregulation, and creationism (Ellerin and Kesten, 1981).

Our definition of social policy is fairly exclusive and distinguishes it from related subjects, including the following:

1. *Law*. Policy and law overlap. Laws are formal and specific rules, while policies are more informal and general plans. Policy can proceed with the law, absent the law, or even contrary to the law. For example, the Reagan administration's policy of denying certification to eligible Social Security disability applicants and of decertifying recipients continued after federal courts ruled that it was illegal.

2. *Administration*. Administration is specific and managerial, while policy is general and conceptual. Administration is the organizational implementation of policy. Policy sets the framework for administration, but administrative execution can enhance, inhibit, or distort policy. In short, while law formalizes the intent of policy, administration manages its implementation. However, administration cannot be neatly separated from policy. Like the distinction between policy and program, the distinction between administration and policy is more analytical than practical. Administrators have discretion in interpreting policy mandates; they can also initiate policy (Anderson, 1987, p. 23). Thus, in our view, social policy is not merely a mechanical instrument of the state. Rather, it is socially constructed (Van der Veen, 1988) through a conflictual fluid process involving

politicians, officials (bureaucrats and professionals), and the public. Furthermore, the public is not amorphous; instead, it is composed of competing groups, including social classes.

Social Policy and Economics

Social policy dominates public expenditure among the three major policy areas: social, economic, and national security. In every major Welfare State social policy expenditure ranks first, accounting for an average of over one-half of the total cost of public policies. Economic and national security policies each account for about one-fourth of public policy costs (Rose and Peters, 1978, p. 68).

Social policy's function of allocating resources within society is closely related to economics. Indeed, the distinctions between society and economy are considerably blurred in reality. Virtually all social policy has economic inputs and impacts. Social policy has been considered an instrument of economic interests at least since the Elizabethan poor laws, which favored landowners and emergent capitalists. Also, social policy frequently includes economic measures. This is especially true in what Titmuss (1968) called *fiscal welfare*, in which taxation is used to provide benefits for some groups. For example, the aged receive tax breaks that are, in effect, indirect income. Income redistribution (discussed in Chapter 5) is a Welfare State feature that is both economic and social in scope. Income taxes are progressive, meaning that tax rates are progressively higher as income increases. The Welfare State then redistributes some of this income downward, in the form of benefits for those with lower incomes.

The origins of the U.S. Welfare State in the 1930s illustrate the importance of economic and political considerations in the formulation of social policy. The principal goal of the New Deal's greatly increased social welfare expenditure was economic: to stimulate the economy by putting money into the hands of consumers. The new policies of the state—public works jobs and welfare payments—were a means of economic recovery from the Great Depression because they provided destitute people with disposable income. These Keynesian (stimulative) economic policies were also meant to defuse the political threat engendered by mass unemployment. Democratic Party policy was oriented to rewarding workers, who were its largest constituency.

The interplay of economics and politics in social policy is also demonstrated by the current situation of the aged:

1. The aged have become a larger proportion of the population, chiefly because of improved life expectancy and declining birth rates. Politically, this means that the aged are an influential constituency if organized. For example, mobilization of the aged forced Reagan to withdraw proposed Social Security cuts in the first year of his administration (Harpham, 1984).
2. The three-generation extended family has declined in favor of the nuclear family and other household configurations, so more older people live alone. Other social trends have contributed to this development: women's entry into the paid

labor force has reduced their abilities to take in their elderly parents; the increased geographical mobility of the population makes for greater distances between elderly parents and their offspring; a declining birth rate makes it less likely that offspring will be available to care for their elderly parents; and increased longevity adds years to the burden of care of the elderly. Together, these factors mean that many of the aged are socially isolated.

3. U.S. production relies more and more on machine and foreign (offshore) labor, creating larger surpluses of domestic labor, including the aged. This means that many of the aged cannot work and depend on financial assistance.

The growth in Social Security is a social policy response to these political, demographic, and economic changes.

THE WELFARE STATE

The mature Welfare State has three salient macro social policies: (1) provision of social entitlements to citizens; (2) public control of the economy; and (3) commitment to full employment (Therborn, 1986, p. 18). Welfare States vary in the extent to which they have developed these meta social policies, a subject that we discuss in Chapter 4.

The premise of Welfare State social policy is that citizens are entitled to social rights as well as to civil rights (such as freedom of speech) and political rights (such as voting). Social rights, according to Marshall (1981, p. 91), are integrative; they "are part of the mechanism by which the individual is absorbed into society (not isolated from it) and simultaneously draws upon and contributes to its collective welfare." Social rights vary considerably in strength in Welfare States. Thus, while education is a more fully legitimated social right in the United States, income security and health care are less so, and housing is only beginning to be defined as a social right.

It is important to understand that the Welfare State has a dual nature: it is both functional for and inimical to the interests of capitalism. Our analysis is not a rigidly functionalist and Marxist one, in which society is considered a puppet theater where the puppeteer is the capitalist ruling class and the Welfare State and the working class are its puppets (Sullivan, 1987, p. 149). Instead, we see less mechanical relationships. The relationship between capitalists and workers is, as noted by Adams (1985, p. 387), based on "a limited and unstable coincidence of interest between capital and labor in social policy, but also a fundamental antagonism." Social policy is the arena in which this fractious relationship is lived out, mediated by the Welfare State. While the Welfare State is not the puppet of capitalists, neither is it evenhanded. Quadagno's (1984, p. 646) analysis of the passage of the 1935 Social Security Act reveals the state's general bias: "The state mediates between various interest groups who have unequal access to power, negotiating compromises between class factions and incorporating working-class demands into legislation on capitalist terms."

In order to appreciate the dual nature of the Welfare State, it is necessary to outline the class structure of capitalism. For our purposes, there are two great classes: a small group of capitalists, who are the primary owners of the production apparatus (factories, land, money); and a large group of workers, who can be subdivided into salaried and professional workers (the middle class) and wage laborers. There are other groups, less central to our analysis: the upper-middle class (including managers), the lower-middle class (usually self-employed), and the lower class (unstably employed workers).

The Welfare State is functional for capitalism in the following ways:

1. The Welfare State reinforces the political power and economic interests of capitalists, that small percentage of the population that owns a greatly disproportionate share of society's resources. By moderating market excesses such as unemployment, the Welfare State picks up the tab for damages done by capitalism. Thus the Welfare State partially compensates for the *diswelfares* (Titmuss, 1968, p. 133) of capitalist production. As noted by Taylor-Gooby and Dale (1981, p. 226), "Thus much of what we refer to as the welfare state consists of mechanisms giving partial compensation for, or insurance against, the diswelfares of urban-industrial capitalism." These Welfare State mechanisms help to assure capitalist profits. The Welfare State protects profit accumulation by transferring certain costs of capitalist production (such as worker unemployment and disability) from the capitalist class to society as a whole. Additionally, the Welfare State helps to sustain capitalist profit by raising the purchasing power of citizens. Welfare State benefits are used by recipients to buy commodities in the market, which promotes aggregate demand and assures capitalists of a regular and major source of profits.

2. The Welfare State helps to discipline the working class. This is achieved primarily through education, training, and socialization that inculcate the values of private property and individualism and predicate the delivery of benefits on work discipline and on moral behavior appropriate to capitalism, such as self-reliance. Workfare programs (discussed in Chapter 5), in which public aid recipients may be forced to take any job at any wage, are an example.

3. The Welfare State maintains social stability by, among other mechanisms, providing minimal benefits and social attachments to people, such as unemployed workers, who might threaten stability. The benefits and attachments are in the form of programs and services, all of which serve to diffuse potential dissent. This is what Habermas (1975) called the *legitimation function* of the state. In order to successfully continue its rule, the government must seem fair and reasonable in its treatment of citizens. The Welfare State publicly demonstrates that the state is concerned about those citizens who are dispossessed by capitalism. If the state were perceived to be totally captured by capitalists, it would become the target of dissent, perhaps even revolution.

We have seen how the Welfare State sustains capitalism. Now we will look at some ways in which the Welfare State has proved to be contradictory to the interests of capitalist profit accumulation.

1. The Welfare State is essentially collectivist in orientation, which serves to undermine the individualistic ethic that is the basis for the capitalists' ideological

dominance. The Welfare State shifts the onus for many problems away from the individual and onto society. Unemployment is no longer viewed as an individual failure but as structural—caused by problems in the economy. Thus higher unemployment rates are experienced in the Snowbelt because of changes in technology and capital investment, and among African Americans because of discrimination and racism.

2. The Welfare State promotes an expanding social wage (discussed in Chapter 5) that tends to undermine the market discipline of wage labor. The social wage is the income received by workers from sources other than their labor—for example, social welfare benefits (Bowles and Gintis, 1982). Since this income source is not directly controlled by employers, the social wage blunts the sometimes harsh labor discipline on which capitalist production relies to secure profits. In effect, Welfare State benefits counteract the coercion of the market because a worker can survive without having to take a low-paying (and often dangerous) job. Thus, just as capitalism collectivizes production, the Welfare State collectivizes consumption.

The social wage benefits nonworkers as well as workers. In capitalist terms, nonworkers are nonproductive. These redundant workers fall into two general categories: (1) former workers in relatively stable jobs who are now retired, disabled, or unemployed; and (2) workers with histories of nonwork or work in unstable jobs (intermittently employed or employed at low wages). Historically, capitalism has segregated these groups of workers into those deserving (the first group) and those undeserving (the second group) of aid. The Welfare State continues this distinction, at least in the United States, in the difference between relatively generous, nonstigmatized social insurance programs such as Social Security and miserly, stigmatized public aid programs such as Aid to Families with Dependent Children (AFDC). However, the Welfare State ultimately undermines this traditional capitalist distinction by tending to adopt universal approaches such as the family allowance. In a family allowance (discussed in Chapters 5 and 6), no invidious distinction is made between deserving and undeserving workers.

There is one feature of the Welfare State that is ambiguous with regard to the interests of capital: its cost. These costs impede profit making by diverting some capital into Welfare State programs as well as by reducing labor discipline. However, the bulk of Welfare State costs is borne by the middle and working classes (through payroll taxes), which amounts to state-mandated recirculation of the resources of these classes. In addition, these costs tend to support capitalists by putting money into the hands of consumers.

The fact that the Welfare State is not merely functional to capitalism is demonstrated by the increasing (and at least implicitly anticapitalist) political role of Welfare State workers and beneficiaries. Organized into professional associations, unions, and interest groups, this sector of the population has been enhancing its ability to force social policy changes, if not its ability to generate social policy. The aged are perhaps the most notable example of this, in their growing political influence over Social Security.

SOCIAL SCIENCE

In addition to its economic and political dimensions, social policy has a social science aspect. Social policy and social practice are related to the generic sociological concepts of social control and social integration. The word *policy* is cousin to the word *police*, which means to regulate order in society. While Welfare State social policy and social practice have been based on moral rationales (a good and just society), they have come to use scientific justifications (a rational society) as well.

The articulation of social policy with social practice presents a unique opportunity for sociological insight. As Mills (1959) pointed out, the sociological imagination involves coupling the structural with the personal. Mills stressed the importance of connecting personal troubles to public issues. Unemployment became a public issue—called *structural unemployment*—in the 1930s, when it reached one-fourth of the labor force and over one-third of the nonfarm labor force. However, there are other means by which troubles can become issues. One is collective action. Thus the situation of the disabled changed in the 1970s because of social movement activity by and on behalf of the disabled, not because of a significant change in the proportion of disabled persons in society. It is one of the tasks of social movements to translate social problems into social policies, to see that social problems constitute claims on society that are to be met through the intervention of social policy (Forester, 1982, p. 45).

Thus new problems are cycled from the micro level of personal troubles to the macro level of public issues. Homelessness (discussed in Chapter 9) is an example. At first it was viewed as a personal trouble for those who experienced it. Their problem was individual failure of character and the remedy, if one was contemplated, was private charity. Next homelessness was seen as an attribute of a specific group: the recently deinstitutionalized mentally ill. This was the critical step in its transition from personal trouble to public issue because deinstitutionalization was a social policy. The proposed remedy was adequate community support such as halfway houses. Now homelessness is acknowledged as a society-wide public issue, produced by structural features such as the lack of low-cost housing. Advocates of the homeless have been arguing in courts, with some success, that adequate shelter is a basic social entitlement. Homelessness rapidly graduated from a personal trouble to a public issue in the 1980s because of the rising numbers and higher visibility of the homeless, and because of social movement activity on their behalf.

Other contemporary problems that have progressed from personal troubles to public issues are child care (analyzed in Chapter 6), illiteracy (Chapter 7), and AIDS (Chapter 8). Some problems remain at the level of public issues, but alternately wax and wane in public visibility. Poverty, discussed in Chapter 5, is a prominent example.

Social policy and social practice are vitally concerned wi
between three levels: the bonds of individuals to groups an
society. Thus the War on Poverty in the 1960s was a social
couraged individual poor persons to band together i
organizations. These organizations, in turn, articulated with society as interest groups. An example of how social science, social work, and social policy
can be united is the development of the major innovation of the War on
Poverty, the Community Action Program, which was based on a new concept for social practice: maximum feasible participation of the poor. The
single most significant input into this social policy was sociological research
on juvenile delinquency conducted by Cloward and Ohlin (1960), which was
cycled through the programs of a social work agency of New York City's
Lower East Side, Mobilization for Youth, to the U.S. Office of Economic
Opportunity.

Social policy and social practice have matured as disciplines at a time
when advanced capitalism has increasingly isolated the individual in society.
The principal source of this increased isolation has been the commodification
and atomization of social life. Individuated commodity consumption has
replaced family- centered entertainment such as conversation and musical instrument playing. Social interaction has been supplanted by manipulation of
objects: radios, televisions, personal computers, stereo systems, and videocas-
sette recorders. Furthermore, these products are aimed at certain age and sex
markets, which tends to segregate families into groups of older and younger,
female and male. Thus, according to a commonly held sociological view (e.g.,
Bellah et al., 1985), Americans are increasingly grouped into superficial lifestyle or consumer clusters rather than into meaningful communities. One
overarching goal of social policy and social practice is the maintenance of some
collective solidarity in the face of the growing social isolation produced by advanced capitalism.

SOCIAL PRACTICE

Both social science and social policy articulate with social practice. Social practice is shaped by organizational—especially bureaucratic—imperatives.
Efficiency is one such imperative. However, although the implementation of
social policy is managed by administrators, it is actually made manifest by
practitioners in relationships with clients. These relationships are between
social workers and clients, doctors/nurses and patients, teachers and
students.

Social practice is determined by the state of the art of the profession as
well as by its norms and culture. Increment in expertise is one such norm.
Administrators and social practitioners conflict over their competing standards of efficiency and expertise. Efficiency is often measured in objective cost-

benefit terms (discussed in Chapter 10), which promote repetition and routine, while expertise is enhanced by experience with the nonroutine, even rare, cases. The administrator is perplexed by the practitioner's extraordinary case, while the practitioner is bored by the administrator's routine case.

It is their social practice that affords Welfare State workers more leverage than other workers with regard to social policy. Although practitioners may have limited influence in setting social policy, they can advance, retard, and shape its delivery. One way in which social practitioners do this is by establishing a gatekeeping function so that, no matter what the social policy mandate is, eligible clients are screened according to professional and agency criteria (Greenley and Kirk, 1973). In addition, Welfare State social practitioners influence the creation of social policy through the collective action of their professional associations, such as the National Association of Social Workers, and of their unions, such as the American Federation of State, County, and Municipal Employees. These organizations can mobilize their memberships to influence public opinion and politicians through lobbying, demonstrations, and other means.

Social practice means dealing directly with human needs. These needs are classified in several ways. There are the "normal" needs of people in extenuating circumstances, such as the income needs of the unemployed. There are the extraordinary needs of disturbed people, such as the mentally ill. There are physical needs, such as the material necessities of life for the destitute. And there are social interaction needs, such as human contact for the isolated. These needs loom large for practitioners, leaving little room for consideration of social policy. Indeed, because of the sheer volume and depth of the need that many Welfare State workers confront daily, they have little time for anything but attention to their clients. The overwork and lack of support that are the lot of many Welfare State workers can lead them to neglect their personal needs, producing burnout (discussed in Chapters 5, 7, and 8) and other pathologies. This situation creates a Sisyphian orientation among many Welfare State workers, who feel they are working under difficult and disabling constraints that constantly undermine their effectiveness. Reagan administration policies were a major force in producing the constraints of higher caseloads, reduced support, and social devaluation.

The social practice of Welfare State workers should include the integration of three tasks, of which only one, helping people, is generally recognized. The other two, unfortunately, are inactive rather than active aspects of daily practice: creating change and maintaining personal growth and integrity. Creating change is periodically recycled as a general task of Welfare State workers, as in the United States in the 1930s and 1960s, but it is not built into daily work. Maintaining personal growth and integrity is rarely even acknowledged as a task of social practice.

The general economic deterioration that is squeezing the middle and working classes, with many people experiencing downward mobility, is affecting Welfare State work. It is undergoing an increasing separation between professionalization at the top (epitomized by private practitioners) and proletarianization at the lower levels (where more workers are hourly wage earners). In response, Welfare State workers at the middle and lower levels have been turning to unionization to defend their collective interests. Public aid workers, discussed in Chapter 5, are a good example of this.

The collective organization of Welfare State workers, in both professional associations and unions, presents the potential for unified social action, perhaps in concert with organized client groups. However, the status gaps between professional and nonprofessional and between worker and client inhibit such collective action. One salient feature of these status gaps is the association between lower position and higher proportions of females and minorities. Thus, in addition to status gaps, gender and racial divisions are impediments to collective action. These divisions encourage people to emphasize their differences rather than their similarities.

Sometimes, however, these social statuses can be the basis for crossing occupational barriers and extending collective solidarity. An example was the development in the 1980s of social services such as child care and counseling by some unions for their members (Martin, 1985). The key determinants were gender and social practice: the efforts of female (and feminist) staff social workers in largely female unions, such as the Amalgamated Clothing and Textile Workers Union, to meet the social needs of their sisters. (This development is also discussed in Chapter 10.)

The social practice of Welfare State workers is a fundamental cohesive bond in modern society. This bond has become more important as the connections of individuals with families and other integrating social institutions have loosened and deteriorated. Unfortunately, social practice is viewed as impersonal and incapable of compensating for the loss of personalistic family and community ties. This impersonality is commonly perceived as the product of the social processes of bureaucratization and professionalization, in which formal relationships replace informal ones. However true this may be, several caveats are in order:

1. The personal/impersonal distinction has been dichotomized, distorted into an either-or proposition. In fact, professionals and bureaucrats do engage in personal relationships with their clients to some extent. Indeed, the best professional/bureaucratic work is that done with a substantial personal touch; for example, the work of beloved teachers and empathetic social workers. Thus the personal/impersonal conflict is more a trade-off or a balancing act than a dichotomy. Moreover, impersonality is often not a conscious choice by the worker. Workers have limited influence over bureaucratic settings, especially workers who deal directly with clients, since they are usually at the bottom of the bureaucratic pecking order.
    In fact, there are many trade-offs in the social practice of the Welfare State. Con-

sider the conflict between worker altruism and self-interest. This presumed dichotomy also involves balancing worker interests (a reduced workload) with client interests (more service). Again, the resolution of the conflict is affected by the worker's position in the Welfare State organizational hierarchy. The lower the worker's position, the less control she has over work conditions, including caseload. At the same time, the lower the worker's position, the more likely it is that she will be dealing with clients on a daily basis and have more demands placed on her altruism.

These presumed dichotomies, which are actually continuums, are also a feature of social interaction and social policy in the larger society. Thus Welfare State social policy must confront trade-offs between democratic participation and bureaucratic efficiency and between collective solidarity and individual freedom.

2. Impersonality produces some positive benefits, including fairness. Impersonality means social distance: the worker is not personally involved with the client. The downside of this is well known and widely denounced: workers may not care about clients and may treat them badly. But there is also an upside: workers have no personal axes to grind. Thus the fact that workers do not respond to clients as unique persons means that clients are not judged by their personal characteristics. The worker cannot refuse to serve a client because she does not like him. In a more personalized and less bureaucratic system, such as a traditional society, personal characteristics determine eligibility and level of service received. Thus personal appearance, personality, and family connections are more important than objective need in deciding whether or not someone will be given help. The point is that some positive benefits flow from bureaucratic impersonality and these include objectivity and fairness. This is not to say that some bureaucratic impersonality is not exaggerated, because it is, or that it is altogether necessary, because it often is not.

3. The impersonality of the Welfare State is produced as much by its position within capitalism as by professional and bureaucratic imperatives and pathologies. This position is marginal: Welfare State programs are viewed, especially in the United States, as adjuncts to the marketplace. This viewpoint produces an underfunded and stigmatized Welfare State, leading to too high caseloads and too little support. Many Welfare State workers cannot work effectively without exaggerated impersonality because, despite overwork, clients must be served, if only minimally, and personal integrity must be maintained. The exceptions are extraordinary workers who manage to make personal connections despite these negative circumstances, and those who operate in the context of the market, such as private-practice psychotherapists, who can limit their caseloads and maximize their personal time.

This negative structural context of much of Welfare State social practice encourages invidious distinctions between groups of clients, as between African Americans and whites, men and women, and the morally deserving and the undeserving. Because with given resources all clients cannot be served well, some are relegated to a lower status and served poorly or not at all. Overcrowded public hospitals are one locale where such distinctions between deserving and undeserving clients have been empirically demonstrated to produce fateful negative results (Roth, 1981; Sudnow, 1967).

REFERENCES

Adams, Paul. 1985. "Social Policy and the Working Class." *Social Service Review* 59:387–402.

Anderson, Charles W. 1987. "Political Philosophy, Practical Reason, and Policy Analysis." Pp. 22–44 in *Confronting Values in Policy Analysis: The Politics of Criteria*, eds. Frank Fischer and John Forester. Beverly Hills, CA: Sage Publications.

Bellah, Robert N., et al. 1985. *Habits of the Heart: Individualism and Commitment in American Life.* Berkeley: University of California Press.

Blumberg, Paul. 1980. *Inequality in an Age of Decline.* New York: Oxford University Press.

Bowles, Samuel, and Herbert Gintis. 1982. "The Crisis of Liberal Democratic Capitalism: The Case of the United States." *Politics and Society* 11:51–93.

Cloward, Richard A., and Lloyd E. Ohlin. 1960. *Delinquency and Opportunity.* New York: Free Press.

Ellerin, Milton, and Alisa H. Kesten. 1981. "The New Right: What Is It?" *Social Policy* 11:54–62.

Forester, John. 1982. "A Critical Empirical Framework for the Analysis of Public Policy." *New Political Science* 3:33–61.

Greenley, James R., and Stuart A. Kirk. 1973. "Organizational Characteristics of Agencies and the Distribution of Services to Applicants." *Journal of Health and Social Behavior* 14:70–79.

Habermas, Jurgen. 1975. *Legitimation Crisis*, trans. Thomas McCarthy. Boston: Beacon Press.

Harpham, Edward J. 1984. "Fiscal Crisis and the Politics of Social Security Reform." Pp. 9–35 in *The Attack on the Welfare State*, eds. Anthony Champagne and Edward J. Harpham. Prospects Heights, IL: Waveland Press.

Hogwood, Brian W., and B. Guy Peters. 1983. *Policy Dynamics.* New York: St. Martin's Press.

MacRae, Duncan, Jr. 1980. "Policy Analysis Methods and Governmental Functions." Pp. 129–151 in *Improving Policy Analysis*, ed. Stuart S. Nagel. Beverly Hills, CA: Sage Publications.

Marshall, T. H. 1981. *The Right to Welfare.* New York: Free Press.

Martin, George T., Jr. 1985. "Union Social Services and Women's Work." *Social Service Review* 59:62–74.

Mills, C. Wright. 1959. *The Sociological Imagination.* New York: Oxford University Press.

Offe, Claus. 1984. *Contradictions of the Welfare State*, ed. John Keane. Cambridge, MA: MIT Press.

Ostrander, Susan A. 1985. "Voluntary Social Service Agencies in the United States." *Social Service Review* 59:433–454.

Quadagno, Jill S. 1984. "Welfare Capitalism and the Social Security Act of 1935." *American Sociological Review* 49:632–647.

Rose, Richard. 1986. "Common Goals but Different Roles: The State's Contribution to the Welfare Mix." Pp. 13–39 in *The Welfare State East and West*, eds. Richard Rose and Rei Shiratori. New York: Oxford University Press.

Rose, Richard, and Guy Peters. 1978. *Can Government Go Bankrupt?* New York: Basic Books.

Roth, Julius A. 1981. "Some Contingencies of the Moral Evaluation and Control of Clientele." Pp. 322–341 in *Social Welfare in Society*, eds. George T. Martin, Jr., and Mayer N. Zald. New York: Columbia University Press.

Sudnow, David. 1967. *Passing On: The Social Organization of Dying.* Englewood Cliffs, NJ: Prentice Hall.

Sullivan, Michael. 1987. *Sociology and Social Welfare.* London: Allen & Unwin.

Taylor-Gooby, Peter, and Jennifer Dale. 1981. *Social Theory and Social Welfare.* London: Edward Arnold.

Therborn, Goran. 1986. *Why Some Peoples Are More Unemployed Than Others: The Strange Paradox of Growth and Unemployment.* London: Verso.

Thurow, Lester C. 1980. *The Zero-Sum Society: Distribution and the Possibility for Economic Change.* New York: Penguin.

Titmuss, Richard M. 1968. *Commitment to Welfare.* London: Allen & Unwin.

Van der Veen, Romke. 1988. "Social Justice by Social Policy." Paper presented at International Conference on Social Justice and Societal Problems, Leiden.

Wilensky, Harold L., and Charles N. Lebeaux. 1965. *Industrial Society and Social Welfare.* 2nd ed. New York: Free Press.

3

The Historical Development of Social Policy

Men make their own history, but they do not make it just as they please; they do not make it under circumstances chosen by themselves, but under circumstances directly found, given and transmitted from the past. The tradition of all the dead generations weighs like a nightmare on the brain of the living.

Marx, *The Eighteenth Brumaire of Louis Bonaparte*, 1852

Social policy had a long history before the emergence of the Welfare State in the twentieth century. In this chapter we will look at the paths that social policy and social practice have taken from the sixteenth century to the present. An awareness of this past is the basis for understanding contemporary social policy and social practice. Because income security has been the central subject, and the social work profession the central actor, in the historical development of Welfare State social policy and social practice, they are the focus of this chapter.

Major changes have occurred in social policy and social practice in the same nation, or type of nation, over time. Nevertheless, through the centuries of change one dominant feature stands out: the expansion of both the scale and the scope of social policy and social practice. This expansion has not been steady and even; it has come in alternating cycles of hyper-growth, incremental growth, and retrenchment. The principal reason for this punctuated growth is that social policy and social practice are responses to and manifestations of social change, which tends to occur in cycles of revolution, reaction, and consolidation. Thus U.S. social policy and social practice in the Welfare State era began with the watershed creativity of the 1930s New Deal. Since then, social policy and social practice have experienced consolidation in the 1940s and 1950s, major expansion through the Great Society programs of the 1960s and 1970s, and retrenchment fostered by Reaganism in the 1980s.

Despite the periodic ups and downs in Welfare State social policy and social practice, the overall trend is expansion. The common empirical measure of the scale of social policy and social practice is the level of public social welfare expenditure in society. In the United States in 1929, right before the advent of the New Deal, public SWE accounted for just 3.9 percent of the gross national product, and only one-fifth of this was federal government expenditure (Martin, 1981b, p. 508). Fifty-six years later, in 1985, public SWE represented 18.5 percent of GNP, nearly a fivefold increase. The federal government accounted for over three-fifths of public SWE in 1985, triple its proportion in 1929. The major expansions of the scope of social policy and social practice occurred with the Social Security Act of 1935, the Economic Opportunity Act of 1964, and the introduction of Medicaid and Medicare in 1965.

We divide the following historical analysis of social policy and social practice into three parts. First, we examine the history of social policy from the sixteenth century English poor laws to the contemporary Welfare State. We focus on the major historical developments that shaped social policy in this period: (1) the decline of feudal society (and of religious authority) and the rise of capitalist society (and of secular authority); (2) the emergence of the modern bureaucratic state; and (3) the rise of a socialist alternative to capitalism. Next we turn our attention to social practice, focusing on its historical development from almsgiving through philanthropy to the contemporary professionalization of helping. Finally, in this walk through the past, we concentrate on developments in the United States and on one of its outstanding social practitioners, Bertha Capen Reynolds, a woman whose social practice extended throughout much of the twentieth century.

SOCIAL POLICY IN HISTORY

Modern social policy has its roots in the dissolution of feudalism and the rise of capitalism (Martin, 1981a, p. 11). This important historical transition is also variously described in terms of rural-to-urban, agricultural-to-industrial, and traditional-to-modern society.

In the transition from feudalism to capitalism, poverty becomes a concern of the state; sometimes it becomes a crime. The English poor laws illustrate this. For example, under Henry VIII, the 1536 Act for the Punishment of Ruffelers, Sturdy Vagabonds and Valiant Beggars authorized a series of escalating penalties: whipping, loss of an ear, branding, enslavement, and death

(De Schweinitz, 1943, p. 22). This act was part of a series of poor laws that began in the fourteenth century and continued into the nineteenth century; their central motif was the social control of surplus labor. The emerging capitalist production system required a large labor force of wage earners (proletarians) who hired their time to its owners (capitalists). These wage earners were a new social class constituted out of the old feudal peasantry. The poverty of peasants was not a crime because the general standard of living was quite low in peasant society. Also, their poverty was cushioned by food production and was not so visible or threatening because peasants were dispersed throughout the countryside. Poverty, then, was routinized and expected among peasants. It was the habitual poverty mentioned in the Bible (John 12:8): "For the poor always ye have with you."

When feudalism broke down and the peasants were uprooted, not all of them were needed in production all the time. Capitalists profited from this surplus of wage earners because it depressed the cost of labor owing to supply and demand forces of the market. On the other hand, the labor surplus was detrimental to workers, for it meant unemployment and lower wages. As a result, workers as a group developed interests that were inimical to the capitalist labor market: work for all at an adequate wage and income security when work was not an option.

Capitalist production was eventually predicated on the concentration of wage earners into an urban factory system. This concentration provided capitalists with powerful production advantages such as mass production (including the economy of scale) and the use of machines. However, the fact that wage earners had been uprooted from their peasant communities and concentrated in urban districts threatened capitalist production in the following ways:

1. Being uprooted was a source of grievance. Leggett's (1968) work on the contemporary Detroit working class demonstrated that uprooted peasants (Poles and Ukrainians) were significantly more likely to be militantly class-conscious and anticapitalist than were other workers.

2. Unlike peasants, workers had nothing to fall back on during times of unemployment and underemployment, common in capitalism. Lacking the cushion of food production, they were more likely to suffer and to see their families suffer. This was a strong incentive for action, including anticapitalist political activism.

3. Concentration produced social interaction and social solidarity among workers, which were the basis for the development of organizations such as unions. These organizations allowed aggrieved, desperate workers to collectively mobilize to improve their situation. Such mobilization has been historically a check on capitalist excess and a crucial ingredient in socialist revolutions. The anticapitalist mobilization of workers was facilitated by their increased literacy, a development that was promoted by the requirements of industrial production.

The poor laws were the first state efforts to address these threats. The surplus laborers were categorized into two groups: those who were capable of work and those who were not. The first group were healthy adult males (the able-bodied poor) and the second were women and children, the infirm, and the aged. The latter were deemed deserving of society's assistance and received "poor relief." The able-bodied poor were deemed undeserving and were forcibly put to work, institutionalized, or turned into vagabonds (Marx, 1967). This policy served to divide workers against one another, helping capitalists to control the most threatening fraction of workers: able-bodied males in the prime of life who could not find work at an adequate wage.

From this miserable start workers have waged centuries of struggle to expand jobs, wages, and income security. Capitalists have responded, not out of altruism, but because of the political threat represented by organized workers. This class struggle between workers and capitalists has been the primary basis for the development of social policy, mediated through the state. Thus the major reason for the first social insurance program, in Germany in the late nineteenth century, was Bismarck's desire to provide workers with an alternative to socialism. In Britain the political influence of the working class through trade unions and the Labour Party was decisive in the creation of the Welfare State. In the United States unions, especially the industrial unions, and the Democratic Party played a similar role.

The view that class struggle was the historical harbinger of the Welfare State is supported by research findings. For example, a study by Dickinson (1986, p. 103) concluded: "The most important objective factor with regard to the evolution of social insurance in Britain and Germany appears to have been the rise of the working class as an independent political force." In Zapf's (1986) analysis the explanation for the rapid implementation of social security programs in Germany in the 1880s was Bismarck's desire to politically control the working class and integrate it into society. Thus the ruling capitalist class was forced to expand social policy in order to guarantee its security in the face of growing working-class political strength.

Although other factors, including economic development, were involved in the emergence of the Welfare State, the role of working-class political organization was crucial. True, the Welfare State emerged in industrially developed nations that did not have a strong social democratic labor movement. The United States is a prime example, but even here labor played an important role in the introduction of Welfare State social policy in the 1930s (Levine, 1989). Also, in virtually all cases the development of the Welfare State was faster and its interclass income redistribution greater in nations where there was a strong labor movement.

The role of the organized working class—organized through unions and political parties—in the emergence of the Welfare State carried over to its later development. Today the most developed and progressive Welfare States, such as Sweden, are societies in which labor has a strong political presence (Shalev, 1983). The organized working class is an important constituency of the Welfare State. The conventional wisdom that links the Welfare State with "welfare" or public aid for the poor is off the mark. The organized working class and the middle class are substantial beneficiaries of the Welfare State (Goodin and LeGrand, 1987). Social Security is perhaps the best example of a Welfare State program whose principal beneficiaries are the working and middle classes.

The variations in adoption of Welfare State social policy among the more advanced capitalist nations such as Germany and Britain resulted from differences in internal politics and history. Thus Germany adopted social insurance before Britain at least partly because the German working class was more independent and radical than the British working class at an earlier point, making it a greater threat (Dickinson, 1986). Other political factors that produced national variations in the timing of Welfare State innovation were the influences of past social policy (in the form of policy feedback) and the dynamics of state formation, both of which were political and bureaucratic processes (Orloff, 1987). Struthers's (1987) study illustrated the roles of political process and policy feedback in the adoption of the Canada Assistance Plan of 1966. Policy feedback is the process by which one policy results, unintentionally, as a consequence of a previous policy.

Stinchcombe's (1985) discussion of the history of social insurance pointed out the dual roles of functionalism (social insurance's positive function in capitalism) and a political selection process. In political selection a social policy is chosen among alternatives by political elites because it gives workers the idea that they are represented and cared for without challenging the basic control by capitalists. Key political advisers in this selection process in Europe in the late nineteenth and early twentieth century were civil servants, professors, and reformers, the wing of traditional (predemocratic) politics that was most responsive to the working class.

After their original adoption, Welfare State social policies create their own momentum, sustained by the bureaucrats and experts who staff programs and by the consumers of benefits. Thus the single most important influence in the lifespan of U.S. Social Security has been the Social Security Administration, which has been "a major force behind every legislative turning point, even the retrenchments" (Tynes, 1987, p. 21).

Thus we can identify the central factor in the sociohistorical emergence of Welfare State social policy as the urban-sited class struggle of industrial capitalism. In addition to producing the modern class struggle, industrial capitalism was the basis for demographic changes, such as the aging of populations, which also furthered the emergence of Welfare State social policy. Empirical research argues for the complementarity of economic, political, and statist explanations for the development of Welfare State social policy. In a cross-sectional analysis of social policies in American states in the 1930s, Amenta and Carruthers (1988) found support for all three factors, and especially strong support for the role of the state. State governments were assessed on the basis of their fiscal and administrative capacities and it was found that a state's revenue strength and its bureaucratic development had a positive effect on the timing of its introduction of emergency relief, unemployment in-surance, and old-age pensions.

SOCIAL PRACTICE IN HISTORY

Social policy and social practice express more than the imperatives of capitalist development and state formation. They also reflect a moral value to care for people who are dispossessed by capitalism. It is in social practice that this ex-pression of human solidarity is manifested.

One useful tool for understanding the underlying basis of social practice is Gaylin's (1981) primal model of social dependency. Human beings univer-sally experience a lengthy infancy of total dependence and this social ex-perience is the foundation of human altruism. Because all humans know the condition of social dependency from personal experience, they respond to de-pendency in others with empathy and caring. Of course, this care is strongly modulated by social ideologies (such as those that create deserving and un-deserving categories of dependent people) and by the quality of one's infant experience. Thus an infant who receives no care or bad care may grow into an adult who does not care or who cares badly.

Historically, social practice can be seen as the progression from charity to social service (Martin, 1981a, p. 14). Under feudalism, the social prac-titioners were clergy and other members of religious organizations who engaged in charitable work. The Webbs (1927, p. 1) emphasized this point at the beginning of their classic study of the English poor laws: "Throughout all Christendom the responsibility for the relief of destitution was, in the Middle Ages, assumed and accepted individually and collectively, by the Church." Today social practice is still infused with religious ideals. However, religious personnel and organizations no longer dominate the vocations of social prac-tice.

If there is a single starting point for modern social practice, it may be the Leisnig (Saxony) Ordinance of a Common Chest in 1519, begun under the in-fluence of Martin Luther and the Reformation. This and similar efforts to create community chests formalized a communal responsibility for poor relief and introduced civil administration as the means of carrying it out (Martin, 1966). The first nonclerical social practitioners were overseers of the poor whose principal tasks were administration of a means test (by which the des-titute had to prove they lacked means of support in order to obtain aid) and surveillance of the poor. The clerical version of overseers were visitors of the poor, who were perhaps more altruistic. In 1633, for instance, Saint Vincent de Paul founded an order of nuns, the Daughters of Charity, whose express purpose was to visit and care for the poor.

Modern social work has its roots in the nineteenth century ascendancy of industrial capitalism, with its attendant social problems. The first expres-sion used to denote what would become the vocation of altruism was "scientific charity" (Chalmers, 1832). Combining the old moral imperative of charity (the expression was coined by a Scottish minister) with the emergent technology (social science) of the post-Enlightenment period, scientific charity became the guiding concept for social work.

With the growth of industrial capitalism and urbanization, social problems increased in visibility, if not also in scale and intensity. This was especially true of unemployment and poverty, social problems produced directly by the capitalist labor market. In New York City in 1843, the Association for Improving the Condition of the Poor was established. It was a forerunner of modern social reform efforts.

The most noteworthy vehicle for the science of charity was the Charity Organization Society (COS) movement that originated in England in 1869 and spread to the United States in 1877. Closely related to the COS was the settlement house movement, in which middle-class practitioners of the new discipline "settled" in working-class districts. The earliest such institution was London's Toynbee Hall, which opened in 1884. The scientific aspect of this social practice is illustrated by Booth's (1892) study of London, in which he found that about one-third of the city's population lived in poverty. All these developments set the stage for the emergence of the social work profession in the early twentieth century. Thus the development of social practice proceeded from almsgiving through overseeing and visiting the poor, through scientific charity, to social diagnosis in the twentieth century (Lubove, 1965).

SOCIAL POLICY AND SOCIAL PRACTICE IN U.S. HISTORY

Social policy and social practice experienced their greatest visibility and most dramatic growth in the United States during three periods: the early twentieth century, the 1930s, and the 1960s. All three periods were characterized by massive social upheaval and social protest. Public attention was focused on the plight of working-class and poor people, as illustrated by the widespread popularity of the following writings that each period produced: Upton Sinclair's *The Jungle* (1905), John Steinbeck's *The Grapes of Wrath* (1939), and Michael Harrington's *The Other America* (1963).

At the beginning of the twentieth century the United States experienced the largest immigration in its history, as well as rapid industrialization, both of which greatly expanded urban areas and social problems. During this period, called the Progressive Era (1895–1917), efforts to moderate the abuses of industrial capitalism multiplied, as did activities to carve a vocation out of these efforts. This in part reflected the growing political strength of the working class, exemplified by advances in unionism. The union movement was bolstered by the influx of immigrants from central, eastern, and southern Europe, where there were socialist traditions. Workmen's compensation and minimum wage laws were passed by several states. The settlement house emerged to meet the social needs of immigrant workers. The most notable set-tlement house in the United States was Chicago's Hull House, founded by Jane Addams in 1889 (Addams, 1961). (The present Jane Addams School of Social Work of the University of Illinois is located at the site of a restored Hull House.)

In 1898 formal training in social work began at the New York School of Philanthropy, which subsequently became the Columbia University School of Social Work. Its first technology was social casework, pioneered by Mary Rich-mond, a COS veteran (Richmond, 1917). In the same period the Chicago School of Civics and Philanthropy was founded; it later became the Univer-sity of Chicago School of Social Service Administration. In 1917 the National Social Workers Exchange was founded, and in 1920 the journal *Social Casework* began publishing. During the 1920s Freudian approaches imported from Europe came to dominate social diagnosis. This was heralded by the forma-tion of the American Association of Psychiatric Social Workers in 1919 and the ascendancy of social casework over the previously dominant social action ap-proach.

Throughout its history social practice has accented one or another of the three worldviews that Lofland and Stark (1965) proposed for defining life problems and needs: religious, political, and psychological. In the nineteenth century a distinctly religious vision marked the development of social prac-tice. However, in the twentieth century, the emphasis has alternated between the political and the psychological worldviews.

The psychological perspective focuses on "retail" practice (Ehrenreich, 1985, p. 64), such as casework, and stresses inner problems. Individual psychotherapy is the preferred vehicle of social practice and the middle-class person is the client of choice. The political viewpoint focuses on "wholesale" practice such as community organization and stresses the problems of human society. Advocacy of group rights is the preferred vehicle of social practice and the working class, including the poor, is the preferred client group. True to the dominant paradigms of twentieth century civilization, the psychologi-cal perspective is Freudian and the political perspective is Marxian. The psychological view has been more important in efforts to professionalize so-cial work, as it is congruent with the clinical model of the highly successful medical profession (discussed in Chapter 8). However, the political view has been more important in the growth of social work and the successes of social policy.

Major innovations and expansion of social practice took place during the 1930s with the New Deal of the Roosevelt administration and during the 1960s with the Great Society of the Kennedy-Johnson administration. Both ad-ministrations employed thousands of social practitioners. The number of so-cial workers doubled during the turbulent 1930s, to about 80,000 by the end of the decade, and social workers were key players among New Deal reformers. For example, Harry Hopkins and Frances Perkins were prime movers behind the Social Security Act of 1935 (Trattner, 1979, pp. 238–239), which became the centerpiece of the Democratic Party's New Deal. The Social Security Act created federalized retirement, survivorship, and unemployment insurance, and public assistance, in order to meet the massive social needs that resulted from the most serious economic depression in U.S. history.

The late 1960s and early 1970s represented a third important period of growth (Martin, 1981b, p. 510). The Food Stamp program was established in 1964 and Medicaid and Medicare began in 1965. The focal legislation of the Great Society was the 1965 Economic Opportunity Act that initiated the War on Poverty. It included the Community Action, Headstart, and Job Corps programs. In 1960 public SWE represented 10.3 percent of GNP, with the federal government accounting for 47.8 percent of the outlays. By 1976 public SWE had risen to 19.3 percent of GNP, and 59.3 percent of the outlays were by the federal government.

This 1965–1976 welfare expansion (discussed in Chapter 5) was spurred by the demands of the civil rights movement and the need to quiet urban unrest (Piven and Cloward, 1971). Just as in the early twentieth century and the Great Depression of the 1930s, expanded social policy and social practice were a response to national political crisis. In each period the crisis increased the influence of leftist and liberal political forces, including social workers and unions, which served as a basis for expansion of social policy and social practice.

The professionalization of social practice has been both a major impetus for the expansion of the Welfare State and a reflection of that expansion. An important dynamic has been the growth of public bureaucracies, which created a structural basis for the helping vocations. Over time, charity became institutionalized as the expertise of a specific secular vocation: social service or social administration. The profession of social service has had no better exemplar than Bertha Capen Reynolds, whose work we will now discuss.

Social Practitioner at Work: Bertha Capen Reynolds (1885–1978)

The social practice of Bertha Capen Reynolds spanned much of the twentieth century and illustrates how individual troubles and social issues can be addressed simultaneously. Reynolds integrated Freudian and Marxian perspectives in her social practice. In fact, she has been called the great synthesizer of social work because she unified the two major tendencies in the field: outward-looking social action and inward-looking social psychology. Reynolds was, in the words of a colleague, "a Freudian and a Marxist, a practitioner and an activist, a psychiatric social worker who was our leading advocate for social change" (Schwartz, 1981, p. 9).

Reynolds was in Smith College's first graduating class in psychiatric social work in 1918. In the 1920s and 1930s she was an educator at Smith's School for Social Work. In the 1930s and 1940s she was a caseworker in the Personal Service Department of the National Maritime Union (NMU) and a leader in the early efforts to unionize social workers. Her work in the NMU in the 1940s laid the basis for a new subdiscipline: industrial social work. Industrial social work is concerned with extending social work practice into work settings. Because of her leftist politics, Reynolds was blacklisted during the anticommunist inquisition of the late 1940s and early 1950s. According to Day (1989, p. 295), "Although she was deeply respected in the profession, she never worked again as a social worker after the McCarthy red scare." However, she lived long enough to see her ideas revived by a new generation of activist social workers in the 1960s and 1970s.

Reynolds's social practice stressed the dynamic quality of helping relationships. For her, helping a client was a reciprocal process. She affirmed the quality of reciprocity in helping relationships in the following comments (Reynolds, 1942, pp. 29–30):

> Helping implies a helper and a helped. If we constantly see ourselves as on the giving end of the relationship between helper and helped, we provide a safe harbor in ourselves for all the unconscious desires to be superior, desires to which science teaches us that we are subject no less than other people. As a corrective to our occupational tendency to deformity (like the rounded back of a farm laborer) we need to take exercises in *being helped*, as well as in helping. We must learn in order to teach, receive in order to give. Indeed, we must receive from those to whom we give, in order to give to them—receive of their understanding, their energies for action, their feelings in the situation which guide our way in it.

Reynolds's integration of Freudian and Marxian perspectives can be seen in her daily social practice. The influence of Freudian principles is evident in her focus on the personal feelings and relationships of clients, the Marxian influence in her stress on the social and material circumstances of clients. In the following description of her work in the NMU, Reynolds (1975, pp. 7–8) explains the importance of relating to both the feelings and the social situations of seamen:

> The caseworkers did have the opportunity to know what seamen and their families found hardest in their lives, how they struggled to make ends meet, how illness wrecked cherished plans, and how distorted relationships made happiness impossible. We knew what they wanted for their children. It was of great importance to know what they were making of the resources they had, personal and social as well as material resources, and how they could use help on their present problems. The caseworkers were constantly concerned with feelings, but always in relation to social situations which urgently needed solution.

To this faculty of sensitivity to the personal problems and nuances of individual clients, Reynolds added an understanding of the social realities of U.S. society. She perceived the major ongoing conflict of the Welfare State and made it clear where her sympathies lay (Reynolds, 1975, p. 174):

> Our explorations have faced us with a choice between contradictory forces in our society: those which are moving toward the welfare of the people, as the people's

own concern and responsibility, and those which destroy human life in preventable misery and war, and relieve poverty only grudgingly to keep the priviledged position they hold.

REFERENCES

Addams, Jane. 1961 [1910]. *Twenty Years at Hull House*. New York: Signet.
Amenta, Edwin, and Bruce G. Carruthers. 1988. "The Formative Years of U.S. Social Spending Policies: Theories of the Welfare State and the American States During the Great Depression." *American Sociological Review* 53:661–678.
Booth, Charles. 1892. *Life and Labor of the People of London*. London: Macmillan.
Chalmers, Thomas. 1832. *On Political Economy in Connection with the Moral State and Moral Prospects of Society*. New York: Daniel Appleton.
Day, Phyllis J. 1989. *A New History of Social Welfare*. Englewood Cliffs, NJ: Prentice Hall.
De Schweinitz, Karl. 1943. *England's Road to Social Security*. New York: Barnes.
Dickinson, James. 1986. "Spiking Socialist Guns: The Introduction of Social Insurance in Germany and Britain." *Comparative Social Research* 9:69–108.
Ehrenreich, John H. 1985. *The Altruistic Imagination: A History of Social Work and Social Policy in the United States*. Ithaca, NY: Cornell University Press.
Gaylin, Willard. 1981. "In the Beginning: Helpless and Dependent." Pp. 1–38 in Willard Gaylin et al., *Doing Good: The Limits of Benevolence*. New York: Random House.
Goodin, Robert E., and Julian LeGrand. 1987. *Not Only the Poor: The Middle Classes and the Welfare State*. London: Allen & Unwin.
Harrington, Michael. 1963. *The Other America: Poverty in the United States*. New York: Macmillan.
Leggett, John C. 1968. *Class, Race, and Labor: Working Class Consciousness in Detroit*. New York: Oxford University Press.
Levine, Rhonda F. 1989. *Class Struggle and the New Deal: Industrial Labor, Industrial Capital, and the State*. Lawrence: University Press of Kansas.
Lofland, John, and Rodney Stark. 1965. "Becoming a World Saver: A Theory of Conversion to a Deviant Perspective." *American Sociological Review* 30:862–875.
Lubove, Roy. 1965. *The Professional Altruist: The Emergence of Social Work as a Career 1880–1930*. Cambridge, MA: Harvard University Press.
Martin, George T., Jr. 1966. "Two Historical Responses to the Question of Community Responsibility in Social Welfare Financing." Unpublished.
_____. 1981a. "Historical Overview of Social Welfare." Pp. 11–17 in *Social Welfare in Society*, eds. George T. Martin, Jr., and Mayer N. Zald. New York: Columbia University Press.
_____. 1981b. "Social Welfare Trends in the United States." Pp. 505–512 in *Social Welfare in Society*, eds. George T. Martin, Jr., and Mayer N. Zald. New York: Columbia University Press.
Marx, Karl. 1967 [1867]. *Capital*, ed. Frederick Engels, trans. Samuel Moore and Edward Aveling. Volume I: *A Critical Analysis of Capitalist Production*. New York: International Publishers.
Orloff, Ann Shola. 1987. "The Political Origins of Canada's Welfare State for the Aged: The State, Political Parties and Policy Feedback." Paper presented at Annual Meeting, American Sociological Association, Chicago.
Piven, Frances Fox, and Richard A. Cloward. 1971. *Regulating the Poor: The Functions of Public Welfare*. New York: Pantheon.
Reynolds, Bertha Capen. 1942. *Learning and Teaching in the Practice of Social Work*. New York: Farrar & Rinehart.
_____. 1975 [1951]. *Social Work and Social Living: Explorations in Philosophy and Practice*. Washington, DC: National Association of Social Workers.
Richmond, Mary E. 1917. *Social Diagnosis*. New York: Russell Sage Foundation.
Schwartz, William. 1981. "Bertha Reynolds as Educator." *Catalyst: A Socialist Journal of the Social Services* 3:5–14.
Shalev, Michael. 1983. "Class Politics and the Western Welfare State." Pp. 27–50 in *Evaluating the Welfare State: Social and Political Perspectives*, eds. Shimon E. Spiro and Ephraim Yuchtman-Yaar. New York: Academic Press.

Sinclair, Upton. 1960 [1905]. *The Jungle*. New York: Signet/The New American Library.

Steinbeck, John. 1972 [1939]. *The Grapes of Wrath*. New York: Viking Press.

Stinchcombe, Arthur L. 1985. "The Functional Theory of Social Insurance." *Politics & Society* 14:411–430.

Struthers, James. 1987. "Shadows from the Thirties: The Federal Government and Unemployment Assistance, 1941–1956." Pp. 3–32 in *The Canadian Welfare State: Evolution and Transition*, ed. Jacqueline S. Ismael. Edmonton: University of Alberta Press.

Trattner, Walter I. 1979. *From Poor Law to Welfare State: A History of Social Welfare in America*. 2nd ed. New York: Free Press.

Tynes, Sheryl R. 1987. "Turning Points in Social Security: Explaining Legislative Change, 1935–1985." Paper presented at Annual Meeting, American Sociological Association, Chicago.

Webb, Sidney, and Beatrice Webb. 1927. *English Poor Law History*. London: Longmans, Green.

Zapf, Wolfgang. 1986. "Development, Structure, and Prospects of the German Social State." Pp. 126–155 in *The Welfare State East and West*, eds. Richard Rose and Rei Shiratori. New York: Oxford University Press.

4

Comparative Perspectives on Social Policy

In short, by this comparison, we are led to know, and to know
scientifically, what is most perfect.
Monboddo, Of the Origin and Progress of Language, 1787

Just as we learn about social policy by understanding its historical development, so do we learn by comparing national variations in social policy. Nations differ politically, culturally, historically, and in other ways, and all these differences are touched on in our comparative analysis. However, our classification of nations is based on a socioeconomic criterion: the level and the mode of production. The level of production determines whether a nation is to be classified as more developed or less developed (or underdeveloped). The mode of production differentiates basically between capitalist and socialist societies. For the purpose of analyzing social policy and social practice, this classification scheme yields three comparisons that are particularly illuminating: (1) rich and poor nations, (2) various Welfare States, and (3) capitalist and socialist nations.

RICH AND POOR NATIONS

One major division in the nations of the world is that between rich and poor countries. Rich nations are those that are highly developed economically, or industrialized. The First World comprises the rich capitalist nations and contains the Welfare States. The Second World comprises industrially developed nations that are socialist. The Second World is less developed than the First World but more developed than the Third World. The Third World comprises poor countries that are primarily agricultural. Some Third World nations are capitalist, some are socialist, and many have mixed economies. There are some anomalies in this scheme. Japan, for example, is a First World nation because of its economic development and capitalist economy, but in geography and ethnicity it shares much with the Third World.

The Third World was colonized and exploited by the First World, the historic basis of their relationship, and has long provided cheap natural resources and labor for the development of First World capitalism. The Third World comprises the bulk of Asia, Latin America, and Africa, and it is the world of colored peoples—black, brown, yellow, and all shades in between. It contains the overwhelming majority of the world's population, nearly four-fifths of the 5.1 billion people on this globe in 1987.

Much of the Third World is exceedingly poor and wracked by compelling social needs. World Bank data show that in 1985 Third World nations had an average per capita GNP of only $610. In the First World in the same year per capita GNP was $11,810. In 1985 the average life expectancy at birth was only fifty-seven years in ninety Third World nations. The shortest life expectancies were in the African nations of Guinea and Sierra Leone: forty years. The longest life expectancy among Third World nations was in socialist Cuba: seventy-seven years. Among twenty-three First World nations the average life expectancy was seventy-five years, led by Australia and France at seventy-eight years. Among nine Second World nations the average life expectancy was seventy-one years.

As indicated by the extraordinary life expectancy of Cuban citizens, Third World nations that are socialist make considerable efforts to meet basic social needs, while those that are not socialist usually do not. A typical example of the latter group is Kenya. In her study of Kenyan social policy Mutiso (1986, p. 207) concluded that

> what we have is a situation of generally inadequate coverage within an extremely complex picture of partial government provision, combined with varying degrees and types of private individual, group, community and/or voluntary organisational and local authority support. Wide variations also exist between what different sectors of the population have at their disposal.

Despite the First World's position of economic superiority, some social problems and needs are more pronounced in the First World than in the Third World. There is consistent evidence, for example, that schizophrenia, a major mental health problem of First World societies, is much less common and much less serious in the Third World. One reason for this is the effects of unemployment and underemployment in developed capitalist nations. The stresses of the labor market are "less destructive as well as less common where wage labor is rare and where most people are involved in subsistence modes of production" (Warner, 1986, p. 52).

Whatever the variations in the level and nature of their social needs, First World and Third World nations differ considerably in the extent of their social policy and social practice. Cutright's (1965) landmark study of seventy-six nations found that the historical development of social security was strongly and positively correlated with higher levels of economic development. Other data point to the same connection between industrial development and social welfare effort. In 1983 central government expenditure for housing, social security, and welfare averaged 41.1 percent of GNP in high-income nations and only 5.8 percent of GNP in low-income nations (Rajapatirana, 1987). Also, in a multivariate analysis for four time points (1960, 1965, 1970, 1975) in forty-eight First and Third World nations, Pampel and Williamson (1985) found that industrialism had a dominant effect in explaining the level of public pension expenditure. Studies such as these are the empirical basis for the industrialism explanation for Welfare State development, which was discussed in Chapter 3.

Another variable associated with the level of economic development, the age structure of society, also has an important bearing on Welfare State expenditure. Wilensky's (1975) research on sixty-four countries demonstrated that the higher the proportion of aged people in a society, the greater was the Welfare State effort, as measured by social security spending. Wilensky's finding was supported by a later study of social welfare spending in Welfare States by Pampel and Williamson (1988), who reported that social insurance spending was most determined by the size of the aged populations in nations. (It is important to note that Pampel and Williamson found that public assistance benefits, as opposed to social insurance benefits, were determined by social class variables.)

Economic development and a high percentage of aged persons in the population are closely associated and are conducive to the development of a Welfare State. Economic development is an important basis for improved longevity (discussed in Chapter 8). In developed nations the aged are the group most vulnerable to the loss of work and most in need of Welfare State benefits, including medical care and pensions.

Economic development is the basis for Welfare State social policy and social practice in three other ways. First, it creates surplus resources, a fraction of which can be used to finance Welfare State benefits. Second, economic development results in a population, including especially the unemployed and the underemployed, that is more vulnerable to social dependency. Third, economic development creates technology such as the mass media and circumstances such as literacy that facilitate the political organization of vulnerable groups. These mobilized groups then press for expanded Welfare State social policy and social practice.

WELFARE STATES

Among Welfare States there is variation in the scale and scope of social policy. Based on a 1974–1984 study of unemployment policies in sixteen Welfare States, Therborn (1986) arrived at the following ranking: 1, Sweden; 2, Belgium, Denmark, Netherlands; 5, Austria, Norway; 7, Finland, France, Italy, U.K., West Germany; 12, Japan, Switzerland; 14, Australia, Canada, U.S. This ranking is generally consistent with others we will examine as we look at social welfare expenditure and income distribution in various Welfare States.

Social Welfare Expenditure

Comparative studies of social welfare expenditure (SWE) usually include the sum of medical care benefits, pensions, family allowances, unemployment compensation, public employee benefits, veterans' benefits, workers' compensation, and maternity benefits. The rankings of nations in various studies show some variability, primarily because of differences in definitions of what constitutes SWE. However, the rankings are remarkably consistent with regard to the nations at the top and at the bottom. Over and over again studies demonstrate that Sweden is a leader and the United States is a laggard in expenditure on social welfare. For example, based on 1981 data from Western Europe's Organisation for Economic Co-operation and Development (OECD), fourteen Welfare States ranked as follows on the basis of public SWE as a proportion of GDP (Johnson, 1987, p. 164): 1, Belgium (public SWE was 37.6 percent of GDP); 2, Netherlands; 3, Sweden; 4, Denmark; 5, West Germany; 6, France; 7, Italy; 8, Ireland; 9, Austria; 10, Norway; 11, Finland; 12, U.K.; 13, Canada; 14, U.S. (public SWE was 20.8 percent of GDP). Other rankings, including those of Rose and Peters (1978, pp. 64, 255) and of Andrain (1985, p. 15), similarly put the United States at the bottom of their lists of Welfare States with regard to public SWE as a percentage of GNP or GDP. The current low position of the U.S. is not new. Historically, the U.S. has been a Welfare State laggard. For example, Glennerster's (1975, p. 48) data showed that the U.S. trailed the U.K. throughout the period 1929–1972 in public SWE as a percentage of GNP.

Including private-sector SWE does not raise the U.S. from its position in the bottom group of Welfare States. Rainwater and Rein (1983, p. 123) devised a comparative measure, social protection expenditure, that included both public and private resources. In 1977 their rank order of nine Welfare States by the percentage of GDP devoted to social protection expenditure was as follows: 1, Netherlands; 2, West Germany; 3, Denmark; 4, Belgium; 5, France; 6, Italy; 7, U.K.; 8, Ireland; 9, U.S.

Two criticisms of the Welfare State often voiced by conservatives are that it impairs the efficiency of the private economy and coerces individuals. These criticisms are challenged by empirical research. Andrain's (1985) analysis documented that higher SWE levels did not impair economic efficiency. Between 1960 and 1980 the four nations that were Welfare State leaders attained greater increases in manufacturing labor productivity than did the three nations that were Welfare State laggards. For example, Sweden's manufacturing productivity grew by an average of 5 percent annually in 1960–1980, while U.S. gains averaged only 2.6 percent per year, and Japan more than tripled social expenditure between 1960 and 1981, yet its economic growth in the same period was more than three times that of the United States (Burtless, 1986, p. 46). Moreover, at the same time that Sweden's economy outperformed the U.S. economy, the standard of living of its citizens improved more markedly than did that of U.S. citizens (Erikson and Aberg, 1987). With regard to civil rights, Welfare State development is historically associated with less government coercion. For example, of seventy-three nations studied in 1945–1966, Iceland, Luxembourg, New Zealand, Norway, and Sweden, in order, had the lowest levels of state coercion of citizens (Feierabend, Nesvold, and Feierabend, 1970). All but one of these nations (New Zealand) are among the more advanced group of Welfare States.

Income Distribution

Three aspects of income distribution are the concern of social policy: income inequality, income redistribution, and poverty. The consensual goal of Welfare State social policy (indeed, one of its distinguishing characteristics) is to reduce income inequality and poverty through income redistribution. The essence of the social policy of income redistribution is that the Welfare State, through a progressive tax system and the provision of social benefits, redistributes income downward. The more advanced Welfare States have less income inequality, more income redistribution, and less poverty than do the more rearward Welfare States.

A commonly used method to assess the degree of income inequality is to look at the share of national income received by quintiles (fifths) of the population, arranged in order of their income. Based on World Bank data, eighteen Welfare States were ranked according to the share of national income received by the poorest 20 percent of households. The rank order was: 1, Japan (8.7 percent of national income went to the poorest 20 percent of the population); 2, Netherlands; 3, Belgium, West Germany; 5, Sweden; 6, Ireland; 7, U.K.; 8, Spain; 9, Finland; 10, Italy; 11, Norway, Switzerland; 13, France; 14, Australia, Denmark; 16, Canada, U.S.; 18, New Zealand (5.1 percent of national income went to the poorest 20 percent of the population). Data from the 1980 Luxembourg income study were generally consistent with this ranking. Among seven Welfare States, Sweden had the lowest inequality in the distribution of disposable income, followed by, in order, Norway, U.K., Canada, U.S., Israel, and West Germany (Hedstrom and Ringen, 1987, p. 236).

Consistent with lagging behind other Welfare States in income equality, the U.S. also trails in two related areas: income redistribution and poverty reduction. With regard to income redistribution, in a study of direct fiscal redistribution (through progressive taxes and income transfers) and indirect fiscal redistribution (through high- or full-employment policy) in thirteen Welfare States, Hicks and Swank (1984) found that the U.S. ranked tenth. The ranking, in descending order of magnitude of redistribution, was as follows: 1, Sweden; 2, Netherlands; 3, Finland; 4, Norway; 5, U.K.; 6, Australia; 7, Japan; 8, Canada; 9, Ireland; 10, U.S.; 11, France; 12, West Germany; 13, Italy.

With regard to poverty, OECD data from the 1970s showed that, using a relative measure of poverty, the U.S. had the highest poverty rate of all but one of ten Welfare States. The three lowest poverty rates were in West Germany (3 percent), Sweden (3.5 percent), and Denmark (5 percent). The three highest poverty rates were in France (16 percent), the U.S. (13 percent), and Canada (11 percent) (Rodgers, 1982, p. 26). Other data demonstrated a similar ranking of nations. Among seven Welfare States measured, the U.S. had the highest poverty rate (16.9 percent), followed by Israel (14.5 percent), Canada (12.1 percent), the U.K. (8.8 percent), West Germany (7.2 percent), Sweden (5.0 percent), and Norway (4.8 percent) (Hedstrom and Ringen, 1987, p. 236).

Sources of Welfare State Variation

The sources of variation in Welfare States are illustrated by the differences between the United States and Sweden. The relative backwardness of the United States is due to its racial and cultural heterogeneity, its political decentralization (Wilensky and Lebeaux, 1965), and its lack of a feudal past—all of which have helped to produce less clearly defined class politics. We saw in Chapter 3 how class struggle and the maturity of working-class political strength are prime movers in Welfare State development. The United States has relatively weak labor unions and no working-class political party. In comparison, Sweden is ethnically homogeneous, is politically centralized, and is a nation with a feudal past. These characteristics helped to produce more clearly defined class politics in Sweden, including a relatively strong labor movement and a working-class (social democratic) political party.

The most important factors behind the development of Sweden's Welfare State have been the strength of Swedish organized labor and its long experience of social democratic political rule (Pontusson, 1983, pp. 46–49). Union strength appears to be a factor generally associated with Welfare State development. Examination of the rates of unionization in twenty Welfare States showed that the more advanced Welfare States also had higher rates of unionization (Sweden—85 percent, the highest), while the laggard Welfare States also had lower rates of unionization (U.S.—25 percent, the lowest) (Therborn, 1984, p. 11). Myles's (1984) analysis of fifteen Welfare States stressed the tenure of socialist (social democratic) rule as the main predictor of Welfare State effort. Social democratic tenure ranged from zero years in the United States, the Welfare State laggard, up to twenty-four years in Sweden, the Welfare State leader.

The United States has much more decentralized government than the other Welfare States. There are three branches (executive, judicial, legislative) and three levels of government (federal, state, local), making the articulation of social policy more problematic than in unitary state structures such as those of Western Europe. Compared to other Welfare States, U.S. social policy and social practice have been constrained by political decentralization. Because the United States is divided into state and local jurisdictions, its social policy is subject to wide variation. For example, in the conterminous United States in 1985 the average monthly payment to a family receiving Aid to Families with Dependent Children ranged from a low of $104 in Mississippi, through a national average of $342, to a high of $514 in California.

The pronounced localism or provincialism of U.S. society has contributed to its more laissez-faire approach to social needs. (Laissez-faire is the idea that the state should not interfere in the market.) Also, individualism is a stronger value in the United States than in other Welfare States, where collective orientations, which are more compatible with Welfare State social policy and social practice, are more entrenched. As Tropman (1989, p. 11) has noted, in the United States "it is more difficult to achieve any objective that relies upon cooperation."

The United States is far more reluctant than other Welfare States to use its national government for social policy goals. For example, not one of ten essential services and key industries is state owned, and only two, electricity and railways, are partially state owned. This contrasts with other Welfare States. In Sweden three essential services and key industries (telecommunications, gas, railways) are state owned and four (electricity, airlines, steel, shipbuilding) are partially owned by the state (Tarpinian, 1986, p. 4). Also, the United States remains the only Welfare State without nationalized health insurance (discussed in Chapter 8) and a family allowance (discussed in Chapters 5 and 6).

A final factor in the Welfare State backwardness of the United States is the militarization of its economy. The United States devotes a considerably higher proportion of its resources to warfare (versus welfare) than do other Welfare States. World Bank data showed that it ranked first among fifteen Welfare States in the percent of total central government expenditure going to defense, while Sweden ranked seventh. In 1985, 24.9 percent of U.S. expenditure went to the military; this was nearly quadruple the comparable figure for Sweden, 6.4 percent. A Department of Defense study showed that in 1988 the U.S. ranked first among sixteen Welfare States in military expenditure. It spent 6.8 percent of its GDP on the military, compared to an average of 3.1 percent for the other fifteen Welfare States. Military spending was $1,164 per person, compared to an average of $293 per person for the other fifteen Welfare States. Of the sixteen Welfare States Japan had the lowest military expenditure; only 1 percent of its GDP was spent on the military, which represented an expense of only $163 per person. Thus, part of the explanation for our backwardness in social policy is that our military commands resources that could go to meeting social needs. This is especially critical in a period like the present, when economic stagnation puts intense pressure on public budgets.

WELFARE STATES AND SOCIALIST NATIONS

There are informative differences and similarities between social policy and social practice in socialist countries and capitalist Welfare States. Capitalist and socialist nations have developed a similar array of social policies, but their relative positions differ. In capitalist nations Welfare State social policy and social practice are, in varying degrees, accessories to the market. One outcome of this difference is that in capitalist nations social policy and social practice go through a cycle of expansion and contraction, following the ups and downs of the economy and the ins and outs of parties, while their development in socialist nations is more even.

Data consistently demonstrate that socialist nations, despite their lower level of economic development, make a greater social welfare effort than do capitalist nations. In this sense socialist nations are truer welfare states than are developed capitalist nations. For example, George and Manning (1980, p. 32) found that in 1970, among three nations ranked by public expenditure on education, health, housing, and social security as a percent of GDP, the U.S.S.R. was first, 22 percent higher than the U.K. and 37 percent higher than the U.S.

Socialist nations also demonstrate lower levels of income inequality than do Welfare States. Based on Page's (1983, pp. 144–145, 191–192) review of 1960s and 1970s research, the rank order among fourteen nations, from low to high inequality, was as follows: 1, Czechoslovakia; 2, Hungary; 3, Poland; 4, Netherlands; 5, Sweden; 6, Norway; 7, U.K.; 8, Japan; 9, Canada; 10, Australia; 11, U.S.; 12, West Germany; 13, Spain; 14, France. Thus the three nations with the lowest income inequality were all socialist. Similarly, data compiled by Taylor and Jodice (1983, pp. 134–136) showed that in the early 1970s socialist nations outdid Welfare States in the percentage of national income devoted to the bottom 40 percent of the population. Again, the top three nations were socialist: Czechoslovakia led, with 27.4 percent of its national income going to the poorest 40 percent of its population, followed by Bulgaria (26.6 percent) and East Germany (26.3 percent). The U.S. ranked nineteenth, with only 15.2 percent of its national income going to the poorest 40 percent of its population.

There are several reasons for the generally higher social welfare effort of socialist nations. Their goals of social policy and social practice greatly differ from those of Welfare States. In Welfare States social policy aims to provide for minimum human needs, while maintaining the essential differences between social classes. In socialist nations, social policy is directed toward the reduction of differences between social classes. Morris (1986, p. 187) summarized this socialist goal as follows:

> ...persistent inequalities in entrepreneurial societies gave rise to socialist alternatives, which rely on a major reordering of the relationships between classes in society. This introduced in the strongest possible manner the rights of *all* persons to more equal shares in national income, to more security and well-being. To this was added a belief in increased equality in conditions among all classes.

Even underdeveloped socialist nations such as the People's Republic of China make relatively high social welfare efforts. Their lack of economic resources is offset by their more egalitarian distribution of what is available.

Socialist societies heavily subsidize the provision of basic social needs such as health care, housing, and transport, so that these goods are either free or very cheap. A study of the physical quality of life (PQL) in 123 nations, including measures of education and health, found that "in 28 of 30 comparisons between countries at similar levels of economic development, socialist countries showed more favorable PQL outcomes" (Cereseto and Waitzkin, 1986, p. 661). One reason for this strong difference is the importance that socialist social policy and social practice attach to major public health and education efforts, including improved nutrition and literacy. Additionally, socialist nations promote a full-employment economy and exert control over wages to reduce income inequality. Thus in the U.S.S.R., the average pay of the highest-paid managers was only 4.1 times the average pay of the lowest-paid workers in 1975 (Yanowitch, 1977, p. 25). In the U.S. this difference was much greater. Moreover, the data indicated that inequality in the U.S.S.R. declined from the 1940s to the 1970s, while inequality in the U.S. remained fairly static.

What are some of the limitations of social policy and social practice in socialist nations? Although in his analysis of social policy in the U.S.S.R. Deacon (1981, p. 54) gave that nation higher marks than Welfare States, he also found that the Soviets have fallen short of achieving a fully socialist social policy and social practice. Social welfare provision in the U.S.S.R. is superior to that of Welfare States in two major quantitative ways: (1) level of state, as opposed to private, provision; and (2) adequacy of funding. The U.S.S.R. falls short of a socialist social policy and social practice in two qualitative dimensions: (1) allocation of benefits by work rather than by the criterion of need; and (2) lack of active participation of citizens (democratization).

A study of social policy in the U.S.S.R. by George and Manning (1980, pp. 167–174) came to several major conclusions about the differences between Welfare States and the U.S.S.R. and the limitations of Soviet social policy. First, social policy is more universalistic and government based in the U.S.S.R. than it is in Welfare States. Second, the U.S.S.R. is explicitly commited to social policy, whereas in Welfare States the commitment is more tenuous and depends on pressure from labor. Third, the reduction of income inequalities in the U.S.S.R. after universal benefits have been provided has been no more successful than in Welfare States. Thus there was a discrepancy between the goals of Soviet social policy and its achievements, and between its achievements and an ideal socialist social policy—gaps that were attributed largely to the inadequate material base (development) of the U.S.S.R. George and Manning found strong support among the people for the achievements of Soviet social policy in education, health, and workers' benefits—support which exists even among dissident refugees.

In summary, it appears that social policy and social practice are influenced strongly by both the level and the mode of production in society. Social policy and social practice are more advanced in societies with higher levels of production and socialist modes of production. The outcomes of social policy in Welfare States and in socialist nations may be similar, particularly in comparison to Third World nations, but the reason is probably not the convergence theory: that industrialism produces similar (convergent) outcomes for capitalist and socialist nations. The Welfare States have advanced social policy and social practice because of very high levels of production and also because of working-class pressure. (In the most conspicuous Welfare State laggard, the United States, this working-class pressure is relatively weak.) The Second World nations have advanced social policy and social practice, despite lower levels of development than Welfare States, because of an ideological commitment to socialist goals and a political commitment to the working class.

REFERENCES

Andrain, Charles F. 1985. *Social Policies in Western Industrial Societies*. Berkeley: Institute of International Studies, University of California.

Burtless, Gary. 1986. "Public Spending for the Poor: Trends, Prospects, and Economic Limits." Pp. 18–49 in *Fighting Poverty: What Works and What Doesn't*, eds. Sheldon H. Danziger and Daniel H. Weinberg. Cambridge, MA: Harvard University Press.

Cereseto, Shirley, and Howard Waitzkin. 1986. "Economic Development, Political-Economic System, and the Physical Quality of Life." *American Journal of Public Health* 76:661–666.

Cutright, Phillips. 1965. "Political Structure, Economic Development, and National Social Security Programs." *American Journal of Sociology* 70:537–550.

Deacon, Bob. 1981. "Social Administration, Social Policy and Socialism." *Critical Social Policy* 1:43–66.

Erikson, Robert, and Rune Aberg, eds. 1987. *Welfare in Transition: A Survey of Living Conditions in Sweden, 1968–1981*. Oxford: Clarendon Press.

Feierabend, Ivo K., Betty Nesvold, and Rosalind L. Feierabend. 1970. "Political Coerciveness and Turmoil: A Cross-National Inquiry." *Law and Society Review* 5:93–118.

George, Vic, and Nick Manning. 1980. *Socialism, Social Welfare and the Soviet Union*. London: Routledge & Kegan Paul.

Glennerster, H. 1975. *Social Service Budgets and Social Policy*. London: George Allen & Unwin.

Hedstrom, Peter, and Stein Ringen. 1987. "Age and Income in Contemporary Society: A Research Note." *Journal of Social Policy* 16:227–239.

Hicks, Alexander, and Duane H. Swank. 1984. "Governmental Redistribution in Rich Capitalist Democracies." *Policy Studies Journal* 13:265–286.

Johnson, Norman. 1987. *The Welfare State in Transition: The Theory and Practice of Welfare Pluralism.* Amherst: University of Massachusetts Press.

Morris, Robert. 1986. *Rethinking Social Welfare: Why Care for the Stranger?* New York: Longman.

Mutiso, Roberta M. 1986. "Kenya and the Future of the Welfare State." Pp. 205–221 in *Comparing Welfare States and Their Futures,* ed. Else Oyen. Aldershot, UK: Gower.

Myles, John. 1984. *Old Age and the Welfare State: The Political Economy of Public Pensions.* Boston: Little, Brown.

Page, Benjamin I. 1983. *Who Gets What from Government.* Berkeley: University of California Press.

Pampel, Fred C., and John B. Williamson. 1985. "Age Structure, Politics, and Cross-National Patterns of Public Pension Expenditures." *American Sociological Review* 50:782–799.

———. 1988. "Welfare Spending in Advanced Industrial Democracies, 1950–1980." *American Journal of Sociology* 93:1424–1456.

Pontusson, Jonas. 1983. "Comparative Political Economy of Advanced Capitalist States: Sweden and France." *Kapitalistate: Working Papers on the Capitalist State,* No. 10/11.

Rainwater, Lee, and Martin Rein. 1983. "The Growing Complexity of Economic Claims in Welfare Societies." Pp. 111–129 in *Evaluating the Welfare State: Social and Political Perspectives,* eds. Shimon E. Spiro and Ephraim Yuchtman-Yaar. New York: Academic Press.

Rajapatirana, Sarath. 1987. *World Development Report.* New York: Oxford University Press/World Bank.

Rodgers, Harrell R., Jr. 1982. *The Cost of Human Neglect: America's Welfare Failure.* Armonk, NY: M. E. Sharpe.

Rose, Richard, and Guy Peters. 1978. *Can Government Go Bankrupt?* New York: Basic Books.

Tarpinian, Greg. 1986. "Deregulation—Deunionization." *Economic Notes* 54:1–4.

Taylor, Charles Lewis, and David A. Jodice. 1983. *World Handbook of Political and Social Indicators.* Volume I: *Cross-National Attributes and Rates of Change.* 3rd ed. New Haven, CT: Yale University Press.

Therborn, Goran. 1984. "The Prospects of Labour and the Transformation of Advanced Capitalism." *New Left Review,* No. 145.

———. 1986. *Why Some Peoples Are More Unemployed Than Others: The Strange Paradox of Growth and Unemployment.* London: Verso.

Tropman, John E. 1989. *American Values and Social Welfare: Cultural Contradictions in the Welfare State.* Englewood Cliffs, NJ: Prentice Hall.

Warner, Richard. 1986. "Hard Times and Schizophrenia." *Psychology Today,* June, pp. 50–52.

Wilensky, Harold L. 1975. *The Welfare State and Equality: Structural and Ideological Roots of Public Expenditures.* Berkeley: University of California Press.

Wilensky, Harold L., and Charles N. Lebeaux. 1965. *Industrial Society and Social Welfare.* 2nd ed. New York: Free Press.

Yanowitch, Murray. 1977. *Social and Economic Inequality in the Soviet Union: Six Studies.* White Plains, NY: M. E. Sharpe.

5

Income Security

Do you call poverty a crime? The worst of crimes. All the other crimes are virtues beside it: all the other dishonors are chivalry itself by comparison. Poverty blights whole cities; spreads horrible pestilences; strikes dead the very souls of all who come within sight, sound, or smell of it.
Bernard Shaw, *Major Barbara*, 1907*

Income security is at the heart of Welfare State social policy and social practice. Income security problems have been a focus of social policy at least since the sixteenth century, when the English poor laws were promulgated to control uprooted and pauperized peasants. Since then, the preeminent agenda of social policy has been to deal with the needs and demands of people who cannot find work or who are unable to work. In the modern Welfare State income security is greatly expanded in scale and is centralized in the national government. The importance of income security is indicated by its magnitude. In 1985 U.S. public expenditure for income security was $1,923 per person: income security expenditure represented 64.3 percent of all public social welfare expenditure, 34 percent of all government outlays, and 11.9 percent of GNP.

Without regular wage labor at an adequate wage, the modern worker is vulnerable to material and social deprivation. Material deprivation is a lack of the physical necessities of life—food, clothing, and shelter. (In modern

*Reprinted by permission of the Society of Authors on behalf of the Bernard Shaw Estate.

society education and health care can also be considered necessities.) Social deprivation stems from a lack of connection to and acceptance by society.

Material deprivation is manifested in, among other hardships, homelessness (discussed in Chapter 9) and hunger. Hunger is a growing world problem. The United Nations Food and Agriculture Organization estimated that the number of hungry people grew from 460 million in 1970 to 475 million in 1980—nearly 10 percent of the world's population. The World Bank estimated the number of hungry people to be between 340 million and 720 million in 1980—from 7 to 14 percent of the world's population. The minimum figure of 340 million represented people whose caloric intake was below what was necessary to prevent serious health risks, including stunted children. Africa is the continent most seriously affected by hunger, and children are its prime victims. In 1987 the UN's World Food Council estimated that about 40,000 children in the world died of hunger-related causes every day (Lewis, 1987).

Hunger is conventionally viewed as a problem for less developed countries of the Third World, where drought and famine command periodic international attention. However, it is also a problem in at least some developed nations. For example, data from the Physicians' Task Force on Hunger indicated that there were up to twenty million hungry people in the United States in 1986, or about 8 percent of the population (Bennett, 1987). New Jersey's Commission on Hunger found that in 1986 about 600,000 people suffered from hunger—7.7 percent of the state's population (Colman, 1986). In capitalist nations such as the United States, where people are dependent on wage labor in order to buy food, the loss of work and inadequate pay for work are major causes of hunger and poverty. The unfortunate reality is that the children of poor workers are most vulnerable to the insecurities of the capitalist labor market. According to the Citizens Commission on Hunger in New England (based at Harvard University), the group hardest hit by hunger in the United States are poor infants and children, many of whom suffer from silent undernutrition, as evidenced by slow growth and extremely low weight-to-height ratios.

Poverty also results in social deprivation. Poor people are set apart from the rest of society and stigmatized or shamed. Areas where they live are demarcated as slums, the "other side of the tracks," shantytowns. Thus economic deprivation produces a social deficit for poor persons (Camasso and Camasso, 1986, p. 388). For example, Jahoda (1982, p. 39) found that unemployment resulted in "the reduction of social contacts, the lack of participation in collective purposes, the absence of an acceptable status and its consequences for personal identity." Dail's (1988) research demonstrated that unemployment has a negative impact on family dynamics, increasing stress (as evidenced in the development of conflict in relationships) and leading to a loss of family and social identity. The social deficit of poor persons can also have negative social-psychological consequences. Poor people may internalize society's negative attitudes about them and become self-abusive. Such a reaction may cause them to become mentally ill, to try to escape reality through mood-altering substances, and to make hostile (sometimes criminal) attacks on one another and on society.

This chapter delineates the major structures and social policy issues of Welfare State income security, beginning with an examination of current U.S. programs. We then discuss the relationship between income security and income redistribution, and analyze poverty, particularly its characteristics and causes. Next we look at specific social policy alternatives that address the problems of poverty and welfare, including workfare, full employment, and the family allowance. Finally, we assess the social practice of income security, concentrating on public aid workers.

INCOME SECURITY AND SOCIAL POLICY

Income security is the provision of benefits to workers (and their dependents) who are not working for various reasons, including unemployment, disability, and retirement. Despite the growth in private-sector expenditure, notably private pension plans, the state still dominates income security. In 1985, 81.5 percent of all income security expenditure in the United States was made by the state. Although income is an economic aspect of life, income security is first and foremost a social policy: it has social goals such as social stability, it is directed at social groups such as the aged and the poor, and it reflects social values such as altruism. Moreover, as Boulding (1967) pointed out, while economic policy is rooted in the concept of exchange or bilateral transfer (trade), social policy uses the grant or unilateral transfer (payment). Income security payments are the principal unilateral transfers in the Welfare State.

Income security provides temporary or long-term replacement income for workers whose incomes have been interrupted and for the dependents of workers who die. It provides a secure source of income in an insecure working environment. It is recognition that workers in capitalism are in a more vulnerable position (because they are economically dependent on uncertain wage labor) and are a greater threat (because they are ecologically concentrated, socially cohesive, and politically organized) to elites than were peasants under feudalism.

Who shall have their incomes maintained, at what level, and for what interruptions of work? Welfare State social policy mandates, ideally, that all citizens shall have their incomes maintained, at least up to the minimum necessary to sustain life. The value that underlies eligibility is universalism: all citizens are entitled to coverage. This works to foster social solidarity and to prevent discrimination against certain social groups, including racial, ethnic, religious, and gender groups.

In addition to universalism, income security in the Welfare State includes the idea of a minimum standard of living based on the material necessities of life. The concept of a minimum has been advanced at least since Rowntree's (1901) work in England at the turn of the twentieth century. Minimum support is rooted in the premise that because of the greater resources and the higher standard of living in modern society, no person should suffer or die for lack of a subsistence income. In the United States the best-known minimum is the poverty line (Orshansky, 1965).

As we shall document in this chapter, many people who receive public income security payments are entirely dependent on them for their livelihoods. While some commentators, especially conservatives, bemoan this social dependency, it is a fact of life in modern society and the Welfare State did not create it. Among other causes (such as the increasing scale and complexity of society), social dependency is a product of the development of capitalist industrialism, especially its market and wage labor features. As citizens of modern society, we are all, in sundry ways and degrees, dependent on state subsidies, direct and indirect, for our education, transport, and health care, as well as for our income. There is no empirical evidence that this dependence in itself influences people's behavior in a negative way. For example, Ellwood and Summers (1986) found that disability payments did not decrease work effort and that public assistance was not a major cause of family dissolution.

Income Security Programs

The Welfare State goal of universal and minimal entitlement is only approximated in the United States. U.S. income security programs can be classified into two broad types: social insurance and public assistance. Social insurance is contributory, and it best realizes the Welfare State goal of universal and minimal entitlement. It is paid for by contributions of workers and employers; benefits are related (loosely) to these contributions. The major social insurance programs are Social Security, officially known as Old Age, Survivors, and Disability Insurance (OASDI), and unemployment insurance (UI).

Public assistance programs are categorical and are paid for out of general tax revenues—local, state, and federal. Their benefits are determined by a means test, which amounts to demonstrating proof of poverty (no visible means of support). The categorical approach means that public assistance programs are not created for everyone (universal), but for specific categories or subgroups of citizens. Those chosen for programmatic attention are deserving or non–able-bodied (unable to work) persons in need, including the aged, children, and the disabled. The major public assistance programs are Aid to Families with Dependent Children (AFDC); Supplemental Security Income (SSI), which serves the aged, blind, and disabled; and General Assistance (GA), a residual program for those who do not qualify for other income security programs.

Categorical programs help their recipients but also stigmatize them and exercise surveillance over them. The recipients are required to pass an often demeaning eligibility test that amounts to a degradation ritual. The shame connoted by the expression "on welfare" exemplifies the stigma. Nichols-Casebolt's (1986) research, based on Panel Study of Income Dynamics (PSID) data collected at the University of Michigan's Institute of Survey Research, found that single-parent women who were AFDC recipients had lower scores on psychological well-being than did single-parent women who were not AFDC recipients. (However, the data were inconclusive as to whether lack of work or receipt of AFDC was the primary source of the felt stigma.) Additionally, a study (Goodban, 1985) of 100 AFDC recipients in New Haven found that many felt guilty, ashamed, and stigmatized.

There are several myths about public assistance, especially AFDC, that help to propagate this stigma. One is that it encourages recipients to have a lot of children. The reality is that in September 1986 the average AFDC family had only 1.95 children. In a 1980–1983 study of 2,796 randomly chosen households receiving welfare, it was found that welfare recipients have a relatively low fertility rate—lower than that of comparable women in the general population. Moreover, the longer a woman remained on welfare, the less likely she was to give birth. Why is this the case? Based on qualitative data from in-depth interviews with the welfare recipients, Rank (1989, p. 302) answered this question as follows:

> The economic, social, and psychological situation that women on welfare find themselves in is simply not conducive to desiring more children. Becoming pregnant and having a child is perceived as making the situation worse, not better.

Another myth is that there is widespread fraud by AFDC recipients. The fact is that less than 1 percent of all AFDC cases involve possible fraud, and a much smaller percentage are proved guilty. The most pervasive fraud in public assistance programs is that committed by third-party providers such as doctors receiving Medicaid payments (Beeghley, 1983, pp. 70–71).

In 1987 U.S. income security programs had about 55 million recipients, representing over one-fifth of the population. Social Security is by far the largest program, reaching over two-thirds of transfer payment recipients. In May 1988 OASDI had 38.4 million beneficiaries, representing about 16 percent of the population. Receiving benefits were 2.8 million disabled workers, 23.6 million retired workers, and 12 million survivors or dependents of workers. In September 1986 public assistance programs had about 18 million recipients, who were around 7 percent of the population. The largest program by far is AFDC; it had 11 million recipients, representing one in every twenty-two Americans. These income security programs transfer income from the state to eligible beneficiaries in the form of a check from the government. In May 1988 the average monthly OASDI benefit was $463 and the average SSI payment was $254 per recipient. The average UI payment in April 1988 was $146 per week. For all of 1986 the average AFDC payment was $358 per family per month.

In addition to income the state supplies in-kind benefits. In-kind programs do not provide cash but a commodity or a service, the supplier of which is the government or is reimbursed by the government. Examples are the Medicare and Medicaid programs. In 1986 Social Security recipients got an average of $2,392 from Medicare, while AFDC and SSI recipients (and others) received an average of $1,827 from Medicaid to cover their medical costs. (The recipients do not actually get the money—it goes directly to health-care providers.) Falling somewhere between income and in-kind benefits are voucher programs, which provide beneficiaries with cash substitutes such as coupons. The most important voucher program is Food Stamps. Originally set up in 1964 to aid farmers by supporting food prices, the Food Stamp program has grown into a large antipoverty effort. People who receive public assistance or whose incomes fall below a certain level are eligible for coupons that can be redeemed for food. In 1986 the average Food Stamp coupon value for the whole year was $546 per recipient and the average number of monthly recipients was 19.4 million.

All these income security programs evolved over time in response to economic conditions, demographic trends, and social changes. We now turn our attention to the major developments in U.S. income security policy since the 1930s.

Changes in Income Security

There have been two noteworthy developments in over fifty years of income security policy in the U.S. Welfare State (Martin, 1981): growth and federalization. These changes are demonstrated by the data in Table 5.1. The data show the growth of Welfare State income security from its inception with the Social Security Act of 1935. The growth occurred in cycles of punctuated expansion—in the 1930s and in 1965–1975—followed by ever-higher plateaus—in the 1940s, 1950s, and in 1975–1985. The data also demonstrate

TABLE 5.1   U.S. Public Income Security Recipients and
             Expenditure, 1940–1985*

	RECIPIENTS		EXPENDITURE	
YEAR	NUMBER (MILLIONS)	% OF POPU- LATION	% OF GNP	% FED- ERAL
1940	7.9	5.9	5.1	39.2
1950	8.9	5.9	2.8	43.1
1960	22.7	12.6	4.7	70.2
1965	27.3	14.1	5.3	73.8
1975	49.5	23.0	10.8	77.2
1980	52.6	23.2	11.3	79.5
1985	53.6	22.4	11.9	79.9

*Includes OASDI, UI, SSI, AFDC, and GA, adjusted for recipients who received both SSI and OASDI.

Sources: *Social Security Bulletin* 51:31–54, 49:56; *Statistical Abstract of the United States* 1972:271, 1974:286, 1988:334–336; and *Historical Statistics of the United States* 1975:341.

that the federal government has increased its role in income security (this is the process of federalization) as compared to local and state government. What the data in Table 5.1 do not show is that the federal government has also increased its role relevant to that of the private sector. Between 1950 and 1985 the federal share of all income security expenditure, public and private, rose from 29.9 to 65.1 percent (Kerns and Glanz, 1988).

Widespread social need during the Great Depression of the 1930s, when unemployment rates were as high as one-third of the nonfarm labor force, acounted for the dramatic growth in Welfare State income security in 1935–1940. There were several factors that caused the accelerated growth in 1965–1975. Wildavsky (1979, pp. 105–106) estimates that the causes (and their shares of the increase) of the 1965–1975 expansion in income security benefits were: (1) rising inflation—40 percent; (2) rising unemployment—10 percent; (3) demographic trends—20 percent; and (4) policy changes (such as broadening coverage and raising benefit levels)—30 percent. The 1960s civil rights movement and other political protest had an effect (limited, in Wildavsky's view) only on the Food Stamp, AFDC, and housing assistance programs.

Other analysts have assigned more importance to political protest. Empirical analysis by Browning (1986) indicates that the 1965–1975 expansion reflected the liberal domestic policies of the Kennedy-Johnson administration, in conjunction with a Congress controlled by non-Southern Democrats. Piven and Cloward (1971) have argued that the Democratic Party's action was based on its desire to meet and control the growing protests and demands of one of its important constituencies: urban African Americans. A large portion of urban African American protest was directed at income security policy; most notable were the activities of the National Welfare Rights Organization, which pushed for higher benefits and easier and broader eligibility for AFDC (Martin, 1972).

The 1965–1975 expansion was also spurred by the culmination of the great migration of African Americans from the rural South, where they had been peasants, to the urban North, where they became proletarians. This migration occurred at the same time that the industrial capitalist factory system was dispersing from the central cities. Thus inner cities lost stable unskilled and semiskilled jobs paying adequate wages just as millions of uneducated and undereducated African Americans poured into them, creating greater demand for income security.

Demographic change, particularly the upturn in the social dependency ratio (SDR), was another important cause of the 1965–1975 expansion. The SDR is the age group 65 and over plus the age group under age 18 (the nonworking or socially dependent populations) as compared to the age group 18–64 (the working population). The combination of greater longevity and the post–World War II baby boom produced a dramatic rise in the SDR, from 0.675 in 1940 to 0.950 in 1965, an increase of 41 percent (Lampman, 1984, p. 155). These were the years immediately preceding the welfare expansion of 1965–1975. In 1965–1975 the SDR declined from 0.950 to 0.828, a drop of 13 percent. These were the ten years immediately preceding the leveling of the recipient population in the late 1970s. Demographic changes, then, increased pressure on income security caseloads in 1965–1975 and decreased pressure from 1975 onward.

Only part of the 1975–1985 leveling in the population receiving income security can be accounted for by Reagan policy, which did not take effect until 1981. The most important reasons for the leveling were a cooling off of political protest and a changing demographic context. The decline in OASDI for survivors and dependents can be attributed to a sharp drop in child recipients. The number of child recipients of OASDI reached a high of 3.6 million in 1975; the number declined by 8.7 percent in 1975–1980 and by 27 percent in 1980–1985. Deceased workers were leaving fewer children, consistent with the declining birth rate and SDR in 1975–1985.

A major impact of Reagan policy was in the OASDI disability population. In 1975–1980 the disability beneficiary population grew by about 15 percent, whereas in the early Reagan years it declined by about 10 percent. This decline can be attributed largely to the Reagan policy of decertifying recipients and denying certification to potential recipients. In Reagan's first year in office continuing disability investigations increased by 29 percent over their average for the previous five years and cessations (terminations) increased by 79 percent (Weatherford, 1984, p. 54). In 1975 only 8 percent of disability applicants were denied benefits; in 1981, the figure was 43 percent. In 1986 the Supreme Court ruled unanimously that the Reagan administration had used a secret and systematic policy to deny benefits to eligible mentally disabled people, in violation of Social Security Administration rules, and the Reagan administration was forced to abandon its assault on the disability program.

The Reagan administration also had a strongly negative impact on the Food Stamp and AFDC programs. Between 1981 and 1986 participation in the Food Stamp program declined by 13 percent. In 1982, for the first time since the program's inception, the authorized spending limit decreased. The total amount cut from the fiscal 1982 Food Stamp budget was $1.7 billion (Weaver, 1984, p. 125). We will discuss the negative effects of Reagan policy for the AFDC program later in this chapter.

In summary, changes in the scale of Welfare State income security result from several factors: economic conditions, political demands, and demographic trends. These factors are beyond the control of presidential power. Thus the efforts of the Reagan administration to undermine Welfare State income security notwithstanding, it remains a major institutional feature of U.S. society. Because of this staying power of Welfare State income security programs, a new term has entered the language of social policy: the social wage.

The Social Wage

It is well known that income security benefits are vital to the financial well-being of many older persons. In 1984, 62 percent of Americans age fifty-five and over received one-half or more of their income from Social Security. For this age group the proportion of total income that came from federal social insurance programs increased from 37 percent in 1962 to 45 percent in 1984. What is not as well known is that public income security payments constitute a sizable and growing source of support for all citizens. This income is referred to as the *social wage*. In 1950 the social wage constituted 4 percent of personal income. By March 1988 it had grown to 13.9 percent, approaching one-seventh of personal income. The social wage is even larger if nongovernment and noncash benefits are taken into account, which Lampman (1984) did with a measure he called secondary consumer income (SCI). This expanded definition more than triples the social wage: in 1950 the SCI was 17 percent of the GNP; in 1980, 29 percent.

Although the U.S. social wage has grown, it still lags behind that in other Welfare States. In a comparison of workers' disposable income (a measure that is related to the social wage) in seven Welfare States, the U.S. ranked seventh, behind France, Japan, Canada, Italy, West Germany, and the U.K. Disposable income (DI) was calculated for a married couple with two children and one wage earner. It equaled gross earnings less income taxes and social security contributions, plus direct cash transfers from government. DI in the U.S. was only 79 percent of gross earnings, compared to 99 percent in France (Hansen, 1984). The major cause of this large difference was that, although workers in the other nations paid more in taxes than U.S. workers, they received considerably more social benefits. Comparative research by Therborn (1984, p. 28) has shown a considerable range in the social wages of eight Welfare States. Measuring the social wage by social security benefits as a percentage of household income in 1980, Therborn produced the following ranking: 1, Netherlands (the social wage was 25 percent of household income); 2, France; 3, Sweden; 4, West Germany; 5, Italy; 6, Japan, U.K., U.S. (each of these three nations had social wages that equaled 12 percent of household income).

The social wage represents a socialization of the costs of the capitalist wage labor system. Capitalists do not bear the brunt of the expense. Rather, the social wage consists largely of income transfers within the working class, from its upper levels (stably employed workers) to its lower levels (intermittently employed, unemployed, and underemployed workers). Tonak's (1987) study has demonstrated that social benefits and taxes for the U.S. working class are roughly equal. The ratio of taxes paid by workers to benefits received by workers averaged 1.13 per year in 1952–1980. This meant that for every $100 workers received in benefits, they paid $113 in taxes.

Because the social wage consists largely of income transfers within the same social class, it results in little or no income redistribution between social classes. This fact is the major reason why so little income is redistributed through Welfare State social policy in the United States, a subject that we now examine.

INCOME REDISTRIBUTION

In addition to universal coverage and minimum support, Welfare State social policy is based on a third ideal: income redistribution, which reduces society's inequality by redistributing some income downward. This is mainly achieved in two fiscal (budgetary) policies: progressive taxation, in which the wealthy pay a higher portion of their income in taxes than others do; and transfer payments, which go disproportionately to the nonwealthy.

The considerable growth in income security has only marginally reduced income inequality in the United States, as the data in Table 5.2 indicate. After very little change in income distribution from 1947 through 1980, a noticeable change occurred in the Reagan years of 1981 to 1986. In that period the four lowest quintiles of the population lost ground to the highest (richest) quintile. Thus a redistribution of income upward to the wealthy increased the already high level of income inequality in the United States, which was discussed in Chapter 4. Data on average, real family income prepared by the Committee on Ways and Means of the U.S. House of Representatives demonstrated that, between 1979 and 1987, the poorest quintile of the population had a 6.1 percent decline to $5,107, while the richest quintile gained 11.1 percent to $68,775 (Primus, 1989).

Our income inequality, although high, is less than our wealth inequality. Wealth consists of what one owns—the net value of one's assets. According to a study by the Joint Economic Committee of Congress, in 1983 only 0.5 percent of Americans owned over one-third of the nation's total wealth, up from one-fourth in 1963 (Smith, 1986). Thus the wealth disparity between the poor and the nonpoor is even greater than their income difference. According to data from the Census Bureau's Survey of Income and Program Participation (SIPP), the median net worth of all U.S. households in 1984 was $32,667. Poor households had a median net worth that was only 15.6 percent (about one-sixth) of the median for all households. By comparison, poor households had a median income that was 20.6 percent (about one-fifth) of the median income for all households (O'Hare, 1987, p. 45).

TABLE 5.2   Distribution of U.S. Family Income, 1947–1986

QUINTILE	1947	1980	1986	UPPER LIMIT (1986)
Lowest	5.0	5.1	4.6	$13,886
Second	11.8	11.6	10.8	$24,020
Middle	17.0	17.5	16.8	$35,015
Fourth	23.1	24.3	24.0	$50,370
Highest	43.0	41.6	43.7	—
Top 5%	17.2	15.9	17.0	—
Highest-lowest gap	38.0	36.5	39.1	

Source: Statistical Abstract of the United States, 1972:317, 1988:428.

It is important to note that by one measure another major inequality in the United States—that between African Americans and whites—does seem to have declined somewhat over time. Based on a statistical analysis of national data, Fossett, Galle, and Kelly (1986) found that overall racial occupational inequality declined in the 1960s and 1970s from the levels that existed in the 1940s and 1950s. The researchers attributed this decline to the social policy innovations of the 1960s.

Why does the United States continue to have a high level of inequality even as it spends more money on social welfare benefits? In a statistical analysis of the redistributive effects of Welfare State transfer payments, Devine and Canak (1986) found that between 1949 and 1977 social insurance served to reproduce the existing maldistribution of income because it bypassed the poor, and public assistance, while essential to the survival of the poor, was too trivial (only about 1 percent of GNP) to have any measurable impact on income distribution. Thus United States social policy is considerably more successful at horizontal redistribution (redistribution within classes over the life cycle), so that the aged fare well, than it is at vertical redistribution (redistribution between classes), so that the poor fare badly.

Still, the redistributive effects of Welfare State income security have probably prevented greater inequality from developing. Also, there has been a modest amount of income redistribution in the United States, owing more to progressive taxation than to transfer payments. How does the United States compare in this area to other, similar nations? As discussed in Chapter 4, the United States ranked tenth among twelve Welfare States in the magnitude of income redistribution through progressive taxes, income transfers, and employment policy.

Inequality has been growing in the United States. In addition to the Reagan legacy, the general economic context has been an important reason. Between 1947 and 1973 the U.S. economy was robust and expansive; it dominated the world economy. Median family income rose between 1947 and 1973 from $14,859 to $29,741 (in 1986 dollars), an increase of 100 percent. The economy began to falter in 1973, and it has been relatively stagnant ever since. The U.S. economy is now challenged internationally by other capitalist nations (especially Japan and West Germany), which outproduce it, and by socialist nations, which often deny large markets and cheap raw materials to capitalism. Since 1973 real income has not grown in the United States. In 1986 median family income was $29,458, a loss of about 1 percent since 1973. This occurred despite the fact that more families had two wage earners.

Data on inequality reveal a sharp split between the rich, who have gotten richer, and the working class and the poor, who have gotten poorer. Thus between 1977 and 1987 consumer prices rose by 94 percent, which meant that merely to stay even with inflation income would have had to rise by 94 percent as well. For workers, income in those ten years rose only 74 percent, which resulted in a real decline in their standard of living. Interestingly, compensation for the chief executives of the top 100 corporations rose by 181 percent in the same period (Batra, 1987).

This growing gap between the top and bottom levels of society is referred to as *class divergence* (Blumberg, 1980) or class polarization (Kloby, 1988). It is the product of the economic deterioration that began in the early 1970s. In the present stagnant economy those with economic assets and political influence (the rich) are able to maximize their position at the expense of those who lack economic assets and political influence, especially when the state adds its power to that of the rich. In the 1980s Reagan administration policies contributed to growing inequality. Danziger, Gottschalk, and Smolensky (1985) have calculated that the Reagan administration's cuts in income security programs accounted for about two-fifths of the 1980–1984 rise in poverty, while deteriorating economic conditions accounted for one-third. In 1980–1983 the percentage of potentially poor persons saved from poverty by income transfers fell from 52.5 percent to 46.3 percent (Danziger, Haveman, and Plotnick, 1986, p. 65).

POVERTY

Inequality is a relative or comparative concept—it measures the shares of income received by various groups. *Poverty,* on the other hand, is a term applied to those at the bottom of society's income distribution and can be measured by either a relative or an absolute standard. Relative measures of poverty assess the position of those at the bottom compared to the general standard of living in a society. One commonly used relative measure is one-half the national median income. By this measure, those earning less than one-half the median income are considered poor.

Poverty is more commonly measured by an absolute standard. In the United States this standard is the poverty line. The poverty line is an absolute standard because one either has enough money to buy life's necessities or one does not—there is no comparison to another group. The poverty line is calculated on the basis of minimum material necessities and adjusted for family size and residence (urban or rural). In 1986 the poverty line for a nonfarm family of four persons was $11,203, and 32.4 million persons, or 13.6 percent of the total population, were below that line.

The overall poverty rate for a given year conceals the fact that considerably more people actually experience poverty at some time during the year. Thus, according to SIPP data, 26.2 percent of the population fell below the poverty line for at least one month in 1984, although the overall poverty rate for the year was only 14.4 percent (O'Hare, 1987, p. 45). The poverty line also underestimates the level of poverty as compared to the level yielded by a relative measure. Thus, if the relative standard is one-half the median income, the number of poor persons increases by as much as 40 percent. Poverty data have been systematically collected since 1959. The highest poverty rate was in 1959—22.4 percent; it declined steadily to 11.4 percent in 1978, its lowest point. In the six years immediately preceding the Reagan administration the average annual poverty rate was 11.9 percent. In the first six years of the Reagan administration the poverty rate averaged 14.4 percent, an increase of over one-fifth.

The level of poverty is determined primarily by two factors: the state of the economy and social policy. Poverty declines in periods when the economy is performing well (as indicated by low unemployment) and rises in periods when the economy is performing badly (as indicated by high unemployment). Poverty also rises or falls as a result of government policy. Thus the U.S. poverty rate declined in the 1960s as a result of a relatively strong economy and because of government policy (the War on Poverty). By contrast, the poverty rate rose in the late 1970s and the 1980s as a result of deterioration in the economy and because of Reagan administration cuts in income security programs.

Social Security benefits have increased sufficiently to keep the incomes of many elderly and disabled persons from falling below the poverty line. The major success of the 1965–1975 expansion in income security was the decline in the poverty rate for the aged, due to Social Security, SSI, Medicare, and Food Stamp benefits. In 1969, 25.3 percent of persons sixty-five years old and older were below the poverty line, compared to 12.1 percent of all persons. In 1986 the poverty rate for the aged had fallen to 12.4 percent, while the poverty rate for all Americans was up to 13.6 percent. The highest poverty rates are for the nonaged and the nonwhite and for those living in female-headed households. In 1983 about 75 percent of the aged poor were removed from poverty by transfers, but only 8 percent of nonwhite females with children were (Danziger, Haveman, and Plotnick, 1986, p. 66).

Public assistance, unlike Social Security, has not expanded enough in coverage or in monetary level to prevent more people from slipping into poverty. In other words, while public assistance payments are *efficient*—a high proportion go to persons whose incomes, without government help, would fall below the poverty line—they are not *effective* in preventing large numbers of people, especially single-parent families, from falling below the poverty line (Burtless, 1986, p. 26). Thus the money that is spent is well spent, but more money is needed in order to substantially reduce poverty.

Government spending on human capital has a much more uncertain impact on poverty than transfer payments and in-kind benefits have. *Human capital spending* refers to expenditure to increase the education and skill levels of workers in order to improve their prospects in the labor market. Some human capital programs, such as the Comprehensive Employment and Training Act (CETA), were particularly beneficial for adult women, who raised their real wages by 25–75 percent as a result of the program's classroom training, on-the-job training, and work-experience components (Burtless, 1986, p. 38). CETA was a casualty of the Reagan administration: more than 300,000 CETA jobs in the public sector were eliminated in 1981, about one-third of them held by African Americans (Blackwell and Hart, 1982, p. 192). Despite CETA's successes, the overall impact of training and education programs, at least at the low-cost levels at which the government has traditionally supported them, have been quite modest. Hoos (1983, p. 156) summarized research on the subject and concluded that the overall economic benefits of training and education programs, such as those that flowed from the Manpower Development and Training Act of 1962, have yet to be empirically demonstrated.

Although the poverty population is mixed in its composition, two large groups of poor persons command the special attention of social policy: the working poor and female-headed households. Although we separate them for purposes of our analysis, it is important to note that the two groups overlap—many female-headed households are among the working poor.

The Working Poor

The working poor compose a substantial portion of the U.S. poverty population. In 1986, 50 percent of the heads of families below the poverty line worked, over 25 percent of them full-time year-round. The working poor are an especially large proportion of the rural poor—in 1984 two-thirds of poor rural families had at least one worker (Duncan and Tickamyer, 1988, p. 244).

For the two million family heads who worked full-time year-round to be poor in 1986 meant that their family income (for a nonfarm family of four) was $11,203 or less, the poverty line that year. How could so many people work full-time all year long and still remain in poverty? Simply, they work for very low wages. For a forty-hour workweek and fifty weeks of work, the poverty line translated in 1986 into an hourly income of $5.60. The minimum wage of $3.35 an hour, if worked at for a comparable time, produced an income of only $6,700. Incredibly, 3.3 million workers earned less than the minimum wage in the United States in 1986; another 3.5 million worked at the minimum wage (Levitan and Shapiro, 1987, p. 50).

The working poor represent a problem—and a large one, at that—of poverty that is in fact a problem of work. The principal cause of poverty among workers is the labor market. The three labor market problems suffered by workers are unemployment, involuntary part-time employment (part-time workers who seek full-time jobs), and low earnings. According to the Bureau of Labor Statistics, the total number of workers with labor market problems was 33.7 million in 1984, of whom 7.1 million lived in poor families (Levitan and Shapiro, 1987, p. 31).

Research by Danziger, Gottschalk, and Smolensky (1985) has demonstrated that Reagan's policies especially harmed the working poor. This group increased by about a half million, or nearly 18 percent, in 1980–1984. One major source of the damage was the 1981 Omnibus Budget Reconciliation Act (OBRA), which changed the AFDC funding formula to restrict eligibility and benefits for working recipients. Thus many working poor were eliminated from the welfare rolls, and for those who remained, tax rates rose considerably (Moffitt and Wolf, 1987). Joe and Rogers (1985, p. 95) concluded that between 370,000 and 507,000 families were dropped from AFDC nationally as a result of OBRA, and that recipients who worked were more likely to lose their benefits.

The Feminization of Poverty

In 1985 about one-half of all poor persons lived in families with female householders, up considerably from 1959, when only about one-fourth of all the poor lived in such families. In 1985 the poverty rate for all persons was 14.0 percent; for those living in households where the head was a female eighteen to sixty-four years old, the poverty rate was 26.8 percent. For children in two-parent families the poverty rate was 11.4 percent; for those in one-parent families, 49.9 percent (Danziger, 1988, p. 7). The term *feminization of poverty* was first applied to this development by Pearce (1978).

Based on an analysis of 1960–1983 national data, Rodgers (1986, p. 52) concluded that increasing rates of divorce, separation, and single parenting were the most important factors in the rise in female-headed households. Between 1970 and 1986 the number of female-headed families with one or more children under eighteen more than doubled, from 3.4 million to 7.8 million. In 1970 these families made up 11.5 percent of all families; in 1986, 23.1 percent. The majority (almost two-thirds in 1986) of these families are white; however, a larger proportion of African American families (about one-half) than of white families (about one-sixth) fall into this category. The growth in female-headed families is not confined to the United States. For example, between 1961 and 1981 the number of one-parent families (about 90 percent of which are female-headed) more than doubled in the U.K. (Graham, 1984, pp. 30–31).

The Reagan administration's 1981 changes in welfare policy reduced the effectiveness of public assistance in relieving poverty among female-headed households. Between 1978 and 1984 the percentage of poor white females with children who were removed from poverty by cash transfers declined from 21.8 percent to 11.7 percent; for poor African American females with children, from 13.3 percent to 8.9 percent (Danziger and Plotnick, 1986, p. 46). Based on a study of women terminated from AFDC because of OBRA policies in six Michigan counties in 1981–1982, Sarri (1985) found that 89 percent ran out of money at least once, and that 62 percent were without money seven or more times. She concluded that the Reagan policy changes were a major factor in increasing poverty among female-headed households.

The chief reasons for the high rate of poverty among female-headed households are low incomes and high rates of underemployment. Poor females raising children on their own are just as likely to work as nonpoor females raising children on their own. Data from the Census Bureau's Survey of Income and Education (SIE) showed that in 1975, among female heads of families with children eighteen years old or younger, there was no significant difference in work experience between the poor and the nonpoor (Ellwood, 1984, p. 41). However, poor women raising children alone work for low wages and get less support from absent fathers than do nonpoor women raising children alone.

Most recipients are on welfare because they need income supplements or substitutes for short periods (Beeghley, 1983, pp. 82–83). They are low-wage workers who are experiencing a temporary drop in or loss of income, usually because of some calamity such as job loss or the breakup of a marriage. Another group of welfare recipients use welfare as a longer-term (several years) income supplement. These are usually stably employed workers in very low-paying jobs. That leaves only a small minority, about 10 percent of recipients, who use welfare as an income substitute for long periods, of four years or more. Most are young females with little education and work experience, who are heading families.

Longitudinal research (Duncan, 1984) has demonstrated that the poor are not a homogeneous and stable group. They are, in fact, representative of the general population, and the turnover in the poverty population is high. However, for a small group of persistently poor people (over a ten-year period), race and sex are salient characteristics; African Americans and families headed by women are disproportionately represented in this group. These findings were echoed for the poor who received public assistance. Most remain on public assistance temporarily. However, for a small subgroup, dependence on public assistance is long term, and race and sex are important factors.

Rank's (1985) study showed that most people used welfare only briefly. About three-fifths of the households studied had been on AFDC less than one year; the average length of welfare use was less than two years. Exit probabilities differed considerably among households. Single-headed households and married-headed households had median exit times of 5.7 and 8.6 months, respectively. However, for female-headed and elderly-headed households, the median exit time was 22.1 months. The principal reasons were that female and elderly heads of households had limited job opportunities and had experienced disruptive life cycle changes (having children or aging).

It is important to recognize that female-headed households that are poor are not so because of changes in family status. In analyzing PSID data, Bane (1986) found that family composition changes made only a trivial contribution to the increase in poverty in the early 1980s. Even though African American poverty is concentrated in female-headed households, the *beginning* of poverty is associated with family changes in only about 17 percent of these households. Poverty in female-headed households is widespread because of three other factors: low earnings capacity, limited financial support from absent fathers, and inadequate welfare payments (Garfinkel and McLanahan, 1988, p. 49).

Another piece of erroneous conventional wisdom is that welfare, especially AFDC, *creates* family dissolution. In an impressive review of the research on this subject, Wilson and Neckerman (1986, p. 251) concluded that neither welfare receipt nor benefit levels affected the frequency of out-of-wedlock births (discussed in Chapters 6 and 7) and that they had only a modest effect on separation and divorce. Thus welfare cannot be blamed for either the rise in female-headed households or out-of-wedlock births. In fact, since the mid-1970s the real value of welfare payments has declined, while the number and proportion of female-headed families has risen. Wilson and Neckerman suggest, instead, that these developments are produced by the increasing labor force problems of African American men, especially young, marriageable men. Largely because of high and rising unemployment rates through the early and mid-1980s, the proportion of African American men in stable jobs has been in a long-term decline. Thus the increasing delay of first marriage and the low rate of remarriage among African American women (compared to white women), which produced more female-headed households, is directly tied to the high rates of joblessness for African American males.

It is certainly true that African American male unemployment is high and rising. In the 1970s the average annual unemployment rate for white males was 4.9 percent; for African American males, 10.4 percent, 2.1 times the white rate. In the years 1980–1986 the African American unemployment rate averaged 16.3 percent, 2.3 times the white rate. Sherraden's (1985) research showed that chronic unemployment (twenty-seven weeks or longer) increased among nonwhites between 1971 and 1982, from 1.2 percent to 4.2 percent of all nonwhite employment. The comparable figures for white chronic unemployment were 0.6 percent in 1971 and 1.5 percent in 1982. Furthermore, the number of discouraged nonwhite workers (those who had given up looking for employment) rose as well, from 2.2 percent of total nonwhite employment in 1971 to 4.5 percent in 1982. The comparable figures for white discouraged workers were 0.8 percent in 1971 and 1.2 percent in 1982. Thus joblessness is a far more serious problem for African American workers than for white workers, and the problem has been worsening.

Wilson (1987a) analyzed the connections among male joblessness, female-headed families, and poverty in inner city African American ghettoes. He constructed a Male Marriageable Pool Index (MMPI) to show the ratio of employed men to women of the same age range (both under forty-five years old). Analysis of changes in the MMPI over time demonstrated that young African American women have confronted a shrinking pool of marriageable men. At the same time, changes in the MMPI for white women have been minimal. Thus between 1960 and 1980, in the North Central states, the African American MMPI (employed men per 100 women) declined by 12.5 percent and African American female-headed families rose by 26.3 percent; for whites, the MMPI declined by only 3.6 percent and female-headed families rose by only 5.8 percent. Similar patterns were found for the other three regions of the United States. Rodgers's (1986, p. 53) analysis also found a connection between male joblessness and female-headed households among African Americans: "The staggering rate of unemployment suffered by black males correlates strongly with rates of poverty among black female-headed households."

Why the increase in joblessness among inner city African American men? There are at least three causes. First, the movement of increasing numbers of the African American middle class to the suburbs has left higher concentrations of the poor in inner city ghettoes. This phenomenon has bereft inner city neighborhoods of resources needed to increase their job potential. Second, inner city ghettoes have been subjected to one devastating invasion after another since the 1950s—the bulldozers and speculators involved in interstate highway construction, urban renewal, and gentrification (discussed in Chapter 9). The resulting displacement further undermined the social attachments of ghetto residents (a job-promoting resource), which had already been weakened by the massive and relatively rapid migration from the rural South (Piven and Cloward, 1987, p. 79).

The third and most direct cause of increasing inner city African American male joblessness is the decline of industrial jobs with low educational requirements. Between 1970 and 1984, for example, New York City lost 492,000 jobs whose workers had a mean educational attainment of less than high school (Wilson, 1987a, p. 40). The deindustrialization of Snowbelt cities had a disastrous effect on African American males, especially young ones: they were more likely to lose their jobs than were white males (Baca Zinn, 1987, pp. 17–18). Based on a statistical analysis of national data, Lichter (1988) concluded that, in central cities, the African American jobless rate increased substantially more than did the white rate between 1970 and 1982. Young, uneducated African Americans were particularly affected. The large migration of African Americans from the rural South to the urban North, especially during World War II, had been pulled by the attraction of available low-skill jobs in expanding industries, including auto and steel. (The migration was pushed by the mechanization of Southern agriculture.) The massive decline in these industries since the early 1970s, coupled with historical job discrimination against African Americans, left many inner city African Americans high and dry. Gunnar Myrdal (1962) was the first to refer to these African American jobless workers as an underclass.

The underclass can be expanded to include people in any combination of four conditions: (1) persistent poverty, (2) not in the labor market, (3) not in a family headed by a married couple, (4) long-term use of public assistance. Although there are little data on this group, it probably constitutes a minority of the poor. One researcher, using a variety of definitions, estimated that the underclass represented from 5 to 24 percent of the poor population (Reischauer, 1987). Actually, the word *class* may be a misnomer for this group of people, for there is no empirical evidence that they demonstrate homogeneous behavior and attitudes that differ from those of the larger population. In fact, people in the underclass share the basic values of the majority of the population. The underclass, in Bane's (1984, pp. 11–12) words, are "the result of a collision of basically mainstream values among the poor with hard luck and difficult circumstances." Among these difficult circumstances we must include racism and high unemployment.

The feminization of poverty, while more acute in the United States, seems to be a problem in other nations as well, perhaps caused by the common failure of capitalist societies to equalize women's opportunities in the labor force, and the failure of both capitalist and socialist nations to equalize men's responsibilities in the family. The United States ranked last in the 1980s among seven Welfare States and socialist nations in social policy measures to deal with female poverty (Goldberg and Kremen, 1987). We can speculate that the problem is more acute in the United States because of two factors: the country's racial divisions and its weak Welfare State.

A comparative study of eight Welfare States by Kamerman and Kahn (1987) found that the United States ranked last in providing income to single-mother families. For nonworking single mothers with two children in Sweden, family income was 93.8 percent of the net wage of the average production worker; this was the highest among the eight nations. The ranking was as follows: 1, Sweden; 2, France; 3, West Germany; 4, Canada; 5, U.K.; 6, Australia, Israel; 8, U.S. In the U.S. single mothers with two children had incomes that were only 44 percent of the net wage of the average production worker. For low-wage single working mothers with two children, Sweden again ranked first—such families had incomes that were 123.1 percent of the net wage of the average production worker. The ranking was as follows: 1, Sweden; 2, France; 3, U.K.; 4, Australia; 5, Canada; 6, Israel; 7, West Germany; 8, U.S. In the U.S. low-wage single working mothers with two children had incomes only 69.2 percent of the net wage of the average production worker. These rankings correspond to national rankings in the level of support for Welfare State activity (discussed in Chapter 4): the more advanced Welfare States did better in providing income security for single mothers. Also, the countries in which universal programs dominated did better than those in which means-tested programs dominated.

The glaring deficiencies of the United States relative to other Welfare States in dealing with poverty point to a need for new social policies.

SOCIAL POLICY ISSUES

A range of social policy innovations is available to reduce the income security problems of tens of millions of Americans. In this section of the chapter we analyze several of these ideas, including a family allowance, socialized child support, workfare, and full employment. In addition, we present a number of reforms that could be made to strengthen current policies and programs. Finally, we discuss the Family Support Act of 1988.

Family Allowance

The major policy weakness of U.S. antipoverty efforts is their categorical nature. Separating subgroups from the general population offends ideals of universality, community, and fairness. Moreover, targeted subgroups like the poor often lack political power, and under our political system, weak constituencies create weak programs. Further, categorical programs are inefficient; sometimes they overlap, and at other times they leave gaps in coverage. Finally, duplication of administrative overhead adds to the inefficiency of income security programs.

Instead of antipoverty policy, what is needed is a comprehensive income security policy that incorporates both the needs of the poor and the needs of other citizens. In Heclo's (1986, p. 308) words, "when developing programs designed to serve the best interests of the poor, we should not think only of the poor." His point was echoed by Wilson (1987b, p. 7), who suggested that the way "to improve the life chances of truly disadvantaged groups such as the ghetto underclass is by emphasizing programs to which the more advantaged groups of all races and class backgrounds can positively relate."

Social Security is a prominent example of the success of comprehensive income security policy. What we need is a similarly successful minimum income policy. Many Welfare States have a legislated universal minimum income policy, including West Germany (since 1961), the Netherlands (1963), the U.K. (1970), Belgium (1974), Israel (1980), Luxembourg (1986), and France (1986). The policies are intended to provide aid to families that are not covered by Social Security. A family allowance (or children's allowance) is one type of minimum income. Under a family allowance policy (discussed further in Chapter 6), families are paid a sum (nationally standardized and indexed for inflation) for each child born, and then monthly payments until the child reaches adulthood. The money is paid on the basis of the presence and number of children, not on the basis of family income.

Socialized Child Support

There are other alternatives to deal with the growing needs of female-headed families. A major problem for female-headed families is securing adequate child support payments from absent fathers. There are two categories of absent fathers who fail to pay child support: (1) those who can pay and do not (a problem of enforcement and collection) and (2) those who cannot pay (a problem of unemployment and poverty).

A study by Oellerich and Garfinkel (1983) indicated that a socialized child support program could substantially reduce poverty among female-headed households. Using data on 3,547 female-headed households from the U.S. Current Population Survey—Child Support Supplement, the researchers found that a perfect collection regime would reduce poverty among support eligible children only marginally, by less than 10 percent. This is because the average child support award is very low, since the fathers of most poor children are also poor. However, if absent parents were required to pay support equal to a certain proportion of their incomes and the state were to make up the difference to a minimum support benefit of $2,000 per year for one child, up to $7,000 for six or more children, the poverty among eligible children would be reduced by a whopping 44 percent.

The development of a socialized child support policy could proceed in several stages (Stuart, 1986, pp. 215–216): (1) application of a uniform formula for support, like that used in Minnesota and other states, rather than continued reliance on individual court-based decisions; (2) mandatory withholding of support from absent parents (as a percentage of their wages), as tested in Wisconsin; (3) federalization of income withholding, in order to improve collection and to standardize payments; and (4) implementation of a federal supplement when support payments fall below the minimum standard. Meanwhile, perhaps poor and absent fathers could be afforded an opportunity to make their support contribution in other than financial ways, such as by sharing more in child rearing and by staffing schools and child-care centers (Amott, 1987).

The Wisconsin experimental child support program, designed at the University of Wisconsin's Institute for Poverty Research, has received good reviews from analysts. Begun as a pilot program in 1983, the experiment combines a mandatory child support payment for absent parents (as a percent of their wages) and a state-guaranteed minimum child support benefit. The difference between what the absent parent pays and the minimum is assumed by the state. In his summary evaluation of this program, Chambers (1986, p. 211) stated:

> The signal genuinely humane aspect of this proposal is its ability to generate a universal benefit and to destigmatize a way of life for an increasing number of women and children while it takes advantage of a method of financing that is proven effective and has, in place, an enforcement capacity that requires no additional expensive personnel or administrative machinery.

Workfare

A historically recurrent reaction to growth in welfare has been mandatory work for its recipients. There are a number of problems with workfare, involving both the work and the welfare recipients, that make it unlikely that it will succeed.

A 1987 study of sixty-one workfare programs in thirty-eight states by the General Accounting Office (GAO) found that in one-half the programs, more than 50 percent of the recipients stayed on welfare after finding work because most of them had ended up in low-wage or part-time jobs. This is a major problem with workfare: the jobs that recipients get pay very low wages—often the minimum wage, which is less income than either the poverty line or the public assistance grant. In 1987, in New York City, the maximum public assistance grant for a family of three was $652 per month, considerably more than a minimum wage job would provide. In addition, working would require the mother to pay for transport, child care, health care, and other expenses. The GAO study concluded that workfare programs did not succeed because welfare recipients were not given the necessary remedial education or train-ing to improve their job skills. (In 1987 only 25 percent of New York City's public assistance recipients had graduated from high school, while more than 90 percent of job openings required at least a high school diploma.)

Even if provision were made for upgrading the skills of welfare recipients, workfare would remain highly problematic. This and other such policies that emphasize training, education, and social services have been found to produce very limited benefits to poor people compared to direct cash or in-kind assistance. According to Morris and Williamson (1986, pp. 2–3) workfare depends on changing personal characteristics such as abilities and attitudes, a very difficult task. These analysts pointed out that successful workfare requires the unlikely fulfillment of all of the following conditions: (1) participants must be motivated and able to learn; (2) their training must be educationally sound; (3) the training must be at a high enough level to provide program graduates with better than poverty-level wages; (4) decent-paying jobs must be available in the participants' communities; and (5) graduates must be able to hold jobs and these jobs must be long term.

Another major problem with workfare is its assumption that there are many malingerers on public assistance. Research has consistently demonstrated that this is not so. One example is Goodwin's (1983) finding that public assistance recipients did not lack motivation to work—rather, they lacked the skills to get jobs at decent wages. His study of 428 AFDC recipients in 1978–1981 led him to conclude that they would have preferred to work, but there were not enough jobs available at wages that would have allowed them to support their families. This conclusion was supported by Duncan's (1984) finding that most recipients used public assistance to supplement their labor market earnings. Only 2 percent of Duncan's national sample were persist-ently dependent on public assistance, defined as receipt of aid amounting to more than one-half of family income in eight or more years of the ten-year study period. Likewise, Rein's (1982, p. 117) study of 206 recipient families, using PSID data, found that over an eight-year period, for the years when the families were on welfare, 30.3 percent of their total household income came from earnings.

Other research (Morris and Williamson, 1987, p. 49) has indicated that even when workfare does have a positive effect, it is quite modest. Gueron's (1987, p. 29) evaluation of feasibility studies of workfare programs in five sites (Arkansas, Baltimore, San Diego, Virginia, and West Virginia) concluded that the programs moved only a small fraction of welfare recipients (in the range of 5 percent) into the work force. The Urban Institute estimated that a nation-al workfare program would reduce its participants' reliance on welfare by only 1 to 5 percent, while raising their earnings by only 3 to 6 percent (Walsh, 1988). The most telling critique of the positive results of feasibility studies is that all of them excluded mothers with children under six years of age. Moreover, a number of the studies limited their samples to new welfare recipients. Thus the studies did not address the problems of the bulk of the

AFDC caseload—female-headed families with young children and long-term recipients (Block and Noakes, 1988).

Workfare reinforces the traditional dominance of the market and tailors its approach to the market: recipients are pressured to take whatever jobs are available at whatever wages employers will pay. In fact, the market is at the heart of the problem, in the widespread economic dislocation and unemployment it creates through the downs of the business cycle, through uneven development (discussed in Chapter 9) that leaves some regions and industries in depression, and through long-term structural change that eliminates whole categories of work.

The most serious obstacle to the success of workfare is the functional need for a capitalist economy to maintain a sizable minority of its labor force in underemployment and unemployment in order to secure economic and social control over workers and their wage demands. When many jobs pay poverty-level wages and many workers cannot find jobs, all workers find it more difficult to get wage increases and to keep their jobs. This is how employers keep their labor costs to a minimum.

Workfare has met with little success in other nations. For instance, an analysis (Evans and McIntyre, 1987) of provincial workfare programs in Canada found that they encouraged a short-term work approach, had important hidden costs, and eroded the entitlement of single mothers to public assistance. Ultimately, workfare cannot measurably reduce poverty in the absence of decent-paying jobs. The availability of such jobs is predicated on an effective full-employment policy and an above-poverty minimum wage, subjects that we now address.

Full Employment

Reducing unemployment is necessary in order to reduce poverty. Corcoran and Hill (1980) demonstrated that the number of persons in poverty would have been reduced by about 10 percent if all the unemployment of household heads had been eliminated. Today the effect would probably be greater, as this research was done in a period (1967–1976) of lower unemployment than the 1980s. Other research has demonstrated that the amount of poverty in a locality reflects the availability of non–poverty-level jobs (Tomaskovic-Devey, 1988).

Unemployment, however, is only part of the job problem. For example, in 1982 the unemployment rate represented only about 60 percent of all job problems among African Americans. The other 40 percent was caused by subemployment (workers not looking for work because they believe it is unavailable) and underemployment by low hours or by low pay (Lichter, 1988). For the entire labor force in 1986, Gross (1987) estimated that, in addition to the 8 million officially unemployed workers, there were 5 million part-time workers seeking full-time jobs and 7 million discouraged workers (unemployed and not looking for jobs), for a total of about 20 million. Additionally, there were an estimated 50 million underpaid workers and workers in insecure jobs, making a total of 70 million people who were directly or indirectly the victims of the job problem in the United States.

A minimum step to meet the large need for secure jobs at adequate wages would be a comprehensive full-employment policy, successful examples of which abound in other Welfare States. As Bell (1983, pp. 5–7) pointed out, a full-employment policy is one of the three cornerstones of the Welfare State that do not exist in the United States. (The other two are national health insurance and a family allowance.) A comprehensive full-employment policy would provide guaranteed jobs and raise wages, thereby assuring workers of a social right to a decent livelihood. At least two Welfare States have been successful at implementing a full-employment policy while maintaining high worker productivity. Between 1980 and 1986 the annual unemployment rate in Japan averaged 2.6 percent of the labor force; in Sweden, 2.9 percent. By contrast, U.S. unemployment rates averaged 8.1 percent in the same period, and labor productivity (as measured by output per hour) was lower than in Japan and Sweden. Of all the capitalist nations Sweden has the largest public sector, the highest taxes, and the most generous Welfare State. At the same time, the nation's economy was among the strongest in the 1980s—inflation fell below 4 percent, unemployment remained below 3 percent, the economy grew at about 3 percent a year, and real wages stayed among the highest in the world (Levine, 1988).

The effectiveness of a full-employment policy was demonstrated by Therborn (1986). His study of sixteen Welfare States found that only five prevented the worldwide economic crisis that began in 1973 from leading to mass unemployment among their people: Austria, Japan, Norway, Sweden, and Switzerland. All these nations had firmly institutionalized full-employment policies (maintaining unemployment rates below 2.5 percent) before the crisis began—policies that stressed adjusting the labor market to achieve full employment. The other eleven nations in the study plunged into mass unemployment because they had no institutionalized full-employment policy or because they adopted anti-inflation or growth policies, neither of which was effective in preventing rising unemployment. These nations were Australia, Belgium, Canada, Denmark, Finland, France, Italy, the Netherlands, the U.K., the U.S., and West Germany.

Strengthening Current Approaches

In order to ensure the success of major innovations such as full employment, changes need to be made in the minimum wage, income security benefits, and the tax codes.

The working poor will be helped primarily by raising the minimum wage. The national minimum wage has been $3.35 an hour since 1981 and is overdue for a raise. In 1938 the minimum wage represented 40.3 percent of the average manufacturing wage; by 1981, 41.9 percent. However, in just six years, from 1981 to 1987, the minimum wage fell to only 33.8 percent of the average manufacturing wage (Stout, 1988). In response to the erosion in the value of the national minimum wage, California in 1988 raised its own minimum wage to $4.25 an hour, making it the highest in the nation. The action affected about 600,000 workers in the state. The national minimum wage should be raised to 50 percent of the average production worker's hourly wage. In June 1988 this would have meant a minimum wage of $4.64. Also, the minimum wage should be indexed (adjusted to changes in the Consumer Price Index) in order to prevent its real value from constantly declining because of inflation.

A number of improvements are needed in present income security programs. A national minimum and indexed (for inflation) AFDC grant should be established by the federal government, comparable to the Social Security benefit. The grants that some states pay are shamefully low. In 1985 the average monthly AFDC benefit was $550 in Alaska, $514 in California, $495 in Minnesota, $490 in Wisconsin, and $453 in New York, the highest-paying states, but only $104 in Mississippi, $113 in Alabama, $134 in Tennessee, $162 in Texas, and $164 in Arkansas, the lowest-paying states. In 1988 the maximum combined AFDC and Food Stamp benefits did not raise a family of three out of poverty in any state. This situation has worsened over time: from 1970 to 1985 the real value of the average AFDC grant declined by about one-third (Abramovitz, 1988). Also, the paperwork required in the AFDC application process is burdensome and unfair to many potential recipients. A study sponsored by the Southern Governors' Association and the Southern Legislative Conference found that in the year ending June 30, 1986, 16 percent of welfare and Medicaid applicants were denied benefits solely because of application problems (Tolchin, 1988). This compared to just 7 percent of applicants who were denied benefits because they earned too much or owned too much to qualify. Furthermore, many potential recipients do not even apply for AFDC because they are unaware of the program or of their potential eligibility.

Social Security needs to be reformed in order to meet the special needs of women, including their longevity, and to compensate for discrimination against women in the labor force. In December 1985 monthly Social Security benefits averaged $530 for men and $383 for women. Schorr (1986, p. 69) proposed the following reforms of Social Security to help women: (1) upgrading benefits for the old old (who are discussed in Chapter 8), perhaps by revising them to increase with age rather than decrease, in real terms, as they do now; (2) liberalizing maximum benefits for families; and (3) restoring a general minimum benefit.

The major problem with unemployment insurance is that it reaches only a minority of unemployed workers. Unemployed people who have never worked, such as youths coming out of high school and housewives looking for work after their children are grown, are not covered by UI. Others not covered are people who have exhausted their benefits (the maximum period of benefits is only twenty-six weeks). Additionally, the Reagan administration placed new restrictions on UI payments. As a result of all these factors, only 25.4 percent of unemployed people received UI in October 1987. According to research done by the Center on Budget and Policy Priorities (Washington, DC), this was the lowest percentage recorded since such data were first collected in 1955.

Finally, we need to reform the federal tax codes to allow the working poor to regain the position they held before the Reagan years. Between 1975 and 1986 the tax-free amount of income as a percentage of the poverty line fell from 122 percent to 82 percent. In 1986 the tax-free income, comprising personal exemptions, the standard deduction, and the earned income tax credit, for a family of four was $9,503. However, the poverty line in 1986 was $11,203 for a nonfarm family of four, which meant that that family had to pay taxes on $1,700 of their income (Terrell, 1986, p. 276). To remedy this situation, the portion of income exempt from taxes can be increased.

The Family Support Act of 1988   The AFDC program was reformed with the passage of the Family Support Act (FSA) of 1988, the provisions of which will be implemented in stages through the 1990s. The act's substantive titles are the following:

I: *Child Support and Establishment of Paternity.* This provision will increase the enforcement of child support payments from absent parents, who are nearly always fathers. Enforcement will be strengthened by, among other measures, withholding support payments from the wages of absent parents, mandating automated tracking and monitoring systems, using Social Security numbers to establish the identities of absent parents, and creating a Commission on Interstate Child Support to deal with jurisdictional problems.

II: *Job Opportunities and Basic Skills Training Program.* This provision will establish a work training (workfare) program.

III: *Supportive Services for Families.* This provision will establish child-care services for participants being trained for work and extend (for one year) transitional child-care and Medicaid benefits to participants who find work.

IV: *Related AFDC Amendments.* Among other changes, this provision will mandate universal coverage of two-parent AFDC families.

V: *Demonstration Projects.* This provision will set up demonstration and research projects that will, among other things, test the effects of early childhood development programs, encourage states to employ AFDC parents as paid child-care providers, and create counseling and social services to prevent pregnancy, suicide, substance abuse, and school dropout among high-risk teenagers.

The FSA addressed two of the major social policy measures we have discussed in this chapter: child support and workfare. The act will no doubt improve enforcement of child support payments by working absent fathers, but it will do nothing to alleviate the problem of absent fathers who do not have the means to pay child support. With regard to workfare, mandatory work will be implemented by the requirement that states enroll 20 percent of their

AFDC recipients in work training programs by 1995. It is significant that this version of workfare will also mandate support services for recipients who participate, including child care and Medicaid benefits. However, the workfare provision still has many of the generic weaknesses of all such programs. We will point out only two of them. First, many AFDC recipients (perhaps the majority) will, rightfully, be excluded from work training, including those who are ill, disabled, or elderly; those who care for an ill or disabled household member; and those who have children under three years of age. Second, the workfare provision of FSA does not actually provide jobs—much less decent, permanent jobs. Also, FSA does not provide follow-up support beyond one year for ex-recipients fortunate enough to find jobs.

The FSA did not address two major social policy measures that we have discussed in this chapter: full employment and the family allowance. Thus the major shortcoming of this act will probably prove to be what it does not do. As Axinn and Stern (1988, p. 161) have noted, the Family Support Act "may be as significant for what it ignores as for what it addresses." While reform of AFDC is welcome, the FSA does not go far enough. For example, the act does not raise the low level of AFDC benefits, nor does it make it any easier for the many eligible poor who are not currently receiving benefits to get them. However, the FSA does provide some hope for future change because it mandates "the study of a new national system of welfare benefits for low-income families with children, giving particular attention to what an appropriate national minimum benefit might be and how it should be calculated" (U.S. Congress, Public Law 100-485, Section 406, p. 2399, October 13, 1988). Finally, the FSA does little to address the needs of the poor who do not qualify for AFDC. Thus the working poor, who constitute the majority of adults below the poverty line, will receive no relief from the Family Support Act.

SOCIAL PRACTICE

Income security policy innovation cannot proceed successfully until the concerns of income security social practitioners are addressed. The largest group of Welfare State workers directly involved in income security are the employees of public assistance offices. In 1985 there were 430,000 public assistance workers—one-fortieth of all public workers. Over one-half of these workers were employed at the local level in county public assistance departments.

Social work practice in large settings such as public assistance has become increasingly industrialized and Taylorized. The principal forces behind this development have been the U.S. fiscal crisis and the Reagan ideology, both of which have eroded the resources for social welfare institutions while increasing their workloads. Taylorism, or scientific management, divides a task into minute, time-limited detail operations and shapes the worker's activity to fit the task. It is a special application of industrial and bureaucratic management, in which work is increasingly routinized and standardized. Fabricant (1985, p. 394) made the following comment on the results of this process: "The work process is increasingly controlled by scientific managers and an assembly-line structure that characteristically deskills the worker, fragments the problem, contests any form of discretionary decision making, and ultimately contributes to burnout." Patry (1978, p. 35) documented the introduction of Taylorism to the Texas Department of Human Resources in 1977; one of the industrial engineers involved in the project complained to the researcher that "workers 'show no respect whatsoever for productivity,' spending as much time as is needed to take care of individual client's needs."

The overall goal of increasing rationalization of social practice—by subdividing and routinizing it—is to cheapen its cost. The overall impact on social practitioners is to dequalify their work (Johnson and O'Donnell, 1981, pp. 47–48). This dequalification of social practice is similar to the deskilling of craft work, as analyzed by Braverman (1974). As managerial control is asserted over social practice, social practitioners become less independent and exercise less discretion. This managerial control is increasingly modeled after corporate management in the private sector, and its negative effects are most evident perhaps in health care (see Chapter 8).

The Taylorization of social practice plays a major role in the development of burnout among social practitioners. Burnout (also discussed in Chapter 7 and 8) is a condition characterized by emotional withdrawal from work and from clients; it is reflected in absenteeism and other symptoms. Burnout can be viewed as a response to the monotony, higher caseloads, and decreased autonomy of social practice (Arches, 1985). It is a sure indication of low work satisfaction among social practitioners.

In a study of the Alabama public welfare agency Teare (1981) found that work satisfaction among its five major job families was lowest for eligibility workers and social service workers (the other three job families were paraprofessionals, supervisors, and administrators). He attributed this low satisfaction chiefly to the conflict between the job demand of accountability (surveillance of recipients) and the personal desire (and professional mandate) to provide service. Contributing factors were the need to try to meet more human needs than the organization's resources permitted, large caseloads, and an immense amount of paperwork.

The negative work situation of public assistance stems partly from the fact that they work with socially devalued clients in an underfunded organization. Bertha Capen Reynolds (1975) noted this limitation nearly forty years ago: "Social workers in public assistance have always been placed by their communities under severe handicaps, with little community understanding of their work and never enough money to make possible a decent standard of living for relief recipients." Public assistance has more than its share of routine "dirty work" (Hughes, 1958), such as terminations and refusals to certify. In addition, the entire clientele is socially stigmatized, and some of this stigma rubs off on public assistance workers, creating a greater sense of devaluation than exists in most other Welfare State bureaucracies.

Public assistance workers use three approaches as antidotes to the regimentation, impersonality, and devaluation of their work:

1. *Professionalization.* This is the caseworker model, and it emphasizes the social service aspect of public assistance work. Lipsky (1980) argued that while professionalization may be a viable route for improving the work conditions and performances of street-level bureaucrats such as public assistance workers, it probably will not improve responsiveness to clients. Moreover, at this point there are two serious limits to professionalization in public assistance (Street, Martin, and Gordon, 1979): lack of professional training and career lines, and the public mandate for surveillance and control of clients. Public assistance workers in the United States have had to turn to other forms of organization. A similar development has occurred in Britain, where the political ineffectiveness of the professional organization has resulted in union growth among social workers (Jones, 1983, p. 135).

2. *Radicalization.* This approach argues that public assistance workers, being strategically located at the edge of the Welfare State, develop anticapitalist ideas and, especially if they are able to act in coalition with their clients, can be agents of institutional and social change (Corrigan and Leonard, 1978). Another reason these workers are likely to have progressive political attitudes is that they are disproportionately minority group members, especially African Americans. Minority group members make up nearly one-fourth of state and local government employees, about twice their representation in the total labor force. Radicalization rejects professionalism in favor of solidarity with clients and with other workers (Withorn, 1984). The success of this advocacy model depends to a large extent on the historical moment. All the successful examples of radicalization and resultant coalition building come from periods of generally heightened protest activity such as the 1930s and 1960s. Then groups of public assistance recipients and workers were able to work cooperatively in a number of local areas.

3. *Unionization.* Public employee unionization grew rapidly between 1965 and 1975. In 1964 there were 1.5 million unionized government workers, representing 8 percent of union workers and 15 percent of government workers. In 1978 there were 3.6 million unionized government workers, representing 17 percent of union workers and 23 percent of government workers. This growth continued into the Reagan era. In 1986 there were 5.9 million unionized government workers, representing 33 percent of union workers and 36 percent of government workers. Between 1964 and 1987 the largest government workers' union, the American Federation of State, County, and Municipal Employees, grew from 235,000 to 1 million members, more than a fourfold rise. The increasing unionization of public employees has, in fact, been the major positive development for the U.S. labor movement, which has been in overall decline. While the proportion of all workers who were unionized fell from 28 percent in 1968 to 18 percent in 1986, the proportion of public workers who were union members rose from 18 percent in 1968 to 36 percent in 1984.

Public worker unions hold out the promise of radicalizing the U.S. labor movement as the Congress of Industrial Organizations (CIO) did in the 1930s

(Yates, 1981). This promise is based on their unique and critical role as instruments of state legitimacy. Public workers are the providers of benefits and services that are a bedrock feature of the state's legitimacy in the eyes of working-class recipients. Adams and Freeman (1980) have argued that if social workers are to be agents of change, they will have to become so in coalition with the labor movement, not with their clients, for only the labor movement can provide social workers with the power base necessary to effect change. Unfortunately, however, the U.S. labor movement has lost substantial power, and anyway, unions tend to focus on bread-and-butter issues (wages and working conditions) rather than on social change. Government employee unions have been relatively successful on bread-and-butter issues. In 1986 unionized government workers made 15 percent more in weekly wages than nonunionized government workers. Also, government social practitioners earn more than those in the private sector. In June 1987, in New York City, the salary of a social worker with a master's degree at a city agency ranged from $24,967 to $30,685. The average salary of comparable workers in private agencies was just $21,806 (Blair, 1987).

However successful unionization has been for the material position of government workers, it has the potential for creating yet another barrier between workers and clients. The Schutt (1986) study of unionization among public assistance workers in Chicago demonstrated that as the union matured, it moved away from identification and joint action with public assistance recipients. There is some hope that this tendency will not generalize because government employee unions are more progressive than other unions on policy questions, certainly on those affecting women and minorities, who are the great majority of public assistance recipients.

Finally, it may be a mistake to assume that professionalization and unionization are mutually incompatible for public assistance workers and for other social practitioners. There are numerous examples of professional social practitioners who are members of effective unions, including unionized professors in higher education. While professionalization has been generally more successful among upper-level social practitioners and unionization among lower-level workers, there is evidence that social practitioners do not view the two types of organization as competing alternatives. A study (Alexander, Lichtenberg, and Brunn, 1980) of 84 MSW (Masters in Social Work) union members in a large U.S. urban area found that though they viewed their work as professional, they saw no incompatibility between unionization and professionalization. Also, Lightman's (1982) study of 121 professional social workers in Toronto reported that a vast majority saw no incompatibility between the two approaches. The respondents clearly outlined a division of labor for unions and professional groups. Wages and job security were identified by the social workers as the two areas of their work that unions could best improve, and professional standards and in-service training and education as the two areas that professional associations could best improve.

Social Practitioner at Work: Janet Johnson

Janet Johnson is a social work specialist in the Cook County (Chicago) Department of Public Aid. She works directly with public assistance recipients, providing counseling and case management services. Her current clients are elderly persons, often homeless, who are referred to the department's Adult Protective Services Unit by the police, other city agencies, and churches and synagogues.

Janet's clients are often socially isolated people who receive no help from family, friends, or other agencies. One client with whom she became very involved she was never able to meet. This elderly woman had been referred to her by another city agency because she had no running water and heat in her apartment and because she was covered with dirt and feces. Janet spent several days making telephone calls and searching for the woman, who never seemed to be home. She contacted the woman's landlord, public agencies, and local hospitals in an effort to restore services to the woman's apartment and to arrange hospital care for her if she needed it. After several days of intensive work on the case, Janet arranged for support from a local hospital's Mobile Crisis Team (psychiatric) and entered the woman's apartment with the help of her brother, only to find her dead. Janet felt bad about the situation, especially since some people mistakenly blamed her for taking too long to help the woman. She did some counseling work with the woman's brother, who had had a major conflict with his sister.

In another case, referred by a visiting nurse, Janet was asked by a woman to place her mother, with whom she was living, in a nursing home. The mother, aged sixty-four, was slowly killing herself through alcoholism and refusal to eat. Janet made several visits to the home and established a beginning relationship with the mother, who said she did not want to live. After some counseling, Janet was able to get the mother to enter a contract in which she agreed to try to live, with Janet's help. Janet arranged for a homemaker from her agency to visit the mother on a regular basis to help her with her physical needs. For a while the mother's condition stabilized, but then her health worsened and Janet convinced her she needed care in a hospital. Once in the hospital, the mother deteriorated rapidly and died. Janet said that "she just gave up; I really wanted her to live." At least, Janet said, the woman developed a real connection with her before she died—she felt a bond with the woman, and believed the woman was making an effort because of that bond. Janet has continued to counsel the woman's daughter, a woman in her early forties who never married and had always lived with her mother. Janet discovered that the daughter resented her mother because she had left her husband (the daughter's father) when the daughter was very young and until recently had claimed that it was the husband who had left her. Janet believed that the daughter's hatred of the mother and the mother's guilt played important parts in the mother's slow suicide.

Janet's work is challenging for a number of reasons. Her clients are often people for whom help from other agencies and sources has either never been extended or has been exhausted. These people are frequently in extreme distress, physically and emotionally, and feel little hope. They are difficult to locate, and once found, they may refuse help, which is their right—assuming they are capable of exercising it, which is a difficult and complicated legal and moral question to resolve. Even if a meaningful and beneficial relationship with a client can be established, the client still may not be able to change, or the resources necessary for change, such as housing and health care, may be nonexistent or inadequate. Finally, as happened in the two examples Janet offered, some clients die during the course of her work with them. Janet has gotten a lot of emotional support from her co-workers, especially in weekly group meetings where workers discuss their feelings about their clients. Unfortunately, not all her supervisors have been willing to support such activities. Usually, the more professionally trained supervisors are more supportive.

Janet said that being a social worker is a natural outcome of her family experience. She was born in 1948 and grew up in an extended family in a small city in the South. She was often the mediator among her four siblings, parents, and grandparents. Janet mediated especially between her parents, who quarreled frequently and eventually divorced. She often found herself defending family members against the moral judgments of other members, as when her grandmother was quite critical of a relative who had a child out of wedlock and wanted to ostracize her. Janet took the position that however one evaluated the woman's action, she needed help in dealing with her situation.

At the University of North Alabama Janet majored in sociology and graduated with a Bachelor of Science degree. She married, moved north with her husband, and took her current job in 1975. After working for about a year, she entered graduate school, where her tuition was paid by the agency. She received her MSW degree in 1977 and returned to the agency. Janet has never done social work anywhere but in public assistance. She finds it very gratifying to know that she is "helping people who really need help and providing services that they would never get" otherwise. Janet's criticism of public welfare work is that a lot of the personnel are not professional social workers and the agency does not emphasize social work. For many workers, it seems to be "just a job."

Janet is an African American woman but she reported that discrimination has not been a major problem for her in public assistance. In her work there are more women and African Americans than in most other kinds of jobs. This, in conjunction with the fact that the agency is a public one, has meant that racist and sexist practices are not so big a roadblock as they are in other jobs. However, Janet has experienced putdowns by white males. After her last promotion she heard some co-workers telling others that she got the new job only because of affirmative action, even though she had more credentials and experience than the white male who had previously held the job.

Janet's clients are poor people. She has learned that poverty is "a very mixed situation," that there are many different kinds of poor people. Janet has known poor people who were wonderful homemakers and parents who sacrificed a lot for their families, and other poor people who were irresponsible and seemed to have given up all desire to change their situation. She has known public assistance recipients who cheated the agency in order to buy shoes for their children, and others who shared in the profits of their children's drug selling. Janet has also seen poverty among the elderly that was caused by self-denial: people with money who refused to spend it on themselves. Thus poor people are, in most ways, just like the rest of us.

With regard to social policy, Janet has definite opinions based on her work experience. She stated that public assistance programs are "just Band-Aids," and that rather than helping the poor escape poverty, "our system just continues to regulate the lives of the poor." Instead of adequately planned and funded programs, public assistance produces "a lot of rules" about what recipients "have to do" in order to get help. One constructive thing that public assistance could do is to provide recipients and potential recipients with education about the agency's programs so that they will know what is available that could help them. This would be a positive approach, stressing what the agency can do for the recipient. The present approach creates a lot of "embarrassment and pain" for clients. In effect, we as a society give up on poor people and then blame and punish them for their lack of progress. Perhaps we need the poor as much as they need us. Janet remembered one co-worker who commented: "What would we do without poor people? What would happen to our jobs?" Janet thinks that we "need an underdog" to make the rest of us feel better.

This is reminiscent of Gans's (1972, p. 281) statement of the functions that poverty serves for society, two of which are to provide jobs for the middle class and to assure the social status of the nonpoor; thus "the poor function as a reliable and relatively permanent measuring rod for status comparison." His was not an argument in favor of poverty; it was, rather, a critique of functionalism. The fact that poverty serves certain functions does not make it desirable or necessary. One alternative is to change society in a direction that reduces the economic and psychological need for poverty. Moreover, it is clear that poverty is dysfunctional for society in at least one way: its high economic and social costs.

Although perfect economic equality may be unrealizable (or even undesirable), it is quite practical to propose that poverty and inequality in the United States can be minimized. Even if there must be some group at the bottom, it does not follow that their lot has to be as miserable as it is in the United States, nor their numbers so large nor their treatment so shameful. Other nations have achieved a higher standard of living for their poor citizens, a smaller poverty population, and a greater acceptance of poor persons. Finally, women, African Americans, Hispanics, and Native Americans are disproportionately represented in the poor population. Poverty is not an equal opportunity status in the United States: white males are underrepresented.

Janet Johnson's comments highlight some important points about public assistance work and public assistance recipients. With regard to poor persons,

Janet's experiences make it apparent that social isolation and acute need are characteristic of public assistance recipients. The isolation and need sometimes overwhelm recipients to the point that they despair. Yet the recipients also display unusual strength in the face of their adversity—far more strength than is required of those of us who are not poor. Also, public assistance recipients are varied in their attitudes and habits. In this respect, the poor are remarkably similar, as a group, to the rich and the middle class. The poor, like the rest of us, are capable of selfishness as well as self-sacrifice, resignation as well as struggle, and sloth as well as industry.

Janet's comments also indicate just how difficult public assistance work can be. Caring for others normally anticipates a reciprocal response: we expect others to return our care about them. In social practice reciprocal caring is not a realistic (or even an appropriate) expectation. However, social practitioners do reasonably desire recognition and gratitude—if only in the form of a "thanks." Unfortunately, many public assistance recipients and other groups of clients are in such an extreme condition of isolation and need that acknowledging the efforts of social practitioners is beyond them.

Normally, institutional and professional rewards compensate social practitioners who work with the most needy and damaged members of society. However, in public assistance, as Janet noted, institutional support is lacking and professional status is ambiguous. Public assistance is underfunded and carries lower status than other social work careers, such as private practice social work. Thus scant institutional and professional resources make Janet's job more difficult.

What is to be done about the difficulties of public assistance work? One, admittedly optimistic, scenario for change is that adoption of the social policies discussed earlier in this chapter will substantially reduce the U.S. poverty population and raise its living standard. This could lead to a reduction in—perhaps even an elimination of—the surveillance presently done by public assistance workers. What would public assistance workers then do? First, the kind of major social policy innovation we have been discussing here would require a lengthy transition period, ensuring that present public welfare workers would retain their jobs. Second, the suggested innovations represent better approaches to the problems of income insecurity, but they will not eliminate them, at least not in the context of a capitalist economy. Thus there will always be a vocation for those who want to work with the personal and social problems created by income insecurity. Even in full-employment capitalist societies such as Japan and Sweden, unemployment rates are in the 2–3 percent range. Also, even in capitalist nations with a minimum income policy, income insecurity remains a problem because benefits are not high enough. The minimum income usually comes to only 30 to 40 percent of the average gross wage of manual workers; the only exception is the Netherlands, where the minimum income amounts to 50 percent of the average gross wage for manual workers (Euzeby, 1987).

Although the social policy innovations we have discussed will not eliminate income insecurity, they may permit the redirection of public welfare work into a more humane course. With fewer recipients, with recipients who are in less extreme isolation and need, and with greater institutional support, public welfare work could be reclaimed as a rewarding social practice, both for its workers and for its recipients.

REFERENCES

Abramovitz, Mimi. 1988. "Why Welfare Reform Is a Sham." *The Nation*, September 26, pp. 221, 238–241.

Adams, Paul, and Gary Freeman. 1980. "On the Political Character of Social Service Work." *Catalyst: A Socialist Journal of the Social Services* 7:71–82.

Alexander, Leslie B., Philip Lichtenberg, and Dennis Brunn. 1980. "Social Workers in Unions: A Survey." *Social Work* 25:216–223.

Amott, Teresa. 1987. "Put Responsibility Where It Belongs." *Dollars & Sense*, October, pp. 17–19.

Arches, Joan. 1985. "Don't Burn, Organize: A Structural Analysis of Burnout in the Human Services." *Catalyst: A Socialist Journal of the Social Services* 5:15–20.

Axinn, June, and Mark J. Stern. 1988. *Dependency and Poverty: Old Problems in a New World.* Lexington, MA: Lexington Books/D. C. Heath.

Baca Zinn, Maxine. 1987. "Minority Families in Crisis: The Public Discussion." Memphis, TN: Center for Research on Women, Memphis State University.

Bane, Mary Jo. 1984. "The Poor in Massachusetts." Pp. 1–13 in *The State and the Poor in the 1980s*, eds. Manuel Carballo and Mary Jo Bane. Boston: Auburn House.

———. 1986. "Household Composition and Poverty." Pp. 209–231 in *Fighting Poverty: What Works and What Doesn't*, eds. Sheldon H. Danziger and Daniel H. Weinberg. Cambridge, MA: Harvard University Press.

Batra, Ravi. 1987. "An Ominous Trend to Greater Inequality." *The New York Times*, May 3.

Beeghley, Leonard. 1983. *Living Poorly in America.* New York: Praeger.

Bell, Winifred. 1983. *Contemporary Social Welfare.* New York: Macmillan.

Bennett, Jon. 1987. *The Hunger Machine: The Politics of Food.* Cambridge: Basil Blackwell/Polity Press.

Blackwell, James E., and Philip Hart. 1982. *Cities, Suburbs, and Blacks: A Study of Concerns, Distrust and Alienation.* Bayside, NY: General Hall.

Blair, William G. 1987. "Workers' Resignations Threaten Quality of Private Social Services." *The New York Times*, December 20.

Block, Fred, and John Noakes. 1988. "The Politics of New-Style Workfare." *Socialist Review* 18:31–58.

Blumberg, Paul. 1980. *Inequality in an Age of Decline.* New York: Oxford University Press.

Boulding, Kenneth E. 1967. "The Boundaries of Social Policy." *Social Work* 12:3–11.

Braverman, Harry. 1974. *Labor and Monopoly Capital: The Degradation of Work in the Twentieth Century.* New York: Monthly Review Press.

Browning, Robert X. 1986. *Politics and Social Welfare Policy in the United States.* Knoxville: University of Tennessee Press.

Burtless, Gary. 1986. "Public Spending for the Poor: Trends, Prospects, and Economic Limits." Pp. 18–49 in *Fighting Poverty: What Works and What Doesn't*, eds. Sheldon H. Danziger and Daniel H. Weinberg. Cambridge, MA: Harvard University Press.

Camasso, Michael J., and Anne E. Camasso. 1986. "Social Supports, Undesirable Life Events, and Psychological Distress in a Disadvantaged Population." *Social Service Review* 60:378–394.

Chambers, Donald E. 1986. *Social Policy and Social Programs: A Method for the Practical Public Policy Analyst.* New York: Macmillan.

Colman, Penny, ed. 1986. "Hunger: Report and Recommendations of the New Jersey Commission on Hunger." Trenton.

Corcoran, Mary, and Martha S. Hill. 1980. "Unemployment and Poverty." *Social Service Review* 54:407–413.

Corrigan, Paul, and Peter Leonard. 1978. *Social Work Practice Under Capitalism: A Marxist Approach.* London: Macmillan.

Dail, Paula W. 1988. "Underemployment and Family Stress." *Public Welfare* 46:30–34.

Danziger, Sheldon. 1988. "The Economy, Public Policy, and the Poor." Pp. 3–13 in *Beyond Welfare: New Approaches to the Problem of Poverty in America*, ed. Harrell R. Rodgers, Jr. Armonk, NY: M. E. Sharpe.

Danziger, Sheldon, Peter Gottschalk, and Eugene Smolensky. 1985. "The Effects of Unemployment and Policy Changes on America's Poor." *Journal of Social Policy* 14:313–331.

Danziger, Sheldon H., Robert H. Haveman, and Robert D. Plotnick. 1986. "Antipoverty Policy: Effects on the Poor and the Nonpoor." Pp. 50–77 in *Fighting Poverty: What Works and What Doesn't*, eds. Sheldon H. Danziger and Daniel H. Weinberg. Cambridge, MA: Harvard University Press.

Danziger, Sheldon, and Robert D. Plotnick. 1986. "Poverty and Policy: Lessons of the Last Two Decades." *Social Service Review* 60:34–51.

Devine, Joel A., and William Canak. 1986. "Redistribution in a Bifurcated Welfare State: Quintile Shares and the U.S. Case." *Social Problems* 33:391–406.

Duncan, Cynthia M., and Ann R. Tickamyer. 1988. "Poverty Research and Policy for Rural America." *The American Sociologist* 19:243–259.

Duncan, Greg J. 1984. *Years of Poverty/Years of Plenty.* Ann Arbor: Institute for Social Research, University of Michigan.

Ellwood, David T. 1984. "The Hope for Self-Support." Pp. 19–48 in *The State and the Poor in the 1980s*, eds. Manuel Carballo and Mary Jo Bane. Boston: Auburn House.

Ellwood, David T., and Lawrence H. Summers. 1986. "Poverty in America: Is Welfare the Answer or the Problem?" Pp. 78–105 in *Fighting Poverty: What Works and What Doesn't*, eds. Sheldon H. Danziger and Daniel H. Weinberg. Cambridge, MA: Harvard University Press.

Euzeby, Chantal. 1987. "A Minimum Guaranteed Income: Experiments and Proposals." *International Labour Review* 126:253–276.

Evans, Patricia M., and Eilene L. McIntyre. 1987. "Welfare, Work Incentives, and the Single Mother: An Interprovincial Comparison." Pp. 101–125 in *The Canadian Welfare State: Evolution and Transition*, ed. Jacqueline S. Ismael. Edmonton: University of Alberta Press.

Fabricant, Michael. 1985. "The Industrialization of Social Work Practice." *Social Work* 30:389–395.

Fossett, Mark A., Omer R. Galle, and William R. Kelly. 1986. "Racial Occupational Inequality, 1940–1980: National and Regional Trends." *American Sociological Review* 51:421–429.

Gans, Herbert J. 1972. "The Positive Functions of Poverty." *American Journal of Sociology* 78:275–289.

Garfinkel, Irwin, and Sara McLanahan. 1988. "The Feminization of Poverty: Nature, Causes, and a Partial Cure." Pp. 27–52 in *Poverty and Social Welfare in the United States*, ed. Donald Tomaskovic-Devey. Boulder, CO: Westview Press.

Goldberg, Gertrude S., and Eleanor Kremen. 1987. "The Feminization of Poverty: Only in America?" *Social Policy* 17:3–14.

Goodban, Nancy. 1985. "The Psychological Impact of Being on Welfare." *Social Service Review* 59:403–422.

Goodwin, Leonard. 1983. *Causes and Cures of Welfare: New Evidence on the Social Psychology of the Poor.* Lexington, MA: D. C. Heath.

Graham, Hilary. 1984. *Women, Health and the Family.* Brighton: Wheatsheaf Books.

Gross, Bertram. 1987. "Rethinking Full Employment." *The Nation*, January 17, pp. 44–48.

Gueron, Judith M. 1987. *Reforming Welfare with Work.* New York: Ford Foundation.

Hansen, Fay. 1984. "Conditions of the Working Class Abroad." *Economic Notes* 52:7, 12.

Heclo, Hugh. 1986. "The Political Foundations of Antipoverty Policy." Pp. 312–340 in *Fighting Poverty: What Works and What Doesn't*, eds. Sheldon H. Danziger and Daniel H. Weinberg. Cambridge, MA: Harvard University Press.

Hoos, Ida R. 1983. *Systems Analysis in Public Policy: A Critique.* Rev. ed. Berkeley: University of California Press.

Hughes, Everett C. 1958. *Men and Their Work.* London: Collier-Macmillan.

Jahoda, Marie. 1982. *Employment and Unemployment: A Social-Psychological Analysis.* Cambridge: Cambridge University Press.

Joe, Tom, and Cheryl Rogers. 1985. *By the Few for the Few: The Reagan Welfare Legacy.* Lexington, MA: D. C. Heath.

Johnson, Dale L., and Christine O'Donnell. 1981. "The Accumulation Crisis and Service Professionals." Pp. 34–53 in *Crisis in the Public Sector: A Reader,* ed. Kenneth Fox et al. New York: Monthly Review Press.

Jones, Chris. 1983. *State Social Work and the Working Class.* London: Macmillan.

Kamerman, Sheila B., and Alfred J. Kahn. 1987. "Universalism and Income Testing in Family Policy: New Perspectives on an Old Debate." *Social Work* 32:277–280.

Kerns, Wilmer L., and Milton P. Glanz. 1988. "Private Social Welfare Expenditures, 1972–85." *Social Security Bulletin* 51:3–10.

Kloby, Gerald S. 1988. "Class Polarization in the United States, 1973–1985." Ph.D. dissertation, Rutgers University.

Lampman, Robert J. 1984. *Social Welfare Spending: Accounting for Changes from 1950 to 1978.* New York: Academic Press.

Levine, David. 1988. "Capitalism, Swedish Style: Managing Full Employment Without Inflation." *Dollars & Sense,* October, pp. 20–22.

Levitan, Sar A., and Isaac Shapiro. 1987. *Working but Poor: America's Contradiction.* Baltimore: Johns Hopkins University Press.

Lewis, Paul. 1987. "World Hunger Found Still Growing." *The New York Times,* June 28.

Lichter, Daniel T. 1988. "Racial Differences in Underemployment in American Cities." *American Journal of Sociology* 93:771–792.

Lightman, Ernie S. 1982. "Professionalization, Bureaucratization, and Unionization in Social Work." *Social Service Review* 56:130–143.

Lipsky, Michael. 1980. *Street-Level Bureaucracy: Dilemmas of the Individual in Public Services.* New York: Russell Sage Foundation.

Martin, George T., Jr. 1972. "The Emergence and Development of a Social Movement Organization Among the Underclass: A Case Study of the National Welfare Rights Organization." Ph.D. dissertation, University of Chicago.

———. 1981. "Social Welfare Trends in the United States." Pp. 505–512 in *Social Welfare in Society,* eds. George T. Martin, Jr., and Mayer N. Zald. New York: Columbia University Press.

Moffitt, Robert, and Douglas A. Wolf. 1987. "The Effect of the 1981 Omnibus Budget Reconciliation Act on Welfare Recipients and Work Incentives." *Social Service Review* 61:247–260.

Morris, Michael, and John B. Williamson. 1986. *Poverty and Public Policy: An Analysis of Federal Intervention Efforts.* Westport, CT: Greenwood Press.

———. 1987. "Workfare: The Poverty/Dependence Trade-Off." *Social Policy* 18:13–16, 49–50.

Myrdal, Gunnar. 1962. *Challenge to Affluence.* New York: Pantheon.

Nichols-Casebolt, Ann. 1986. "The Psychological Effects of Income Testing Income-Support Benefits." *Social Service Review* 60:287–302.

Oellerich, Donald T., and Irwin Garfinkel. 1983. "Distributional Impacts of Existing and Alternative Child Support Systems." *Policy Studies Journal* 12:119–130.

O'Hare, William P. 1987. "Poverty in America: Trends and New Patterns." *Population Bulletin* 40:1–45. Washington, DC: Population Reference Bureau, Inc.

Orshansky, Mollie. 1965. "Counting the Poor: Another Look at the Poverty Profile." *Social Security Bulletin* 28:3–29.

Patry, Bill. 1978. "Taylorism Comes to the Social Services." *Monthly Review* 30:30–37.

Pearce, Diana. 1978. "The Feminization of Poverty: Women, Work and Welfare." *Urban and Social Change Review* 11:28–36.

Piven, Frances Fox, and Richard A. Cloward. 1971. *Regulating the Poor: The Functions of Public Welfare.* New York: Pantheon.

———. 1987. "The Contemporary Relief Debate." Pp. 45–108 in *The Mean Season: The Attack on the Welfare State,* ed. Fred Block et al. New York: Pantheon.

Primus, Wendell. 1989. "Background Material and Data on Programs Within the Jurisdiction of the Committee on Ways and Means." Washington, DC: U.S. Government Printing Office.

Rank, Mark R. 1985. "Exiting from Welfare: A Life-Table Analysis." *Social Service Review* 59:358–376.

————. 1989. "Fertility among Women on Welfare: Incidence and Determinants." *American Sociological Review* 54:296–304.

Rein, Mildred. 1982. *Dilemmas of Welfare Policy: Why Work Strategies Haven't Worked*. New York: Praeger.

Reischauer, Robert D. 1987. "America's Underclass." *Public Welfare* 45:26–31.

Reynolds, Bertha Capen. 1975 [1951]. *Social Work and Social Living: Explorations in Philosophy and Practice*. Washington, DC: National Association of Social Workers.

Rodgers, Harrell R., Jr. 1986. *Poor Women, Poor Families: The Economic Plight of America's Female-Headed Households*. Armonk, NY: M. E. Sharpe.

Rowntree, B. S. 1901. *Poverty: A Study of Town Life*. London: Macmillan.

Sarri, Rosemary C. 1985. "Federal Policy Changes and the Feminization of Poverty." *Child Welfare* 64:235–247.

Schorr, Alvin L. 1986. *Common Decency: Domestic Policies After Reagan*. New Haven, CT: Yale University Press.

Schutt, Russell K. 1986. *Organization in a Changing Environment: Unionization of Welfare Employees*. Albany: State University of New York Press.

Sherraden, Michael W. 1985. "Chronic Unemployment: A Social Work Perspective." *Social Work* 30:403–408.

Smith, James D. 1986. "The Concentration of Wealth in the United States: Trends in the Distribution of Wealth Among American Families." Washington, DC: Joint Economic Committee, U.S. Congress.

Stout, Hilary. 1988. "Propping Up Payments at the Bottom." *The New York Times*, January 24.

Street, David, George T. Martin, Jr., and Laura Kramer Gordon. 1979. *The Welfare Industry: Functionaries and Recipients in Public Aid*. Beverly Hills, CA: Sage Publications.

Stuart, Archibald. 1986. "Rescuing Children: Reforms in the Child Support Payment System." *Social Service Review* 60:201–217.

Teare, Robert J. 1981. *Social Work Practice in a Public Welfare Setting: An Empirical Analysis*. New York: Praeger.

Terrell, Paul. 1986. "Taxing the Poor." *Social Service Review* 60:272–286.

Therborn, Goran. 1984. "The Prospects of Labour and the Transformation of Advanced Capitalism." *New Left Review*, No. 145.

————. 1986. *Why Some Peoples Are More Unemployed Than Others: The Strange Paradox of Growth and Unemployment*. London: Verso.

Tolchin, Martin. 1988. "Welfare Denied to Many of Poor over Paperwork." *The New York Times*, October 29.

Tomaskovic-Devey, Donald. 1988. "Industrial Structure, Relative Labor Power, and Poverty Rates." Pp. 104–129 in *Poverty and Social Welfare in the United States*, ed. Donald Tomaskovic-Devey. Boulder, CO: Westview Press.

Tonak, E. Ahmet. 1987. "The U.S. Welfare State and the Working Class, 1952–1980." *Review of Radical Political Economics* 19:47–72.

Walsh, Joan. 1988. "It's the Rage on Capitol Hill, but Does Workfare Work?" *In These Times*, September 14–20, p. 2.

Weatherford, Bernadyne. 1984. "The Disability Insurance Program: An Administrative Attack on the Welfare State." Pp. 37–60 in *The Attack on the Welfare State*, eds. Anthony Champagne and Edward J. Harpham. Prospect Heights, IL: Waveland Press.

Weaver, Mary. 1984. "The Food Stamp Program: A Very Expensive Orphan." Pp. 111–129 in *The Attack on the Welfare State*, eds. Anthony Champagne and Edward J. Harpham. Prospect Heights, IL: Waveland Press.

Wildavsky, Aaron. 1979. *Speaking Truth to Power: The Art and Craft of Policy Analysis*. Boston: Little, Brown.

Wilson, William Julius. 1987a. *The Truly Disadvantaged: The Inner City, The Underclass, and Public Policy*. Chicago: University of Chicago Press.

————. 1987b. "The Hidden Agenda." *The University of Chicago Magazine* 80:2–11.

Wilson, William Julius, and Kathryn M. Neckerman. 1986. "Poverty and Family Structure: The Widening Gap Between Evidence and Public Policy Issues." Pp. 232–259 in *Fighting Poverty: What Works and What Doesn't*, eds. Sheldon H. Danziger and Daniel H. Weinberg. Cambridge, MA: Harvard University Press.

Withorn, Ann. 1984. *Serving the People: Social Services and Social Change.* New York: Columbia University Press.

Yates, Michael D. 1981. "Public Sector Unions and the Labor Movement." Pp. 220–239 in *Crisis in the Public Sector: A Reader,* ed. Kenneth Fox et al. New York: Monthly Review Press.

6

The Family

Family life not only educates in general but its quality ultimately determines the individual's capacity to love. The institution of the family is decisive in determining not only if a person has the capacity to love another individual but in the larger sense whether he is capable of loving his fellow men collectively.
Martin Luther King, Jr., *Address*, 1965

Welfare State social policy and social practice help to secure social survival, which is the reproduction of society through time. Social reproduction is an ongoing, re-creative, multifaceted process. The reproduction of human society requires much more than sexual propagation. Humans are not programmed by instinctual inheritance; they have a large capacity to learn over their entire lifetimes. Learning begins in an extended period of infancy when we are helpless to fend for ourselves. This period of social dependency requires that other humans nurture and teach us. So in order to reproduce human society, social relationships such as parent-child and social institutions such as the family also have to be reproduced. Human families, in turn, are reproduced through social groups—clans, tribes, racial, ethnic, and class clusters—that also are renewed through the generations. Society is the central structure through which all these diverse human associations are articulated. Thus the reproduction of society entails an elaborate re-creation of human behaviors and values through social relationships, groups, and institutions.

This continuous re-creation of society is not an automatic process—social reproduction does not mold citizens in a cookie-cutter fashion. Social reproduction is a problematic activity that involves ambiguity, contradiction, and struggle. It is an interactive process between society and its members, as individuals and as aggregates. These individuals and groups have quite diverse interests for economic, cultural, and other reasons. There is considerable conflict between groups that revolves about the issues of whose values shall dominate in society and whose interests shall be rewarded. Thus those who favor freedom of choice in reproduction (including abortion) conflict with those who oppose abortion. The position adopted by society, as represented by its legislation and judicial decisions, is a key focus of this conflict.

The most salient group conflict that bears on social reproduction is that between those in society who have superior positions with regard to wealth and power and those who have inferior positions. In Welfare States this division corresponds to the cleavage between the owners of the production system (capitalists) and the workers (discussed in Chapter 2). Indeed, one neo-Marxist view reserves the concept of social reproduction to refer specifically to the social renewal of human labor in capitalist society. According to this perspective, labor power is the sole essential commodity in capitalism that cannot be produced capitalistically (for profit). It is this peculiarity that accounts for the radical separation of work (production) and home (reproduction) in capitalist society (Dickinson and Russell, 1986). Work is the realm in which laborers produce commodities at a profit to capitalists. Home is the realm in which laborers themselves are produced and sustained so that they can work. The control and reproduction of labor power is problematic because workers resist their domination by capitalists and this resistance yields social change. The Welfare State is itself a product of social change; it evolved as mature capitalism's effort to reproduce labor under modern conditions (discussed in Chapter 2). The result of social reproduction, then, is not the continuation of the identical society through history. Societies change and innovate; they also stagnate and decline.

The principal process of social reproduction is learning, carried out largely through the family and the school. Learning is a dynamic process in which learners modulate the content of education and a reciprocal process in which learners and teachers both learn. We become moral persons through the process of learning. Once learned, morality becomes part of us; it is internalized. We monitor our moral compliance through such sentiments as embarrassment and guilt, which, although intensely personal feelings, are socially produced. Sociologists refer to social learning as socialization. The specific content of socialization varies considerably among different class, gender, racial, ethnic, and national groups. However, there is a common core content, which comprises the most general and basic values shared by the whole society or the values of the dominant group in society. In addition to socialization, society has recourse to a related means of social reproduction: social control, both informal (such as peer pressure) and formal (such as commands from authorities), which is the enforcement, often coercive, of socially appropriate behaviors. A pertinent example of social control is compulsory schooling. The family and the school are primary arenas for the exercise of social control as well as for socialization.

In this chapter we analyze the family with regard to social policy. (In Chapter 7 we discuss education and social policy.) Our analysis of the family focuses on changes in its structure and social role, on the new social needs these changes have precipitated, and on the social policies necessary to address these needs. We conclude the chapter with a discussion of the nature of social practice in the family and an interview with a state worker who is involved in the sensitive and difficult task of helping abused children.

THE FAMILY IN TRANSITION

There is widespread concern, even alarm, about the condition of the American family. What is happening is that the structure and purpose of the family are changing, creating new social needs and the necessity for new social policies. If there is a crisis of the family, it is in fact a crisis of social policy, which lags behind the new forms and needs of families. The process by which some family functions have been externalized (removed from the family) plays a central role in the current transition in the family. To the extent that such activities become publicly sponsored they are socialized as well as externalized. An example is compulsory free public schooling, which externalized and socialized a major part of the family's social reproduction activity. The emergence and development of extra-familial child care represents an extension of the same trend.

We are not witnessing the death of the family but the emergence of variations of the family. The traditional family, in which females marry and have children while being supported by and subordinated to male breadwinners, has been the model for social policy. Thus throughout history married women and previously married women have received better treatment under social policy than have single women and unwed mothers (Abramovitz, 1988). The contemporary transition is from one dominant model for the family to a series of diverse models. In addition to the patriarchal model of married father/husband/breadwinner and mother/wife/housewife living with their children, other forms of the family are growing in absolute and relative numbers, including divorced and remarried families, single-parent families, and families in which both father/husband and mother/wife are breadwinners. We can reasonably estimate that the traditional intact patriarchal family declined as a proportion of all families from about one-half in 1950 to only about one-tenth in 1985. This change is not unique to the United States; it is also occurring in other Welfare States, including the U.K. (Pascall, 1986).

There are specific historical, economic, and social changes that are the driving forces in the current transition in family form and purpose, subjects to which we now turn our attention.

Changes in Family Functions

For most of human history it was the family that fulfilled social production (economic) tasks. Capitalism and urbanization have steadily encroached on this purpose of the family. Products formerly made for use in the family are now produced by corporations for profit. In the not-distant past families produced much of their own food, clothing, and shelter. At home, butter was churned, buildings were raised, bread was baked, clothing was sewn, gardens were cultivated, and vegetables were preserved for winter. No longer is this true. For example, the proportion of all flour that was used for commercial purposes in the United States rose from one-seventh in 1899, to two-fifths in 1939, to nine-tenths in 1977. Today even farmers buy their bread.

In losing its production function, the family lost something else. The enormous labor required for production required the services of all family members. (The loss of its production function was a major factor in the decline in the number of children in families, as their labor was no longer needed.) Production was an important focus for social life, necessitating social cooperation and interaction; it was the activity around which intra- and interfamily communal life was organized. Consider canning, or the preservation of food. When canning time came, all family members gathered, for a lot of work had to be done in a short period of time. The vegetables had to be prepared in large quantities and at the moment when they were at their natural best. Neighboring families rotated from one kitchen to another, assisting one another and socializing at the same time.

Thus, in addition to losing its productive function, the family lost a focus of its solidarity: the cooperative dependence of its members. Solidarity comprises those communal activities that unite the family in a mutual social life, with each other and with other families. A good example is recreation. In the past recreation was family produced and family focused; whole families and neighboring families participated in singing and playing musical instruments, telling stories, and picnicking. Today recreation is often conducted outside the context of the family and has become a major market for capitalism. Recreation is purchased in the marketplace in the form of cassettes, records, equipment, tickets, and other commodities. In addition, recreation is marketed for subgroups, so that the family does not consume it as a unit. Different generations separate into different leisure activities: parents go to museums and bars, while their children frequent rock concerts and video arcades. Part of the current stress experienced by the family stems from these centrifugal pressures. Family members are more individuated than they used to be, and families are more isolated from other families. This produces stress, but it is stress caused by the encroachments of corporate capitalism, not by any presumed moral decline in society.

The diminution of its production activities has not meant the end of the family. Two purposes have grown in importance to replace production: consumption of commodities and provision of emotional support. The family has always consumed, of course, but now consumption is a paramount social function of the family and it is producing some negative consequences. The family consumes commodities that are not produced for its need, but for capitalist profit. Through advertising and marketing, families are urged to consume many products that they do not need and that may be detrimental to their health. Take food, for example. Constantly barraged by messages to buy packaged or fast food, family members lose the organic connection between food and nutrition. Many people overeat or eat badly. Studies by the American Academy of Pediatrics found that the proportion of overweight children in the United States increased more than 50 percent in the 1970s and 1980s. Also, the President's Council on Physical Fitness and Sports reported that in 1986 one-third of boys and one-half of girls from six through twelve years of age could not run a mile in less than ten minutes. Society as a whole pays for this, in the form of lost labor and of resources spent on remedial health care for diet-related problems such as heart attacks and strokes. These health problems are sometimes referred to as the diseases of civilization, because they are the result of sedentary lifestyles and of affluent diets that contain high levels of animal fat, sugar, salt, and cholesterol (Eckholm and Record, 1977). The diseases of civilization are chronic degenerative diseases that entail enormous health-care costs (see Chapter 8).

The consumption of commodities is a major focus of family social life, whether in the form of eating out at family restaurants or consuming TV dinners at home. However, unlike traditional family production, which was active and required mutual cooperation, consumption is passive and fosters isolation. This is another way in which the advance of capitalism has infringed on an important aspect of family integrity.

In addition to promoting passive consumption, capitalism has remolded the family into a sanctuary from the travails of modern life—a "haven in a heartless world" (Lasch, 1977). It is now the responsibility of the family to provide the emotional connections that citizens miss in their public lives, where they experience alienation or separateness. Zaretsky (1976) analyzed this development of a personal life apart from society and work as a new basis for the oppression of women: they are now responsible for the maintenance of everybody's personal life. They do it in the family as unpaid mothers and wives. They do it outside the family as low-paid secretaries and waitresses. And they do it in the Welfare State as underpaid social practitioners—caseworkers, nurses, and teachers. We will return to this issue later in the chapter when we discuss social practice.

Its new sanctuary function puts great strain on the family and adds to its instability. The transition to a smaller family unit (discussed later in the chapter) has left the family understaffed at a time when considerably more emotional work is required. The modern family has only two adults (increasingly, only one), and the woman, the one who is charged with the responsibility for emotional work, is likely to be working in the paid labor force. This is the double burden of the modern woman: underpaid work in the paid labor force and unpaid labor in the home. To seek a high level of emotional support from only one overworked adult is a precarious undertaking. One advantage of the larger family was that there were others—grandparents and older siblings, for instance—to turn to for emotional support when mother/wife was unavailable, unwilling, or incompetent.

In the past more family labor was communally shared, including child care. Because of the isolation of the modern family, the task of parenting has become considerably more individualized and privatized. Maher (1987) analyzed the contemporary loneliness of parenting and argued that it has eroded the emotional connections between parents and children. Modern parents are isolated from the kinds of social relationships and social supports that existed in the precapitalist community. The result is increased stress on, and alienation of, parents and, quite likely, increased symptoms of depression and mental disorder. It should come as no surprise, then, that the modern family is a crucible, producing much heat and dissolution. The current transition in the family reflects the development of new forms that are adaptations flowing from this crucible.

Changes in Family Composition and Structure

Related to the changes in the family fostered by capitalist development are certain demographic changes. The birth rate has declined. In 1960 there were 118.0 births per 1,000 women aged 15–44; in 1985 there were only 66.2, a reduction of 43.9 percent. In addition to having fewer children, women are marrying later in life. In 1950 the median age at first marriage for women was 20.3 years; in 1984 it was 22.8 years. Never-married females 18 years old and older were only 11.9 percent of all females in 1960; in 1986, they were 18.3 percent. The greatest increase in never-married females occurred for the age group 25–34, in which the proportion more than doubled. When they cohabitate, couples today are less likely to marry. In 1970 there were 87 married couples for each unmarried couple; in 1986 there were only 23. Slower to marry and less inclined to bear children, women are also more likely to divorce. In 1960 there were 42 divorced females per 1,000 married females; in 1986, 157, nearly a fourfold increase. Finally, there has been a steady rise in female family householders (discussed in Chapter 5), from 9.8 percent of all family householders in 1960 to 16.2 percent in 1987. (U.S. Bureau of Census projections for the year 2000 indicate that female households will constitute nearly 20 percent of all family households.) As a result of these and other changes, the average family size has declined. In 1987 the average family had 3.19 members, a decline of 11.1 percent from 1955.

It is reasonable to expect these changes to remain with us, although they do show signs of stabilizing at current levels. The demographic changes are here to stay largely because of the participation of women in the paid labor force, which is expected to continue to increase. The female labor force as a percentage of the female population rose from 31.4 percent in 1950 to 55.4 percent in 1987. The increase for wives with children under six years old was even more dramatic. Of this group, only 11.9 percent were in the paid labor force in 1950; by 1987 the proportion had more than quadrupled, to 56.9 percent.

As a result of these changes, the proportion of wives who are economically dependent on their husbands has declined markedly. Analysis of the Public Use Sample of the U.S. Census by Sorensen and McLanahan (1987) showed that for nonwhite couples, the proportion of wives who were 100 percent economically dependent on their husbands declined from 68.5 percent in 1940 to 27.1 percent in 1980. For white couples the change was even more dramatic. In 1940, 83.7 percent of white wives were totally dependent on their husbands; in 1980 only 30.6 percent were.

Although there have been other reasons for current changes in the family, none has been more important than the enormous increase in the number of women working for pay outside the home. The fact that women have entered the paid labor force in such large numbers has contributed to family change in at least three ways:

1. *Lower birth rate.* Bearing (and raising) children is still largely a private and female responsibility, putting great claims on women—claims that are often incompatible with the demands of work.
2. *Postponement of marriage.* Increasingly, success at work requires higher education and an early start in a career, requirements in conflict with the traditional responsibilities of married women, such as housework and child care.
3. *Higher divorce rate.* Working in the paid labor force has provided wives with resources that reduce their economic dependence on their husbands and enable them to terminate marriages. In the past, when women were without such resources, they had to remain in marriages, no matter how bad.

Despite these major changes in the family, it remains an irreplaceable and highly popular social institution. It is irreplaceable as the principal locus of biological reproduction and socialization, and its popularity is reflected in the fact that the remarriage rate has generally risen along with the divorce rate (Bane, 1976, p. 34). The modern pattern of serial marriage has led to one of the new varieties of the family: the multifamily, in which multiple stepparent-stepchild relations are prominent. Thus the family adapts and survives, but in variegated forms, which present new and growing social needs.

SOCIAL NEEDS OF THE FAMILY

One consequence of higher family dissolution rates and of female longevity is the emergence of a large group of "displaced homemakers." These are women

women who have not worked outside the home and who are left with few resources by divorce or separation, or by the death, disability, or unemployment of their spouses. In 1980 there were 11.4 million such women in the United States, and 40 percent of them lived below the poverty line. These women are largely unprepared for work outside the home; 56 percent lack a high school education.

The social needs of displaced homemakers are extensive and unprecedented. Among other things, these women require job counseling and financial assistance (Brozan, 1987). In 1987 only twenty-two states had social policies directed to displaced homemakers. Nationally, these policies support programs that serve 300,000 women—only about 3 percent of those who need them. In order to secure jobs one of the principal needs of displaced homemakers and of other contemporary mothers is child care. The nation's unmet child-care needs are immense and growing, largely as a result of the mass entry of mothers into the paid labor force. A Children's Defense Fund study estimated that 15 million preschool children and 35 million school-age children will have mothers in the paid labor force by 1995 (Tarpinian, 1988, p. 2). Child-care services constitute the fourth-largest expenditure for families with children, after food, housing, and taxes (Kahn and Kamerman, 1987, p. 2). In 1982, 5.1 million children under five years of age needed child care from a person in addition to their mothers, and millions of school-age children required nonmaternal care for at least part of the day. How is this large child-care need being met? There has been a shift away from family care toward group care since the 1960s, largely because of the unavailability of family caretakers (Wilkie, 1987, pp. 158–160). Data on the child-care arrangements of working mothers are presented in Table 6.1.

As the data in the table indicate, child-care arrangements are largely informal—relatives, neighbors, and friends are recruited for the job. These arrangements are often both undependable and expensive. They are also quite uneven in quality. In addition to teenagers who do it for pocket money, many

TABLE 6.1   Child-Care Arrangements for Children Under 5 of Full-Time Employed Mothers, 1984–1985

ARRANGEMENT	PERCENT
Total	100.0
Care in child's home, subtotal	24.4
By relative	19.4
By nonrelative	5.0
Care in another home, subtotal	42.2
By relative	14.7
By nonrelative	27.5
Organized child-care facility	28.0
Other	5.4

Source: Statistical Abstract of the United States 1988: 357.

women operate jerrybuilt group child-care facilities in their homes. Regrettably, there is even a very small proportion of young children who are obliged to take care of themselves. This small group increases with the age of the child. Of children five to fourteen years old in 1984–1985, 2.7 percent took care of themselves at least part of the day. The great need for child care is not being met adequately under these ad hoc arrangements. For example, New York State's Commission on Child Care reported in 1986 that although as many as 1.2 million children needed child care, there were fewer than 135,000 licensed spaces available. The lack of child care is a particularly acute problem in cities. According to a survey of fifty-two cities by the U.S. Conference of Mayors, an estimated 45 percent of the demand for child care for children under six years of age went unmet in 1988.

The current arrangements have different implications for various social groups. The lack of child-care facilities penalizes the working class, poor and non-poor. Sidel (1986, p. 130) pointed out that these groups are more likely than better-off groups to face long waiting lists, overcrowded facilities, and high turnover in caregivers. Thus, for those groups with the greatest child-care needs (because mothers are more likely to have to work), adequate facilities are fewest. For most parents child care is now like any other product bought in the marketplace: those with few resources have to settle for cheap and inferior child care or forgo it altogether.

Because the unmet national need for child care is so large and so vital to both the family and society, it cries out for new policy initiatives from government. Child care is far too important to be left to the vagaries of the marketplace.

In sum, today's family is confronted with new problems. Conservative claims notwithstanding, the state of the contemporary family does not reflect moral decline and the solutions to its problems do not lie in reasserting the authority of the biblical patriarch. The patriarchal model declined because of social changes, such as the entry of women into the paid labor force and feminism, and these changes are irreversible. The American family is not in moral decline; it is in desperate need of new social policy initiatives.

TOWARD A FAMILY POLICY

The family's current social needs highlight the lack of attention given to the family in U.S. Welfare State social policy, which has traditionally focused on the labor force and on special categories of citizens, such as the unemployed and the aged. When the family was more stable and uniform, the lack of a family social policy was not as glaring an omission as it is now that the family is in transition and is more needy. The United States is one of only five nations in the world that do not have a family policy; the other four are New Guinea, South Africa, South Korea, and the Sudan. Folbre's (1988, p. 72) comments give us some idea of the scale of the social needs: "In the US today, less than 40 percent of all women workers are covered by any contractual provisions for pregnancy leave, very few men have a paternity leave option, and many workers forced to take time off to cope with family illness lose their jobs."

There are four cornerstones of a national family policy: (1) a family allowance of cash benefits to supplement the incomes of adults who raise children; (2) comprehensive prenatal and maternity health services; (3) paid work leaves for parents to care for newborns and for ill children; and (4) a child-care program (Lubeck and Garrett, 1988). Austria provides a good example of a national family policy (Busch et al., 1986). In the first half of the 1980s Austria, along with France and the Netherlands, led Welfare States in resources devoted to families. In Austria family social policy is composed of three major components:

1. Cash payments and benefits-in-kind that compensate parents for the expense of raising children. These include a family allowance, maternity benefits, and educational benefits for children.
2. Payments, benefits, and regulations that enable working women to take one-year leaves upon the birth of a child.
3. Benefits and programs to improve general conditions for birth and for rearing and educating children, including health clinics and child-care facilities.

Although a comprehensive U.S. family policy would have numerous elements, we shall focus here on two needed initiatives: child care and family allowance policies. (The family allowance as an income maintenance measure was also discussed in Chapter 5.)

There is precedent and support for a government child-care policy in the United States. During World War II, when many women worked in wartime industries, child-care facilities flourished with federal, state, and local government sponsorship. They vanished after the war ended; in 1946, 2,800 child-care centers, serving over 1.5 million children, were closed (Frohmann, 1978, p. 12). Today a majority of Americans support renewed government involvement in child care. In a national poll by *Time* magazine (June 22, 1987) 54 percent of Americans said that the government should do more to provide child care. A 1988 national survey by *Working Mother* magazine found that the overwhelming majority of 2,304 respondents believed that their child-care options were not ideal and that the government should take a more active role in providing affordable and quality child care (Satran, 1988, p. 55). The majority that favored greater government involvement was composed of women in different social classes and circumstances. Greater government involvement in child care was advocated by well-to-do women as well as by women with moderate and low incomes, by women with postgraduate degrees as well as by women with high school diplomas, and by women who were content with their child-care arrangements as well as by those who wished they could stay home with their children. One reason that women overwhelmingly favor publicly sponsored child care is that the present lack discriminates against them because of their traditional responsibility for children. Research indicates that about one out of every five or six unemployed women is not working because she is unable to make satisfactory child-care arrangements (U.S. Commission on Civil Rights, 1984, p. 96.)

(The government needs to play a leadership role in providing child care for nonpoor and poor alike because the private sector is unable or unwilling to meet the large child-care needs of society. For example, although employer-sponsored child care has been increasing, less than 1 percent of employed women were served by it in 1986. There are several reasons to expect that employers will not substantially increase their effort in this area: child care is costly, is used by only a minority of workers, and may encourage pregnancy. These monetary considerations will outweigh the positive benefits of on-the-job child care for employers, which include lower employee absenteeism, tardiness, and turnover, as well as greater employee satisfaction and productivity (Burud, Aschbacher, and McCroskey, 1984, pp. 21–48; O'Connell and Bloom, 1987, p. 12). Like education, child care is too important and large a task to be left to the private sector.

The first, minimal step toward comprehensive government involvement in child-care policy is licensing to assure at least minimum standards of care. Licensing provides for the state regulation of child care, which has a positive effect on quality. For example, of the eighteen substantiated cases of child abuse at child-care centers in New York City in 1988, seventeen occurred at unlicensed facilities (Faludi, 1988, p. 18). In New York City licensing requires background checks on the criminal or child abuse history of providers, on-site assessment, and periodic monitoring, all done by the city's Human Resources Administration and its Health Department. Currently, the overwhelming majority of child-care facilities in the United States are not licensed; only about one-eighth of the three- to five-year-olds who receive care are in licensed facilities (Levitan and Belous, 1981, p. 101). In New York City only about 8 percent of 25,000 child-care providers were licensed in 1987.

What about the effects of child care on children? Quality child care has few, if any, negative effects, and may even benefit children. Research indicates that good child care does not disturb parent-child bonds and does not result in emotional problems. Furthermore, child care can enhance the development of children, at least those from poor families, and it can benefit parents as well (Rescorla, Provence, and Naylor, 1982; Trickett et al., 1982). Research has found that the social and intellectual development of children in child care was six to nine months ahead of that of children who remained at home (Faludi, 1988). Belsky (1985, p. 250), a leading researcher in the field, summarized work on the effects of child care on child development as follows:

> In response to the policy-oriented question, "Is day care bad for children?", it seems appropriate to conclude that it usually is not and certainly does not have to be, but that it can be. In view of this conclusion, the policy orientation is forced

to shift from one of day-care effects to the conditions of care that produce different consequences.

Although older children probably benefit from child care, research results are more ambiguous with regard to its effects on infants in the first year of life.   ((   )'

Of course, the key condition is *quality*. The essential ingredient in quality is a focus on the developmental (or learning) needs—emotional, social, and intellectual—of children, not just on their custodial needs. A developmental focus requires certain minimal material and personnel standards. Summarizing studies on the issue, Rutter (1982, p. 17) noted that what is necessary to ensure quality is "to individualize care as far as possible; to keep staff changes to a minimum; to provide suitable training for those serving as caregivers; to ensure adequate staffing, space, and play facilities; and, by suitable recruitment and adequate remuneration, to ensure that care is provided by people with the necessary qualities."

Unfortunately, the current haphazard child-care arrangements are not high in quality. Based on a national study, Keyserling (1972, p. 120) found that 69 percent of child-care facilities provided only custodial care. A major reason for this is the low esteem in which society holds child care, which is traditionally women's work. In 1986 the first comprehensive study of child-care pay in New York State (done by the Center for Public Advocacy Research in New York City) reported that it ranged from $4.26 to $6.23 an hour. The highest pay, $6.23 an hour, was earned by head teachers, 84 percent of whom were college educated (Collins, 1986). Low pay breeds great turnover among child-care workers (an annual rate of 40 percent); most workers stay in their jobs for three years or less.

Of all licensed child-care centers in 1970, 51 percent were proprietary, or private-sector facilities. Many of these providers are involved in child care for profit, which means it is in their interest to minimize their costs by, among other things, hiring inexperienced staff and paying them low wages. Substantial differences in quality between for-profit and not-for-profit facilities were documented in the Keyserling (1972, p. 120) study: of for-profit child-care centers, only 16 percent were rated superior or good, while 50 percent were rated poor; of nonprofit centers, 37 percent were rated superior or good and only 11 percent were rated poor. The nonprofit child-care facilities included programs operated by Head Start (discussed in Chapter 7), community agencies, hospitals, and religious organizations. Quality of care was assessed by observation and by review of adult-child ratios, services available, salaries paid, staff training, parental participation, and physical facilities of child-care centers.

Thus the Reagan policy of privatization is not the answer to the child-care needs of the United States. (Privatization is also discussed in Chapters 9 and 11.) Privatizing has resulted in lower and less frequently enforced minimum standards of care. Privatizing the regulation of child care has led to a decline in standards and enforcement. Privatizing the financing of child care has produced greater hardship for low-income families (Kahn and Kamerman, 1987, p. 113). Perhaps the most noticeable outcome of the Reagan legacy of privatization has been the proliferation of "McDaycare"—profit-seeking, franchised, bare-bones child care (Bricker-Jenkins and Sindos, 1986, p. 50).

Greater government involvement will serve to widen coverage and to upgrade minimum quality. It should be noted that, unlike education, child care will be voluntary, not compulsory. The exception, unfortunately, will be mothers on public aid who are forced to work (through a workfare program), an issue discussed in Chapter 5.

Two other considerations besides quality are cost and convenience. To be fully utilized, child care must be accessible, affordable, and accountable (Ackerman et al., 1987). Only government is capable of setting and enforcing quality standards of care (accountability). Only government can make child care available nationally as well as locally (accessibility). Only government can subsidize child care (affordability). One major government institution, the public school, is already in place to meet this standard of accessibility, affordability, and accountability. The use of public schools as child-care facilities and for other social needs is discussed in Chapter 7.

Increasing government involvement in child care can be achieved by several specific measures: expansion of the Head Start program, an increase in the federal child-care tax credit, and revitalization of the federal Interagency Day Care Requirements (Nelson, 1982). These requirements were made moot when the Reagan administration ended the federal role in standard setting by channeling child-care support in block grants to states, even though some states have no statutory regulation of child care.

The principal objection to publicly sponsored child care is its cost. However, the cost can be contained by, among other steps, using already available public facilities such as schools. Moreover, we are paying a considerable price as a nation now for not adopting a universal child-care policy, including the loss of labor of parents who could work (or could work full-time) if they had child care. The most needful in this category are single parents, especially single mothers of young children, many of whom are presently receiving public welfare. Finally, universal quality child care can improve the life chances of children, particularly those who are poor.

The reluctance to fund needed child care is penny wise and pound foolish. A good example is provided by the Head Start program. Largely because of lack of adequate funding, only 20 percent of eligible children participate in the program. If Head Start were adequately funded, society would gain economically, by forgoing large future costs. A 1987 analysis by the Select Committee on Children, Youth and Families of the U.S. House of Representatives found that for every $1 spent on Head Start, $4.75 was saved in later social costs through the program's success in increasing school achievement and employability.

Other steps need to be taken to help families meet their child-care needs. One is flextime: allowing workers to put in their required hours at flexible times so that they can arrange their work hours around available child care. Only a small minority of white-collar employers provide flextime, but government could legislate it as an opportunity for all workers. Government could also guarantee working mothers the right to a leave of absence after the birth of a child. The United States is the only industrialized nation that does not have this guarantee. At present, only about 40 percent of working women are assured this right by their employers.

Finally, the concept of maternity leave needs to be expanded to one of parental leave. The United States and South Africa are the only developed capitalist nations with no parental leave policy. Sweden has had such a social policy, Parental Benefit Insurance, since 1974. It provides for up to nine months of any combination of maternity and paternity leave at 90 percent of pay, and guarantees jobs upon return to work. Additionally, either parent can receive full pay for working six-hour days until the child is eight years old. Furthermore, fathers can take ten days off immediately after birth to care for their families, and either parent may take leave to care for an ill child. In Hungary employed new mothers are entitled to 20–25 weeks of leave at full pay, reduced work hours for breast-feeding, and up to 60 days of leave per year to care for ill children under six years of age. In addition, Hungarian parents benefit from a child-care grant for three years after birth, at 65 to 75 percent of the pay of the parent who stays home (Fried, 1988, p. 15).

In 1987 Minnesota became the first state to provide parental leave rights. All companies with twenty-one employees or more must offer up to six weeks of unpaid leave to the father and mother after the birth or adoption of a child. Both parents can take leave at the same time, and their jobs are guaranteed upon their return. Oregon passed a similar law, effective in 1988, and twenty-eight other states have parental leave legislation under consideration. Although this legislation falls short of the Swedish and Hungarian plans because it allows only relatively brief and unpaid leaves, it is a progressive step for U.S. social policy.

It is in society's interest to assure the adequate socialization of its young. Publicly sponsored child-care and parental leave policies would promote that interest and would support the family at a time when it is in transition. Society cannot, without high social costs, continue to rely on the unpaid labor of mothers for this socialization as these women increase their full-time responsibilities outside the home. It is time for U.S. social policy to catch up with that in the rest of the developed nations by legitimating child care as valuable and paid labor.

Family Allowance

In addition to child care, a comprehensive family policy requires the provision of income supplements to those adults who raise children. An income allowance has a positive effect on all aspects of child development. In a reanalysis of the four experimental tests of the negative income tax (NIT) in cities in New Jersey and Pennsylvania; rural areas in Iowa and North Carolina; Gary, Indiana; and Seattle/Denver, Salkind and Haskins (1982) found evidence that in families that received income supplements fewer infants were born with low birth weight, children's nutritional intake was higher, and so were their school attendance, grades, and achievement test scores.

The major objection to the family allowance is that it would create a work disincentive: beneficiaries would not work, or would work less, if they received this income. The four major NIT experiments, however, did not demonstrate a significant work disincentive for the poor families that received money. Chambers (1986, p. 104), after reviewing the research, summarized its effect on work as follows: "A conservative conclusion, faithful to the facts the experiment reveals, would be that the effect is there but very slight—probably insignificant to most people." If there is a substantial work disincentive that affects poor people, it lies in the work they do. The jobs available to poor people pay very low wages, offer little possibility of advancement, and are often dirty and dangerous. What is needed to improve the work prospects of the poor, who demonstrate as much motivation to work as do other groups in society, is more jobs, better jobs, and jobs that pay adequate wages (discussed in Chapter 5). Finally, family allowances have been adopted in virtually all Welfare States except the United States without evidence that work incentives were negatively affected.

The first family allowance was introduced in France in the 1930s. Finland, Sweden, and several other nations followed suit in the 1940s. Currently sixty-seven countries provide a family allowance as a supplement to the income of adults who are raising children. Family allowances are a substantial portion of income—between 5 and 10 percent of the median wage in families where there is one child, and considerably more for single mothers and for families with several children (Kamerman, 1984, p. 62).

The United States has a program, the Earned Income Tax Credit (EITC), that could serve as the base for a family allowance. The EITC, which dates from 1975, provides an annual earnings supplement to parents who maintain a household for a child, provided they fall below a specified income. If parents do not owe any taxes, or owe a tax lower than the EITC, they receive a payment from the IRS. A couple with two children that earned a poverty-level income of $12,368 in 1988 owed no federal taxes and received an EITC refund of $663. With expansion, the EITC could approximate the family allowances found in other Welfare States (Rodgers, 1988, pp. 46–47).

SOCIAL PRACTICE

Caring work is central to the reproduction of society and a critical aspect of any analysis of social policy. Caring is directed to all sorts of people, but is particularly focused on those who are in a state of partial or total social dependency, including the young, the old, the disabled, and the unemployed.

These people are the principal constituents of the Welfare State. Although caring work is done throughout the Welfare State, it is most familiar in the family, where it is originally learned. In the United States caring work, whether in the family or in the Welfare State, is women's work. In 1980 about 70 percent of social welfare jobs (including those in education) were held by women. These jobs made up about one-fourth of all female employment (Ehrenreich and Piven, 1984, p. 50).

Why do women have a special affinity for caring work? One explanation, based on the work of Chodorow (1978) and Gilligan (1982), is that the special caring capacity of women develops out of their early and uninterrupted attachments to their mothers, who are of the same gender. For boys this connection is considerably more problematic because of Oedipal conflict and because boys are gender differentiated from their mothers. As a result of their different experiences with their mothers, women develop a stronger capacity and need to connect to and empathize with others, while men develop a stance of separation and autonomy. Women also develop a worldview that emphasizes personal relationships and responsibilities, while men focus more on impersonal abstractions and rights. In this view, caring is nurturing, and nurturing is mothering. Thus girls' identification with their mothers is identification with being a carer. It has to be noted that despite this developmental difference between gender groups, there are individual exceptions. Although caring is generally a female activity, some women are not good at it, while some men are.

In addition to the affinity that women have for caring work because of their psychosocial backgrounds, women are given the responsibility of caring by their families and by society. An additional perspective on caring work comes from Hochschild (1983, p. 165), who analyzed it as emotional work that women do—"the work of affirming, enhancing, and celebrating the well-being and status of others." Hochschild argued that emotional work is more important to women than to men at least partly because of their subordinate status in society. Women's emotional work is a social resource that is exchanged for material resources, and it is also a way of showing deference. In the labor force jobs requiring emotional work make up only 25 percent of the jobs that men do, but over 50 percent of women's jobs. Thus, for women, caring work represents both a self-identifying expression of love and a duty to other people. The result is that women are both motivated to provide care and exploited to furnish it without pay (Ungerson, 1987).

Although women are central to all caring work, it is in Welfare State activities where their role is most noticeable. While 44 percent of all jobs are held by women, they hold 70 percent of Welfare State jobs. The caring hand of woman is ubiquitous in social reproduction. Women are primarily responsible for socialization both in the family and in the school (discussed in Chapter 7); they do most of the caring work that is so essential to successful learning. In 1986, 96.5 percent of the 762,000 child-care workers (outside of private households) were women. In a study of largely white, middle-class

Americans, Googins and Burden (1987) found that married female parents who worked full-time outside the home did 20 hours of housework and 26 hours of child care per week, for a total of 46 hours. Their counterparts, working and married male parents (with employed spouses), did only 11 hours of housework and 14 hours of child care, for a total of 25 hours—46 percent less than women did.

Social practice in the family and the Welfare State can be significantly improved only by confronting structures of male domination. This domination ensues from the patriarchal ideology that women and their work are dependent and devalued, both in the family and in the labor force. Miller (1987, p. 290) explained male domination in private life and in public arenas as follows:

> Control is maintained through the sexual division of labor and the institution of marriage, with men in the public sector and women in the private sector in service to the public sphere. When women venture into the public arena, the dualities are maintained through the occupational segregation of women, the differentiation of tasks in the workplace, and economic control through lower pay.

The goal is not for women to become more like men—to relinquish their nurturing role and to forgo their caring skills. Rather, the aim is, as Morell (1987, p. 151) noted, to prevent such caring from remaining a basis for their subordination. Compassion is a trap for women when it operates within unequal relationships, where the caring is one-sided. Overcoming gender domination requires changes for both men and women. The United States can take a cue from Sweden, where there is a sex role debate rather than a women's movement, and where social policy is aimed at men as well as at women (Davidson and Gordon, 1979, pp. 242–252). Ultimately, gender domination can only be overcome by men and women sharing more fairly the work of caring—in the family, in the Welfare State, and in the labor force at large. It is the role of social policy to provide incentives for men to become full members of their families and to eliminate the barriers to women becoming full members of the labor force.

Social Practitioner at Work: Michael Vanzetti

Mike Vanzetti is a family service specialist with the Division of Youth and Family Services (DYFS) of the state of New Jersey. Mike was born to an Italian working-class family in Paterson, New Jersey; both his parents worked in the city's textile and silk factories. His interest in social work began right after he received his Bachelor of Arts degree, when he became a volunteer at a day camp for children who lived in public housing in Paterson. Mike discovered that he liked doing social work, especially with kids. His first paid job in social work began in late 1975, when he was hired by the Senior Outreach of Catholic Family Services, a CETA (Comprehensive Employment and

Training Act, discussed in Chapter 5) program that did advocacy work for senior citizens who were having difficulties with public agencies, especially the welfare and housing departments. In this job Mike advocated the interests and rights of elderly citizens who were facing eviction and having problems obtaining welfare benefits and medical care. He stayed at this agency until 1979, when he moved to DYFS, where he renewed his work with children.

At DYFS the formal term for Mike's clientele is "families under stress." Mike works on behalf of abused children—unborn to age eighteen—in these families. The families are referred to DYFS by a variety of sources, including law enforcement agencies, neighbors, and relatives of abused children. "Families under stress" translates into many dysfunctional situations and practices, including physical, sexual, and emotional abuse, mental retardation, substance abuse, and medical neglect. Most of Mike's clients are poor; many receive public assistance. He rarely gets middle-class clients. Although child abuse is a problem in middle-class families as well as in poor ones, middle-class families are usually served by private agencies.

Mike's work with families consists of a four-step process: (1) assessment, (2) support, (3) stabilization, and (4) termination. Assessment involves a determination of what supportive services are needed by the family. Supportive services are oriented to improving daily coping skills and include homemaker, child-care, and counseling services, as well as advocacy work on behalf of the family. Support also involves referring clients for specialized mental health help such as psychotherapy. The need for mental health services for the young extends well beyond the population of abused children, although they are among the most desperately in need. One out of eight American children suffers from a mental health problem serious enough to warrant treatment. But the Congressional Office of Technology Assessment found that in 1986 about 75 percent of these children were not receiving mental health services.

Mike continues supportive services until the family is stabilized and the presenting problem is resolved. The last step—termination—has one of four outcomes, ranging from most preferred to least preferred: (1) stabilization, (2) placement of the child with other family members, (3) placement of the child in foster care, or (4) termination of parental rights and placement of the child for adoption.

When Mike gets a new case from the screeners at DYFS (who do a preliminary assessment and assign cases to workers), he first reads all the paperwork on the family and decides if the child is in imminent danger—defined as likelihood of severe physical abuse or any sexual abuse. If the child is in imminent danger, Mike visits the family's home within twenty-four hours. If not, he visits within forty-eight hours to one week. At the home Mike interviews all the family members, including the reportedly abused child, and investigates material conditions, especially the state of the bedding and the food supply. In almost all cases in which the child was deemed to be in imminent danger, the abuse proves to have actually happened. However, actual abuse is found in only about one-half of all other cases. Adults—usually the parents—cannot prevent Mike's entry because his visit is backed by the legal authority of the state of New Jersey. When necessary, he is accompanied by police officers, but Mike prefers not to resort to the police but to rely on persuasion instead. However, he has had to call on police officers on many occasions because the parents refused him entry.

If a child shows physical signs of abuse and the parents do not provide an adequate reason for the signs (such as an accidental fall) or do not assure Mike that the abuse will not be repeated (as, for example, when it was caused by an estranged parent who will henceforth be denied entry to the home), Mike has the authority to remove the child from the home on his very first visit. Mike removes all children if the abuse clearly is crippling, debilitating (such as starvation), or sexual, or if the parents are indifferent or noncooperative. Initial removals are not common; they occur in only about 15 percent of Mike's cases. Removals at any point in the process happen in about 25 percent of his cases. Thus in the great majority of Mike's cases, about 75 percent, the child is not taken from the family. In these cases Mike supervises family care of the child and arranges for support services and referrals for family members. In almost all cases Mike terminates his role after six months to one year of work.

Most of the child abuse Mike deals with consists of neglect, such as not caring for a child's medical needs, or minimal physical abuse, such as bruises and minor lacerations. In the roughly 15 percent of his contacts that result in removing the child, the abuse is severe. Severe abuse can be emotional (such as locking up a child) or physical (such as major bodily trauma). Any inappropriate sexual activity by an adult with a child is considered severe abuse.

If Mike has to remove a child, he first tries to find other family members who can care for the child, such as its grandparents. If that is not possible, then he arranges for foster care. The state of New Jersey operates its own foster care services. It selects, trains, and supervises foster parents, and provides Medicaid and a board rate for the care of the child. Mike finds the quality of foster care to be uneven; it ranges from extraordinarily good to criminally abusive. At times he has even had to remove children from foster parents who abused them. One problem is that many foster families, like Mike's clients, are poor and live in stressful situations. Foster parents are recruited from the same general community as that of clients, in part to make the transfer less traumatic for the child. Another problem is that the supply of foster homes is limited and there are many kids to place.

The most fateful action involved in Mike's work is the termination of parental rights (TOPR). TOPR may be either voluntary or involuntary. If it is involuntary, it is done through the legal authority of the Family Court. After parental rights have been severed, the child is placed for adoption. Foster parents may eventually adopt the child they care for if they are positively recommended by DYFS. In a few TOPR cases the child ends up in a psychiatric institution or a residential school instead of with another family.

Why do parents abuse their children? In Mike's experience they themselves do not know why—it is a thoughtless act. Some of the explanations Mike has heard are: "I was sleeping when the kid drank the poison," "I was out when the kid knocked the pot off the stove on himself," "I didn't know my strength," "I just couldn't stop her from crying," "I love my kid but sometimes she just drives me crazy."

Parents always deny sexual abuse of their children. How common is it? According to an analysis of national data by the University of New Hampshire's Family Research Laboratory, roughly 1 in 275 children under six years of age has suffered sexual abuse. (Young children were more than fifteen times as likely to be sexually abused at home as in child-care centers.) Other research indicates that in any single year from 1 percent to 1.5 percent of children are abused (Goleman, 1989). In Mike's experience, adults rarely get punished for child abuse. Only in the most severe cases, such as crippling or killing a child, does the law prosecute, and even then the punishment is usually minor. The typical result of a conviction is six months' probation.

In Mike's opinion, some people, poor and middle-class alike, just should not be in charge of children. They are not fit, or are not yet ready, for the task of parenting. Many of the parents in Mike's caseload are barely more than children themselves. Also, many families break down because they are overwhelmed by the problems of daily life. Thus some people who are fit and ready to parent may not be able to because of a combination of desperate circumstances—no work, lousy housing, and bad health.

Mike believes his work is far too reactive to symptoms and should be much more concerned with preventive steps. For example, lack of housing and poor housing are major problems for adults who end up abusing children. Unhealthy living conditions such as extreme overcrowding, which results in kids and adults sleeping together, is an incubator for tension. Mike has found that many abusive parents were themselves abused children. Research confirms Mike's impression. Studies indicate that about one-third of child abusers were abused in their childhoods (Goleman, 1989). Mike has been with his agency long enough to have had to take children away from parents whom he had removed from abusive parents when they were kids. Thus, although there is no excuse for abusing a child, there are circumstances that make it more likely. In addition to low-cost decent housing, the families with whom Mike works are in urgent need of birth control information and resources. About 80 percent of his cases involve families headed by a single female, often a teenager. In about one-half of these cases the child abuse is committed by the mother.

Out-of-wedlock births (also discussed in Chapter 7) became a public issue in the United States in the 1980s. The birth rate per 1,000 unmarried women rose from 21.6 in 1960 to 32.8 in 1985, an increase of about 50 percent. For unmarried women aged 15 to 19, the rise was even more dramatic—from 15.3 to 31.6, more than a 100 percent increase. There is some indication that the out-of-wedlock birth rate is stabilizing. However, even if the U.S. teenage pregnancy rate, including out-of-wedlock pregnancies, were to stop rising, it would remain the highest for all the Welfare States (Barron, 1987). In other Welfare States unwanted teenage pregnancies are not a major problem, largely because of the widespread state provision of sex education and contraception. The Alan Guttmacher Institute (New York City) calculated the number of pregnancies and births for each 1,000 women 15 to 19 years old for six Welfare States in 1981. The United States led both in pregnancies (96) and in births (54). Comparable figures for the other five Welfare States were as follows: the U.K. (45 pregnancies and 31 births), Canada (44 and 28), France (43 and 25), Sweden (35 and 16), and the Netherlands (14 and 9). Sweden's low rate of unwanted teenage pregnancy is credited to its sex education program in schools and to the easy availability of contraception in its state health clinics. Swedish teenagers have a considerably lower pregnancy rate than American teenagers despite the fact that they are sexually active at a younger age (Lohr, 1987).

Research indicates that the most effective and efficient vehicle for reducing teenage pregnancy is sex education in the public school system (Gilchrist and Schinke, 1983). Furthermore, the overwhelming majority of Americans favor sex education in public schools. However, only four states (Kentucky, Maryland, Nevada, and New Jersey) require it in all schools. A problem with existing sex education in the United States is that it often does not include information about contraception. The common message to teenagers is: "Don't do it." Clearly this policy is not working. What is needed is federal leadership for a thorough and honest sex education policy.

Mike is quite conscious of the fact that his work is considered women's work. Only about 10 percent of the caseworkers in his office are males. Mike feels a certain sense of loneliness as a male in his job. Issues that are important to him as a man are not addressed by the agency; for example, he is not a father and his inexperience with infants was not taken seriously. It took a lot of time for Mike to overcome his insecurity about physically handling infants. His female supervisors trivialized his concern, saying, "All men are like that," and "Just go on and do it." The women in Mike's office are much better than the men at mutual support and providing resources for one another. Unfortunately, they do not easily accept the men into their network. For one thing, Mike's female co-workers, perhaps unconsciously, look down upon the men, just as society does, for doing women's work. They "prefer to date lawyers and businessmen" rather than their fellow social workers. Mike's friends outside of work occasionally suggest to him that he should become a lawyer or a psychologist, that his experience is a good background for either career and law or psychology would be more suitable for him. Mike believes that if more men did his kind of work, much of the loneliness and devaluation he feels would disappear.

Another major problem in Mike's office is that there are not enough African American workers, especially males, to meet the demands of the African American caseload. Although whites do serve African American families, Mike has found that the racial difference creates one more barrier that has to be overcome in the course of an already difficult job. Usually,

African American workers have more understanding of, and get more acceptance from, African American clients. In Mike's agency, even though the caseload is disproportionately African American and Hispanic, the workers are disproportionately white. Worse yet, the agency hierarchy in Trenton is almost entirely white male, and the local office hierarchy is mostly white female.

Mike feels that the worst things about his job are danger and stress. The danger is real and physical; it comes from both the families he deals with and the neighborhoods in which they live. Mike has been threatened by adults who have tried to intimidate him from doing his job. He is dealing with an explosive situation (removing children from families) that is compounded by racial and class differences. He often feels scared in inner city neighborhoods and has learned to rely on his sixth sense. Over the years he has developed an acute smell for danger. He has only one choice in dangerous situations—to retreat and return another time, perhaps with support.

The danger of Mike's work is one source of stress. Another is the high caseload and the need to deal every day with the intense personal traumas of other human beings. It is a job tailor-made for burnout (discussed in Chapters 5 and 8). Mike copes with the stress by doing regular physical exercises and by cultivating interests related to, but somewhat removed from, his job, such as children's literature. Co-workers help one another with their stress. They have a strong sense of fellowship—a *"MASH* camaraderie"—that helps them keep things in perspective. As in the TV show, gallows humor is a good tonic for work stress.

Why does Mike stay on in his job? He likes being on the line, doing what he and his co-workers call "trench casework." What appeals to him is the thrill of actually being able to see, and to see soon, the concrete results of his work. He also believes that job conditions are improving somewhat, principally because of unionization. (Mike's office has been unionized by the Communications Workers of America for about six years.) Ultimately, Mike feels that the good things about his job outweigh the bad. High on the list of good things is working with the kids. "When you have a successful case—getting an abused child in a good placement—it's really rewarding." The kids are wonderful—affectionate, strong, and resilient. Mike feels personally rewarded when he sees kids through to a good and final placement and can watch them recover. Because his agency is the last hope for many poor and abused children, Mike knows that he has truly rescued them and changed the course of their lives.

REFERENCES

Abramovitz, Mimi. 1988. *Regulating the Lives of Women: Social Welfare Policy from Colonial Times to the Present.* Boston: South End Press.

Ackerman, Frank, et al. 1987. "It's All in the Family: How Government Influences Family Life." *Dollars & Sense*, March, pp. 6–9.

Bane, Mary Jo. 1976. *Here to Stay: American Families in the Twentieth Century.* New York: Basic Books.

Barron, James. 1987. "Learning the Facts of Life." *The New York Times*, November 8.

Belsky, Jay. 1985. "The Science and Politics of Day Care." Pp. 237–262 in *Social Science and Social Policy*, eds. R. Lance Shotland and Melvin M. Mark. Beverly Hills, CA: Sage Publications.

Bricker-Jenkins, Mary, and Louise Sindos. 1986. "Making Capital on Kids: The Economic Context of Day Care Policy Debates." *Catalyst: A Socialist Journal of the Social Services* 5:37–51.

Brozan, Nadine. 1987. "Former Wives: A Legion of the Needy." *The New York Times*, July 29.

Burud, Sandra L., Pamela R. Aschbacher, and Jacquelyn McCroskey. 1984. *Employer-Supported Child Care: Investing in Human Resources*. Dover, MA: Auburn House.

Busch, Georg, et al. 1986. "Development and Prospects of the Austrian Welfare State." Pp. 178–191 in *Comparing Welfare States and Their Futures*, ed. Else Oyen. Aldershot, U.K.: Gower.

Chambers, Donald E. 1986. *Social Policy and Social Programs: A Method for the Practical Public Policy Analyst*. New York: Macmillan.

Chodorow, Nancy. 1978. *The Reproduction of Mothering*. Berkeley: University of California Press.

Collins, Glenn. 1986. "For Child-Care Workers, Poverty-Level Wages." *The New York Times*, November 24.

Davidson, Laurie, and Laura Kramer Gordon. 1979. *The Sociology of Gender*. Chicago: Rand McNally.

Dickinson, James, and Bob Russell. 1986. "The Structure of Reproduction in Capitalist Society." Pp. 1–20 in *Family, Economy and State*, eds. James Dickinson and Bob Russell. New York: St. Martin's Press.

Eckholm, Erik, and Frank Record. 1977. "The Affluent Diet: A Worldwide Health Hazard." *The Futurist*, February, pp. 32–42.

Ehrenreich, Barbara, and Frances Fox Piven. 1984. "Women and the Welfare State." Pp. 41–60 in *Alternatives: Proposals for America from the Democratic Left*, ed. Irving Howe. New York: Pantheon.

Faludi, Susan. 1988. "Are the Kids Alright?" *Mother Jones*, November, pp. 15–19.

Folbre, Nancy. 1988. "Whither Families? Towards a Socialist-Feminist Family Policy." *Socialist Review* 18:57–75.

Fried, Mindy. 1988. "Who's Minding Our Children?" *Dollars & Sense*, July/August, pp. 12–16.

Frohmann, Alicia. 1978. "Day Care and the Regulation of Women's Work Force Participation." *Catalyst: A Socialist Journal of the Social Services* 1:5–17.

Gilchrist, Lewayne D., and Steven Paul Schinke. 1983. "Teenage Pregnancy and Public Policy." *Social Service Review* 57:307–322.

Gilligan, Carol. 1982. *In a Different Voice: Psychological Theory and Women's Development*. Cambridge, MA: Harvard University Press.

Goleman, Daniel. 1989. "Sad Legacy of Abuse: The Search for Remedies." *The New York Times*, January 24.

Googins, Bradley, and Dianne Burden. 1987. "Vulnerability of Working Parents: Balancing Work and Home Roles." *Social Work* 32:295–300.

Hochschild, Arlie Russell. 1983. *The Managed Heart: Commercialization of Human Feeling*. Berkeley: University of California Press.

Kahn, Alfred J., and Sheila B. Kamerman. 1987. *Child Care: Facing the Hard Choices*. Dover, MA: Auburn House.

Kamerman, Sheila B. 1984. "Child Care and Family Benefits: Policies of Six Industrialized Countries." Pp. 60–67 in *Families and Change: Social Needs and Public Policies*, ed. Rosalie G. Genovese. New York: Praeger.

Keyserling, Mary Dublin. 1972. *Windows on Day Care*. New York: National Council of Jewish Women.

Lasch, Christopher. 1977. *Haven in a Heartless World: The Family Besieged*. New York: Basic Books.

Levitan, Sar A., and Richard S. Belous. 1981. *What's Happening to the American Family?* Baltimore: Johns Hopkins University Press.

Lohr, Steve. 1987. "Swedes Instill a Sense of Responsibility." *The New York Times*, November 8.

Lubeck, Sally, and Patricia Garrett. 1988. "Child Care 2000: Policy Options for the Future." *Social Policy* 18:31–37.

Maher, Thomas F. 1987. "The Loneliness of Parenthood." *Social Service Review* 61:91–101.

Miller, Dorothy C. 1987. "Children's Policy and Women's Policy: Congruence or Conflict?" *Social Work* 32:289–292.

Morell, Carolyn. 1987. "Cause *Is* Function: Toward a Feminist Model of Integration for Social Work." *Social Service Review* 61:144–155.

Nelson, John R., Jr. 1982. "The Politics of Federal Day Care Regulation." Pp. 267–306 in *Day Care: Scientific and Social Policy Issues*, eds. Edward F. Zigler and Edmund W. Gordon. Boston: Auburn House.

O'Connell, Martin, and David E. Bloom. 1987. "Juggling Jobs and Babies: America's Child Care Challenge." Washington, DC: Population Reference Bureau, Inc.

Pascall, Gillian. 1986. *Social Policy: A Feminist Analysis*. London: Tavistock.

Rescorla, Leslie A., Sally Provence, and Audrey Naylor. 1982. "The Yale Child Welfare Research Program: Description and Results." Pp. 183–199 in *Day Care: Scientific and Social Policy Issues*, eds. Edward F. Zigler and Edmund W. Gordon. Boston: Auburn House.

Rodgers, Harrell R., Jr. 1988. "Reducing Poverty Through Family Support." Pp. 39–65 in *Beyond Welfare: New Approaches to the Problem of Poverty in America*, ed. Harrell R. Rodgers, Jr. Armonk, NY: M. E. Sharpe.

Rutter, Michael. 1982. "Social-Emotional Consequences of Day Care for Preschool Children." Pp. 3–32 in *Day Care: Scientific and Social Policy Issues*, eds. Edward F. Zigler and Edmund W. Gordon. Boston: Auburn House.

Salkind, Neil J., and Ron Haskins. 1982. "Negative Income Tax: The Impact on Children from Low-Income Families." *Journal of Family Issues* 3:165–180.

Satran, Pamela Redmond. 1988. "Who Shares the Care?" *Working Mother*, April, pp. 55–57.

Sidel, Ruth. 1986. *Women and Children Last: The Plight of Poor Women in Affluent America*. New York: Penguin.

Sorensen, Annemette, and Sara McLanahan. 1987. "Married Women's Economic Dependency, 1940–1980." *American Journal of Sociology* 93:659–687.

Tarpinian, Greg. 1988. "Child Care." *Economic Notes* 56:1–6.

Trickett, Penelope K., et al. 1982. "A Five-Year Follow-Up of Participants in the Yale Child Welfare Research Program." Pp. 200–222 in *Day Care: Scientific and Social Policy Issues*, eds. Edward F. Zigler and Edmund W. Gordon. Boston: Auburn House.

Ungerson, Clare. 1987. *Policy Is Personal: Sex, Gender, and Informal Care*. London: Tavistock.

U.S. Commission on Civil Rights. 1984. "Equal Opportunity and the Need for Child Care." Pp. 92–105 in *Families and Change: Social Needs and Public Policies*, ed. Rosalie G. Genovese. New York: Praeger.

Wilkie, Jane Riblett. 1987. "Marriage, Family Life, and Women's Employment." Pp. 149–166 in *Women Working: Theories and Facts in Perspective*, eds. Ann H. Stromberg and Shirley Harkess. 2nd ed. Palo Alto, CA: Mayfield.

Zaretsky, Eli. 1976. *Capitalism, the Family and Personal Life*. New York: Harper & Row.

7

The School

In my eyes the question is not what to teach, but how to Educate.
Kingsley, *Letters*, 1849

Education, in the family and in the school, is the principal way by which society assures its own reproduction. As Durkheim (1956, p. 123) noted, education "is above all the means by which society perpetually recreates the conditions of its very existence." While the family (discussed in Chapter 6) is the private and informal domain of education, the school is its public and formal sphere. Whereas the family is the locus of particular, elemental learning in a small group of kinfolk, the school is the assigned place for a universal, elaborated learning experience in a larger group of dissimilar students.

The principal subjects of education are the young. They must learn society's ways and byways, for these are not known innately. Through education, the young learn not only the culture and language of society but its expected norms of behavior as well. The result is the development of conscience, which represents an integration of individual and society: "When our conscience speaks, it is society speaking within us" (Durkheim, 1961, p. 90). However, teachers do not implant modules of conscience in the fallow characters of the young. Education is not a mechanical process by which new citizens are stamped out of the same mold. As humans, we have considerable scope with regard to what we learn and how we learn, and we recast both the contents and the processes of our educations.

Because education is an essential task and because the school is its common ground, the school is an important and oft-used locale of social policy. For example, in the United States the social policy of universal free public schooling serves as a means by which a large and diverse population can be integrated into a coherent society. In the same vein the school serves as a means of fostering racial desegregation, which is another integrative social policy. Thus, while "getting an education" is the acknowledged purpose of schooling, the school is also an agency of social policy. Because of this fact the contentious political nature of social policy is reflected in the school.

Our analysis of the school focuses on its role in society and on its relationship to current social policy issues, including child care and literacy. In our analysis we examine historical changes in the school, especially its increasing federalization, and we discuss social changes that have had fateful consequences for the school, such as the suburbanization of the white population. We also join the ongoing debate about the school by siding with the democratists who espouse an egalitarian extension of quality education, and against the elitists who defend the classical notion of a quality education restricted to a relative few. The chapter concludes with a discussion of social practice in the school, including an interview with a third-grade teacher in a public school.

THE SCHOOL IN SOCIETY

For most of human history the educational function so important to society was fulfilled solely by the family. It was only in the past few hundred years that public institutions of education emerged. The establishment of free public schools in the nineteenth century represented an unprecedented democratization of education and signaled a sea change in society. The public school fostered the emergence of mass literacy: the extension of the ability to read and write to all levels of society. Before the advent of the public school, literacy was restricted to a small elite in society. Labor unions played a pivotal role in the struggle for public schools in the United States, because they were the only way the children of workers could have access to formal education. Support also came from middle-class WASP (white Anglo-Saxon Protestant) reformers, who saw public schools as a vehicle for Americanizing the non-WASP immigrants who began arriving in the United States in large numbers in the mid-nineteenth century (Collins, 1979).

The public school is the most localized—that is, the most decentralized—of all the institutions of the Welfare State. It is largely a creature of local school boards. However, the federal government has played an increasingly larger role in public education, especially since the creation of the National Science

Foundation and the passage of the National Defense Education Act (NDEA) of 1958. Spurred by the success of the Soviet space program, the NDEA sponsored the creation of new and expanded curricula in mathematics and science. It was through such programs that the federal government increased its previously small influence in education and first pressed the development of "a national curriculum" (Lora, 1986, p. 106). The subsequent mobilization of the school in the 1960s to deal with the domestic crises of racial segregation, racial conflict, and poverty further expanded the federal role. Prominent among the new federal initiatives in that period were the Elementary and Secondary Education Act (ESEA) of 1965 and the Civil Rights Acts of 1964 and 1965.

Data indicate the growth of the education sector in society and the increased role of the federal government in education. Between 1950 and 1980, school expenditure grew from 4.1 percent to 6.2 percent of the gross national product. During the same period, the public share of school expenditure held steady at about four-fifths of the total. However, the federal share of school expenditure grew from only 1.7 percent in 1950 to 11.5 percent in 1980; it then fell back to 8.5 percent between 1980 and 1985. The relative decline in the federal role in education in 1980–1985 was due to Reagan administration policies. In 1980 education represented 5.9 percent of federal budget outlays; in 1985 the figure had fallen to 4.1 percent.

The state's role in the provision of education grew partly out of the fact that the school is a universal institution, reaching all citizens. It is a lever by which diverse groups can articulate with one another and with society. The school serves a number of latent social policy purposes that are oriented to socialization and societal integration. One of these purposes is the provision of a means of social mobility, a subject to which we now turn our attention.

Allocation and Equality

In addition to its tasks of socialization and societal integration, the school performs another critical activity of social reproduction: allocation, or the sorting of persons and groups into a hierarchy of various social roles and statuses. Allocation reproduces social stratification and inequality, and it is done largely through the school and the occupational structure. Tracking in schools and among schools is one method of allocation. For example, students are directed into college preparatory or vocational courses (or schools) in high school, and later into elite colleges, state colleges, junior colleges, or the labor force. Such tracking reproduces stratification and inequality because it is based preeminently on social class. Thus college prep in high school and then elite colleges and state colleges are largely for the upper and middle classes. Vocational education in high school and then junior colleges or the labor force are primarily for the working class.

Occupational attainment in the United States is a reflection of original social class. The most important intervening or connecting factor between original social class and occupational attainment is education. This means that social class is more important for later educational achievement than any other single influence, including individual attributes such as mental ability and motivation, and group attributes such as race and ethnicity (Parelius, 1987).

Because of the critical intermediary role that education plays between social background and occupational success, it is the focus of social policy aimed at achieving social mobility and equality of opportunity. The public school is viewed as a route by which children of the working class, poor and nonpoor, can become upwardly mobile. Thus social policy has focused on trying to ensure equal access to quality education through such measures as school desegregation.

How important really is the school as a vehicle for upward mobility? Although there are dissenting opinions, the bulk of research indicates that the positive effects of the school on upward mobility have been exaggerated. For some Americans education is a vehicle for upward mobility, but for most it is not. Research supports the view that the school does not compensate for low socioeconomic status, that it does little more than replicate and legitimate existing stratification patterns (Bowles and Gintis, 1976; Coleman et al., 1966; Jencks et al., 1972). Schools, then, have little real effect in overcoming socioeconomic inequality between social groups. Only fundamental economic redistribution can achieve this goal.

Even if overall social class inequality has not been substantially reduced by equal opportunity in the school, marginal gains have resulted for racial equality. With regard to increased racial equality in schools in the late 1960s and early 1970s, Kirp (1982, p. 278) noted the following:

> As compared with a quarter-century ago, blacks and whites are more likely to attend racially mixed schools; resources are more equitably shared by black and white students; blacks are far more likely to stay in school beyond the minimum leaving age (indeed, the college attendance rates of blacks and whites are essentially the same), and the gap between the educational achievement of blacks and whites, although still sizable, has narrowed considerably.

The fundamental reason why equality of opportunity in the school is a desirable social policy is moral: It is the right thing to do. Even if the school cannot eliminate social inequality, it is imperative to have the school exert whatever influence it does have in opposing inequality. The school has substantial symbolic relevance to equal opportunity, and symbolic value is important because it reflects on group status within society. Devoting the school to the goal of equal opportunity puts the state squarely behind the efforts of previously disenfranchised groups to gain status and power. Nonetheless, the social policy of equal opportunity, even if fully realized, cannot redress the fundamental cause of social inequality: social origins. Equal opportunity may guarantee a fairer race, but it cannot assure a fair outcome so long as the working class, poor and nonpoor, and minorities start out handicapped compared to middle-class WASPs.

Excellence and Universality

Although the public school has not eliminated social class inequality, it has succeeded in universalizing citizenship. The public school provides a common learning experience for citizens, and this is an impressive and unprecedented accomplishment, perhaps the most successful social policy in U.S. history. It is perhaps the only Welfare State social policy in which the United States has been a world leader rather than a laggard. The public school has provided the basis for citizenship: the common egalitarian values that are essential for the functioning of a democratic political culture. These values foster an informed and thoughtful citizenry.

Evidence amply supports the achievement of mass education in the United States. In 1870 only 2.1 percent of persons 14 to 17 years old were in school; in 1986 the figure was 95 percent. In 1870 only 1.7 percent of persons 18 to 21 years old were in college; in 1986 the figure was 46.3 percent. Between 1940 and 1986 the median years of schooling for Americans 25 years old and older rose from 8.6 to 12.6 years. According to research done in the 1960s, other developed nations (France, Japan, the U.K., the U.S.S.R., and West Germany) do not approach the United States in the percentages of relevant age groups completing secondary school and university education (Collins, 1979, p. 92). The United States leads all nations in the mean years of schooling of its labor force: 12.6 years. The nations that come closest to this standard are East Germany, 11.9 years; Canada and New Zealand, 11.7 years; and Czechoslovakia, 11.5 years (Psacharopoulos and Arriagada, 1986).

In recent years this achievement of mass or democratic schooling has been criticized under the banners of excellence and standards (*Action for Excellence*, 1983; *A Nation at Risk*, 1983; Ravitch, 1983). The gist of the criticism is that the public school sacrificed quality for equality, standards for coverage, and excellence for universality. The policy recommendations emanating from these critiques included returning to basics, tightening and upgrading standards, implementing competency tests, and other measures that would reduce coverage. The critics tend to blame the curriculum (too soft) and teachers, rather than their lack of resources and their work conditions, for the perceived decline of standards (Kelly, 1985). In rebuttal, Bastian et al. (1986, p. 163) have argued that these criticisms are elitist and reinforce the logic of the contemporary capitalist economy: to lower expectations and to reduce the life chances for the majority in order to preserve the privileges of a minority.

The conservative critique of education is reflected ideologically in the work of Bloom (1987) and others who represent "the literature of cultural despair" (Botstein, 1988). Theirs is a reactionary response to the democratic expansion of education that began in the 1960s; they yearn for the restoration of a more elitist educational system.

This elitist criticism of public education buttressed the conservative policies of the Reagan administration, of corporations whose interest is in fitting students to the narrow, technocratic needs of the labor market, and of the major universities (Altbach, 1985, p. 26). Privatization of education, through such policy ideas as the voucher system, has been one policy advocated by conservatives. Privatization is not so easily achieved, however, because the boundaries between private and public education are quite blurred in the Welfare State. For example, Hogwood and Peters (1983, p. 195) pointed out that when the Reagan administration made major cuts in student loan and other programs, students were forced to choose public higher education over the considerably more expensive private alternative. The result was a somewhat smaller proportion of students attending private colleges and universities.

A voucher system in which parents could choose among private and public schools for their children has three serious flaws (Gutmann, 1987, pp. 64–70). First, such a system challenges the primacy of the public interest in education. Parents already have a private domain for education, especially moral education: the family. Society has a preeminent interest in the public schools precisely because individual families cannot provide for the collective interest in a common education for citizenship. Second, a voucher plan would have to be regulated in order to ensure that schools did not discriminate on the basis of race and other factors and that they did furnish a minimal level of instruction. Such regulation would lead to more centralization and bureaucratization than we already have. Finally, a voucher plan would almost certainly make education less democratic because the children of knowledgeable middle-class parents with the resources to shop and compare would end up in better schools than the children of the poor and working classes.

Even more reactionary proposals to remold public schooling to conform to traditional values and authorities have come from the New Right. Their effort revolves around attempts to put religion back into the public schools, to censor books, and to promote creationism.

Aronowitz and Giroux (1985) have attributed the conservative attack on the public schools to a backlash against the egalitarian educational developments of the 1960s and 1970s. These achievements included the expansion of public schooling to include masses of African Americans. For example, the median years of school completed for African Americans twenty-five years old and older rose by 50 percent between 1960 and 1980 (for whites, it rose by 15 percent). Aronowitz and Giroux propose a left strategy for further advances in public education. Left critiques of the school focus on its repressive and authoritarian nature and advance liberating alternatives, including critical thinking and Freire's (1970) idea of "dialogic education." The latter is achieved through teacher-student conversation based on the teacher's respect of the student's experience and willingness to learn from the student.

Besides these criticisms from right and left, the public school has been debilitated by a major social change in recent years. The mass suburbanization (discussed in Chapter 9) of the white population has resulted in a market-driven public education system (Katznelson and Weir, 1985). Quality education is now a commodity that is bought by those who can afford to move to suburbs, while those who cannot, predominantly African Americans and

Hispanics, end up paying more (relative to income) for education and getting less from it.

This fragmentation has resulted in a situation similar to that which existed before the egalitarian reforms of the 1960s and 1970s. Before then, the public school was a two-track system, with better-off (mainly white) students using the upper track and less well-off and African American students using the lower track. Today there are three tracks: a suburban track and a city upper track for better-off and white students, and a city lower track for less well-off and African American students (Kirp, 1982, p. 301). The major difference is that now African Americans exert political influence over the lower track.

Fragmentation and segregation have produced a highly variable public school system in which the common core of democratic citizenship is threatened. The real problem is not a lack of standards, but a lack of balance and an increasing bifurcation into have and have-not schools. The evidence of this trend is clear. Egalitarian policies helped to produce a decline in the proportion of African Americans enrolled in predominantly minority schools, from 76.6 percent in 1968 to 62.4 percent in 1976. The decline stopped in the late 1970s, however, and the proportion stood at 63.5 percent in 1984. For segregation of African Americans Illinois led all states (84 percent of African Americans attended predominantly minority schools), followed by Michigan (83.8 percent), New York (81.7 percent), Maryland (79.2 percent), and California (74.8 percent). For segregation of Hispanics, New York led (85.1 percent of Hispanics attended segregated schools), followed by Illinois (79.2 percent), Texas (77.9 percent), and New Jersey (75.1 percent). The highest levels of segregation exist in states with higher proportions of suburbanization. Desegregation is difficult to achieve in such states, where numerous small suburban school districts isolate themselves from central cities (Orfield, Monfort, and George, 1987).

In reality, the problem is not a school problem but a social problem, in that the school reflects basic social and economic inequalities in society.

THE SCHOOL AND SOCIAL POLICY

Educational social policy can address the question of excellence without compromising the vital goals of equality and universality. What social policy initiatives are needed to deal with the social problems impinging on the school? To relieve the large disparity between city and suburban schools, government has to play an active role. One way to proceed is exemplified in New Jersey, where legislative and judicial authorities have mandated an equalization of resources among public school districts. Under New Jersey's plan, state subsidies will be used to bring poorer school districts up to the state average of expenditure per pupil. Nationally, desegregation policy has to be strengthened after being weakened under the Reagan administration. Segregation means inferior schools for minority groups, the people most in need of superior schools. Research indicates that desegregation enhances minority student learning and opportunity for adult achievement (Crain and Carsrud, 1985, p. 221). Finally, other social policy initiatives are needed in the areas of illiteracy, child care, and health care.

Literacy

Despite its educational achievements, the United States lags behind comparable nations in literacy. In 1981 the United States ranked 18th among 154 nations in male literacy, and 13th among 143 nations in female literacy. The top seven nations in female and male literacy were the same; in order, they were Australia, Finland, Luxembourg, the Netherlands, the U.S.S.R., Switzerland, and Austria (Kurian, 1984, pp. 356–359). The U.S. Department of Education reported that between 20 and 26 million Americans suffered from illiteracy in 1988, and the number is growing by 2.2 million a year. Literacy is defined as the ability to read and write well enough to meet the basic requirements of everyday life, including work. According to the Business Council for Effective Literacy, about 23 million American workers read at no better than an eighth-grade level in 1988, while 70 percent of the reading material required in jobs was written for at least a ninth-grade comprehension level.

Far too little is being done about illiteracy in the United States. In 1980 this country ranked 32nd among 157 nations in percentage of GNP spent on education (Kurian, 1984, pp. 357–358, 378). Adult Basic Education is the largest literacy program in the United States, and it enrolls only a fraction of its target population—perhaps as few as 5 percent of functionally illiterate adults (Gutmann, 1987, p. 274).

Although it will take money to reduce illiteracy—perhaps $200 to $400 per year for remedial education for each illiterate person (whose numbers may be as high as one-third of all adults)—the cost of doing nothing is considerably higher. A major study by Kozol (1985) detailed the economic and human costs of illiteracy. The economic costs, direct and indirect, add up to several hundred billion dollars, including income security payments to illiterate adults unable to secure work and the loss of tax revenues from wages. As for the human costs, illiteracy narrows people's horizons and limits their participation in democratic politics. It may also contribute to crime: one estimate is that 60 percent of the state and federal prison population cannot read above the sixth-grade level (Berger, 1988). Only the federal government is capable of providing the leadership and funding necessary for a comprehensive social policy to promote literacy. An adequate social policy to address illiteracy will also serve to upgrade minimum educational levels. To the extent that this is achieved, excellence will be promoted without sacrificing—indeed, by extending—coverage.

Other nations, including those with far fewer resources than the United States, have reduced their illiteracy rates substantially. For example, in the first year after the overthrow of the Somoza dictatorship, the Sandinista government of Nicaragua initiated a National Literacy Crusade that reduced the country's illiteracy rate from about 50 percent to 12.9 percent (Collins, 1987). For this major achievement the United Nations Educational, Scientific, and Cultural Organization (UNESCO) awarded Nicaragua the 1980 prize for distinguished and effective contributions to literacy. A key element in this successful campaign was the recruitment and training of 80,000 volunteers to teach literacy, only 10,000 of whom were professional teachers. The lasting impact of this success was demonstrated by the fact that in 1985 nearly one-third of Nicaraguans were enrolled in some educational program.

Besides improving literacy levels, we need to expand the concept of literacy from one of "functional literacy" to one of "empowering literacy." While functional literacy refers to reading and writing skills, empowering literacy focuses on dialogue and critical thinking (Freire, 1970), and its goal is to teach people how to assume greater control over their lives (Carlson, 1985, p. 174). As important as functional literacy is, it has limitations. As Aronowitz (1981, p. 54) argued, its minimalist focus overlooks the connection between lower and higher education: "Gains made in measures of reading in the early grades are wiped out as higher grades demand comprehension and critical intelligence." Functional literacy is also limited because of its dependent linkage to the labor market, which is characterized by a lot of low-paying, low-skill jobs, especially in the service sector. Functional literacy may be sufficient to sell fast food, but more education is needed for occupational advancement. Thus functional literacy is an essential first step, but it should not be thought of as the final goal of education, which is the development of the ability to think.

Schools as Child-Care and Health-Care Centers

We would greatly benefit as a nation from social policy initiatives that directed the extensive facilities of the public school to other social needs. One such initiative would take advantage of the strategic location and ample facilities of schools to use them as child-care and health-care centers. The public school is ideal for this use on three grounds: accessibility (neighborhood placement), affordability (the necessary infrastructure is already present), and accountability (public control).

Public schools already provide child-care services for children age 5 and older to a large number of working mothers; about three-fourths of children are in school during the hours when their mothers work (Lubeck and Garrett, 1988, p. 36). But the reality of working mothers has increased the demand for preschool care for 3- to 5-year-olds. Between 1965 and 1986 the proportion of this age group enrolled in preprimary school rose from 27.1 percent to 55 percent. However, the increase was unevenly distributed between social classes. In fact, a large preschool education gap has developed in the United States. While about three-fourths of 3- and 4-year-olds from families with incomes above $25,000 per year attend preschool, only 29 percent of poor 3- and 4-year-olds do. As Walsh (1988, p. 12) noted, this gap "is undermining the nation's commitment to universal public education."

Another socially useful role for the public school is to serve as a location for programs aimed at pregnancy prevention. Gilchrist and Schinke (1983), in a study of the social problem of teenage pregnancy, pointed to the success of clinics in high schools in St. Paul, Minnesota, staffed by social workers, nurses, and doctors, which provide pregnancy testing, contraception, and treatment of STDs (sexually transmitted diseases). Three-fourths of students requested these services, which helped to produce a 40 percent decline in unwanted pregnancies. Although the level of sexual activity of U.S. teenagers is about the same as that of teenagers in other Welfare States, we have a much higher rate of teenage pregnancy (discussed in Chapter 6). The difference is largely accounted for by the easier access to sex education and contraception in the other Welfare States. Studies have demonstrated that family planning education for adolescents is more successful if conducted within the school (Rodgers, 1986, pp. 123–124).

A prototype of the potential of the public school for child care and health care is the Beethoven Project in Chicago, a pre-Head Start program designed to provide special developmental services to the kindergarten class that will enter Beethoven Elementary School in 1993 (Teltsch, 1986). Some 150 expectant mothers are receiving comprehensive training in prenatal and infant care, including nutrition education and family counseling. The novelty of the project lies in its provision of comprehensive coordinated services over a five-year period. It is supported by the U.S. Department of Health and Human Services (DHHS), the Illinois Department of Public Aid, the Illinois Department of Children and Family Services, the Chicago Housing Authority, and other public agencies, as well as by private funding from the Ounce of Prevention Fund, the Chicago Urban League, and other sources. The project, which will be evaluated by researchers at the University of Chicago, is sited in one of the twenty-eight high-rise buildings of the Robert Taylor Homes, the world's largest public housing development, where 20,000 to 40,000 African Americans live in poverty. The Beethoven Project is staffed chiefly by local laywomen, who have been trained to serve as mentors to the young mothers.

Preschool education has proved effective for poor children. An analysis of eleven preschool experiments by the Consortium for Longitudinal Studies found that poor kids who attended preschool were much less likely to be left back a grade or to drop out of school than peers who did not attend preschool. Although it is unclear exactly why preschool works so well for poor kids, it is probably not because kids get smarter, but rather because they learn very young to like school, to be responsible students, and to persevere to graduation.

The national model for preschool education is Head Start, the most successful initiative of the War on Poverty of the 1960s. Head Start is designed to provide a preschool experience for poor kids in order to meet their large educational, nutritional, and health needs. Parental involvement, as staff and as volunteers, is mandated. In 1985, according to a DHHS report, one-third of

Head Start staff were parents of current or former students. Despite its demonstrated success and its widespread public support, Head Start remains only a shadow of what it could be. In 1986 the program served 448,000 poor children aged three to five, only a small portion of the children whose poverty qualified them for enrollment.

Three major initiatives are needed to expand Head Start. First, funding should be increased to enable the program to serve more poor preschoolers. Substantial increases are needed just to reach a simple majority of poor preschoolers and their parents. Part of this expansion should be an upgraded outreach service by Head Start because the traditional recruitment methods are not reaching a critical group of potential beneficiaries: teenage single mothers (Walsh, 1988). Second, Head Start should be converted from a half-day to a full-day program. Third, the age at which children can enter Head Start should be lowered from three to two years old.

There is also a large social need to utilize the public schools as after-school child-care facilities. A national Harris Poll of parents and teachers in 1987 found that 51 percent of teachers cited the isolation and lack of supervision of pupils after school as the major reason they have difficulties in school. Forty-one percent of parents reported that their child was often alone from the end of school until 5:30 P.M. A majority of parents said that they would enroll their child in an educational after-school program at school if one were available. The use of schools as child-care centers is widespread in the European Welfare States. The centers are usually free, universal, and used by anywhere from 75 percent to 98 percent of different age groups (Kahn and Kamerman, 1987, p. 154).

Finally, it is apparent that new social needs are being created for the school. Not only the United States, but all industrialized nations, capitalist and socialist alike, are faced with an emerging need for educational policies that respond to the aging of their populations. Some nations, including France, Italy, and Poland, have already initiated social policies to deal with the educational needs of the aged (Coombs, 1985, p. 60). Haubert (1986) reported on the success of adult education policies in Latin America that use a pedagogical strategy of "participatory action-research." In this method, education involves apprenticeship, research, and social action. It is a technique that stresses learning by doing, a tactic well-suited for adults, who have considerable experience and skills. In the United States, adult education needs are growing rapidly. In only six years, between 1980 and 1986, the school enrollment of persons thirty-five and older rose from 1.3 to 1.9 million, an increase of 46 percent. The school enrollment rate for this age group increased from 1.4 percent to 1.8 percent.

Social policy initiatives for the school are desirable, but how would they operate in the context of an institution that is already severely handicapped by a lack of resources? Social practitioners, primarily teachers, are struggling with work overload and other debilitating conditions. So before inaugurating any new social policies through the school, it is imperative to deal with this and other issues involved in current social practice in the school.

SOCIAL PRACTICE

Teachers are the largest single group of state and local government employees. In 1985 the four million public school teachers in the United States represented 29.3 percent of all state and local government employees. The majority of teachers are females. Of teachers at all levels in 1986, in the public and private sectors, 67.7 percent were women; that same year women occupied 44.4 percent of all jobs in the labor force. In all social welfare work, including teaching, in 1980 women held 67.6 percent of jobs, a figure that has been remarkably consistent since at least 1920 (Dressel, 1987, p. 297).

Despite this responsibility carried by women, it is men who control the institutions of learning. Even after the changes precipitated by the feminist movement, it is still men who dominate the school and other social welfare institutions. For example, 30 percent of all male social welfare workers in 1984 were administrators, compared to only 13 percent of all female social welfare workers (Dressel, 1987, p. 298). In educational jobs the proportion of women declines sharply as one goes up the hierarchy of status, pay, and authority. In 1986, 98.3 percent of prekindergarten and kindergarten teachers, 85.2 percent of elementary teachers, 54.9 percent of secondary teachers, and 36 percent of college and university teachers were women. Furthermore, while women occupy over two-thirds of teaching positions, they hold less than one-half the administrative positions in education.

To fully understand the social practice aspect of the school, it is necessary to analyze the work and the subordination of women. Wilson (1977, p. 15) was among the first to point out the connections between education and the subordination of women:

> The whole socialization and education process, at home and in the school, is of crucial importance in raising children who are both trained in particular ways to fit them for the various kinds of work necessary and available under capitalism, and trained to a belief in the naturalness and inevitability of this process. It is this process that the Welfare State is concerned to guide and promote, and in order to do this successfully it has had to develop a particular attitude towards women and the family.

The caring work that women do in the school is difficult and demanding. The term *caring work* means that the worker not only does a job, such as teaching, but also is also expected to care about the job—to invest emotional energy in relating to students. Because of its devaluation by society, caring work features low pay and high workloads. In 1986 the average starting salary of public school teachers in the United States was $16,500, considerably less than the starting pay for other college graduates—42 percent less than that for engineers, 37 percent less than that for computer science majors, 32 percent less than that for chemistry majors, 31 percent less than that for mathematics majors, 26 percent less than that for economics and finance majors, 23 percent less than that for business majors, and 22 percent less than that for accounting and liberal arts majors. Largely because of these negative features, a sizable proportion of teachers regret their decision to make teaching a career. In 1986 about one-third of all elementary and secondary teachers reported that they certainly or probably would not become a teacher again if they were given the chance to start over.

One consequence of the high demands and relatively low rewards of teaching is burnout. Burnout is a general problem for helping professionals that was first analyzed by Freudenberger (1974, 1975). (Burnout among social practitioners is also discussed in Chapters 5 and 8.) A 1977 empirical study of public school teachers in Houston found that burnout was "a significant driving force in the plans of teachers to quit their careers" (Dworkin, 1987, p. 64). This study defined burnout as a form of alienation in which one's work was felt to be meaningless and one was powerless to make it more meaningful. The research found that the role of the school principal was a critical factor in the etiology of burnout: teacher burnout was higher when the principal was seen as unsupportive.

One general approach to dealing with burnout among social practitioners is to recognize the salience of women and their subordination and the relevance of feminism. Morell (1987, p. 151) was speaking of social work when she made the following comment, but it is pertinent to teaching:

> We are a male-dominated women's profession, doing for women what is largely viewed as women's work and generally paid at a women's wage. The project of feminism speaks directly to our experience.

Here a valuable lesson from the feminist movement is contained in the axiom: The personal is political. It helps female teachers recognize the subordination that occurs in their personal relations with male administrators and to work at overcoming it through peer support groups and alternative institutions. Both are relevant to social practice in the school.

One specific method to restructure the social practice of teachers in a positive direction is the use of students as tutors, an ancient practice that has periodically experienced renewed popularity (McNett, 1981). One-to-one peer tutoring has demonstrated its effectiveness in improving academic achievement for tutors as well as tutees, though, regrettably, it has been treated as a remedial rather than a basic tool of teaching. Using student tutors promises gains in areas other than academic achievement, including individualizing instruction for widely divergent students and recruiting teachers-to-be from among the student population. In addition, this strategy makes positive changes in the social practice of teachers. It allows them to better use their skills to plan curriculum and to structure the learning environment—in effect, to manage the educational experience. Thus, in one stroke, teaching loads can be reduced and teachers can expand their professional horizons, at little cost (Hedin, 1987).

By freeing up resources, the peer-tutoring strategy enables public schools to expand and to innovate, especially valuable at a time when school budgets are under pressure. For example, the San Francisco Peer Resource Program trained students to be peer helpers in providing AIDS education in their high schools. The student-peer helpers used their skills in communicating with their fellow students in a number of ways. They led small group discussions and presented dramas, all of which candidly discussed such relevant issues as abstinence and safe sex (Riessman, 1988, p. 3).

Social Practitioner at Work: Terry Murphy

Terry Murphy teaches third grade at an elementary school in a New Jersey suburb of New York City. He was born in 1950 and grew up in Newark, the son of Irish working-class parents. While in high school he was caught up in the mass cultural and political activities of the 1960s, and in college his views as a political progressive crystallized. After graduating from college Terry held a number of jobs in teaching and social welfare: he worked in a nursing home, at a day-care facility in a hospital, and as a school volunteer. The job he liked best was assistant teacher at the Ironbound Community School in Newark. His experience there influenced him to make a career of teaching, and he received his master degree in education from Bank Street College in New York City in 1985, as well as certification to teach in New York and New Jersey.

What Terry likes so much about teaching is being with kids, especially sharing information with them and learning things together. The eight-year-olds he teaches are "developmentally at a new, open stage," beginning to move beyond self-absorption to involvement with the world. Terry said that it is like seeing people open a new vista in their lives and that it is "real exciting to be there and see it, to help it open." Children at this age are still innocent, eager to learn, and not yet cynical. They "really get excited about what is around them, outside them, and learning all about it."

Terry enjoys living down the stereotypes about teachers and about males. He disagrees with the traditional role expectation of the teacher as the one who gives knowledge and who is always right. He tries to share knowledge with his pupils rather than dispense it. He aspires to be a teacher who is open to learning from kids, who admits to making mistakes, and who is "a regular human being." Terry also strives to be a male who combines the traditional masculine virtue of strength with the virtue of gentleness. He is the only male teacher in his school and reports that the experience has been "wonderful, for everyone is supportive and appreciative of a male doing this—it makes it more important." Being a male in a female environment is an issue that has faded over time: "After a while, I just became another member of the staff." However, Terry sometimes feels uncomfortable in this situation and misses being with other men more regularly. He believes that men and women are different because of how they were brought up, and that their teaching styles also differ. Male teachers are more focused on individual kids and more goal oriented, while female teachers are more nurturant and more oriented to the whole class. Terry believes that there are strengths in each approach, and he tries to combine them in his teaching.

Terry's biggest dislike about his work is having to do too much. He feels that he is being asked to teach too many subjects (social skills as well as intellectual ones, reading as well as social studies) and that his work suffers from the overload. Another thing he dislikes is the occasional personality conflict he has with a kid. Although this seldom involves more than one kid in a class, it takes up a lot of his time and is frustrating. Also, because eight-year-olds are not fully rational, he has to spend too much of his limited time on discipline rather than on teaching and on sharing.

Terry has taught in both private and public schools and he sees a lot of differences between them. In private schools education is seen more as a commodity and "the parents want their money's worth." Consequently, mothers and fathers are more involved in the school. Also, because of resources, philosophy, and size, private schools have lower teacher-pupil ratios, more progressive (less traditional) curricula, and less bureaucracy. On the other hand, the public schools have more support activities and support personnel, such as specialized teachers, and a much greater social mix in the pupil population. The public schools, Terry said, provide a "social education" that private schools cannot. Kids in public schools learn to relate to kids from many different racial, ethnic, social class, and religious backgrounds. Finally, Terry found that private schools do not pay nearly as much as public schools and tend to be much more authoritarian toward teachers. In a private school the administrator "tells you what you will make in a one-on-one session, and that is it." In the public school where he now teaches, salaries are public information and are negotiated between the school board and the teachers' union, which is affiliated with the New Jersey Education Association and the National Education Association.

Terry would like to see more innovation in the public schools. He favors team or dual teaching and would like to have more opportunities to do it. He would also like to see more after-school programs, provided they are educationally sound and employ devoted and trained personnel. Terry's special interest is social studies and he advocates more social studies curricula for elementary schools, especially in the areas of conflict resolution and peace studies. Peace studies are becoming more popular in higher education. In 1979 only 14.6 percent of U.S. colleges and universities offered majors, minors, concentrations, or classes in peace studies; in 1985, the proportion had risen to 46 percent (Stout, 1987). Since Terry prefers an experiential rather than a textbook approach to teaching, he favors using simulations and other teaching aids that involve kids in conflict resolution, rather than books that tell them how to do it.

Terry is interested in educational and social policy but is too absorbed in his daily teaching to keep up with all the issues. He is not directly affected by the AIDS crisis (discussed in Chapter 8), for his school has no kids with the disease, but he sees a potential problem that no one wants to deal with. His school is supposed to be developing and implementing a special educational curriculum for AIDS, but it is not really happening, mostly because "controversial issues are a no-no in school." The suburb in which Terry works is populated by people with conservative middle-class values, and everyone in the school is afraid of a big backlash from them about AIDS education. Hence, although the school administration is in favor of AIDS education, no one is pushing it.

Terry believes his union is honestly interested in issues such as AIDS and that he can have his greatest impact on social policy through the union. The biggest personal boon the union has brought him, Terry says, is that he feels he has someplace to go if he has a problem. In the private schools where he used to teach, he felt isolated and vulnerable. In addition to protecting its members, Terry's union runs a lot of programs and seminars to help teachers improve their skills and it takes positions on major national social policy issues. The union is one reason Terry likes his work so much and feels that he has found a rewarding career.

REFERENCES

Action for Excellence. 1983. Washington, DC: Education Commission of the States, Task Force on Education for Economic Growth.

Altbach, Philip G. 1985. "The Great Education 'Crisis.' " Pp. 13–27 in *Excellence in Education: Perspectives on Policy and Practice,* eds. Philip G. Altbach, Gail P. Kelly, and Lois Weis. Buffalo, NY: Prometheus Books.

A Nation at Risk: The Imperative for Educational Reform. 1983. Washington, DC: National Commission on Excellence in Education.

Aronowitz, Stanley. 1981. "Toward Redefining Literacy." *Social Policy* 12:53–55.

Aronowitz, Stanley, and Henry A. Giroux. 1985. *Education Under Siege: The Conservative, Liberal and Radical Debate over Schooling.* South Hadley, MA: Bergin & Garvey.

Bastian, Ann, et al. 1986. *Choosing Equality: The Case for Democratic Schooling.* Philadelphia: Temple University Press.

Berger, Joseph. 1988. "Price of Illiteracy Translates into Poverty and Humiliation." *The New York Times,* September 6.

Bloom, Allan. 1987. *The Closing of the American Mind.* New York: Simon and Schuster.

Botstein, Leon. 1986. "Education Reform in the Reagan Era: False Paths, Broken Promises." *Social Policy* 18:3–11.

Bowles, Samuel, and Herbert Gintis. 1976. *Schooling in Capitalist America: Educational Reform and the Contradictions of Economic Life.* New York: Basic Books.

Carlson, Dennis. 1985. "Curriculum and the School Work Culture." Pp. 171–181 in *Excellence in Education: Perspectives on Policy and Practice,* eds. Philip G. Altbach, Gail P. Kelly, and Lois Weis. Buffalo, NY: Prometheus Books.

Coleman, James S., et al. 1966. *Equality of Educational Opportunity.* Washington, DC: U.S. Government Printing Office.

Collins, Randall. 1979. *The Credential Society: An Historical Sociology of Education and Stratification.* New York: Academic Press.

Collins, Sheila. 1987. "Education in Nicaragua: What Difference Can a Revolution Make?" *Social Policy* 18:42–53.

Coombs, Philip H. 1985. *The World Crisis in Education: The View from the Eighties.* New York: Oxford University Press.

Crain, Robert L., and Karen Banks Carsrud. 1985. "The Role of the Social Sciences in School Desegregation Policy." Pp. 219–236 in *Social Science and Social Policy,* eds. R. Lance Shotland and Melvin M. Mark. Beverly Hills, CA: Sage Publications.

Dressel, Paula. 1987. "Patriarchy and Social Welfare Work." *Social Problems* 34:294–309.

Durkheim, Emile. 1956 [1922]. *Education and Society*, trans. Sherwood D. Fox. New York: Free Press.

———. 1961 [1925]. *Moral Education: A Study in the Theory and Application of the Sociology of Education*, ed. Everett K. Wilson, trans. Everett K. Wilson and Herman Schaurer. New York: Free Press.

Dworkin, Anthony Gary. 1987. *Teacher Burnout in the Public Schools: Structural Causes and Consequences for Children*. Albany: State University of New York Press.

Freire, Paulo. 1970. *Pedagogy of the Oppressed*, trans. Myra Bergman Ramos. New York: Seabury Press.

Freudenberger, Herbert J. 1974. "Staff Burn-out." *Journal of Social Issues* 30:159–165.

———. 1975. "The Staff Burn-out Syndrome in Alternative Institutions." *Psychotherapy* 12:73–82.

Gilchrist, Lewayne D., and Steven Paul Schinke. 1983. "Teenage Pregnancy and Public Policy." *Social Service Review* 57:307–322.

Gutmann, Amy. 1987. *Democratic Education*. Princeton, NJ: Princeton University Press.

Haubert, Maxime. 1986. "Adult Education and Grass-Roots Organisations in Latin America: The Contribution of the International Co-Operative University." *International Labour Review* 125:177–192.

Hedin, Diane. 1987. "Students as Teachers: A Tool for Improving School Climate and Productivity." *Social Policy* 17:42–47.

Hogwood, Brian W., and B. Guy Peters. 1983. *Policy Dynamics*. New York: St. Martin's Press.

Jencks, Christopher, et al. 1972. *Inequality: A Reassessment of the Effect of Family and Schooling in America*. New York: Harper & Row.

Kahn, Alfred J., and Sheila B. Kamerman. 1987. *Child Care: Facing the Hard Choices*. Dover, MA: Auburn House.

Katznelson, Ira, and Margaret Weir. 1985. *Schooling for All: Class, Race, and the Decline of the Democratic Ideal*. New York: Basic Books.

Kelly, Gail P. 1985. "Setting the Boundaries of Debate About Education." Pp. 31–42 in *Excellence in Education: Perspectives on Policy and Practice*, eds. Philip G. Altbach, Gail P. Kelly, and Lois Weis. Buffalo, NY: Prometheus Books.

Kirp, David L. 1982. *Just Schools: The Idea of Racial Equality in American Education*. Berkeley: University of California Press.

Kozol, Jonathan. 1985. *Illiterate America*. Garden City, NY: Anchor Press/Doubleday.

Kurian, George Thomas. 1984. *The New Book of World Rankings*. New York: Facts on File Publications.

Lora, Ronald. 1986. "Education, Public Policy, and the State." Pp. 105–131 in *American Choices: Social Dilemmas and Public Policy Since 1960*, eds. Robert H. Bremner, Gary W. Reichard, and Richard J. Hopkins. Columbus: Ohio State University Press.

Lubeck, Sally, and Patricia Garrett. 1988. "Child Care 2000: Policy Options for the Future." *Social Policy* 18:31–37.

McNett, Ian. 1981. "Youth Teaching Youth." *Social Policy* 12:30–37.

Morell, Carolyn. 1987. "Cause *Is* Function: Toward a Feminist Model of Integration for Social Work." *Social Service Review* 61:144–155.

Orfield, Gary, Franklin Monfort, and Rosemary George. 1987. *School Segregation in the 1980s*. Chicago: National School Desegregation Project, University of Chicago.

Parelius, Robert J. 1987. *The Sociology of Education*. 2nd ed. Englewood Cliffs, NJ: Prentice Hall.

Psacharopoulos, George, and Ana Maria Arriagada. 1986. "The Educational Composition of the Labour Force: An International Comparison." *International Labour Review* 125:561–574.

Ravitch, Diane. 1983. *The Troubled Crusade: American Education 1945–1980*. New York: Basic Books.

Riessman, Frank. 1988. "Transforming the Schools: A New Paradigm." *Social Policy* 19:2–4.

Rodgers, Harrell R., Jr. 1986. *Poor Women, Poor Families: The Economic Plight of America's Female-Headed Households*. Armonk, NY: M. E. Sharpe.

Stout, Hilary. 1987. "Peace Studies Rise." *The New York Times*, April 12.

Teltsch, Kathleen. 1986. "A Cradle-to-Kindergarten Aid Plan in Chicago." *The New York Times*, December 28.

Walsh, Joan. 1988. "Giving Kids a Head Start." *In These Times*, October 19–25, pp. 12–13.

Wilson, Elizabeth. 1977. *Women and the Welfare State*. London: Tavistock.

8

Health

Should untun'd Nature crave the Medic art, what Health can that
contentious Tribe impart?
Pomfret, *Poetical Works*, 1702

U.S. health care is languishing in a debilitating condition, the main symptoms of which are runaway costs and a shameful lack of attention to many ill citizens. American society does not receive fair value for the vast sums of money it devotes to health care. The time is ripe for social policy initiatives to remedy this malady by creating the basis for a health-care system that is both more efficient and more effective. Before we turn to a discussion of required social policy measures, however, we need to examine the nature of the health-care system's problems.

One of the major problems is the distortion caused by the elaboration of costly high-tech interventions that have low benefit for the general population, such as organ transplants. This stress on glamorous technology comes at the expense of more ordinary projects that promise higher social return, including public health policies to eliminate destructive diseases and to reduce environmental toxins. A specific example of how technology skews health care is the proliferation of neonatal intensive care units (NICUs) for the treatment of tiny (1,500 grams or less) premature infants (Guillemin and Holmstrom, 1986). The NICUs do reduce the death rate for infants; however, they distort health care in two ways. First, a number of negative consequences flow directly from NICU technology, including the fact that infants thus treated are highly susceptible to serious permanent neurological and congenital disabilities. The resulting rehabilitative and medical costs are exorbitant—the neonatal care alone of some cases has cost a quarter of a million dollars. Also, there is evidence that death in some instances is only delayed until childhood. Moreover, the consequences of technological treatments can be damaging, including blindness from oxygen therapy. (This is an example of iatrogenic disorders, which are discussed later in the chapter.) Second, there is an indirect adverse result of the emphasis on NICU technology: it drains material resources and public attention from other strategies to deal with premature births. Probably the most efficient and effective way to reduce prematurity is through a universal prenatal program that provides for the health and nutrition needs of pregnant women.

Another problem of the U.S. health-care system is its social class bifurcation: the system performs considerably better for the middle and upper classes than it does for the working and poor classes. Research has consistently demonstrated that people in the lower classes have higher disability, morbidity (sickness), and mortality (death) rates than those in the upper classes (Hadley, 1982; Syme and Berkman, 1986). Race is another differentiating factor in health, with Native Americans, African Americans, and Hispanics suffering from a lower quality of health than Asian Americans and whites. In 1985 African Americans had a mortality rate (age adjusted) 49 percent higher than whites, a life expectancy 5.8 years lower than whites, and an infant mortality rate almost double that of whites. African Americans, Hispanics, and Native Americans have higher rates of health problems principally because they are more likely to be poor than are Asian Americans and whites, a fact that underscores the importance of social class.

Part of the reason why health is differentiated by social class is that health care is rationed according to ability to pay, our first subject in this chapter. After we look at this rationing then we analyze the medical-industrial complex, concentrating on the role of corporations and their control of technology. Following this, we analyze priority policy issues for health care: the crisis that is acquired immune deficiency syndrome (AIDS) and the need for health security and an ecological strategy for health care. Next, we examine the social practice of health care workers, with a focus on nurses. Finally, we take up health-care innovations emanating from holistic health practices, the women's movement, and public health initiatives in the workplace.

RATIONING

Hollingshead and Redlich (1958) did a pioneering study that demonstrated the middle class receives favored mental health care and the working class receives disfavored care. The researchers found that neurotic patients who were upper and middle class were more likely to see private practitioners and to receive psychotherapy, while neurotic patients who were working and lower class were more likely to use public clinics or to be hospitalized in a state institution and to receive shock treatments and sedation.

The root cause of this bifurcation is that access to health care in the United States is constrained by market forces and driven by profit motives. Thus quality of health care is determined by the ability to pay. Summarizing data on the differences in overall health care between the haves and have-nots, Dutton (1986, p. 52) concluded that "despite the increased access provided by public entitlement programs, the poor still have lower rates of utilization among children, fewer services at all ages relative to illness levels, less preventive care, more reliance on hospital-based clinics, and greater financial and organizational barriers to access."

In 1988, thirty-seven million Americans had no public or private health insurance coverage, up from thirty million in 1980. Most uninsured people are in the working and poor classes. About one-half of all uninsured persons work for employers who do not provide health insurance. The other one-half are not poor enough to qualify for Medicaid but too poor to buy private insurance (Tolchin, 1988b). Poor people are twice as likely to be uninsured as middle-class people and three times as likely to be uninsured as upper-class people (Arendell, 1988, p. 55). About one-fourth of persons below the poverty line have no private or public insurance coverage (Starr, 1986, p. 107). The Medicaid program, which was legislated to meet the health needs of the poor as the insurance of last resort, was available to less than one-half of poor people in 1985. In 1980–1985 average annual health insurance expenditure was $257 for the poorest 20 percent of the population. For the richest 20 percent the expenditure was $430, 67 percent more.

Women are especially likely to lack health-care insurance because so many of them are low-wage workers in jobs that do not provide medical coverage. Indeed, being married is a better predictor of health insurance coverage for women than is their employment. The fact that proportionately fewer women are married today has increased their vulnerability (Arendell, 1988, p. 56). Also, Reagan administration policies exacerbated the vulnerability of poor women. The Omnibus Budget Reconciliation Act of 1981 (discussed in Chapter 5) led to the termination of many female-headed families from Aid to Families with Dependent Children, which meant the loss of health insurance (Medicaid) for these families at the very time that their health risks (as measured by morbidity) were increasing (Sarri and Russell, 1988).

African Americans as well as women are harmed by the rationing of health care. For example, research has demonstrated that white men receive a greatly disproportionate share of transplanted kidneys. White men are twice as likely to receive a new kidney as African Americans of either sex, and one-third more likely to receive a new kidney as white women. The disparity exists even when patients from the same socioeconomic group are compared.

The disparity is in the opposite direction from the social need. African Americans have a rate of kidney failure that is three times that of whites (Blakeslee, 1989).

Empirical research (McKinlay et al., 1983) has concluded that an inverse law applies to health care in the United States: The availability of good care varies inversely with the need for it. This is, of course, just the opposite of what a just social policy would produce. The inverse care law was originally postulated as a general principle of the profit-driven allocation of health care in capitalist societies by Hart (1971), who argued that market distribution of medical care is primitive and historically outdated. However, market forces, although they have lost some ground, are still dominant in U.S. health care. Between 1970 and 1986 total U.S. health care expenditure rose from 7.4 percent to 10.9 percent of GNP. In the same period public expenditure rose from 37 percent to 41.4 percent of the total expenditure on health care and the federal share of this went from 63.6 percent to 70.6 percent. Thus, in 1986, 58.6 percent of total health-care expenditure was private, 29.2 percent was federal, and 12.2 percent was state and local.

The root cause of rationing is the fact that the U.S. health-care system is undersocialized and overprivatized. It is dominated by profit-seeking health-care corporations, proprietary hospitals and nursing homes, and private practice physicians, and as a result, American consumers pay more for and get less from health care than do citizens of other nations. In absolute terms the U.S. health-care system is the world's most expensive, costing $458.2 billion in 1986. In relative terms, according to 1985 World Bank data, the United States ranked eighth among the world's nations in the percentage of all central government expenditure that went for health. However, this relatively high expenditure did not result in correspondingly high indices of health. In the same year the United States ranked eleventh in life expectancy, twentieth (tied with three other nations) in population per physician, seventeenth (tied with one other nation) in population per nurse, and seventeenth (tied with three other nations) in infant mortality rate. Six nations ranked higher on at least three of these four major indices of health, and all achieved their superior positions with relatively lower expenditure than the United States. The six nations were Australia, France, the Netherlands, Norway, Spain, and Sweden. All have health-care systems that are more socialized than ours.

Additional data demonstrate the comparative shortcomings of U.S. health care. Weller's (1986) analysis of the health-care systems of Canada and the United States found the Canadian system superior in several respects. First, health levels are somewhat higher in Canada. Second, Canada's health-care system is less expensive than ours, and costs are better controlled. Third, in Canada there is greater equitability of access to health-care services for low-income persons. The superiority of the Canadian system is due largely to its socialized and universal structure: health-care insurance and reimbursement are a public monopoly.

While the United States compares unfavorably to other Welfare States in achieving better health at lower cost, Welfare States generally lag behind socialist nations. For example, a major comparative study of health care in socialist East Germany and capitalist West Germany found that "the East German healthcare system is considerably more efficient, producing similar figures of morbidity and life expectancy with about half as much of the GNP as the West German system uses" (Klinkmuller, 1986, p. 53). The greater cost of the West German health-care system is due to its emphasis on high-technology cures, its neglect of preventive and occupational medicine, and its domination by the medical profession. In contrast, the more efficient East German health-care system stresses intensive preventive programs and occupational medicine, and it links health care with housing, the workplace, and schools. The East German system is state controlled; the medical profession has been effectively neutralized and the profit motive does not exist (Light, 1986, p. 583).

The rationing of U.S. health care raises a grave question of social justice. Great amounts of money are spent on marginally improving the quality of life for some people—through cosmetic surgery, for example—while many other Americans are deprived of even adequate health care. The starkest examples are indigent people who are turned away from one hospital emergency room after another because they lack insurance—some of whom die before they reach an institution that will admit them (McMullen, 1987).

The rationing of health care by social class is a perversion, on a societal scale, of the triage system used in disaster and battlefield situations. In triage, where there are scarce resources to meet emergency needs, casualties are sorted into three groups according to the prognoses for their injuries. Those whose lives can be saved by intervention are the first to be treated. Those who must wait are placed in two groups: casualties with relatively minor injuries who will survive with delayed treatment, and those with severe injuries who will likely die. Triage is morally defensible because the decision as to who will live and who will die is made on the basis of a universalistic criterion—medical prognosis. Rationing of health care by price is unjust because the decision as to who gets care and who does not is based on ascriptive criteria—race and social class. If rationing is necessary, it should, like triage, be based on fair criteria. For example, in the U.K.'s National Health Service costly technology is explicitly rationed so that it pays for very little elective surgery, and dialysis for chronic kidney failure is unavailable to patients over fifty-five (Mechanic, 1986, p. 73). However, access to general health care is readily available to everyone at little or no cost (Churchill, 1987, pp. 113–118).

Rationing has been empirically demonstrated to be a common phenomenon in areas of the U.S. Welfare State other than health care. For example, Gruber's (1980) study of the institutional population showed how rationing of services by race and social class replicated the stratification system. The institutional population included residents of correctional and mental health facilities, as well as residents of institutions for the aged, unwed mothers, and persons with chronic diseases. Nonwhites and the poor were passed from higher-prestige services to lower-prestige ones in an organizationally induced pattern of downward mobility. This rationing of higher-quality services was accomplished through the organizational mechanisms of intake, diagnosis, and referral. These organizational mechanisms reflect the rationing technique of bureaucratic disentitlement (Lipsky, 1984), in which services are reduced and circumscribed through apparently routine actions and through inaction. Consolidation of neighborhood services into one central office is an example of an organizationally routine action (ostensibly to reduce administrative costs) that penalizes the poor as a result of travel costs for some and inaccessibility for others. A decision not to publicize the availability of benefits is an example of bureaucratic disentitlement by inaction that falls most heavily on the poor, because of constraints on their ability to gain information on their own.

Increased socialization of health care promotes social justice, for its basic goal is to provide for the greater good of the greater number. Socialization means that institutions and services are publicly owned or controlled and are operated at cost, not for profit. This reduces the disparities caused by profit-taking providers who seek the well-off and avoid the poor. A policy of health-care socialization redirects resources away from high-cost and only marginally helpful treatments that benefit the few to social and public health programs that help the large majority of people. The most powerful opposition to health-care socialization comes from the profit-taking providers who make up the medical-industrial complex.

THE MEDICAL-INDUSTRIAL COMPLEX

The term *medical-industrial complex* was first used to describe the health-care system in 1970 (Ehrenreich and Ehrenreich, 1970). This complex comprises a range of social actors who dominate the health-care system and operate it with their own interests chiefly in mind. These social actors form three groups of health-care providers: primary providers, such as doctors and hospitals that supply direct care; secondary providers, such as medical schools and drug companies that produce personnel and technology; and insurance providers. These interest groups dominate by owning, financing, and managing the health-care system. They use their considerable resources to influence government, which funds, regulates, and operates a large number of health-care institutions and activities. Through their lobbying of government and their contributions to politicians, health-care providers seek support for their favorite programs: research and training grants for medical schools, construction monies for hospitals, and reimbursement for insurers (Litman, 1984, p. 13). The medical-industrial complex hinders the progressive development of health-care policy because it monopolizes limited social resources for its private, profit-seeking endeavors and because it steadfastly opposes socialization. The two dominant themes in the ascendancy of the medical-industrial complex are the corporatization and the medicalization of health care.

Corporatization

A large and growing sector of the medical-industrial complex is composed of corporations. This corporatization is highlighted by two major developments: the growth of for-profit hospitals at the expense of nonprofit voluntary (largely religious) and public hospitals; and the concentration of the whole range of health-care services, including laboratories and nursing homes, into national conglomerates (Starr, 1982, pp. 420–449). For-profit hospital chains have grown dramatically and have become the "McHospitals" of health care in that their profits depend on the large scale of their operations. In 1971 for-profits operated only 6.2 percent of hospital beds; in 1986, 13 percent; in 1990, 19 percent (Altman, 1986, p. 108). The growth of the for-profit sector is associated with growth in the size of facilities. Between 1971 and 1982 the proportion of all hospitals and nursing homes with seventy-five or more beds rose from 32.9 percent to 40.9 percent.

Health maintenance organizations (HMOs) are among the most visible vehicles of corporatization. HMOs are prepaid group plans that deliver comprehensive health-care services for a fixed price. Since their inauguration with the Health Maintenance Organization Act of 1973, HMOs grew from 175 in 1976 to 595 in 1986, while their enrollment increased from 6 million to 23.7 million persons. The proportion of HMOs operated for profit more than doubled between 1981 and 1984. Evidence (Petchey, 1987) indicates that HMOs have increased the concentration of health services and decreased their costs. However, the cost reductions have been achieved through reduced use by low-income persons rather than through greater efficiency. This is likely to increase inequalities in health care that favor the well-to-do and disfavor the poor.

Health care has attracted the interest of capitalists because of several structural factors that promise profitability: (1) a large and growing captive market, (2) high priority for consumers, (3) control over valuable technology, and (4) guaranteed payment by the state (McKinlay, 1984, p. 5). In addition, involvement in health care enables profit-hungry corporations to project a benevolent public image. For-profit hospital chains had profit margins ranging from 15 to 30 percent in the early 1980s (Abramovitz, 1987, p. 411). It should come as no surprise, then, that corporatization has not reduced the high cost of health care in the United States. In fact, as Starr and Marmor (1984, p. 248) have pointed out, one of the skills of corporate health managers, "reimbursement maximization," promises to raise costs to both government and patients.

Reimbursement maximization is apparently adaptable to new cost-containment measures as they appear. A specific example is the latest public effort to control rising medical costs: diagnostic related groups (DRGs). In the DRG payment system, enacted in 1982 as an amendment to Medicare legislation, federal reimbursement for medical care is a set amount based on a formula by which each patient's stay is placed in a category that includes diagnosis, complications, age, sex, and certain other factors. If the actual cost of caring for a particular patient is less than the reimbursement, the hospital keeps the difference; if the actual cost is more than the reimbursement, the hospital must make up the difference. The DRG system was designed to provide a monetary incentive for hospitals to reduce their costs.

So far results are mixed. There is some evidence that the DRG system has reduced hospital use and cost and has promoted increased home care (Budrys, 1986, p. 70; Siu and Brook, 1987, pp. 25–27). On the negative side, it has expanded the hospital fiscal bureaucracy and has resulted in the premature discharge of many seriously ill people (Hiatt, 1987, p. 86). The greatest danger of the DRG system may be its tendency to encourage hospitals to reduce their accessibility to patients who are sicker than average or for whom DRG reimbursement is lower than average (Churchill, 1987, p. 131). The overriding problem with the DRG system is that its success is predicated on the profit motives of hospitals. Thus there is evidence of "DRG creep," which is the deliberate labeling of case mix to maximize reimbursement (Eastaugh, 1987, p. 23).

The principal danger of corporatization is that it makes health care into a business guided by profit motives rather than by health concerns. Thus, in a survey of 8,298 nursing homes, the overwhelming majority of which were operated for profit, the General Accounting Office found that more than one-third were repeatedly deficient in care in 1981–1985. In response to this problem, Congress passed a law in 1987 to improve the standards of care in nursing homes. However, the Reagan administration failed to carry out the law, in large measure because of the cost it would entail for the nursing home industry (Tolchin, 1988a). Another example of the negative effect the profit motive has on health care is provided by hospitals. In the interest of minimizing labor costs, for-profit hospitals use fewer workers. In 1985, among all nonfederal short-term hospitals (the basic community hospital), for-profit hospitals had the lowest rate of personnel usage—408 staff per 100 patients. State and local government hospitals had 470 staff per 100 patients, and nongovernmental nonprofit hospitals had 466.

An illustrative case of the precedence that corporations place on profit is the proliferation of coronary care units (CCUs) for the treatment of myocardial infarctions (Waitzkin, 1986). Large corporations developed elaborate technology, including cardioventers and defibrillators, and then promoted the CCU as the place to use it, in the interest of profit. This was done without clear evidence that CCUs are more health effective than hospital wards or home care, both of which cost less.

For-profit hospitals, unlike voluntary and public hospitals, can be selective about their clientele. In the interest of maximizing profit, their managers prefer privately insured patients, whose payments are more generous and automatic, over Medicare, Medicaid, and noninsured patients (Starr, 1982,

p. 436). Selectivity is especially pronounced with regard to homeless people. (Homelessness is discussed in Chapter 9.) In New York City in 1986, of the 18,100 emotionally disturbed people, largely indigent and homeless, picked up off the street by police, only 2 percent were treated at private hospitals. For-profit hospitals also prefer patients with problems that require lab tests, drugs, and similar technologies that are common, quickly administered, and involve low overhead, because they generate volume and greater profit. All these practices add up to a skimming of the most profitable clients by private hospitals, while less profitable and unprofitable patients are dumped on public hospitals (Hiatt, 1987, pp. 46–47, 90).

Dumping is the practice by which private hospitals transfer unwanted patients to public hospitals. In a study of transfers to Cook County (Chicago) Hospital, Schiff and his colleagues (1986, p. 556) determined the following:

> We conclude that patients are transferred to Cook County Hospital from other hospital emergency departments predominantly for economic reasons. The fact that many patients are in a medically unstable condition at the time of transfer raises serious questions about the private health sector's ability to consider the condition and well-being of patients objectively, given the strong economic incentives to transfer the uninsured. The delay in providing needed medical services as a result of the transfer process represents a serious limitation of the access to and quality of health care for the poor.

For-profit hospital chains "demarket" the poor also by making them feel unwelcome, by closing emergency facilities that are used so often by poor people, and, most effectively, by locating in areas where few poor people live (Starr, 1986, p. 129).

Thus corporate profit interests contradict the general health interests of society, producing a triumph of self-interest over altruism. Relman (1980, p. 969) described the general contradiction as follows:

> The private health-care industry is primarily interested in selling services that are profitable, but patients are interested only in services that they need, i.e., services that are likely to be helpful and are relatively safe. Furthermore, everything else being equal, society is interested in controlling total expenditures for health care, whereas the private health-care industry is interested in increasing its total sales.

Corporatization is a principal contributor to the increasing cost of health care in at least two ways: the drive for profits encourages the use of unnecessary and expensive procedures and technologies, and profits must be taken in addition to the cost of treatments.

It is important to recognize that the corporatization of health care is international—in fact, it creates even more serious problems in the Third World. A case analysis (Glucksberg and Singer, 1982) of seven transnational drug corporations doing business in Zaire in 1980 revealed that 75 percent of imported drugs were expensive (on average, 300 percent more than generic drugs) and nonessential. Because of the nation's poverty, the expense of these nonessential drugs increased the scarcity of needed imported items. Also, two drugs were imported that were rarely used in developed nations because of their potentially fatal complications. The drug corporations were able to take advantage of a weak government in Zaire that was highly corrupt.

Medicalization

Medicalization is the propagation of the medical model. The word *medical* refers to the administration of remedies, often medicinal substances such as drugs. In the United States, only doctors of medicine (MDs) have the state-legislated authority to prescribe drugs, which is a principal basis for their influence. They are the primary agents of the medical model. In some other societies, health care is in the hands of various practitioners; for example, in the People's Republic of China, premodern medicine such as herbalism and acupuncture coexist with modern medicine.

The medical treatment model is remedial rather than preventive, professional rather than lay, and oriented to the application of technology to individuals rather than to the change of social conditions and processes. Medicalization is illustrated by the rise of neonatal intensive care units, discussed at the beginning of this chapter; they are one aspect of the general medicalization of the birth process, which has changed it from a family event to a medical crisis.

Medicalization advanced through the collective power of MDs. Historically, the American Medical Association (AMA), the professional organization of allopathic MDs, has been a powerful social actor in the medical-industrial complex. It is one of the richest sources of political campaign contributions and legislative lobbying efforts in the United States. After its establishment in 1847, the AMA gradually gained monopoly status in health care, pushing aside the rival claims of midwives and other health practitioners. Professional aggrandizing by the AMA is sometimes unscrupulous. A Chicago federal district judge ruled in an antitrust case in 1987 that the AMA had led a conspiracy to destroy the chiropractic profession. The AMA effort included boycotting chiropractic referrals and labeling chiropractic practice as cultist and unscientific. The instrument of this conspiracy was the AMA's Committee on Quackery, formed in 1962 and disbanded in 1974. Although the AMA contended that its antichiropractic effort ended in 1980, the judge noted that the organization had refused to acknowledge its past action or to affirm that it is now generally considered ethical for MDs to associate with chiropractors. In another tactic to hinder competition, the AMA managed to prevent optometrists (competitors of opthalmalogists) and chiropractors (competitors of general practice MDs and orthopedists) from qualifying for reimbursement as Medicare providers (Feldstein, 1984, p. 237). This has had the effect of raising the price of alternative practitioners.

An important basis for the ascendancy of MDs has been their expertise with medical technology, which increased substantially in scope and complexity in the twentieth century. MDs are the masters of modern medical machines and medications just as herbalists and midwives were the masters of traditional remedies. The hospital also owes much of its increased importance to the expansion of medical technology. It provides the space to house large, expensive medical machinery, such as computerized axial tomography (CAT) scanners, and it is the central place for medical treatment. Medical technology is so expensive (a CAT scanner costs about $1 million) that it has provided leverage for the growth of corporations, which have expanded the function of hospitals as machine garages. Health-care corporations have the capital resources necessary to invest in costly technology and the high volume of use (by the nonpoor) needed to extract profit from it.

The CAT scanner illustrates other issues with regard to medical technology. It is a powerful diagnostic tool, especially for brain and pelvic tumors. Also, it is popular because it is a prestige item and is relatively simple to use. However, the CAT scanner is quite expensive, both to purchase and to operate. As a result, CAT scanners are concentrated in large university hospitals, which limits their availability to the general population. Finally, despite the diagnostic gain the CAT scanner represents, it is questionable that it has improved health. Great progress has been made in the diagnosis of brain and pancreatic tumors since the introduction of the CAT scanner, but almost none in treatment (De Kervasdoue, Kimberly, and Lacronique, 1984, pp. 95–98).

There are other explanations besides professional monopoly for the sanctification of the medical approach to health and health care. One is its scientific basis. Science has replaced religion as the principal source of legitimation in modern society, and MDs speak with the authority of science. They are the contemporary equivalents of traditional priests, for they possess knowledge of the biological facts of life to which the general public does not have access, and this gives them great power. MDs also have skill. As well as knowing how the body works (science), they use their hands to repair it (art). In this respect the MD is the modern equivalent of the shaman and other healers in premodern societies. Underlying the ascendancy of MDs are the common human fears of uncertainty, of the future, and especially of death. Like the oracles and shamans of old, MDs give people the illusion of certainty and control and offer the possibility of postponing death.

The final and perhaps most important reason for the dominance of the medical model is its symmetry with capitalism. Medical treatment, in its one-on-one, fee-for-service, clinical, and remedial structure, conforms to the individualist ideology and market economy of capitalism. As Navarro (1986, p. 196) noted, the "medical ideology and position became hegemonic because it complemented and reproduced the dominant class ideology." Capitalist individualism is the dominant class ideology, and medicine endorses it by locating the cause of illness within the person and by advocating curative individual remedies rather than preventive public health policies.

The medical model not only dominates health care, it pervades society. Social life has been infused with medical jurisdictions. More and more spheres of life have become subject to medical definition and intervention, including leisure (the prescribed role of exercise), sex (à la the Masters and Johnson [1966] treatment), and child care (parenting instructions, beginning with Dr. Spock [1946]). Medicalization has also incorporated some of the marginal statuses in society. Alcoholism and homosexuality, for instance, have been transformed from moral (evil) categories to medical (sick) ones. In the process MDs expanded their areas of control as sorting and treatment agents. A good example of how a social status can be transformed into a medical diagnosis is the transition from the category *hyperactive children* to the diagnosis *hyperkinesis*, or *minimal brain dysfunction* (MBD). Until the 1950s hyperactivity was an antisocial behavior, controlled primarily by parents and teachers. With the development of psychoactive drugs, such as Ritalin, that treated the symptoms of hyperactivity, a deviant behavior was redefined as a medical problem (Conrad and Schneider, 1980, pp. 155–161). The major impetus for this transformation came from the pharmaceutical industry, which used aggressive advertising to promote the use of drugs to treat the problem.

Medicalization increases the sheer number of labeled individuals. One category of deserving Welfare State clients labeled through medicalization is the disabled (Stone, 1984). Disability is a medical category, while the traditional categories of Welfare State clients, such as the poor, are social in nature. One has to be diagnosed and certified by an MD in order to receive disability benefits from Welfare State programs.

Medicalization produces social good as well as negative effects. Deviant behaviors are no longer defined in moral terms and punished. To be labeled a victim of a disease or a biological aberration is a more sympathetic social position than to be branded as immoral. Consider the changed social position of parents of babies who have died in their sleep. Until relatively recently the baby's death was often attributed to accidental suffocation, leading to criticism of parents (especially mothers) for neglect. Now crib death has been medicalized; it is referred to as "sudden infant death syndrome" (SIDS) and research indicates that its cause is a neurological abnormality that probably arises during fetal development (Johnson and Hufbauer, 1982).

Medicalization does not always prevent a negative evaluation, however. If behavior that was once called immoral is now labeled unhealthy, to be unhealthy can also be a stigmatized status. With regard to hyperactivity, for example, the stigma was transformed from "bad" to "sick." Moreover, medicalization may result in more fateful consequences than moral judgment of a behavior because it produces an official dossier that follows the sick person throughout life and because the drugs that often go with it can have long-term side effects.

Medicalization can reduce human suffering, as in the use of drugs to relieve chronic pain. It can also prolong human life, as in the early detection and treatment of cancer. However, medicalization itself has become a source of a whole class of illnesses: iatrogenic disorders (Illich, 1976, p. 14). Iatrogenic illnesses and injuries are those that are medically induced—that is, caused by MDs in their clinical practice. There may be as many as a million such cases each year in the United States. Overreliance on technology and its misuse contribute to iatrogenic outcomes. For example, Riessman and Nathanson (1986, p. 271) found that electronic fetal monitoring in childbirth requires the laboring woman to lie in bed. This may prolong labor, which in turn may lead to more pain and painkilling medications and procedures that increase the risk for mother and fetus. In addition, electronic fetal monitoring produces many false-positive indications of fetal distress, which cause unnecessary caesarean deliveries (Eastaugh, 1987, p. 475) that result in more cost, risk, trauma, and hospitalization. A program at a Chicago hospital demonstrated that the caesarean birth rate can be reduced by as much as 40 percent without adverse effects on mother or infant. Nationally, the cost of a caesarean delivery is more than twice the cost of a vaginal birth (Freudenheim, 1989).

The pathological consequences of modern medical practice have led some researchers to conclude that it creates more problems than it cures. This is an oversimplification. In and of itself medicalization is neither bad nor good; it has a great many positive as well as negative consequences. But it unquestionably has created social problems that are not being addressed by social policy.

Ironically, the corporatization of health care is now challenging the authority of MDs. Freidson (1986) and Salmon (1984) have argued that as a result of increasing state review and standardization of medical practice, beginning with the adoption of Medicare and Medicaid, and increasing corporatization, which has put many MDs in the salaried worker class, the influence of MDs is declining. Even if corporatization does not produce a proletarianization of MDs on the industrial model, it will result in MDs having less control over important aspects of medical practice (Derber, 1984). The control of rapidly growing health-care corporations is vested in businesspersons, not MDs; standardized management and accounting procedures are the means of control, not professional relationships and associations. For-profit corporations employ MDs and the medical treatment model to their financial advantage.

POLICY ISSUES

Corporatization and medicalization are major obstacles to needed policy innovations in health care. Established medicine is not meeting the challenges of modern health care. Medicine has not adapted successfully to the current transition in society's health problems. The acute infectious diseases such as smallpox that plagued the world in the past were brought under effective control by immunization and sanitation—at least in the developed nations. Thus modern society's greatest health challenges are posed by chronic illnesses (diseases of civilization) that cannot be cured but can be managed. Medical treatment has only a negligible impact on the chances of surviving the two major diseases of developed societies, cancer and heart disease (Hart, 1985, p. 9).

Perhaps for the first time in history long life has become a problem. The old old, defined as persons eighty-five years of age and older, represented 1 percent of the U.S. population in 1980. According to Bureau of Census projections, they will be 1.8 percent of the population in 2000, 2.8 percent in 2030, and 5.9 percent in 2080. This group has chronic health problems and extraordinary social needs. Nearly one-fourth of the old old are institutionalized, and one-half of those who are not institutionalized need someone else's help in order to cope with everyday life (Suzman and Riley, 1985). In its single-minded focus on extending life through technology, medicine has ignored the quality of life. The pressing issues of chronic illness are personal and social, not medical; they include family disruption, stigmatization, and loss of bodily integrity (Strauss, 1979).

Corporate medicine's impersonal and technological methods raise the monetary and human costs of health care. Recently there has been some movement away from unnecessary technology and toward more humanistic practice, apparent in insurance providers' requirements for second and third opinions before major medical interventions, in the provision of institutional ombudspersons to represent patients, and in the development of human relations curricula in medical schools. Hospital ombudspersons, usually referred to as directors of guest relations or patient representatives or advocates, are now employed at the majority of U.S. hospitals. One of their functions is to restore the human touch to hospitals. While they perform important services for people, including providing information and emotional support, ombudspersons are hired principally as a public relations gesture by hospitals, and as a means to improve billing and housekeeping procedures and to ward off legal suits (Brody, 1987). While ombudspersons' efforts are to be applauded, they are only remedial responses.

In order to resolve the problems of profit-driven technologies, of human fragmentation and depersonalization, it is necessary to address the fundamental structural problems in U.S. health care: the distorting influences of the medical-industrial complex, medicalization, and the marketplace. The pressing health-care needs of the poor, of women, of workers, and of persons with AIDS will not be fully met until these distortions are corrected by comprehensive health security and ecological policies, both of which require active state intervention. Historical study (Hart, 1985, p. 35) has demonstrated that the health standards of the most vulnerable populations have risen most when the state played a more active role in the economy and in society.

AIDS

AIDS is the quintessential social disease because of the number of people it affects, its mode of transmission, and its impact on society (Velimirovic,

1987). For this reason, AIDS exposes major shortcomings of the corporatization and medicalization of health care. With their stress on remediating the clinical symptoms of individuals at a profit, corporatization and medicalization are unsuitable for dealing with epidemics. Epidemics require strategies that are preventive, social, and socialized in nature—preventive in that a major effort is made to curtail the spread of the disease; social in that successful prevention depends on massive public education and counseling for the entire society; socialized in that the government must take the leading role in providing for research and treatment. Private efforts alone can never be sufficient to overcome a growing social disease such as AIDS. A major failure of the Reagan administration was its reliance on private efforts to deal with AIDS. An expert committee of the National Academy of Sciences concluded in a 1988 report that the most serious deficiency in the struggle to control the AIDS epidemic is the gross inadequacy of federal efforts, including an absence of strong federal leadership (Boffey, 1988). For capitalism, AIDS is just another arena for investment. Profit-seeking companies have indeed made major investments in the treatment of AIDS, but the resulting treatments are very costly and are rationed by ability to pay. AZT (the antiviral drug azidothymidine) costs about $10,000 for a year's supply. Ironically, although AZT is owned by a drug corporation, its basic research and development were carried out with federal grants (Kingston, 1987, p. 409).

AIDS is caused by a virus—the human immunodeficiency virus (HIV), which leads to two diseases, AIDS and ARC (AIDS-related complex). Although it is a communicable disease, AIDS is not highly contagious. Its virus is not airborne, and contracting it requires a specific exchange of bodily fluids, including blood and semen. The disease has a high fatality rate. For people diagnosed before January 1983, the fatality rate by 1985 was over 75 percent (Curran et al., 1985, p. 1352). Few people live as long as three years after contracting the disease (Gorman, 1986, p. 158). AIDS has been spreading rapidly. In 1979 only 7 cases and 6 deaths were recorded for AIDS in the United States (Center for Disease Control, 1985). By early in 1989, cumulative cases had reached 90,990; deaths, 52,435. According to the Center for Disease Control (CDC), by 1992 the United States will have accumulated 365,000 cases and a death toll of 263,000. AIDS has the potential to become the modern equivalent of the Black Death. The World Health Organization (WHO) reported that as of August 1, 1988, there were 108,176 AIDS cases worldwide. However, because underreporting is a problem in many countries, the true total was close to 250,000 (Mann et al., 1988, p. 85). The United States is the most severely affected nation, while the U.S.S.R. had only 4 cases and the People's Republic of China just 1.

Although AIDS has appeared in every state, it is concentrated in a few cities. Of all reported cases in 1981–1983, nearly three-fourths were located in only five cities: New York (46.4 percent of total cases), San Francisco, Los Angeles, Miami, and Newark. The AIDS incidence (cases per million population) in these five cities ranged from a high of 66.1 in New York City to 12.4 in Los

Angeles, compared to an incidence of 1.8 for the rest of the United States (Foege, 1983, p. 12).

In the United States AIDS is concentrated in a few groups. Of all reported cases through July 1988, 63 percent were homosexual or bisexual persons without an intravenous (IV) drug history, 19 percent were heterosexual persons who were IV drug users, and 7 percent were homosexual or bisexual persons who were IV drug users (Heyward and Curran, 1988, p. 78). The remaining 11 percent included transfusion recipients and infants. Even though presently concentrated in a few social groups, AIDS is not limited to these groups. Its incidence among heterosexual Haitians who do not use IV drugs is a clear indication of this fact (Landesman, 1983). AIDS has entered the heterosexual population through bisexual men and needle-using prostitutes. The awareness of this fact brings a sense of danger to almost every sexual encounter except long-established monogamous ones. African Americans and Hispanics are disproportionately afflicted by AIDS, largely because of the higher IV drug use within their communities. As of July 1988, 40 percent of reported adult cases were African Americans and Hispanics, whereas African Americans and Hispanics together represented about 18 percent of the total population. Moreover, the average life expectancy after diagnosis for a white person with AIDS was 24 months, but for a person of color it was only 19 months (Hammonds, 1987, p. 31). A report (Caputo, 1985) by a social practitioner on his work in 1981–1984 revealed that the overwhelming majority of adults with AIDS served at public clinics were IV drug users and people of color. The practitioner noted that this group has so little sense of community that it is difficult for them to form the self-help support groups that have worked so well for homosexual victims of the disease. In addition to deterioration from AIDS, their substance abuse is a major problem.

AIDS attacks in the prime years of life—nearly 90 percent of cases occur in people aged 20 to 49 (Center for Disease Control, 1985, p. 91). Therefore it is having a major impact on the life expectancy of some demographic groups. Using a measure of premature mortality called YPLL (years of potential life lost before age 65), Curran and his colleagues (1985) found that in never-married men aged 25 to 44, AIDS ranked fourth as a premature killer in 1984, behind accidents, homocide/suicide, and cancer. In Manhattan and San Francisco it ranked first.

AIDS is correctly perceived as a major health threat by the public. In the World Future Society's informal survey of 1986 publications, AIDS was ranked fourth among the fears held for the future, moving up considerably from its tenth position in 1985. In 1986, the only fears that loomed larger than the fear of AIDS were economic collapse, nuclear war, and environmental damage. A December 1986 national survey by the American Association of Blood Banks found that AIDS had replaced heart disease as the second most serious health problem in the public's mind, behind cancer. In the previous year's survey AIDS had ranked third, behind heart disease and cancer. Only a year later a 1987 Gallup Poll found that 68 percent of Americans believed that AIDS was the country's most serious health problem; 14 percent named cancer and 7 percent named heart disease.

Although AIDS is contagious, it has a relatively low infectivity potential compared to other diseases. Thus the public fear of AIDS has considerably outstripped the actual threat (Conrad, 1986, p. 53). Some of this fear stems from the fact that AIDS is usually transmitted through sexual contact and sex is a highly charged psychosocial area of life. Also, many people with AIDS are homosexual and homophobia adds to the fear. Moreover, AIDS *is* a communicable disease, and in some ways a throwback to the plagues that have historically decimated human society. Because of its higher incidence in gay and minority communities (already marginalized in homophobic and racist America), AIDS is a potent stigma akin to leprosy. Indeed, the hysterical reaction to AIDS in some sectors of society recalls the initial reaction to cholera in the nineteenth century—it was seen "as a scourge of God, which would strike only those who were filthy, intemperate, and immoral" (Glaab, 1963, p. 116). Because of the public reaction it arouses, privacy and confidentiality rights are salient considerations in the treatment of AIDS, especially with regard to testing for the virus.

In addition to protecting the privacy rights of people with AIDS, social policy has to be directed to three general areas (Gorman, 1986, pp. 167–168): (1) primary prevention to reduce exposure and to stem the epidemic; (2) secondary prevention to detect carriers at an early stage; and (3) tertiary prevention to develop an effective remedy with which to treat victims. In order to be effective, prevention must be federalized. In her in-depth analysis of the shortcomings of the U.S. effort to combat AIDS, Panem (1988) concluded that a strong and centralized federal leadership that provides for strategic planning and for widespread public education is essential from the beginning for dealing with such an epidemic.

Until a cure for AIDS is found, education will remain the principal method of prevention, and it must be universalized. Public schools can be used to house health clinics (discussed in Chapter 7). These clinics can dispense sex education information and technologies that inhibit sexually transmitted diseases, including condoms. Methadone and sterile needles can be made easily available to IV drug users. Hospices and home-care arrangements can be expanded to treat people with AIDS. According to the New York State Department of Health, as many as 2,000 people in New York City will need such hospital care by 1991, at an average daily cost of $1,000 per patient (Sullivan, 1987). Public counseling and education programs would do well to emulate the examples of the Gay Men's Health Crisis in New York City, the Shanti Project in San Francisco, the AIDS Action Committee in Boston, and similar voluntary agencies in other cities, which have been successful in gay communities in helping to change sexual behavior to reduce the incidence of STDs such as rectal gonorrhea. These agencies have also provided assistance, comfort, and advocacy for people with AIDS and their families, and have instituted AIDS telephone hotlines (Fineberg, 1988, p. 132).

The success of community organizing and education campaigns in San Francisco became a model (the "San Francisco experience") for other communities. Beginning in 1983 with grants from the city health department, gay and lesbian community organizations, especially in the Castro district, lobbied and campaigned for help to people with AIDS and for changes in sexual practices in the gay community. As a result, the HIV transmission rate associated with gay sexual contact dropped from 12 percent to less than 2 percent between 1983 and 1986 (Shaw, 1988, pp. 84–85).

Ultimately, AIDS may precipitate a needed expansion of the role of the Federal government in making health care available to the poor because a disproportionate number of persons with the disease are poor and its treatment is expensive.

Health Security

Because health is a basic human right that should not be rationed by price and because health problems are national in scope, modern health-care systems should be socialized and universalized, a task that requires leadership by government. Government-sponsored national health insurance is a social policy that meets a basic criterion of health-care effectiveness: availability, regardless of the geographic location or income of users. In the United States a good name for national health insurance might be Health Security, comparable in health care to what Social Security is in the area of income security.

Health Security has been an inevitable development in the modern world. Bismarck introduced the first such policy in Germany in 1883. Since then, benchmark policies were developed in the U.S.S.R. in 1921, the U.K. in 1946, and Canada in 1958–1971. Today the United States is the single major exception among developed nations to this worldwide trend. Actually, the United States already has an implicit form of Health Security, for the government funds, directly or indirectly, the bulk of health-care costs and operates the major insurance program, Medicare (Fuchs, 1986). However, explicit socialization is needed so that no one lacks essential health care. The inadequacies of the present jerrybuilt insurance system are all too apparent. For example, according to a study by the Department of Health and Human Services, one-fourth of the elderly's medical expenses in 1984 were not covered by any insurance (Pear, 1987).

Health Security would need to be adapted to the decentralized political conditions in the United States. Control over policies such as eligibility and minimum benefits must be vested in the federal government in order to assure universal, equal treatment, but local influence could be maintained in the implementation of national policies and in decisions about provider payment, regulation, quality control, and claims administration (Feder and Holahan, 1980). It may even be possible to have a series of coordinated state programs instead of a single national program (Fein, 1986). Whatever the details of implementation, an effective Health Security policy must incorporate several basic principles (Gill, 1986): uniform distribution of quality care with public accountability.

The American public favors Health Security, even if it is costly. In an analysis of fifteen national polls conducted in 1981–1984, Blendon and Altman (1984, p. 613) found that two-thirds of Americans believed that federal spending for health care should be increased and that three-fifths favored some form of national health insurance, even if it resulted in a tax increase. The major opposition to Health Security comes from the medical-industrial complex, which fears a loss of control and profits.

Health Security reduces inequalities in access to health care. In Canada, where general conditions are more comparable than in any other nation to those in the United States, empirical study (Marmor, Hoffman, and Heagy, 1983, p. 182) has demonstrated that national health insurance produced greater access for the poor, while access for the nonpoor remained stable. Moreover, Canada's program has been successful at stabilizing health-care costs, especially administrative expenses, at the same time that it has equalized access (Hiatt, 1987). Before, administrative costs of medical payments ranged from 10 percent to 50 percent of private premiums. The costs are down to about 3 percent of health expenditure. In the United States, 11.1 percent of private medical premiums and 3.2 percent of public health program revenues went to administration in 1984.

There is reason to believe that adoption of Health Security in the United States will be another step in an incremental process that can be dated to the introduction of Medicare and Medicaid in 1965. The next logical step in this process might be the introduction of health insurance for those at the youngest end of the age spectrum. Marmor (1983), for example, has suggested an insurance plan for children, called Kidcare, beginning with catastrophic illness protection for all children modeled on the catastrophic illness program for the elderly that was enacted into law in 1988, and expanding with preventive programs such as prenatal care and child care (discussed in Chapter 6).

Health Security will hardly be a cure-all. According to Wildavsky (1979, p. 284), only about 10 percent of an individual's health is affected by medical care (MDs, hospitals, technologies). The remaining 90 percent is determined by lifestyle choices such as smoking and exercise, environmental factors such as pollution, and societal factors such as income distribution. Thus improved medical care and resources do not necessarily result in improved health. This fact has been documented repeatedly in different nations, including Canada, the U.S., the U.K., and the U.S.S.R. (Fuchs, 1986, pp. 274–276).

The experience of the British National Health Service (NHS) indicates that its positive effects have been limited by social inequalities that bear on health, including disparities in income, housing, education, and employment. Even though the NHS brings the money price of health care down to zero, other costs discriminate against lower social classes. For example, Cuyler (1980, pp. 125–126) has shown that time prices, including travel, waiting, and loss of working time, are higher for the lower social classes than for the higher ones. Also, the NHS has been no panacea for the racist and sexist aspects of health care. For example, it replicates traditional medical and patriarchal tendencies to view pregnancy and childbirth as illnesses to be controlled (Gray, 1982).

Health Security, then, will not overcome or compensate for the fact that a large number of Americans are poor and discriminated against, lack housing and education, and cannot secure decent jobs. It would expand the scope of prevention within health care, and that indeed would be progress, but prevention of illness in the first place depends on the radical expansion of policies that affect other areas of society. One example is income redistribution from the better-off to the poorer members of society (discussed in Chapter 5).

An Ecological Strategy

The twentieth-century corporatization and medicalization of health care have led to a disintegration of the concept of disease prevention (Ratcliffe et al., 1984). Formerly, disease prevention integrated three targets: (1) the physical environment (e.g., through sanitation); (2) the social environment (e.g., through regulation of working conditions); and (3) specific diseases (e.g., sanatoriums to treat tuberculosis). Medicalization fostered professional and institutional boundaries between curative and preventive health care. Medicine emphasizes a curative approach that focuses on individuals after they become ill. This model has become so dominant that it constitutes health care in the public mind. Preventive medicine, a more socialized approach to health care that maximizes state intervention to prevent disease, is by comparison neglected.

While clinical medical services consume the lion's share of health-care resources, public health measures such as family planning, nutrition education, and environmental protection that would produce greater health benefits remain underfunded (Miller, 1987). Beyond these preventive activities lies a social agenda that bears on the health of the nation. Thus if poverty (discussed in Chapter 5) were to be substantially reduced, the health of society would be profoundly improved. In his analysis of the prevention and treatment of disease in English history, Gray (1979, p. 12) noted that "poverty has always been a common preventable cause of disease." Research has repeatedly demonstrated that individual health interacts with social environments so that, for example, unemployment rates are directly related to mortality rates (Ratcliffe et al., 1984, p. 70).

The acknowledged limitations of corporatization and medicalization argue logically for an ecological strategy in health care—one that could be based in an expanded version of public health. An ecological strategy emphasizes preventive treatment of the environmental factors that are responsible for 90 percent of health problems. In an ecological strategy prevention is a multifaceted concept that operates at various levels: at the individual level, in medical prevention such as vaccination; at the lifestyle level, in behavioral prevention such as regular exercise; and at the social level, in structural prevention such as control of environmental toxins (Conrad and Kern, 1986). A specific example is the most common cause of morbidity and mortality in the developed world—cardiovascular diseases, of which coronary artery disease (CAD) is the biggest problem. In an epidemiological analysis of CAD Ledingham (1987, p. 57) concluded that "any form of treatment for established disease is of limited value and that the most practical and sensible approach is to concentrate on *prevention* by changes in diet and lifestyle." Ledingham added that immense expenditure on heroic resusitation measures such as coronary artery bypass grafting are unwise. Redirection of such expenditure to preventive health policies would produce better results for society.

It is quite possible that the current fixation on medical services is a passing stage in a social cycle. This appears to be the case with treatments for one major health problem, alcoholism (Walsh and Hingson, 1987). In the first stage treatment was legal and moral: alcoholism was defined as an evil and attacked with punitive policies—Prohibition (1919–1933) being the most noteworthy example. The second stage was medicalization: alcoholism was redefined as an individual disease and treated medically, which included using drugs such as antabuse. The third stage in this cycle is only now emerging and is consistent with a general demedicalizing trend in health and society: ecological treatment based on epidemiological data about the diversity of drinkers and drinking contexts. These data have led to the understanding that excessive drinking is produced not only by an individual (the alcoholic) but also by environments—physical, social, and emotional. Ecological treatments of alcoholism include greater public control of alcohol advertising and the provision of widely available, nonstigmatized counseling and education programs, especially for certain at-risk populations such as college students and the offspring of alcoholics.

Society's experience with another major modern health problem, mental illness, also supports a transition to an ecological strategy. The shortcomings of the medical approach to mental health were analyzed by Klerman (1987), who pointed out that the principal determinants of mental health are psychosocial factors such as family history and social conditions such as poverty, not the presence and quality of direct services to those already ill. An effective preventive policy in mental health would include epidemiological investigation and control of environmental hazards, racism, and poverty. That such a policy can be effective is demonstrated by the improved mental health of women, which can be attributed in part to their enhanced position in society stemming from the changes wrought by feminism and other social forces since the late 1960s. Thus females as a proportion of the inmates in mental hospitals and residential treatment centers, which had risen slowly during the 1950s, declined from 46.7 percent in 1960 to 38.8 percent in 1980.

Primary prevention can become the fourth revolution in mental health, after the humanization of treatment, the emergence of psychodynamic frameworks, and the use of community settings. These three recognized shifts in mental health care focused on people who were already ill. Primary prevention, in contrast, seeks to forestall illness. Primary prevention has two general strategies: (1) structural approaches that reduce environmental stress and increase life chances and (2) individual approaches that enhance people's coping abilities. One example of individual primary prevention is the proliferation of programs to help people who experience stressful life events such as divorce. Generally, people who develop mental health problems, such as chronic depression, as a result of these events are treated only after their problems have become substantial. Primary prevention anticipates such stressful events and provides support and coping skills to preclude the development of serious problems (Cowen, 1985). This distinction between structural and individual prevention parallels the distinction between health protection that alters socioeconomic structures and health promotion that alters individual behavior.

One epidemiological tool that illustrates the ecological approach is the use of measures of health outcomes, as analyzed by Miller (1987). For child health the measures include rates of infant mortality, lead toxicity, low birth weight, and congenital disorders. Accurately collected and analyzed, these health indicators reveal a diagnosis for a given community and nation. This diagnosis can then be used to identify and treat specific health problems in given areas. Additionally, the community diagnosis can be the basis for an ecological strategy to prevent the recurrence of health problems.

In the twentieth century many national governments have developed policies to promote health through direct action in environments, including fluoridation of water and bans on smoking. Historically, health has been more improved by these upstream ecological efforts than by downstream efforts dealing with already developed disease (McKinlay, 1986). Sweden has been particularly successful in implementing ecological health policies. One reason for that country's very low infant mortality rate is that the government makes maternal health services available to all mothers, regardless of their incomes. In the first two years after giving birth almost all Swedish mothers visit local free clinics. Also, public schools provide extensive family planning information, which helps to prevent teenage pregnancy. The result is that more children are born to women who are twenty to thirty-five years of age, the prime years for childbirth, which further reduces infant mortality (Andrain, 1985, p. 96).

The major argument against an ecological and a socialized health-care system has been that it would be more expensive than a medical, market approach. However, research indicates the opposite. Andrain (1985, p. 116), in a comparative study of Canada, France, Sweden, the U.K., the U.S., and West Germany, found that where there were more public and centralized health-care systems, there were greater cost savings. In countries where the private sector has the greatest influence, health-care costs were highest, especially for administration. Furthermore, investment in prevention is cost-efficient over time. For example, studies estimated that $1 spent on childhood immunization in the U.S. saved $10 in subsequent costs, and that $2 spent on the Women, Infants and Children program saved $3 in subsequent hospital costs (Moberg, 1987).

Health Security and an ecological strategy are compatible with capitalism as long as they conform to its private economic demands. However, capitalism constrains and stunts the full development of an ecological strategy because its ideology places great responsibility on the individual and his or her lifestyle and tends to ignore structural problems. Thus in the United States there is a strong focus on smoking as a cause of cancer while environmental pollution is neglected (Taylor, 1986). Even where structural approaches can be taken to lifestyle problems, as in bans on smoking, capitalist business interests and ideology mitigate against their use. The result is continued mass manufacture and promotion of cigarettes, which are lethal products. The Center for Disease Control calculated that 315,120 Americans died from diseases attributable to cigarette smoking in 1984.

Although existing socialist societies suffer from problems of industrialization, bureaucratization (Eyer, 1984), and stunted economic development, socialism is better placed than capitalism to achieve the health security of all its citizens for several reasons (Renaud, 1975). Socialist ideology is fully compatible with an ecological and socialized health policy; there are no private economic interests to pervert health policy. Disease and medicine are not merely technical issues to be resolved by technology. Ultimately, they are ideological constructs and they occur within social contexts. Thus socialist Cuba, using the same technology against malaria as nonsocialist Third World nations, succeeded in reducing the disease, while the other nations did not (Stark, 1982, p. 429).

SOCIAL PRACTICE

An analysis of policy issues in health-care would be incomplete without an examination of the social practice of health-care workers. Indeed, the problems of health-care practitioners are policy issues.

Health-care workers constitute an expanding sector of the U.S. labor force. Their proportion of all employed workers rose from 5.7 percent in 1970 to 7.4 percent in 1986. Projections by the Bureau of Labor Statistics (BLS) are that several health-care occupations will be among those with the largest absolute and relative growth up to 2000, including registered nurses (RNs), nursing aides and orderlies, licensed practical nurses (LPNs), and medical assistants. A little more than one-half of all health-care workers are employed by hospitals, while large numbers work in nursing homes and doctors' offices.

The growing demand for nurses is not being met. The American Hospital Association reported that between 1985 and 1986 the vacancy rate on hospital nursing staffs more than doubled, to 13.5 percent. According to the

National League of Nursing, nursing school enrollment fell by about one-fifth from 1983 to 1987 (Lewin, 1987). Several factors are behind this growing shortage of nurses: (1) nurses' pay is not commensurate with their educational and skill levels; (2) nursing is women's work (only 5.7 percent of RNs were men in 1986) and thus culturally devalued; and (3) because of the gains of feminism, women are now able to enter higher-paying male professions.

The structure of nursing work also contributes to the shortage. Nursing demands high responsibility but provides low authority; it has become increasingly routinized and less autonomous. Corporatization of health care has brought with it Taylorization (discussed in Chapter 5), in which work is increasingly subdivided into smaller tasks and workers are expected to perform more of these simplified tasks. This standardization and routinization of health-care work reduces its cost to owners, but also decreases its intrinsic worth to workers.

Health-care occupations have a high proportion of female and African American workers. In 1986 women were 76.7 percent of all workers in health-care occupations, but only 44.4 percent of the total labor force. In the same year African Americans accounted for 13.6 percent of health-care workers, but 9.9 percent of the total labor force. Even though women predominate in most health-care jobs, they are a minority in its most powerful occupation. In 1986 only 17.6 percent of MDs were women; only 3.3 percent were African Americans. In the lower-paying health-care occupations, the proportions of women and African Americans are considerably higher. For example, 90.5 percent of all nursing aides, orderlies, and attendants were females in 1986; 29.5 percent were African Americans.

Thus health-care work is highly stratified by occupation, gender, and race. At the top are MDs, who are overwhelmingly white and male. As one moves downward in this layered structure, there are larger proportions of women, and at the bottom are minorities. Sidel and Sidel (1986, p. 215) described this stratification as follows:

> Thus we may view the typical structure of a large medical institution as a pyramid with the usually white, male physician at the top, his orders carried out by middle-level professionals who are generally women, and with the patients and "dirty work" left to low-paid, frequently alienated, largely black female paraprofessionals at the bottom of the pyramid.

The plight of health-care workers at the base of this pyramid is exemplified by home-care workers. An estimated 3.5 million Americans—largely elderly, chronically ill, and disabled people—receive health-care assistance in their homes (Wolff, 1987). Home care has grown enormously in recent years because of the rise in the AIDS and elderly populations, whose care at home is less expensive and more congenial than it would be in institutions. A major problem for home-care workers is very low pay. In 1987 the median annual income of home-care workers in New York City was $8,000. A Hunter College School of Social Work study found that 94 percent of the home-care workers were African American or Hispanic women, and that 76 percent were the primary earners for their families (Tarpinian, 1988).

Social Practitioner at Work: Hannah Engel

Hannah Engel is a nurse midwife at a state teaching hospital in New York City and assistant professor in its Clinical Nurse Midwifery Educational Program. In addition to her duties in the Obstetrics Department, Hannah works in the Maternal and Infant Clinic (MIC).

Hannah was born in 1941 and grew up in New York City. She received an Associate in Applied Science degree in nursing from a community college and a Bachelor of Science degree in nursing from Hunter College. She trained in the Nurse Midwife Program at the Downstate Medical Center, Brooklyn, New York, from which she received a certificate in nurse midwifery. After working a number of years at Harlem Hospital, Hannah obtained a Master of Science degree in nursing from Columbia University. She worked at New York City's Roosevelt Hospital until 1984, when she moved to her present position.

The MIC, where Hannah spends much of her time, provides prenatal, postpartum, and infant (up to two years of age) care, as well as family planning services. The clientele, which numbers 1,200, is entirely adolescent, poor, and predominantly African American and Puerto Rican. Medicaid covers the program's cost for 80 percent of MIC clients. The remaining 20 percent pay on a sliding scale. The staff uses the team approach, involving MDs, nurse midwives, nutritionists, nurse counselors, and social workers. The clinic encourages family members to participate with the expectant mother and it operates a successful fathers' group. About 90 percent of the mothers have at least one family member who comes with them to the program, and 80 percent of fathers participate in the birthing process. The MIC program is based on federal legislation that was enacted in 1972. Nationally, there is empirical evidence that the program has been successful in reducing the number of babies with low birth weight, a condition that is linked to higher rates of birth defects and infant mortality (Rodgers, 1986, p. 90).

Hannah originally got interested in nurse midwifery as a result of having three children herself. She was simultaneously thrilled by the experience and put off by the medical practices surrounding childbirth. What she likes best about her work is the "intense, intimate, incredibly gratifying experience" of sharing birth with families. The personal connection she feels with mothers compensates for the overwork. Hannah's strongest dislike about her work is "having to fight the same battles, year in and year out," such as the problem of first-year medical residents who do not accept her midwifery expertise. Although some of these battles are getting easier to win, others are not; for example, it is a constant struggle to get birthing rooms (as opposed to delivery rooms and tables) and permission for bed births from MDs and hospital administrators.

Midwifery is an ancient practice whose contemporary popularity is rooted in home birth advocacy, feminism, and holistic health. As nurse midwives have gained legitimacy, they have achieved more autonomy from MDs and hospitals and have become more innovative. Hannah reported that the explosive growth of the natural childbirth movement in the 1960s and 1970s played an important role in helping to legitimate nurse midwifery in the eyes of the public and of the medical and nursing professions. The professional association of nurse midwifery, the American College of Nurse Midwives, increased its membership by 67 percent between 1968 and 1982 (Pickard, 1986, p. 96). As an indication of the growing popularity of nurse midwifery, Hannah noted that when she changed jobs in 1984, there were thirty-seven openings for nurse midwives in New York City.

Hannah feels solidarity with holistic health practitioners. Midwifery and holistic practice have a lot in common, she said, including a focus on the interplay of mind and body, respect for normal bodily processes, and reliance on nature. Midwifery differs sharply from conventional medical practice in that it considers childbirth a condition of health rather than an illness. Midwifery emphasizes that professionals should only rarely intervene with nature at birth. Thus Hannah believes that episiotomy, a common surgical procedure used by MDs at birth, is generally unnecessary. Professional intervention should focus on the prenatal and postpartum periods, and even then methods should rely on education and nutrition rather than on drugs and other technologies.

Hannah believes that technology does have its place and should not be rejected out of hand. However, it should always be used with caution and in conjunction with counseling and active participation by the patient. For example, she noted that amniocentesis can reveal the presence of an "anomalous fetus"—one that is seriously damaged or incomplete. Technology can save the fetus in some cases, but should it? The mother must be involved in this decision.

Hannah has definite opinions about social policy. She thinks that the cutbacks in federal support for health programs under the Reagan administration overloaded health-care workers in public settings, with the result that many people who need help cannot be served and others get a once-over-lightly treatment. Hannah believes that this country needs a national health insurance program. The major reason, she argued, is that the millions of working poor people who do not qualify for Medicaid and cannot afford private insurance put off going for treatment, and when they finally do go because of an acute medical situation such as childbirth, they often have other health problems that might never have developed if they had had access to inexpensive and preventive health care in the first place.

With regard to AIDS, Hannah said that the clinic where she works has a few cases and that many health practitioners are afraid of working with them. She reported that AIDS education is included in all aspects of the midwifery curriculum at her medical school. She believes that mandatory testing is unwise for it will only drive people underground because "they are afraid of becoming lepers. Massive education and counseling programs are needed. We need earlier and better sex education from kindergarten on, about all aspects of sex, including STDs and AIDS." Hannah added that, like childbirth, "sex is a healthy and normal activity."

Hannah's comments about the dangers of an uncritical application of technology to the birth process agree with a general trend in society to demedicalize health care, a trend that we now analyze.

DEMEDICALIZATION

The American public is dismayed by the escalating costs, increases in iatrogenic abuses, and pervasive depersonalization of patients by hospital bureaucrats and MDs (Crawford, 1984, pp. 74–75). The effects of this growing public skepticism are demystification of medicine and a movement to demedicalize health and society (Fox, 1986). One prominent example of demedicalization of social life is the American Psychiatric Association's 1974 vote removing homosexuality from its diagnostic manual. There have been other, disparate efforts to challenge the dominance of health care by MDs and hospitals. We focus on three of these efforts: Environmentalism, holism, and feminism.

One such effort is the focus on the environmental origins of disease, illness, and injury. Estimates are that from 2 to 50 percent of various cancers are attributable to occupational carcinogens and some 3 percent to environmental carcinogens (Prout, Colton, and Smith, 1987, pp. 142–143). Medicalization, intent on remediating clinical symptoms, almost entirely neglects environmental causes of ill health. For that, we have to look to epidemiological or public health approaches involving the identification and control of toxins and other perils in three environments: the natural environment, including air and water; the work environment; and the residential environment, where the dumping of hazardous wastes is a major social problem (Freudenberg, 1984).

The effort to clean up natural and residential environments is led by environmentalists, community activists, and public health advocates, who are pressing for a strong regulatory policy by government, especially by the Environmental Protection Agency (EPA). The EPA, established in 1970, was itself a result of these efforts. The campaign to make working environments cleaner, safer, and healthier is led by labor activists and public health advocates, who secured the passage of the Coal Mine Health and Safety Act of 1969 and the Occupational Safety and Health Act of 1970. The latter legislation created a federal regulatory agency, the Occupational Safety and Health Administration (OSHA), and a research facility, the National Institute of Occupational Safety and Health (NIOSH). Later in this chapter we examine further these efforts to make working environments cleaner and safer.

A second kind of demedicalization is oriented not to societal, or macro, measures, but to alternative provision of health care at the delivery, or micro, level. These micro approaches, which grew out of the 1960s counterculture, reject the technological and hierarchal character of medicine but retain its clinical and remedial features. However, they differ from established medicine in two ways: they advocate the minimum effective treatment, and they stress that the overriding maxim of practice has to be: Do no harm. This reduces the use of unnecessary, risky, and costly technological and procedural interventions. Two of these demedicalizing approaches are the holistic health movement and the women's health movement.

Holistic Health

Holistic health grew out of several social developments of the 1960s: (1) the turn to premodern healing practices, particularly the naturalism and spiritualism of Native Americans; (2) the importation of Eastern methods and philosophies, including meditation and Buddhism; (3) the popularization of non-Freudian psychologies, especially those of Jung (1968) and Reich (1972); and (4) the emergence of alternative health care. Study has shown that alternative healing groups stress an experiential and spiritual approach; they search for an explanation of illness that is beyond the physical body (McGuire, 1988). Holistic health consists of many alternative practices, including yoga, naturopathy, homeopathy, biofeedback, visualization, and body work (Bliss, 1985). Holism (from the word *whole*) is the view that the entire person has a reality independent of, and greater than, the sum of her or his constituent parts.

Holistic health practice is based on the following motifs, all of which are in counterpoint to the medical paradigm: Health is not an either-or condition, but ranges along a continuum extending from wellness to illness. Health is not merely the absence of objective clinical symptoms; one's subjective perceptions and feelings are also important determinants of wellness. Health care does not cure disease but heals persons. Healing is integrative; wellness is the result of the mind, body, and spirit functioning together in an organic fashion. Instead of relying on technology, holistic health stresses natural methods, including lifestyle and social supports. The principal methods of holistic health can be mastered by many people and incorporated into their daily lives, including meditation, regular exercise, and diet. Dieting is not short-term in order to lose weight, but lifelong in order to be well.

Because of medical monopolization of health care, many nonphysician practitioners of holistic health have had to work without licenses, risking arrest in the course of doing so. These practitioners include some herbalists, nutritionists, and acupuncturists (Ullman, 1983). However, as holistic health grew in appeal, it gained advocates within conventional medicine, especially among younger physicians and nurses. The American Holistic Medical Association, composed of holistic MDs, increased its membership from 220 in 1978 to over 2,000 in 1982. Some holistic health practices are in transition from marginal to mainstream status. An example is behavioral or psychosocial medicine. Based originally on biofeedback, psychosocial medicine uses mental techniques such as relaxation to treat physical ailments, including asthma and hypertension (Goleman, 1987). Its premises are that the mind can be used to heal the body and that people should be actively involved in their own healing.

The strength of holistic health and its greatest relevance to social policy lie in its focus on the whole person and its stress on natural treatments. These practices are alternatives to the medical paradigm, which emphasizes invasive technological treatments, specialization of knowledge, and fragmentation of the person (different MDs for different parts of the body and for different medical problems). A more balanced and effective health-care system can use technology without overusing it and harming people in the process, and can reap the rewards of specialization without promoting a callous disregard for personal integrity. Specialization can lead to depersonalization, which is illustrated by such common expressions as "the gall bladder" or "my appendectomy" by MDs in describing their patients. This impersonal treatment of patients has been frequently documented and analyzed in medical settings (Taylor, 1982). In contrast, holistic practitioners extend personal feelings such as sympathy and reassurance to their patients (DiMatteo, 1982, p. 27), and this personal support can have a positive psychophysical impact (Freund, 1982).

A drawback of holistic health practice is that as yet there are few reliable and valid data on its methods. It is essential that holistic health practitioners develop practice standards and some means of regulation (Pizer, 1982). The regulation need not be by the conventional medical establishment, but it must create accountability for holistic practices in order to ensure the confidence and safety of the public and to provide clients with a means for redressing grievances.

The major shortcoming of holistic health is its individualistic reactive aspect, which sustains the health-care system's favoritism toward the middle and upper classes. Holistic health patients have to be relatively educated and sophisticated, and possessed of enough time and money to control their work schedules. Obviously, this is considerably easier for executives and professionals than it is for assembly-line workers and secretaries, let alone the poor and uneducated. Moreover, holistic health treats individual reactions to environments rather than the environments directly, and its one-to-one, fee-for-service practice re-creates the rationing of the capitalist marketplace.

Holistic health is close to the women's health movement in several respects. Both advocate natural and personal approaches over technological and impersonal ones. Moreover, holism's practitioners and clients are overwhelmingly female and disproportionately feminist.

Women and Health

The feminist movement developed a major critique of conventional medical practice that focused on its hierarchal, impersonal, and sexist aspects, as well as on its reliance on cold technology (machines) to the exclusion of warm nature (hands) in treatment. The social influence of the women's health movement was signaled by the publication of an educational guide about women's bodies by the Boston Women's Health Collective in 1970.

Medicalization affects women in more ways and more negatively than it does men. Women are the primary subjects of health care. In 1985, 64.7 percent of patient days of care by hospitals in the United States were for women. In 1985 females averaged 6.1 visits to physicians; males, 4.4. The woman's body and its functions are a special subject of medicalization, including sexual dysfunctions (frigidity), fetal care, fertility, menopause, childbirth, abortion, and contraception. This focus continues in the medicalization of menstruation through the diagnosis of premenstrual syndrome and of weight control through cosmetic surgery and drug treatments (Riessman, 1983). It is interesting that competition from the women's health movement forced the medical establishment to take another look at the real premenstrual suffering that some women endure. Out of that reexamination came hormone research and medication to even out hormone levels over the monthly cycle.

Women's problems in health care are exemplified by the traditional patriarchal practice of gynecology. Despite changes in recent years, the field of gynecology remains overwhelmingly male though, of course, all the clients are female. Until challenged by feminists, gynecological textbooks supported sexist stereotypes of gender roles in which the male dominated the female; in these books women were "consistently described as anatomically destined to produce, nurture, and keep their husbands happy" (Scully and Bart, 1981, p. 350). In other areas of health care, where there are both male and female patients, females are more likely than males to have negative experiences. Thus Lack's (1982) research in a hospital pain unit found that female patients were referred later and experienced pain longer than male patients. Almost all the attending physicians were males. For all the reforms, medicine continues to assert its patriarchal domination over women's bodies in many areas and to expand it into others. Analysis by Riessman and Nathanson (1986) demonstrated how medicine maintains control over birth through the invocation of risk, despite evidence that out-of-hospital birth is quite safe for many women. Also, the hospital setting structures the birth experience in ways that are unrelated to the birth process itself (Rothman, 1983). For example, the timing of hospital birth is dependent on the availability of physicians and technology, which are not under the mother's control.

In response to these negative aspects of medicalization, the women's health movement, inspired and nurtured by the feminist movement, fostered several innovative approaches to health care: self-help, monitoring, and support for feminist health principles and practitioners. Monitoring refers to the establishment of evaluation and referral networks to disseminate information about the availability and quality of feminist health care in given areas. Support for feminist health principles and practitioners includes using feminist doctors (some of whom are male) and feminist alternative care such as midwives. Women's self-help groups include a wide range of activities: consciousness raising, learning about one's own body, alternative health care, and clinics. Regardless of their specific goals, all these groups are united in a quest for health education by and for women, and for women's self-fulfillment. The groups tend to cluster around the organizing roles of women's lives (mothers, workers, wives) and around rehabilitation, behavior change, primary care, or prevention of specific health problems (Gartner, 1985). Self-care or self-help groups have demonstrated positive results for their members (Petrakis, 1988). In a review of the results of experimental studies of self-help groups, both professionally supported and autonomous, Powell (1985) found consistently positive outcomes for participants as compared to nonparticipants. Much of the success of the whole movement is due to its provision of an opportunity for mutual assistance. Self-help enables individuals to overcome their isolation and powerlessness by participating in a social network that informs and empowers them (Levine, 1988).

Feminist self-care espouses not only new techniques but a new conception of health care as well. This new concept stresses the commonality of providers and patients and minimizes power and status differences between them that are based on professionalization. Feminist health care is not just medical, but personal, social, and political as well (Ruzek, 1981). Thus the women's health movement saw that a battered wife needed more than medical treatment for her physical wounds. In a self-care group she got psychological support, information about shelters and legal actions, and advice about supportive doctors and social workers. Out of such groups emerged advocates who achieved needed changes in legislation and police procedures in cases of domestic violence. Such advocacy also resulted in public funding for shelters and social services for battered wives. The women's health movement has also brought about changes in conventional medical practices. Examples are the popularization of nurse midwifery, childbirth education for both parents, less use of drugs in delivery, the introduction of birthing rooms in hospitals, and the development of sensitivity training curricula in medical schools.

Feminist self-care does have limitations (Withorn, 1980). One is its emphasis on an individualistic approach to the neglect of social change, which can result in a subtle form of blaming the victim. For example, Millman (1982) analyzed how self-care ideology blames the lifestyle of the obese for a problem that may well be organic in nature. At least some people's obesity is due to physiological factors, such as an inherited low metabolic rate—the process by which food is changed to energy (Ravussin et al., 1988). Another flaw of self-care is that, ironically, it re-creates medicine's fragmentation by fostering specialized groups for each health problem. Thus there are separate groups for rape victims, battered wives, sexually abused daughters, mastectomy clients, and many others. Such an approach stresses the singularity of people rather than their similarity, and this runs counter to the general feminist principle of emphasizing the common human qualities of people. Furthermore, problem specialization reinforces patient isolation and the tendency of patients to be possessive about their problems, as in the attitude that "only we who have the problem can understand it."

Although self-help has the potential to challenge the impersonal and undemocratic character of bureaucratized and professionalized state services, it is by no means intrinsically radical. States are adept at coopting and depoliticizing self-help initiatives. The conservative governments of a number of Welfare States actively promote self-help as a way of reducing public expenditure and the role of the state, as well as a way of social control. As Johnson (1987, p. 106) pointed out, "While self-help groups may give a voice to consumers, and to some extent challenge professional dominance, no great disturbance of power relationships is involved."

Self-care cannot possibly meet the widespread health needs of society. It is restricted to people who have the resources to take advantage of it, which up to now has meant the exclusion of working-class and poor persons. In fact, at least some feminist health-care approaches are for the middle class only. For example, Nelson's (1983) research with 322 women in a New England hospital demonstrated that feminist-inspired natural childbirth is largely irrelevant to the social realities of working-class women.

Still, there may be ways to make self-care relevant to the working class. In a discussion of the Yale Self-Care Education Demonstration Project, Savo (1983) reported that self-care was extended to a working poor population through some innovative approaches, which included seeking out and relying on a local community's natural helpers. These were neighborhood residents to whom others ordinarily turned for advice and assistance, among them the secretary of a tenants' organization, a young mother, and the wife of a local clergyman. Another approach of this program was to use lay health resources—people who had learned to manage their health problems and who were willing to work with others who had similar problems, including bulimia and STDs.

Another example that demonstrates promise for reducing the structural barriers to women's health care for low-income persons is birth centers (Riessman, 1984). Birth centers increased in the United States from 3 in 1975 to over 100 in 1982. They were pioneered by nurse midwives as facilities separate from hospitals where prenatal, peripartum, and neonatal care for low-risk pregnancies could be provided. In about one-half the centers the primary care providers are nurse midwives. Birth centers are licensed and usually have cooperative agreements with a laboratory, an ambulance service, and a hospital. They improve access for the poor by reducing health-care costs and by being more convenient to reach. Not surprisingly, birth centers have been endorsed by the American Public Health Association but not by the American College of Obstetrics and Gynecology, composed of MDs, which remains opposed to birth outside hospitals.

The social policy implications of self-care are only beginning to crystallize. The general applicability of self-care depends on a number of factors, including whether self-care makes a difference in health, whether it is risky, and whether it proves teachable. Research has only begun to address these questions, but in a study of the curricula of sixteen diverse self-care programs, DeFriese and Woomert (1982, p. 56) concluded that the curricula consisted "of skills the majority of which are significant to health, relatively low in risk when performed by a layperson, and easily taught to persons without professional health backgrounds."

Social policy has far to go to guarantee women the basic right to control the functions of their bodies. The frontiers of reproduction include surrogate motherhood, artificial insemination, and in vitro fertilization, issues for which doctors and lawyers are empowered to represent the interests of children-to-be, fathers, and society. Social policy can buttress maternal rights by taking reproduction out of the courts and the hospitals. History demonstrates that medical and state control discriminates against women and endangers their lives (Gordon, 1987).

Work and Health

Work can be dangerous. In 1985, according to National Safety Council data, 11,600 American workers were killed on the job and 2 million were disabled. Other data from the Bureau of Labor Statistics show that there were 5.5 million cases of occupational injury or illness in 1985—and the BLS counts only highly visible illnesses that have no latency period, which obscures the occupational origin of many cancers, for example (Kotelchuck, 1987, p. 2). Much of the danger of work results from unsafe working conditions, including breakdowns in equipment because of deficient maintenance and human breakdowns because of overwork. In addition to being dangerous, work can be unhealthy. Approximately 400,000 new cases of occupational disease occur annually in the United States. One prominent example of the health hazards of work is coal mining. Some 100,000 miners suffer from debilitating black lung disease, contracted at work from breathing coal dust, and about 4,000 people a year die from it (Ritzer and Walczak, 1986, pp. 415–422). Overall, it is estimated by NIOSH that more than 100,000 deaths result annually from occupationally related causes, the majority of which are attributable to employer negligence or disregard of safety and health standards (Hills, 1987, p. 5; Shanker, 1983).

The Reagan administration pursued a policy to considerably reduce the ability of OSHA to deal with workplace dangers. A national study of changes in OSHA's enforcement vigor (standardized for the number of civilian workers) between Carter's term in office (1977–1980) and part of Reagan's (1981–1983) showed that the number of compliance officers fell by 17 percent, the number of citations declined by 27 percent, and the number of serious citations dropped by 27 percent (Thompson and Scicchitano, 1985). A study by the National Safe Workplace Institute in Chicago found that an OSHA inspector in 1980 was three time more likely to issue the agency's strongest sanction than was an inspector working in 1981 to 1987. Calavita's (1983) analysis suggests that the Reagan administration's deliberate weakening of OSHA was part of a general strategy to revoke gains made by labor in the 1970s. This strategy was made possible by the problems of the U.S. economy, which were used as an excuse to further the interests of capitalists (Szasz, 1986). As a result of the gutting of OSHA's enforcement by the Reagan administration, the long-term improvement in workplace safety and health was stopped in the 1980s.

In addition to stark physical perils, work in modern capitalist industrial society has produced a whole new class of subtle psychosocial health problems—what Freund (1982, p. 133) refers to as "the somatic consequences of social control." The study of workers' health began with the development of industrial capitalism in the nineteenth century, highlighted by the work of Marx (1967) and Engels (1968). Both documented the adverse physical conditions of work under capitalism and developed a concept with which to analyze its psychosocial burden: alienation. Sociology subsequently devoted much research to worker alienation and its consequences. This research focused on the structure of work under capitalism—social activity owned and managed by private interests (capitalists), in which workers are depersonalized and treated as commodities, or proletarianized (Erikson, 1986). In Braverman's (1974, p. 340) words, workers (in this case, clerical workers) are "so many mechanical eyes, fingers, and voices whose functioning is, insofar as possible, predetermined by both rules and machinery." Alienation is the basis for many of the psychosocial health problems of contemporary workers, including the burnout syndrome (Maslach, 1982). Job stress is the principal factor in burnout, and it comes from work disruptions (such as unemployment), time pressures, intense competition, and the hierarchal controls of work under capitalism. (Burnout is also discussed in Chapters 5 and 7.)

According to a thorough review of research data by House and Cottington (1986), several psychosocial aspects of work bear on worker morbidity and mortality, including high demands, lack of personal control, absence of social support, and lack of participation in decision making. Levi, Frankenhaeuser, and Gardell (1986), in another view of research data, found an additional stressor that they called *qualitative underload*, which is produced by the narrow and unsatisfying routines of work. Management has largely resisted acting on these findings. Profit seeking drives companies to avoid the expense of improving the workplace until the data are overwhelming, and even then reform is less than wholehearted (Levine and Lilienfeld, 1987, p. 5).

One major illness that is connected to both the physical and the psychosocial conditions of modern work is hypertension (high blood pressure), a silent and slow killer that afflicts some fifty million American adults. Eyer (1975) has argued that hypertension is a disease of modern society (it appears far less frequently in premodern society) and that the features of modern society that contribute to it are community disruption through mobility and migration, and increased work pressures. Epidemiological studies have implicated workplace physical factors, such as exposure to noise, and psychosocial factors, including time pressure, in hypertension (Schnall and Kern, 1986). Of course, genetic inheritance, diet, and lack of exercise also play roles in the etiology of hypertension, but it is becoming clearer that one of its key under-examined sources is job stress.

The United States lags behind other nations in addressing the health needs of its work force. In a major comparative analysis of occupational safety and health, Elling (1986) found that the United States ranked last or was tied for last for five of the six components of effective occupational safety and health: national policy mandate, worker control, worker education, organization of services, worker information, and level and worker control of financing. On a scale of 0 to 10, the summary score for the U.S. was 1.5, compared to 3.5 for West Germany and the U.K., 6.5 for Finland, and 8.5 for Sweden and East Germany. In Sweden and East Germany the conception of worker health comprises not only physical conditions but also psychosocial factors, including the stresses of shift work. Additionally, these nations have socialized health-care systems that emphasize prevention and general access. East Germany's excellent record in worker safety is also due to an active role by unions. An extensive network of union occupational safety representatives at the shop floor and enterprise levels helps to enforce a three-tier system of inspection: daily safety checks by the foremen and union representatives, weekly checks by the division heads and union representatives, and monthly checks by the enterprise directors and the chairs of union safety committees (Willim, 1987).

One social policy that is needed to address workplace safety and health in the United States is universalization of publicly sponsored workers' clinics. At present there are some sixty such clinics that provide diagnoses and health care to workers with job-related health problems. Many are based at hospitals and university medical schools, such as New York's Mount Sinai Center, San Francisco's General Hospital, Chicago's Cook County Hospital, and the Yale–New Haven Hospital. A few operate without hospital support, including the Greater Cincinnati Occupational Health Foundation; these clinics are supported by unions, public health advocates, and local governments. Another initiative necessary to increase protection for workers is a right-to-know policy that mandates the identification, notification, and counseling of all workers who are exposed (or who were exposed in the past) to a high risk of disease in their jobs (e.g., workers exposed to known causes of cancer such as asbestos, vinyl chloride, and benzene).

The demedicalizing thrusts of the holistic, women's, and workers' health movements have produced important gains for U.S. health care and point the way to the future. If the efforts of all three groups can be united to promote a socialization of health care through the adoption of Health Security, we may someday have a health-care system that is effective, efficient, and just.

REFERENCES

Abramovitz, Mimi. 1987. "Privatizing Health Care: The Bottom Line Is Society Loses." *The Nation,* October 17, pp. 410–412.

Altman, Drew E. 1986. "Two Views of a Changing Health Care System." Pp. 100–112 in *Applications of Social Science to Clinical Medicine and Health Policy,* eds. Linda H. Aiken and David Mechanic. New Brunswick, NJ: Rutgers University Press.

Andrain, Charles F. 1985. *Social Policies in Western Industrialized Societies.* Berkeley: Institute of International Studies, University of California.

Arendell, Teresa. 1988. "Unmarried Women in a Patriarchal Society: Impoverishment and Access to Health Care Across the Life-Cycle." Pp. 53–81 in *Poverty and Social Welfare in the United States,* ed. Donald Tomaskovic-Devey. Boulder, CO: Westview Press.

Blakeslee, Sandra. 1989. "Studies Find Unequal Access to Kidney Transplants." *The New York Times,* January 24.

Blendon, Robert J., and Drew E. Altman. 1984. "Public Attitudes About Health-Care Costs." *New England Journal of Medicine* 311:613–616.

Bliss, Shepherd, ed. 1985. *The New Holistic Health Handbook: Living Well in a New Age.* Lexington, MA: The Stephen Greene Press. (Distributed by Penguin Books; originally published by the Berkeley Holistic Health Center.)

Boffey, Philip M. 1988. "Expert Panel Sees Poor Leadership in U.S. AIDS Battle." *The New York Times,* June 2.

Boston Women's Health Collective. 1970. "Women and Their Bodies: A Course." Boston: New England Free Press.

Braverman, Harry. 1974. *Labor and Monopoly Capital: The Degradation of Work in the Twentieth Century.* New York: Monthly Review Press.

Brody, Jane E. 1987. "Ombudsmen: Helping the Patient Turns Out to Be Good for the Hospital as Well." *The New York Times,* April 1.

Budrys, Grace. 1986. *Planning for the Nation's Health: A Study of Twentieth-Century Developments in the United States.* New York: Greenwood Press.

Calavita, Kitty. 1983. "The Demise of the Occupational Safety and Health Administration: A Case Study in Symbolic Action." *Social Problems* 30:437–448.

Caputo, Larry. 1985. "Dual Diagnosis: AIDS and Addiction." *Social Work* 30:361–364.

Center for Disease Control. 1985. *Reports on AIDS.* Atlanta, GA: Public Health Service, U.S. Department of Health and Human Services.

Churchill, Larry R. 1987. *Rationing Health Care in America: Perceptions and Principles of Justice.* Notre Dame, IN: University of Notre Dame Press.

Conrad, Peter. 1986. "The Social Meaning of AIDS." *Social Policy* 17:51–56.

Conrad, Peter, and Rochelle Kern. 1986. "Prevention and Society." Pp. 468–470 in *The Sociology of Health and Illness: Critical Perspectives,* eds. Peter Conrad and Rochelle Kern. 2nd ed. New York: St. Martin's Press.

Conrad, Peter, and Joseph W. Schneider. 1980. *Deviance and Medicalization: From Badness to Sickness.* St. Louis, MO: C. V. Mosby.

Cowen, Emory L. 1985. "Primary Prevention in Mental Health." *Social Policy* 15:11–17.

Crawford, Robert. 1984. "A Cultural Account of 'Health': Control, Release, and the Social Body." Pp. 60–103 in *Issues in the Political Economy of Health Care,* ed. John B. McKinlay. London: Tavistock.

Curran, James W., et al. 1985. "The Epidemiology of AIDS: Current Status and Future Prospects." *Science* 229:1352–1357.

Cuyler, A. J. 1980. *The Political Economy of Social Policy.* New York: St. Martin's Press.

DeFriese, Gordon H., and Alison Woomert. 1982. "The Policy Implications of Self-Care." *Social Policy* 13:55–58.

De Kervasdoue, Jean, John R. Kimberly, and Jean-François Lacronique. 1984. "Technology and the Need for Health Care Rationing." Pp. 85–109 in *The End of an Illusion: The Future of Health Policy in Western Industrialized Nations,* eds. Jean de Kervasdoue, John R. Kimberly, and Victor G. Rodwin. Berkeley: University of California Press.

Derber, Charles. 1984. "Physicians and Their Sponsors: The New Medical Relations of Production." Pp. 217–254 in *Issues in the Political Economy of Health Care,* ed. John B. McKinlay. London: Tavistock.

DiMatteo, M. Robin. 1982. "New Perspectives on a Science of the Art of Medicine." Pp. 21–97 in *Contemporary Health Services: Social Science Perspectives*, eds. Allen W. Johnson, Oscar Grusky, and Bertram H. Raven. Boston: Auburn House.

Dutton, Diana B. 1986. "Social Class, Health, and Illness." Pp. 31–62 in *Applications of Social Science to Clinical Medicine and Health Policy*, eds. Linda H. Aiken and David Mechanic. New Brunswick, NJ: Rutgers University Press

Eastaugh, Steven R. 1987. *Financing Health Care: Economic Efficiency and Equity*. Dover, MA: Auburn House.

Ehrenreich, Barbara, and John Ehrenreich. 1970. *The American Health Empire: Power, Profits, and Politics*. New York: Random House/Vintage Books.

Elling, Ray H. 1986. *The Struggle for Workers' Health: A Study of Six Industrialized Countries*. Farmingdale, NY: Baywood Publishing.

Engels, Friedrich. 1968 [1845]. *The Condition of the Working Class in England*, eds. and trans. W. O. Henderson and W. H. Chaloner. Stanford, CA: Stanford University Press.

Erikson, Kai. 1986. "On Work and Alienation." *American Sociological Review* 51:1–8.

Eyer, Joseph. 1975. "Hypertension as a Disease of Modern Society." *International Journal of Health Services* 5:539–558.

———. 1984. "Capitalism, Health, and Illness." Pp. 23–59 in *Issues in the Political Economy of Health Care*, ed. John B. McKinlay. London: Tavistock.

Feder, Judith, and John Holahan. 1980. "Administrative Choices." Pp. 21–71 in *National Health Insurance: Conflicting Goals and Policy Choices*, eds. Judith Feder, John Holahan, and Theodore Marmor. Washington, DC: The Urban Institute.

Fein, Rashi. 1986. *Medical Care, Medical Costs: The Search for a Health Insurance Policy*. Cambridge, MA: Harvard University Press.

Feldstein, Paul J. 1984. "Health Associations and the Legislative Process." Pp. 223–242 in *Health Politics and Policy*, eds. Theodor J. Litman and Leonard S. Rubins. New York: John Wiley & Sons.

Fineberg, Harvey V. 1988. "The Social Dimensions of AIDS." *Scientific American* 259:128–134.

Foege, William. 1983. "The Natural Pattern of AIDS." Pp. 7–17 in *The Aids Epidemic*, ed. Kevin M. Cahill. New York: St. Martin's Press.

Fox, Renée C. 1986. "The Medicalization and Demedicalization of American Society." Pp. 390–394 in *The Sociology of Health and Illness: Critical Perspectives*, eds. Peter Conrad and Rochelle Kern. 2nd ed. New York: St. Martin's Press.

Freidson, Eliot. 1986. "The Medical Profession in Transition." Pp. 63–79 in *Applications of Social Science to Clinical Medicine and Health*, eds. Linda H. Aiken and David Mechanic. New Brunswick, NJ: Rutgers University Press.

Freudenberg, Nicholas. 1984. *Not in Our Backyards! Community Action for Health and the Environment*. New York: Monthly Review Press.

Freudenheim, Milt. 1989. "The Effort to Curb Caesarean Rate." *The New York Times*, January 10.

Freund, Peter E. S. 1982. *The Civilized Body: Social Domination, Control, and Health*. Philadelphia: Temple University Press.

Fuchs, Victor R. 1986. *The Health Economy*. Cambridge, MA: Harvard University Press.

Gartner, Audrey. 1985. "A Typology of Women's Self-Help Groups." *Social Policy* 15:25–30.

Gill, Derek. 1986. "A National Health Service: Principles and Practice." Pp. 454–467 in *The Sociology of Health and Illness: Critical Perspectives*, eds. Peter Conrad and Rochelle Kern. 2nd ed. New York: St. Martin's Press.

Glaab, Charles N. 1963. *The American City: A Documentary History*. Homewood, IL: The Dorsey Press.

Glucksberg, Harold, and Jack Singer. 1982. "The Multinational Drug Companies in Zaire: Their Adverse Effect on Cost and Availability of Essential Drugs." *International Journal of Health Services* 12:381–387.

Goleman, Daniel. 1987. "The Mind over the Body." *The New York Times Magazine*, September 27, pp. 36–39, 59–60.

Gordon, Linda. 1987. "Reproductive Rights for Today." *The Nation*, September 12, pp. 230–232.

Gorman, E. Michael. 1986. "The AIDS Epidemic in San Francisco: Epidemiological and Anthropological Perspectives." Pp. 157–172 in *Anthropology and Epidemiology: Interdisciplinary Approaches to the Study of Health and Disease*, eds. Craig R. Janes, Ron Stall, and Sandra M. Gifford. Dordrecht, Neth.: D. Reidel.

Gray, Alastair McIntosh. 1982. "Inequalities in Health. The Black Report: A Summary and Comment." *International Journal of Health Services* 12:349–380.

Gray, J. A. Muir. 1979. *Man Against Disease: Preventive Medicine.* Oxford: Oxford University Press.

Gruber, Murray L. 1980. "Inequality in the Social Services." *Social Service Review* 54:59–75.

Guillemin, Jeanne Harley, and Lynda Lytle Holmstrom. 1986. *Mixed Blessings: Intensive Care for Newborns.* New York: Oxford University Press.

Hadley, Jack. 1982. *More Medical Care, Better Health? An Economic Analysis of Mortality Rates.* Washington, DC: The Urban Institute Press.

Hammonds, Evelynn. 1987. "Race, Sex, AIDS: The Construction of 'Other.' " *Radical America* 20:28–36.

Hart, Julian Tudor. 1971. "The Inverse Care Law." *The Lancet,* February 27, pp. 405–412.

Hart, Nicky. 1985. *The Sociology of Health and Medicine.* Ormskirk, UK: Causeway Press.

Heyward, William L., and James W. Curran. 1988. "The Epidemiology of AIDS in the U.S." *Scientific American* 259:72–81.

Hiatt, Howard H. 1987. *America's Health in the Balance: Choice or Change?* New York: Harper & Row.

Hills, Stuart L. 1987. "Introduction." Pp. 1–10 in *Corporate Violence: Injury and Death for Profit,* ed. Stuart L. Hills. Totowa, NJ: Rowman and Littlefield.

Hollingshead, August B., and Frederick C. Redlich. 1958. *Social Class and Mental Illness: A Community Study.* New York: John Wiley & Sons.

House, James S., and Eric M. Cottington. 1986. "Health and the Workplace." Pp. 392–416 in *Applications of Social Science to Clinical Medicine and Health Policy,* eds. Linda H. Aiken and David Mechanic. New Brunswick, NJ: Rutgers University Press.

Illich, Ivan. 1976. *Medical Nemesis: The Expropriation of Health.* New York: Pantheon.

Johnson, Michael P., and Karl Hufbauer. 1982. "Sudden Infant Death Syndrome as a Medical Research Problem Since 1945." *Social Problems* 30:65–81.

Johnson, Norman. 1987. *The Welfare State in Transition: The Theory and Practice of Welfare Pluralism.* Amherst: University of Massachusetts Press.

Jung, Carl G. 1968. *Man and His Symbols.* New York: Dell.

Kingston, Tim. 1987. "The Unhealthy Profits of AZT." *The Nation,* October 17, pp. 408–409.

Klerman, Gerald L. 1987. "Psychiatric Epidemiology and Mental Health Policy." Pp. 227–264 in *Epidemiology and Health Policy,* eds. Sol Levine and Abraham M. Lilienfeld. London: Tavistock.

Klinkmuller, Erich. 1986. "The Medical-Industrial Complex." Pp. 53–71 in *Political Values and Health Care: The German Experience,* eds. Donald W. Light and Alexander Schuller. Cambridge, MA: MIT Press.

Kotelchuck, David. 1987. "Worker Safety and Health in the 1980s." *Economic Notes* 55:1–5.

Lack, Dorothea Z. 1982. "Women and Pain: Another Feminist Issue." *Women & Therapy* 1:55–64.

Landesman, Sheldon H. 1983. "The Haitian Connection." Pp. 28–37 in *The Aids Epidemic,* ed. Kevin M. Cahill. New York: St. Martin's Press.

Ledingham, J. G. G. 1987. "Alternative Treatments and Outcomes for Patients with Cardiovascular Diseases." Pp. 34–60 in *Medicine and Society: Clinical Decisions and Societal Values,* ed. Eli Ginzberg. Boulder, CO: Westview Press.

Levi, Lennart, Marianne Frankenhaeuser, and Bertil Gardell. 1986. "The Characteristics of the Workplace and the Nature of Its Social Demands." Pp. 54–67 in *Occupational Stress: Health and Performance at Work,* eds. Stewart Wolf and Albert J. Finestone. Littleton, MA: PSG Publishing.

Levine, Murray. 1988. "How Self-Help Works." *Social Policy* 19:39–43.

Levine, Sol, and Abraham M. Lilienfeld. 1987. "Introduction." Pp. 1–14 in *Epidemiology and Health Policy,* eds. Sol Levine and Abraham M. Lilienfeld. London: Tavistock.

Lewin, Tamar. 1987. "Sudden Nurse Shortage Threatens Hospital Care." *The New York Times,* July 7.

Light, Donald W. 1986. "Conclusion: Values and Health in the Two Germanies." Pp. 571–585 in *Political Values and Health Care: The German Experience,* eds. Donald W. Light and Alexander Schuller. Cambridge, MA: MIT Press.

Lipsky, Michael. 1984. "Bureaucratic Disentitlement in Social Welfare Programs." *Social Service Review* 58:3–27.

Litman, Theodor J. 1984. "Government and Health: The Political Aspects of Health Care—A Sociopolitical Overview." Pp. 3–40 in *Health Politics and Policy,* eds. Theodor J. Litman and Leonard S. Rubins. New York: John Wiley & Sons.

Mann, Jonathan M., et al. 1988. "The International Epidemiology of AIDS." *Scientific American* 259:82–89.

Marmor, Theodore R. 1983. "Rethinking National Health Insurance." Pp. 187–206 in *Political Analysis and American Medical Care: Essays*, ed. Theodore R. Marmor. Cambridge: Cambridge University Press.

Marmor, Theodore R., Wayne L. Hoffman, and Thomas C. Heagy. 1983. "National Health Insurance: Some Lessons from the Canadian Experience." Pp. 165–186 in *Political Analysis and American Medical Care: Essays*, ed. Theodore R. Marmor. Cambridge: Cambridge University Press.

Marx, Karl. 1967 [1867]. *Capital*, ed. Frederick Engels, trans. Samuel Moore and Edward Aveling. Volume 1: *A Critical Analysis of Capitalist Production*. New York: International Publishers.

Maslach, Christina. 1982. *Burnout—The Cost of Caring*. Englewood Cliffs, NJ: Prentice Hall.

Masters, William H., and Virginia E. Johnson. 1966. *Human Sexual Response*. Boston: Little, Brown.

McGuire, Meredith B. 1988. *Ritual Healing in Suburban America*. New Brunswick, NJ: Rutgers University Press.

McKinlay, John B. 1984. "Introduction." Pp. 1–9 in *Issues in the Political Economy of Health Care*, ed. John B. McKinlay. London: Tavistock.

———. 1986. "A Case for Refocussing Upstream: The Political Economy of Illness." Pp. 484–498 in *The Sociology of Health and Illness: Critical Perspectives*, eds. Peter Conrad and Rochelle Kern. 2nd ed. New York: St. Martin's Press.

McKinlay, John B., et al. 1983. "Mortality, Morbidity, and the Inverse Care Law." Pp. 99–138 in *Cities and Sickness: Health Care in Urban America*, eds. Ann Lennarson Greer and Scott Greer. Beverly Hills, CA: Sage Publications.

McMullen, Martha. 1987. "State Law Acknowledges 'Patient Dumping' a Crime." *Guardian*, October 28, p. 9.

Mechanic, David. 1986. *From Advocacy to Allocation: The Evolving American Health Care System*. New York: Free Press.

Miller, C. Arden. 1987. "Child Health." Pp. 15–54 in *Epidemiology and Health Policy*, eds. Sol Levine and Abraham M. Lilienfeld. London: Tavistock.

Millman, Marcia. 1982. "The Ideology of Self-Care: Blaming the Victims of Illness ." Pp. 83–91 in *Contemporary Health Services: Social Science Perspectives*, eds. Allen W. Johnson, Oscar Grusky, and Bertram H. Raven. Boston: Auburn House.

Moberg, David. 1987. "The Time Is Right for Public Investment." *In These Times*, November 25–December 8, p. 2.

Navarro, Vicente. 1986. *Crisis, Health, and Medicine: A Social Critique*. London: Tavistock.

Nelson, Margaret K. 1983. "Working-Class Women, Middle-Class Women, and Models of Childbirth." *Social Problems* 30:284–297.

Panem, Sandra. 1988. *The AIDS Bureaucracy*. Cambridge, MA: Harvard University Press.

Pear, Robert. 1987. "Rising Costs of Health Care Still Outstrip Medicare Gains." *The New York Times*, November 1.

Petchey, Roland. 1987. "Health Maintenance Organizations: Just What the Doctor Ordered?" *Journal of Social Policy* 16:489–507.

Petrakis, Peter. 1988. "Research Report of the Surgeon General's Workshop on Self-Help and Public Health." *Social Policy* 19:36–38.

Pickard, Myrna R. 1986. "Changes in White: Health-Delivery Options in a Time of High Cost." Pp. 91–110 in *Urban Policy Problems: Federal Policy and Institutional Change*, ed. Mark S. Rosentraub. New York: Praeger.

Pizer, Hank. 1982. *Guide to the New Medicine: What Works, What Doesn't*. New York: William Morrow.

Powell, Thomas J. 1985. "Improving the Effectiveness of Self-Help." *Social Policy* 16:22–29.

Prout, Marianne N., Theodore Colton, and Robert A. Smith. 1987. "Cancer Epidemiology and Health Policy." Pp. 117–156 in *Epidemiology and Health Policy*, eds. Sol Levine and Abraham M. Lilienfeld. London: Tavistock.

Ratcliffe, John, et al. 1984. "Perspectives on Prevention: Health Promotion vs. Health Protection." Pp. 56–84 in *The End of an Illusion: The Future of Health Policy in Western Industrialized Nations*, eds. Jean de Kervasdoue, John R. Kimberly, and Victor G. Rodwin. Berkeley: University of California Press.

Ravussin, Eric, et al. 1988. "Reduced Rate of Energy Expenditure as a Risk Factor for Body-Weight Gain." *The New England Journal of Medicine* 318:467–472.

Reich, Wilhelm. 1972 [1933]. *Character Analysis*, trans. Vincent R. Carfagno. 3rd ed. New York: Simon and Schuster.

Relman, Arnold C. 1980. "The New Medical-Industrial Complex." *New England Journal of Medicine* 303:963–970.

Renaud, Marc. 1975. "On the Structural Constraints to State Intervention in Health." *International Journal of Health Services* 5:559–571.

Riessman, Catherine Kohler. 1983. "Women and Medicalization: A New Perspective." *Social Policy* 14:3–18.

———. 1984. "The Use of Health Services by the Poor: Are There Any Promising Models?" *Social Policy* 14:30–40.

Riessman, Catherine Kohler, and Constance A. Nathanson. 1986. "The Management of Reproduction: Social Construction of Risk and Responsibility." Pp. 251–281 in *Applications of Social Science to Clinical Medicine and Health Policy*, eds. Linda H. Aiken and David Mechanic. New Brunswick, NJ: Rutgers University Press.

Ritzer, George, and David Walczak. 1986. *Working: Conflict and Change*. 3rd ed. Englewood Cliffs, NJ: Prentice Hall.

Rodgers, Harrell R., Jr. 1986. *Poor Women, Poor Families: The Economic Plight of America's Female-Headed Households*. Armonk, NY: M. E. Sharpe.

Rothman, Barbara Katz. 1983. "Midwives in Transition: The Structure of a Clinical Revolution." *Social Problems* 30:262–271.

Ruzek, Sheryl K. 1981. "The Women's Self-Help Health Movement." Pp. 563–570 in *The Sociology of Health and Illness: Critical Perspectives*, eds. Peter Conrad and Rochelle Kern. New York: St. Martin's Press.

Salmon, J. Warren. 1984. "Organizing Medical Care for Profit." Pp. 143–186 in *Issues in the Political Economy of Health Care*, ed. John B. McKinlay. London: Tavistock.

Sarri, Rosemary C., and Carol Crill Russell. 1988. "Health and Poverty in Single-Parent Families: The Consequences of Federal Policy Change." Pp. 194–221 in *Poverty and Social Welfare in the United States*, ed. Donald Tomaskovic-Devey. Boulder, CO: Westview Press.

Savo, Cynthia. 1983. "Self-Care and Empowerment: A Case Study." *Social Policy* 14:19–22.

Schiff, Robert L., et al. 1986. "Transfers to a Public Hospital: A Prospective Study of 467 Patients." *New England Journal of Medicine* 314:552–557.

Schnall, Peter C., and Rochelle Kern. 1986. "Hypertension in American Society: An Introduction to Historical Materialist Epidemiology." Pp. 73–89 in *The Sociology of Health and Illness: Critical Perspectives*, eds. Peter Conrad and Rochelle Kern. 2nd ed. New York: St. Martin's Press.

Scully, Diana, and Pauline Bart. 1981. "A Funny Thing Happened on the Way to the Orifice: Women in Gynecology Textbooks." Pp. 350–355 in *The Sociology of Health and Illness: Critical Perspectives*, eds. Peter Conrad and Rochelle Kern. New York: St. Martin's Press.

Shanker, Renee. 1983. "Occupational Disease, Workers' Compensation, and the Social Work Advocate." *Social Work* 28:24–27.

Shaw, Nancy Stoller. 1988. "Preventing AIDS Among Women: The Role of Community Organizing." *Socialist Review* 18:76–92.

Sidel, Victor W., and Ruth Sidel. 1986. "Health Care and Medical Care in the United States." Pp. 175–187 in *The Sociology of Health and Illness: Critical Perspectives*, eds. Peter Conrad and Rochelle Kern. 2nd ed. New York: St. Martin's Press.

Siu, Albert L., and Robert H. Brook. 1987. "Allocating Health Care Resources: How Can We Ensure Access to Essential Care?" Pp. 20–33 in *Medicine and Society: Clinical Decisions and Societal Values*, ed. Eli Ginzberg. Boulder, CO: Westview Press.

Spock, Dr. Benjamin. 1946. *Baby and Child Care*. New York: Simon & Schuster Pocket Books.

Stark, Evan. 1982. "Doctors in Spite of Themselves: The Limits of Radical Health Criticism." *International Journal of Health Services* 12:419–457.

Starr, Paul. 1982. *The Social Transformation of American Medicine*. New York: Basic Books.

———. 1986. "Health Care for the Poor: The Past Twenty Years." Pp. 106–132 in *Fighting Poverty: What Works and What Doesn't*, eds. Sheldon H. Danziger and Daniel H. Weinberg. Cambridge, MA: Harvard University Press.

Starr, Paul, and Theodore Marmor. 1984. "The United States: A Social Forecast." Pp. 234–254 in *The End of an Illusion: The Future of Health Policy in Western Industrialized Nations*, eds. Jean de Kervasdoue, John R. Kimberly, and Victor G. Rodwin. Berkeley: University of California Press.

Stone, Deborah A. 1984. *The Disabled State*. Philadelphia: Temple University Press.

Strauss, Anselm L. 1979. "Chronic Illness." Pp. 97–113 in *Where Medicine Fails*, ed. Anselm L. Strauss. 3rd ed. New Brunswick, NJ: Transaction Books.

Sullivan, Ronald. 1987. "Bill of $1 Billion for Treating AIDS Seen in New York." *The New York Times*, May 22.

Suzman, Richard, and Matilda White Riley. 1985. "Introducing the 'Oldest Old.'" *Milbank Memorial Fund Quarterly* 63:177–186.

Syme, S. Leonard, and Lisa F. Berkman. 1986. "Social Class, Susceptibility, and Sickness." Pp. 28–34 in *The Sociology of Health and Illness: Critical Perspectives*, eds. Peter Conrad and Rochelle Kern. 2nd ed. New York: St. Martin's Press.

Szasz, Andrew. 1986. "The Reversal of Federal Policy Toward Worker Safety and Health." *Science & Society* 50:25–51.

Tarpinian, Greg. 1988. "The Politics of Bargaining: Home Care Workers Take on the System." *Economic Notes* 56:10–13.

Taylor, Rosemary C. R. 1986. "The Politics of Prevention." Pp. 471–484 in *The Sociology of Health and Illness: Critical Perspectives*, eds. Peter Conrad and Rochelle Kern. 2nd ed. New York: St. Martin's Press.

Taylor, Shelley E. 1982. "The Impact of Health Organizations on Recipients of Services." Pp. 103–137 in *Contemporary Health Services: Social Science Perspectives.*, eds. Allen W. Johnson, Oscar Grusky, and Bertram H. Raven. Boston: Auburn House.

Thompson, Frank J., and Michael J. Scicchitano. 1985. "State Enforcement of Federal Regulatory Policy: The Lessons of OSHA." *Policy Studies Journal* 13:591–598.

Tolchin, Martin. 1988a. "U.S. Fails to Carry Out Law to Improve Nursing Homes." *The New York Times*, December 9.

———. 1988b. "Turning to the Biggest Gap in U.S. Health Coverage." *The New York Times*, December 25.

Ullman, Dana. 1983. "Medical Monopoly vs. Alternative Health Care." *Social Policy* 14:27–28.

Velimirovic, B. 1987. "AIDS as a Social Phenomenon. " *Social Science & Medicine* 25:541–552.

Waitzkin, Howard. 1986. "A Marxian Interpretation of the Growth and Development of Coronary Care Technology." Pp. 219–231 in *The Sociology of Health and Illness: Critical Perspectives.* eds. Peter Conrad and Rochelle Kern. 2nd ed. New York: St. Martin's Press.

Walsh, Diana Chapman, and Ralph W. Hingson. 1987. "Epidemiology and Alcohol Policy." Pp. 265–291 in *Epidemiology and Health Policy*, eds. Sol Levine and Abraham M. Lilienfeld. London: Tavistock.

Weller, Geoffrey. 1986. "Common Problems, Alternative Solutions: A Comparison of the Canadian and American Health Systems." *Policy Studies Journal* 14:604–620.

Wildavsky, Aaron. 1979. *Speaking Truth to Power: The Art and Craft of Policy Analysis*. Boston: Little, Brown.

Willim, Horst. 1987. "Trade Unions and Occupational Safety in the German Democratic Republic." *International Labour Review* 126:329–336.

Withorn, Ann. 1980. "Helping Ourselves: The Limits and Potential of Self-Help." *Social Policy* 11:20–27.

Wolff, Craig. 1987. "Health Care at Home: A Mixed Blessing." *The New York Times*, October 31.

9

The City

What is the Citie, but the People? True, the People are the Citie.
Shakespeare, *Coriolanus*, 1623

The city is humankind's built environment and the central theater where the performances of social policies are most visible. The flagrant disparities and social problems of capitalist society are dramatized on the public stage that is the city. It is where homeless people live in cardboard boxes on sidewalks in front of luxurious mansions of the wealthy. It is in the city and its environs that the large majority of people in developed nations reside. This multitudinous cast of characters living in close proximity provides a readily observable and vivid display. They make the city the primary locus of political power, in the form of masses of organized and organizable citizens. Consequently, much social policy is city centered—directly in public housing and similar urban policies, indirectly in policies such as public welfare that are for people who are mostly city residents.

Urbanization has been a master trend in modern times. In 1800 only 3 percent of the world's population was urban; in 1900 it was still only 14 percent. By 1980, however, 41 percent of the people of the world were urbanites, and in 2000 the proportion is expected to be 51 percent. Then, for the first time in history, a majority of people will live in urban areas (Palen, 1987, pp. 3–4). Urbanization is linked to industrialization and to the emergence of the Welfare State. In 1985,

75 percent of the population of the nineteen most industrialized nations was urban, compared to only 22 percent of the population of the thirty-four least industrialized countries. Welfare States are among the most heavily urbanized nations. In 1985 the ten most urbanized nations were 1, Singapore (100 percent urban); 2, Belgium; 3, Kuwait, U.K.; 5, Israel; 6, Netherlands; 7, Australia, Denmark, Sweden, West Germany (all four at 86 percent urban).

In addition to its importance as the place where more and more people live, the city is dominant as a cultural and political center. The city is the site of the world's major cultural facilities—universities, museums, libraries, and centers for the performing arts. The principal cultural mediums—film, publishing, television—of modern society are decidedly urban in context and outlook. The capitals of the world are cities, and from them emanate the political decisions that reverberate in the hinterland. The datelines of world news have a familiar ring: London, Paris, Moscow, Tokyo, and other great capitals. Even in largely rural nations cities are the cultural and political centers—viz., Delhi, Beijing, Jakarta, and Lagos.

The United States is one of the world's most urbanized nations. About three out of every four Americans live in an urban area. The United States first became a majority urban nation with its 1920 census. Today its great cities are among the largest and most important in the world—truly world-class in size and influence: New York City, Los Angeles, Chicago, Philadelphia, and San Francisco, each with at least five million metropolitan residents and each an international economic and cultural center. In 1986 these five cities and their environs contained more than one in every five Americans.

To begin our analysis of the city, we discuss the connections among social science, social policy, and the city. Next we look at the contemporary urban transformation and the emergence of the corporate city and its dominant attributes—urban sprawl, city-suburb inequality, and the fiscal crisis. Then we examine a major urban social problem that challenges social policy—homelessness—as well as the related subjects of deinstitutionalization and gentrification. Following this, we interview a social practitioner who works with homeless people. The chapter then moves to an examination of current urban social policy initiatives and options. We end with an analysis of the relationship between the city and social change, in which we highlight urban social movements.

SOCIAL SCIENCE, SOCIAL POLICY, AND THE CITY

The modern connection between social policy and the city goes back to the nineteenth century, when capitalist industrialization and urbanization led to a host of social problems—widespread disease, poverty, unemployment, and homelessness. These problems were tackled by social reformers and reform movements, including the settlement house movement, notably through the work of Jane Addams (1961) at Hull House in Chicago. Reformers' efforts spurred local and state government involvement, which led eventually to federal policies. Today the same social problems of disease, poverty, un-employment, and homelessness, although ameliorated, are pressing social policy issues for the city.

Three broad paradigms of the city have developed in social science, each of which is linked to alternative social policy perspectives: the social psychologi-cal (or cultural), the ecological, and the Marxist (or political economy) models. The social psychological paradigm posits a distinctly urbane culture and focuses on the situation of the individual person in the city. It is a "city life" model and its roots can be traced to the work of Georg Simmel (1964). Urbanization and the money-commodity economy of capitalism are the basis for modern in-dividuality and cosmopolitanism, which result in high levels both of personal freedom and of personal isolation. Because of this presumed isolation, applied social psychological perspectives stress the study of local communities, includ-ing urban neighborhoods (Gans, 1962) and suburbs (Gans, 1967).

The Chicago School of the early twentieth century bridged, in the work of Wirth (1938), the social psychological and ecological paradigms. The ecological perspective contemplates the geographic community and the relationship be-tween urbanites and their physical environment. It is a "city space" model and it originated in the Chicago School (Park and Burgess, 1967), of which the work of Suttles (1968) is a contemporary exemplar. The great size and density of urban populations foster territorial processes such as racial, ethnic, and class segrega-tion and succession. These processes, which are the medium of urban growth, radiate outward through concentric zones from the city core, its central business district (CBD). (The process resembles the ripple effect one gets from tossing a stone into still water.) City planing is an applied art that shares human ecology's interest in the arrangement of physical and social environments; its contem-porary roots go back to a late-nineteenth-century book by Ebenezer Howard, *Garden Cities of To-Morrow* (1965), and to Le Corbusier's *The City of To-Morrow and Its Planning* (1971) and Mumford's *The Culture of Cities* (1938). These three men's work is the basis for the focus in city planning on physical order, gardens, open spaces, high-rise buildings, and regionalism. Contemporary city planning has been sharply criticized, notably by Jacobs (1961), for its bureaucratic and or-thodox approach and for its lack of concern for livable neighborhoods.

The third paradigm of the city stresses economics and politics and is Marxist; it is the "city conflict" model and is based on the work of Engels (1979), Marx (1967), and Marx and Engels (1975). In this model the city is the locale for capitalism's political conflicts, the most fundamental of which is be-tween the interest of the working class in economic security, including ade-quate housing, and the interest of the owning class in economic profit. Long dormant, Marxist analysis of the city has flourished since the 1970s, revital-ized by the work of Manuel Castells, David Harvey, and Henri Lefebvre.

Castells (1977) has researched and analyzed the displacement of class struggle between workers and owners into urban social movements for col-lective consumption of housing and other social goods. The genesis of these movements is struggle between workers and the state, which supplies social goods in the form of the social wage (discussed in Chapter 5). Harvey's (1973) work has concentrated on the city as a built environment colonized by capitalists, especially financial capitalists such as bankers, so that profit can be secured by stimulating new markets—as the development of suburbs created a demand for single-family dwellings and autos. Gottdiener (1985) has amplified Lefebvre's (1969, 1971) work on urban culture and space (for example, as they constitute the bases for ghettoes) and on the production of space as a commodity that is bought and sold in capitalism. Within this perspective of the social production of space, advanced capitalism is seen as creating a distinctive urban space that performs several functions. It serves as a means of production, an object of consumption, and a property relationship between social groups (Deutsche, 1988, p. 27).

Marxist analysts stress, in varying ways and degrees, the role of class struggle (based on the international capitalist economy) and of the state and its social policy, as well as the use and control of space, as the major factors that shape the contemporary city. Thus, for example, uneven economic development is reflected in spatial and social disparities. While some areas and groups prosper from the infusion of capital, others are left to decline for want of investment. Mingione (1981) referred to the examination of this process as *socioterritorial study*—the sociological study of the territorial division of labor (Lebas, 1982, p. 101). Our analysis in this chapter is rooted in such a Marxist perspective: we highlight conflicting class interests in the city. The middle and upper classes compel social policy to remake the city in their image and at the same time to maximize their economic position. These middle- and upper-class plans for social policy conflict with the interests of the poor and working classes in stable neighborhoods and in affordable, decent housing. We expand the Marxist analysis to include concerns for the quality of city life (its culture) and for the organization of city space (its ecology).

URBAN TRANSFORMATION

In Welfare States the city underwent a major transformation in the twentieth century from a vibrant, expanding industrial center, through economic decline and population outmigration, to its present form, which is characterized by decay and increased inequality. This transition constitutes what is commonly referred to as the *urban crisis*. We view this crisis as flowing from changes in the capitalist economy that affected the city through three developments: (1) the emergence of a new city form—the corporate city; (2) the radical partition between city and suburb; and (3) the fiscal crisis of government. We examine each of these developments in turn.

The Corporate City

Contemporary American cities can be divided into three broad categories. The first comprises old industrial cities that are in decline, including Detroit and St. Louis. The second comprises emergent (since World War II) corporate cities that are expanding through service employment in corporate offices. Representative of this group are Dallas and Los Angeles. The final category includes old industrial cities that are making a transition to the new corporate form—Boston, Chicago, and New York City are examples (Mollenkopf, 1983, p. 40). These three cities epitomize the "converting city" that was discussed by Fainstein and Fainstein (1982).

This tripartite classification of cities is not peculiar to the United States. Declining industrial cities in other Welfare States include Glasgow and Liverpool in Great Britain. New corporate cities in the capitalist world outside the United States include Hong Kong and Singapore. The old industrial cities that are making a transition to the new corporate form fall into two subcategories: (1) global command cities, of which London, New York, and Tokyo are clearcut representatives; and (2) corporate and governmental administrative centers (national and regional), of which Chicago, Amsterdam-Rotterdam, Sydney, Toronto, San Francisco, and Frankfurt are examples (Williams and Smith, 1986, pp. 208–211).

Other analysts present a similar picture. For example, work by Cohen (1981) indicates that two U.S. cities have emerged as global centers for both corporate and banking business—New York and San Francisco. Chicago and Houston are in transition from national to international centers, while other U.S. cities have remained national or regional hubs of the new international spatial division of labor. Remaining cities will either atrophy or be satellitized. In the increasingly precarious international economy all cities are more vulnerable to cycles and dislocations. The politically unstable Third World, with its factories, such as *maquiladoras* in Mexico, and resources, such as oil, has become ever more important to the world economy. The huge debts of so many Third World countries add to the perception that this new international economy is a prodigious house of cards.

The corporate city was produced by the transformation of the national capitalist economy into one of global production in the twentieth century. This internationalization of the capitalist economy was rooted in two factors. First, developments such as the elaboration of detailed operations radically decentralized production by enabling it to be "scientifically managed" (discussed in Chapter 5) from a far center. Second, advances in the spatial division of labor that were based on computers and electronic communications made possible the rapid accessibility of former peripheral areas in the Third World as locations of massed cheap labor (Hill, 1984, p. 132). In the new worldwide economy the corporate city is the node, the command center. Its central business district is dominated by corporate headquarters that control farflung production and distribution facilities.

The development of the corporate city in the United States was based principally in a progrowth, redevelopment coalition, in which the main social actors were real estate owners and developers, construction firms and unions, and financial enterprises. The agencies of redevelopment were city halls, and its social policies were urban renewal and zoning. The focus of redevelopment was narrow: construction of office space and a supporting infrastructure in CBDs for the management of worldwide corporate operations. This infrastructure included necessary support facilities such as highways and parking lots for commuters. The scale of human displacement caused by these policies is indicated by the fact that the construction of just one interstate highway in New York City displaced about 50,000 persons in only one borough (Berman, 1987, p. 426). The labor force that resulted from this corporatization of the city is top-heavy with highly paid executives and professionals, most of whom live in the suburbs.

Urban renewal, as expanded under the 1949 Federal Housing Act, was the principal policy for remaking the CBDs of older cities into suitable areas for corporate facilities. Between 1949 and 1967 over 400,000 housing units—the bulk of them low-rent—were destroyed through urban renewal, while only about 40,000 replacement units were built (Friedland, 1983, p. 85). What happened in North Philadelphia exemplifies the negative impact of urban renewal on housing stock. Between 1950 and 1980 the following changes, largely as a result of urban renewal, occurred in North Philadelphia: (1) total dwelling units decreased by 33 percent, (2) vacant dwelling units increased by 572 percent, and (3) property values declined as a proportion of the city's average (Kleniewski, 1987, p. 96). The removal of the poor in favor of capitalist enterprise is a recurrent urban phenomenon. Marx (1967, p. 657) noted it over a hundred years ago: " 'Improvements' of towns, accompanying the increase of wealth, by the demolition of badly built quarters, the erection of palaces for banks, warehouses, &c., the widening of streets for business traffic, for the carriages of luxury, and for the introduction of tramways, &c., drive away the poor into even worse and more crowded hiding places."

The physical city that resulted from redevelopment is highly decentralized rather than compact, as was its predecessor, the industrial city (Gordon, 1984). The new corporate city is characterized by downtown areas given over to high-rise office buildings, parking lots, and related corporate structures. The streets of this downtown are often deserted at night, as commuting workers are in their suburban homes and entertainment and other former CBD functions have largely moved to suburbs and to outlying airport areas. The corporate city emerged in the age of the auto and its mediums—expressways, parking lots, shopping malls, and highway commercial strips. The proliferation of these mediums attests to an environment built for the auto, as does the lack of public transportation. The overall structure of the city is dominated by a horizontal sprawl—giving rise to the term "fragmented metropolis" (Fogelson, 1967), which was first applied to Los Angeles.

Socially, the corporate city is auto-ized. Instead of congregating and walking in the streets, residents cruise the streets in autos, stopping occasionally at drive-in restaurants and other commercial outlets. In the corporate city even the vital social intercourse of religious organizations has been diluted by drive-in churches and, incredibly, drive-in funeral parlors. This auto-ized existence produces a social life that is more atomized, encapsulated, and privatized than that of the traditional city.

The rise of the corporate city was linked to suburbanization. In fact the corporate city has been described as a thousand suburbs in search of a city. The bridging factors between development of the corporate city and of the suburbs were technological (the auto), economic (decentralization of production), and political (prosuburb policies). The result is a large social gap between city and suburb. Thus the corporate city represents a major contradiction and source of strain for corporate capitalism. The social and economic costs of managing the corporate city have become prohibitive, but the highly centralized administration of the corporate capitalist economy depends on its existence. This contradiction is reflected in the fiscal crisis of cities, in environmental degradation, and in a rising population of redundant workers (Mingione, 1981, pp. 130–131). We now turn to an examination of these and other social problems that are based in the development of the corporate city.

City and Suburb

Suburbanization succeeded urbanization in the United States. Between 1950 and 1980 the proportion of the population residing in suburbs rose from 26.9 percent to 44.8 percent, while the proportion living in central cities declined from 35.6 percent to 30 percent, and the proportion living in nonmetropolitan areas declined from 37.5 percent to 25.2 percent. Thus about one-half of the population now lives in suburbs, while the other one-half is nearly equally divided between residents of cities and residents of rural areas.

The roots of mass suburbanization go back to the post–World War II decentralization of employment. The original research on this subject by Kain (1970) found that between 1948 and 1963 the suburban share of employment in forty metropolitan areas increased dramatically, from 33.1 percent to 51.8 percent in manufacturing, with similar increases in wholesale, retail, and service employment. The suburban share of population in these forty metropolitan areas rose from 36.0 percent to 54.3 percent in the same period. These data suggest that the population shift was led by the employment shift.

Suburbanization has been accompanied by a changing regional balance in the population. In 1950 the Snowbelt (the Northeast and Midwest) had 55.5 percent of the U.S. population, while the Sunbelt (the South and West) had 44.5 percent. In 1980 a majority of Americans—52.3 percent—lived in Sunbelt states. By 2000 the Sunbelt is projected to be the home of 58.4 percent of Americans. Thus the prototypical corporate city is in the Sunbelt and is highly suburbanized: Los Angeles.

Suburbanization resulted in city-suburb racial and class segregation. In 1980 the central cities of urban areas were 33.3 percent African American and Hispanic, while the suburbs were only 11.5 percent African American and Hispanic. Per capita money income in 1979 was 13.5 percent lower in central cities than in suburbs. In 1983, 16.3 percent of city residents were poor, compared to 7.8 percent of suburban residents. Segregation by race and social class, with minorities and the poor in cities and the white and better-off population in suburbs, is even more dramatic for the declining industrial cities of the Snowbelt. For example, in 1980 African Americans and Hispanics together were 65.5 percent of Detroit's population but only 5.6 percent of the population of Detroit's suburbs. Per capita income for residents of Detroit's suburbs was 50.3 percent higher than for residents of the city itself.

These inequalities between city and suburb are an extension of the historical process of uneven development under capitalism, which originally referred to the expansion of the city at the expense of the countryside. Now it is the urban fringe, especially the area beyond the suburb that is referred to as the exurb, that flourishes while the inner city deteriorates. Modern capitalism is based on uneven development between city and countryside, between suburb and city, and between regions, as well as between developed and underdeveloped nations. Capital is increasingly mobile in the form of the transnational corporation. Uneven development means that major spaces and sectors of society, and entire societies in the Third World, are exploited and then left to stagnate as capital moves on to new locales.

In addition to its negative effects on cities, uneven development impacts adversely on the poor and working classes, while it advantages the middle and upper classes. Middle- and upper-class people are mobile and thus can follow capital investment, even gaining occupationally in the process. They are also likely to be capital investors as well as salaried employees, so they are able to profit from any economic gains that accrue from uneven development. Finally, middle- and upper-class people profit from the speculation that highly mobile capital produces. Based on their study of New Haven, Detroit, New Orleans, Denver, and San Francisco, Fainstein and her colleagues (1983, pp. 274–275) concluded that "The opportunities for speculative gain afforded by centrally located, devalorized property can redeem the fates of property owners and business managers, but they only heighten the difficulties of low-income populations already injured by earlier disinvestment."

Growing city-suburb inequality is driven by corporations seeking private economic advantage and is supported by favorable social policies, including tax and zoning incentives. Post–World War II policies that promoted suburbanization include interstate highways, which greatly facilitated commuting, and Federal Housing Authority (FHA) and Veterans Administration loans, which channeled money into suburban housing. Additionally, urban renewal cleared low-income housing in the cities to make way for parking lots and freeways for suburban commuters. Logan (1983, p. 88) concluded from a national study of suburbanization that "Market processes have gone hand in hand with collective action and public policy in order to segregate races and social classes in space, to concentrate job creation in certain areas, and to tie these patterns to severe disparities in the life chances of different communities."

Parker (1985) researched forty-one metropolitan areas and created a central city–to–suburban hardship ratio, based on size of the socially dependent population (less than eighteen and over sixty-four years old), crime rate, overcrowded housing (greater than one person per room), percentage of population with less than a high school education, unemployment rate, per capita income, and percentage of population in poverty. Of the forty-one metropolitan areas, the most equivalent city-suburb hardship ratios were in Sunbelt cities: Greensboro had a 1.08 ratio (near equivalency for its central city and suburbs); San Diego, 1.12; Houston, 1.24; San Francisco, 1.25; Ft. Lauderdale, 1.27; Los Angeles, 1.29. The metropolitan areas with the highest ratios of city-to-suburb hardship were all in the Snowbelt: Newark had a 3.02 ratio, meaning the city's hardships were 3.02 times the hardships of its suburbs; Cleveland, 2.32; St. Louis, 2.19; New York, 1.99; Rochester, 1.96. The researchers concluded that federal response to central city hardship declined noticeably during Reagan's administration.

Glaring city-suburb inequalities overshadow the inequalities that exist within cities and suburbs. Political fragmentation produces two distinct kinds of suburb, wealthy and poor, each accounting for 15 to 20 percent of all suburbs. The stereotypical white middle-class suburb is actually a residual category for mixed suburbs. The rich suburbs are the ones that gain in the unequal distribution of public goods and services (Schneider and Logan, 1981). In the city residential segregation separates the upper and middle classes, who live in CBD luxury housing and in near-suburban neighborhoods of single-family dwellings, from the poor and working classes who live in public housing, tenements, and the streets.

The Fiscal Crisis

The same factors that produced city-suburb inequality led to the fiscal crisis of cities. The corporate decentralization of production resulted in declines in the stable working-class population, economic activity, and the tax base of cities. Policy also played an important role, as the FHA encouraged private investment in suburban housing and discouraged it in cities. Although municipal unions are frequently blamed for the fiscal crises of the 1970s and 1980s, they were not responsible for them. A study of 127 cities by Rodgers and Straussman (1986) found that public employee union demands did not by themselves explain fiscal crises. Nonetheless, the municipal unions became a convenient scapegoat and remain so to this day.

Although the fiscal crisis became pervasive throughout all levels of government in the 1970s (O'Connor, 1973), the situation was most desperate in cities, where increasing budgetary shortfalls led to retrenchment of city services, deterioration of urban social and physical infrastructures, and increased reliance on state and federal aid. The fiscal crisis had important implications for social policy. It reduced the city's capacity to take ameliorative action because many factors were out of local control, including the economic changes that produced the fiscal crisis in the first place and the federal relief on which cities had come to depend (Gurr and King, 1987, p. 79).

The root cause of city-suburb inequality and the fiscal crisis of the city is the fact that capital is mobile, while the city is stationary. As capital concentrated into larger units and became transnational, its allegiance to specific locales evaporated. Now advanced technology has increased capital mobility so that it is continually migrating to places where it can maximize profits— places with low tax rates, cheap nonunion labor, and large plots of real estate at low cost. Meanwhile, the city, because it is first and irreducibly a built and unmovable environment, decays.

One of the most visible signs that the city is suffering serious damage is the spectacle of thousands of citizens living on its streets and in its public facilities. We now turn to an analysis of the homelessness problem.

HOMELESSNESS

Homelessness represents a naked failure of social policy. A major misconception about homelessness is that it was created by deinstitutionalization and that, consequently, most homeless people are mentally ill. In fact, homelessness is primarily the result of changing economic conditions and the failure of housing policy. This conclusion is elucidated below, together with an analysis of the homeless population and of social policy ideas to deal with homelessness.

The Homeless Population

Because of the inherent difficulty of counting homeless people and because their presence is an embarrassment to incumbent politicians, gauges of their number vary considerably. Estimates of the U.S. homeless population ranged in the late 1980s from a low of 250,000 to a high of 5 million. The low estimate, which was by the Department of Housing and Urban Development (DHUD), used a restrictive definition of homelessness (Rivlin, 1986, p. 3). Additionally, there are millions of people on the verge of homelessness. In New York City alone it was estimated in 1987 that there were about 100,000 poor families doubled up with relatives and friends, facing the possibility of immediate eviction (Daley, 1987). These "couch people" constitute the hidden homeless, and they have not yet drawn the attention of society. The overwhelming majority of the homeless are poor and are long-term unemployed persons; however, a small but growing minority are middle class. One reliable estimate was that 5 to 15 percent of New York City's homeless shelter population in 1988 were middle-class people (Polner and Schwartzman, 1988).

The biggest concentrations of homeless people are in large cities: in 1986, 60,000 in New York City, 50,000 in Los Angeles, 27,000 in Detroit, 25,000 each in Houston and Chicago, and 20,000 in Baltimore (Pear, 1986). Although homelessness exists in other Welfare States, their homeless populations are much smaller than ours; for example, there were an estimated 3,000 homeless people in London and 500 in Tokyo in 1987 (Barbanel, 1987). The National Coalition for the Homeless estimated that, in 1987, 20 percent of homeless Americans were children, many of whom did not attend school. In 1987 the New York City Board of Education reported that only one-half of the ap-proximately 6,000 school-age homeless children temporarily housed in wel-fare hotels were known to be attending school. Families, especially female-headed families, constitute an increasing proportion of the homeless population. A 1987 national survey by the Conference of Mayors reported that between 1986 and 1987 the number of families that requested emergency shel-ter increased by 31 percent. A 1987 survey of forty-seven cities by the Partner-ship for the Homeless (located in New York City) found that between November 1986 and March 1987 the number of homeless families with children rose by 25 percent and now makes up 35 percent of the homeless population.

Although still primarily a problem of the cities, homelessness is also growing rapidly in the suburbs. Local public officials estimated that between 1984 and 1987 the number of homeless people living in the suburbs of New York City doubled, to between 30,000 and 54,000 people (Schmitt, 1987). This is still about 40 percent less than the estimated number of homeless people in New York City, but the suburban homeless population is expected to continue to rise as affordable housing and federal housing assistance become increas-ingly scarce. Although the data are unconfirmed, official figures indicate that a major difference between city and suburban homelessness is that many sub-urban homeless people—about 20 percent of the total—have jobs and are among the working poor, while virtually none of New York City's homeless people are employed.

Causes of Homelessness

The causes of contemporary homelessness are threefold. In order of im-portance, the decline in the U.S. economy since the early 1970s ranks first. This decline produced higher rates of poverty and unemployment, which are the principal factors in creating homelessness. It also produced lower-paying jobs and higher proportions of the working poor. One estimate is that 44 percent of the jobs created between 1979 and 1984 paid poverty-level wages (Marcuse, 1987).

The second most important cause of homelessness is a critical shortage of affordable housing. For example, in New York City in 1987 the overall vacancy rate was 2 percent, but in low-rent housing it was only 1 percent. Be-cause public housing construction was virtually stopped by the Reagan ad-ministration, the New York City Housing Authority had a waiting list of 200,000 households in 1987; at 1987 turnover rates, this meant an eighteen-year wait (Dumpson, 1987). In a study of eleven large cities Wright and Lam

(1987) found that, from the late 1970s to the early 1980s, the number of poor people increased by 36 percent, while the number of low-income rental housing units declined by about 30 percent.

Much of this general shortage of affordable housing results from urban renewal, the development of the corporate city, and gentrification, all of which eliminated large numbers of low-rent housing units in favor of office buildings, parking lots, expressways, and luxury housing. According to data compiled by the Neighborhood Reinvestment Corporation, between 1974 and 1983 low-rent housing declined at a rate of about 120,000 units a year nationally, while the number of households that needed low-rent housing increased by an average of about 330,000 a year. This growing gap between social need and social provision is projected to produce a deficit of 3.7 million low-rent housing units by 1993 and 7.8 million by 2003.

The third most important cause of contemporary homelessness is the deinstitutionalization of the mentally ill, wrongly assumed by the public to be the major, or even sole, cause of homelessness.

We now turn to discussions of two specific sources of homelessness, gentrification and deinstitutionalization. Following these discussions, we analyze social policy issues in housing and the Reagan legacy for housing.

Gentrification Gentrification of city neighborhoods has been a major cause of the decline in low-income housing. Gentrification is the process by which low-income housing in lower-middle-class, working-class, and poor neighborhoods is converted to middle-class and upper-class housing. (*Gentry* is an old English word for people of hereditary high social rank.) Research has confirmed that gentrifiers are young, white, affluent, and single or childless couples (LeGates and Murphy, 1984). However, gentrification is more than a lifestyle phenomenon in which yuppies (young, upwardly mobile professionals) move into an area and conspicuously consume commodities such as housing and food. Beneath this surface, gentrification is produced by capitalist economic processes, including uneven development, so that gentrifiable housing is rented at lower-than-potential market rent, yielding opportunities for investment and speculation (Beauregard, 1984, p. 61). Gentrification is based on real estate speculation, on housing conversion from low-rent flats to condominiums and other expensive housing, and on commercial conversion from businesses serving the former poor and working-class residents, such as mom-and-pop stores, to businesses serving an upscale clientele, such as gourmet food stores.

Empirical analysis by LeGates and Hartman (1986), based on sixteen displacement studies, has demonstrated that gentrification is widespread. They conservatively estimate that annual displacement in the United States is about 2.5 million persons. This displacement has resulted in hardships for the out-movers. A large number experienced increased rents and decreased quality in their new housing. The data on gentrifiers confirmed the yuppie stereotype. However, the yuppies did not, as commonly assumed, come from the suburbs. The majority moved from within the same city. Marcuse's (1986, p. 164) work also demonstrated that, in four gentrifying areas of Manhattan, gentrification did not result from "a massive influx of additional well-to-do in the city, but rather from a spatial reshuffling of a relatively constant or even declining number."

The overall economic cause of gentrification is the dichotomizing of American society, which is starkly illustrated in the city. At the upper end of the stratification system is great prosperity, highlighted by substantial corporate profits and the emergence of nouveau-riche yuppies. At the lower end of the system is increasing deprivation and misery, dramatized by the rising numbers of homeless, unemployed, and working-poor Americans. In the middle of the stratification system are many middle-class and stably employed working-class people, who are under intense economic pressure and threatened by a decline in their real standards of living.

Continued gentrification holds the potential for creating a sharply polarized city, divided into a core that is a bourgeois playground of upscale recreational and entertainment facilities such as health spas, trendy clubs, and boutiques, and a surrounding city that is home to the working class and poor (Williams and Smith, 1986, pp. 217–219). In fact, this is exactly what is happening in New York City: the core, Manhattan (especially below 96th Street), is dominated by middle-class and upper-class residential areas and pricey restaurants and shops, with its remaining poor, lower-middle-class, and working-class areas undergoing gentrification. The Manhattanization of city cores into elite enclaves is paralleled by increasing ghettoization of the working class and poor, especially minorities, into peripheral areas. Such polarization is a potential source of major social and political conflict for cities and for Welfare States.

Deinstitutionalization Most of the homeless are not deinstitutionalized mentally ill persons. An epidemiological study of 979 homeless people in Ohio found that under one-third of the sample was in need of mental health services. Moreover, the data suggested that mental illness may be a result of homelessness as well as a cause of it (Bean, Stefl, and Howe, 1987). A 1987 survey of twenty-nine cities conducted by the Conference of Mayors did not list deinstitutionalization among the three principal causes of homelessness. The causes, in order of importance, were: (1) lack of affordable housing, (2) lack of jobs, and (3) inadequate public welfare benefits. Local data from New York City also support the view that homelessness is caused primarily by economic factors. In 1987 the city's Human Resources Administration reported that about 25 percent of adult shelter residents had a history of mental illness, while 40 percent were homeless because they had lost their jobs. A 1988 study of homeless individuals in twenty cities by the Urban Institute (Washington, DC) found that only 20 percent had a history of mental hospitalization.

Attributing homelessness to deinstitutionalization of the mentally ill is a form of blaming the victim, or what Marcuse (1988, p. 88) calls *specialism*.

Specialism defines the social problem of homelessness as one caused by individuals with a special characteristic—mental illness. In fact, homelessness is a product of general economic and social changes, which deinstitutionalization contributed to but did not create.

Between 1955 and 1980 the state mental institution population in the United States declined from 559,000 to 138,000 (Gudeman and Shore, 1984). This deinstitutionalization was rooted in four factors that coalesced in the late 1950s and 1960s. First, the development of antipsychotic, neuroleptic drugs enabled medicine to stabilize (or somnambulize) mental patients outside the confines of institutions. The most prominent example was thorazine, a phenothiazine used to treat the symptoms of schizophrenia (Scheff, 1985, p. 257). Second, investigators exposed the dungeonlike conditions of mental institutions, stirring up public and official response. Numerous reports described the inhumane, overcrowded, and unsanitary conditions of state mental institutions and likened them to human warehouses (Edgerton, 1982, pp. 223–224). Third, civil libertarians and mental patients' rights groups pressed the legal rights of the mentally ill. Legal suits by and on behalf of inmates resulted in court mandates enforcing their rights to effective treatment, to refuse treatment, and to refuse institutional labor. A landmark case was *Donaldson vs. O'Connor* in 1975, in which the U.S. Supreme Court ruled that nondangerous inmates who were not receiving treatment should be released (Brown, 1985, p. 196).

Fourth, government wanted to staunch the rising costs of institutionalization. This was the principal cause of deinstitutionalization according to an analysis by Scull (1984, pp. 157, 159). He argued that the expensive system of segregative control of the mentally ill was curtailed in favor of extending public welfare payments to enable the mentally ill to be supported outside institutions, largely to save costs. Scull ascertained that the transfer of patients from state hospitals to boarding homes in California in 1970 resulted in a net savings of $4,300 per patient per year. Principally as a result of this deinstitutionalization, California mental health expenditure declined from 2.6 percent of the state budget in 1959 to 1.7 percent in 1970.

We should stop here to note that deinstitutionalization is *not* a failed policy. Based on a study of Massachusetts, Gudeman and Shore (1984) concluded that only 4 to 5 percent of patients have been inappropriately deinstitutionalized since 1959. The great majority of mentally ill people do not require institutional care. In an analysis of ten experimental studies Kiesler (1985) found that alternative care was at least as effective as inpatient care. He concluded that the majority of patients now being treated in mental institutions could have outside care that would be at least as effective. The key is alternative *care*—meaning quality treatment that emphasizes social support and skill training. Under those conditions, deinstitutionalization of most mentally ill persons is viable—in fact, it is the preferred policy for effectiveness as well as for quality-of-life reasons.

Keeping in mind the need to protect the constitutional rights of the mentally ill and the goal of a normalized life for them, social policy should favor, in descending order, the following: (1) independent living, (2) living with family or friends, (3) supervised community living, (4) community residential facilities (with less than sixteen beds), (5) large institutions with community programs, and (6) small units in large institutions (Lerman, 1982, p. 170). Reinstitutionalization of the mentally ill is plainly not the right moral, legal, or therapeutic choice, although it may be preferred by public officials who are under pressure to do something quickly about homelessness and who lack the resources to provide adequate noninstitutional care.

The *apparent* failure of deinstitutionalization was actually a failure to reintegrate former inmates into the fabric of society. In short, the mentally ill were pushed out of institutions without being given the resources to maintain themselves—namely, adequate housing, jobs, and medical care. The federal government bears a major responsibility for this failure. The overall effect of federal policies, especially Medicare and Medicaid, has been to limit the development and use of community support for the mentally ill (Bassuk and Gerson, 1985, p. 137). Instead, federal policies channeled the mentally ill into nursing homes, inadequate housing, and the streets, with minimal opportunities for psychiatric, occupational, and social rehabilitation. Carrying this conclusion further, Scull (1982, p. 247) has argued that, with the help of federal funds, "mental patients have been transformed into a commodity from which various professionals and entrepreneurs extract a profit." It will be difficult to improve this situation without the adoption of a national health insurance policy (discussed in Chapter 8).

Homelessness and Social Policy

To meet the needs of homeless people, housing policy has to generate a large number of low-rent units. Temporary shelter is no solution. Shelters for the homeless are notorious for their lack of privacy, sanitation, and safety, all of which force many homeless people to stay on the street (Fabricant and Kelly, 1987, p. 27). The need for a home is not a temporary need. Only permanent, decent, affordable housing in livable neighborhoods can resolve the problem.

One resolution to the housing problems of formerly institutionalized persons is the group home. A group home is a publicly subsidized and supervised residence for a small number of mentally retarded or mentally ill people who can live outside an institution if they have proper support. The residences are regular homes in urban and suburban neighborhoods. Unfortunately, resistance by local home owners is often strong enough to prevent the establishment of group homes (Mechanic, 1989, p. 209). Some group homes have even been maliciously burned to the ground. However, New York has demonstrated an effective legal remedy for this impasse. The state passed the Padavan Law in 1978 to enable group homes to bypass local zoning regulations, as long as they meet state codes. The law also controls the siting of group homes so that they are spread out and do not saturate one or two neighborhoods. The state provides 100 percent financing for the purchase of a group home by a nonprofit agency. Largely as a result of the law, in the years 1978–1988, the number of beds for the mentally ill in group homes in New York State grew from 308 to 6,354 (Winerip, 1988).

One promising technique for preventing at least some homelessness is case management service, used by the King Center in Tacoma (discussed later in this chapter) and other agencies. As noted earlier, a cause of homelessness was the deinstitutionalization of chronically mentally ill persons without the provision of adequate community support. The current dominance of the medical model (discussed in Chapter 8) in the treatment of mental illness stresses clinical services, partial hospitalization, day treatment, and medication, all performed by professionals. Although such services may be necessary, they are by no means sufficient to prevent the problem of homelessness among the chronically mentally ill. Medical treatment is too expensive to be widely effective, and it does not address the environmental problems of the potentially homeless, including lack of adequate housing and work. These problems call for social treatment, of which case management service is an example.

Case managers are nonprofessional or preprofessional workers with training and experience who serve as personal helpers for the chronically ill in the community. The model of case management developed by Rapp and Chamberlain (1985) focuses on the social problems of the mentally ill rather than on their illnesses. This focus is consistent with research findings about the needs of the chronically mentally ill, as noted by Burt and Pittman (1985, p. 69): "The evidence from numerous studies strongly suggests that many basic needs of chronically mentally ill persons lie not in therapy or treatment for a mental condition, but in shelter, food, clothing, medical care, and provision of structure to their days, delivered within a rehabilitation framework." The help that case managers offer is therapeutic in that symptoms are reduced when social problems such as unemployment are ameliorated.

Rapp and Chamberlain (1985) used preprofessional workers (both workers with Bachelor of Social Work degrees and graduate students in Master of Social Work programs) as case managers and stressed community outreach rather than deskwork. In an exploratory study of this approach, Rapp and Chamberlain followed nineteen chronically ill persons (fifteen had histories of multiple hospitalization) served by case managers over a six-month period in a Kansas community. The results were positive: Seventeen people reported satisfaction with the service and none were hospitalized or became homeless during the six months. Case management service can be linked to community homes for the chronically mentally ill to prevent homelessness. This combination provides supportive housing and a surrogate family for the mentally ill person. It combines the direct personal touch of case managers with the availability of medical care on an outpatient basis.

An ironic contradiction of contemporary urban life is the juxtaposition of thousands of unoccupied buildings and thousands of homeless people. In

New York City in 1987, while 28,000 homeless people were placed nightly in municipal shelters and welfare hotels, there were 72,000 empty apartments. One grass-roots response to this contradiction is squatting, which is most highly developed in the Netherlands (Van Weesep, 1984). Squatting is the illegal occupation of abandoned public-owned buildings. Squatters do not pay rent but do invest in improvements in buildings, largely through sweat equity. Although it is difficult to estimate their number because their success often depends on secrecy, there are probably at least 8,000 squatters in Amsterdam alone. The majority are young, poor, and either students or unemployed. Some squatters are eventually legalized when the government converts the occupied property into low-income housing. Squatting has been successful enough in the Netherlands to generate classified newspaper ads in which squatters propose swaps of apartments and buildings.

Squatting has also met with some success in U.S. cities, although it is difficult to mobilize and to sustain. In the late 1970s and early 1980s local community activists and the national Association of Community Organizations for Reform Now (ACORN) organized hundreds of North Philadelphia residents to occupy vacant, single-family, DHUD-owned houses. Most squatters, after much work, eventually received title to the homes at nominal cost or else became renters from DHUD (Borgos, 1984). Their success was attributed in part to the recognition that the morality of homeless or ill-housed people occupying vacant houses outweighed its illegality. However, after the initial success of the squatting movement in North Philadelphia, local pressure from the conservative Rizzo administration forced DHUD to take an antisquatting position, which resulted in the movement's demise (Gendrot, 1982, p. 294). Nevertheless, squatting continues to be a widespread indigenous phenomenon, and ACORN is its national advocate.

Current policies are heavily weighted against squatting. Even the federal homesteading program adopted in the Housing and Community Development Act of 1974, which is supposed to encourage such developments as the conversion of vacant housing, is opposed to squatting. The current federal policy is not mass housing for people who need it—the poor, the homeless, and the unemployed—but showcase rehabilitation of housing for middle-class applicants, none of whom are homeless and many of whom are merely speculating in property.

The conservative legacy Thus far homelessness in the United States has been dealt with in a traditionally conservative style that focuses on voluntary efforts, especially from religious groups, and is rooted in the concept of charity. This traditional treatment may help to explain why homelessness exploded into national consciousness as a social problem in the early 1980s (Stern, 1984). It dovetailed with the ascendance of Reaganism.

The conservative Reagan administration turned its back on the needs of cities for housing. Between 1980 and 1987 DHUD's budget plunged from $35.7 billion to $14.2 billion. The budget cuts were especially harmful to low-income persons. Federal subsidies for low-income housing fell by 60 percent between 1982 and 1987 (Riordan, 1987, p. 26; Schwartz, 1984, p. 163). We now turn to critiques of two major Reagan administration urban policies, privatization and enterprise zones.

Privatization of public services (also discussed in Chapters 6 and 11) was a favored policy of the Reagan administration, following from its conservative goals to reduce the size and influence of government and to increase the role of the private marketplace. Privatization is the reverse of the social democratic policy of nationalization. The conservative version of privatization simply transfers public functions to the marketplace. Thus government activities are sold to private, profit-making businesses. This version of privatization does not contemplate transferring public functions to private but nonprofit interests, such as cooperatives and community organizations.

Three empirical studies cast considerable doubt on the efficacy of privatization. First, in a study of refuse removal in Tucson, Marlowe (1985) found that private subscription service cost 60 percent more than municipal provision and that there were no significant differences in consumer evaluation of the two methods. A second example of the problems of privatization was the collapse in the mid-1970s of the private, for-profit reprocessing of radioactive waste. Campbell's (1987) comparative analysis demonstrated that the private approach in the United States failed at nuclear waste management, while the public approach in France succeeded. While the nuclear waste industries in both nations eventually operated at a financial loss, in France the industry survived in the form of a government-owned company. In the United States, largely because of private requirements for profit, the industry collapsed. In a third study Drew (1984) looked at three test cases of human service subcontracting: Area Agencies on Aging (AAAs) in Chicago, Detroit, and Philadelphia. AAAs were established under the 1973 Amendments of the Older Americans Act of 1965 to fund a range of services for the elderly, including referral, transportation, nutrition, and homemaker services. Research demonstrated that the economic self-interests of the for-profit subcontractors reinforced competition and reduced coordination, and that the lack of central control over subcontractors produced fragmented services and program failure.

A centerpiece of Reagan's privatization policy was the housing voucher. Vouchers are provided by the government to low-income families to use for their housing. Under the 1987 federal formula, a family of four earning less than $14,750 (in the New York region) qualified for $134 per month in rent supplements to be used on housing of the family's choice. Vouchers, however, do nothing about the central problem: lack of decent low-rent housing. Thus three of every four vouchers distributed in New York from 1983, when Congress authorized the program, to 1987 were returned because the holders could not secure affordable apartments that met federal quality standards (DePalma, 1987).

In addition to vouchers, the Reagan administration pushed strongly for the sale of public housing units to their occupants in an effort to privatize public housing. This effort, too, failed, because of the basic economic problems of the poor people who occupy public housing. This tenant population does not have the income necessary to pay for the operation and maintenance of public housing developments at their current levels. Rent payments cover only about two-thirds of these costs; the remainder is subsidized by government. If title on these buildings were transferred to tenants, they would incur drastic maintenance costs that would force most of them out of public housing.

Urban enterprise zones are another conservative policy that tried to use the for-profit private sector to resolve social problems. These zones were areas of high unemployment and poverty in cities that were designated by government to attract new business. Government recruited business by reducing taxes and regulation. Enterprise zones have been tried for some forty years in Third World countries without any sustained success (Hill, 1983, p. 12). The general pattern is for businesses to move in when enterprise zones are opened, to take advantage of the incentives, and then, when economic development begins to take off and wages and taxes rise, to seek cheaper labor and lower taxes elsewhere. The end result is the return of decline and stagnation to the enterprise zone.

Enterprise zones have failed to revive the economic health of older industrial cities for another reason. In a study of the 130 largest U.S. cities Kennedy (1984) found that efforts to promote private investment through social investment expenditure by government (such as for police and fire protection) did not produce the expected results; in fact, these expenses became a primary source of fiscal strain. The reason was that the autonomous suburban communities that hem in the city were able to keep their taxes low, enabling them to capture industry from the city and to become the residence of executive and professional employees. The same problem did not exist in the newer corporate cities, where social investment expenditure slightly reduced fiscal strain.

Other factors have contributed to the failure of enterprise zone policy. From its inception, the policy was targeted for small areas rather than neighborhoods. There was no integrated perspective on urban aid and neighborhood development. All the things that make a local area a neighborhood—social and political factors, including an active community role in implementation—were ignored. Local issues were not addressed and local government was not brought in, as both were considered barriers to free market development (Clarke, 1982). Reagan administration enterprise zones preferred to rely exclusively on the uninhibited workings of the private marketplace.

Perhaps the most important reason for the failure of enterprise zones is that public incentives in a private market can never attract enough investment to permanently turn around an area's decline because business relies on many other factors when deciding where to locate, including availability of needed material resources, transportation, and real and potential markets. As Walton (1982) pointed out, public incentives are often unnecessary windfalls to private corporations that have already made a site decision on other grounds.

If enterprise zones are ever to succeed, it will be because of the active involvement of government, not reliance on the private sector. After a comprehensive analysis of enterprise zones in the Reagan years, Bendick and Rasmussen (1986, p. 98) concluded that "enterprise zones can help revitalize distressed inner-city areas, but they do so largely through state-initiated programs that bear little resemblance to the original concept endorsed by the Reagan administration."

We have seen how the social problem of homelessness worsened under the Reagan administration. We now look at that problem from the perspective of social practitioners who work with the homeless.

SOCIAL PRACTICE

In 1984 there were 2.8 million municipal employees in the United States. About one-half worked in education, public safety, hospitals, and utilities. City workers represented 17.3 percent of all government employees and 2.7 percent of all employed workers in the United States. Only 1.8 percent of municipal employees worked in housing, a total of 43,000 workers. In addition, in 1985 DHUD had 12,289 employees, or 0.4 percent of the federal civilian work force. This relatively low number of workers stems from two factors: housing is a commodity, not a service such as education that requires deliverers; and housing is dominated by the private sector, not by government.

Nowhere are the privatization and middle-class bias of U.S. housing policy more apparent than in the presence of millions of homeless people in the streets and public spaces of our cities. Moreover, since the early 1980s, when contemporary homelessness emerged as a major problem, little or no improvement has been made in these people's situation. Indeed, it is a reasonable conclusion that the conservative social policies of the 1980s helped to create and now help to sustain homelessness. Progressive initiatives in dealing with homelessness are grass-roots efforts. The following presentation of the work of Maureen Howard in Tacoma, Washington, is a good example.

Social Practitioner at Work: Maureen Howard

Maureen Howard has been director of the Martin Luther King Ecumenical Center in Tacoma, Washington, since 1982. The Center was founded in 1969 by three local churches—African Methodist Episcopal, Catholic, and Episcopal—to serve the social needs of the neighborhood in Tacoma with the largest proportions of minority (African American, Mexican American, and Native American) and poor people. It is a private, nonprofit agency supported by grants and contributions from the three churches, as well as from foundations, government, and the United Way. In addition, the Center earns income from a farm that it manages outside Tacoma. Martin's Farm is eight acres devoted to growing vegetables, herbs, and flowers, and to employing the homeless. About thirty homeless people work for the Center; in addition to working on the farm, they staff all its other activities, including its clothing bank and housing programs. The Center's goal is to provide permanent housing and employment, not just a temporary handout, to the homeless.

Maureen grew up in a small town in Washington State. She received a Bachelor of Arts degree in Education from Eastern Washington University and a Master of Arts in Theology from Notre Dame University. She was hired at the Center after several years of work in adult basic education among urban illiterate people. Maureen's interest in helping others is motivated by a strong sense of social justice. She was attracted to this ideal originally through the teachings of the Catholic Church. In addition to her work at the Center, Maureen teaches human service courses at Tacoma Community College. She likes her work because its grass-roots nature provides her with the "creativity and freedom to look at things differently" from the way they are seen by large institutions.

Although Maureen finds her work satisfying, it has its drawbacks. The Center operates in continual insecurity; it is dependent on "soft" money (contributions and grants) that is raised on a year-to-year basis. Also, it is always short of needed resources such as telephones. Maureen finds the constant fund-raising and grant-writing part of her work challenging but frustrating as well, because it takes time from her work with homeless people.

The Martin Luther King Ecumenical Center operates three distinct programs for the homeless in several dozen sites: temporary, transitional, and permanent housing. Temporary housing consists of the Last Chance Shelter and Mandela House for overnight stays and Sojourner Housing for stays up to thirty days. The Last Chance Shelter accommodates seventy-five single men; it also houses a Healthcare for the Homeless Clinic. Mandela House is for single women without children. Sojourner Housing is for homeless families with children, and ill and disabled persons. The Center's temporary housing is deliberately small in scale to avoid the congestion that characterizes many shelters for the homeless, in which there are as many as 1,200 beds separated by no more than inches. Large, overcrowded shelters create "a workhouse-like atmosphere that reduces homeless people to the station of a cheaply stored commodity" (Fabricant, 1988, p. 49).

The Center's transitional housing is for families, and keeps people from one month to two years. Here the families receive case management services, which are personalized social services that help them acquire clothing, enroll their kids in school, and get on public aid. One transitional housing site, The White House, is specifically reserved for the hard-to-reach homeless who are often mentally ill or alcoholic. The Center operates a street-level outreach program to recruit these hard-to-reach homeless and serves as their advocate in applying for social benefits from Social Security and local public assistance departments. In 1987 the Center established a nonprofit corporation, the Martin Luther King Housing Development Association, to acquire and rehabilitate vacant housing. The restored housing is let at low rent to home-less families until they can secure permanent housing.

The third program is permanent housing, which Maureen called "the only real, true solution to the problem" of homelessness. The Center's per-manent housing program is Project Second Chance; it is a joint venture with the Pierce County Housing Authority. Homeless people who qualify are provided vouchers that entitle them to rental public housing. This program is reserved for homeless family heads who are presently unemployed but who are capable of work, as they will eventually have to pay rent. The Center provides social services, including employment counseling, as well as hous-ing. Many of the family members are given work on the Center's farm and in other staff jobs, but this is regarded as only a temporary solution to their employment problems.

Maureen described her job as "seeing the faces" behind the numbers and statistics on which policymakers rely. She likes having personal contact with the people she is helping and thinks that policymakers could gain from having it as well. She believes that social policy is often "disconnected to the realities of people's lives." Maureen is concerned that even reasonably conceived so-cial policies fail to live up to their potential because their implementation does not consider the experiences of the people being served. She sees her contribu-tion to social policy as facilitating the upward flow of ideas and feelings—up-ward from the homeless to those who make and implement social policies. The creativity of her work, Maureen stated, is "to ask the people who have the problem to voice their solutions."

For Maureen, current social policy for homelessness is woefully inade-quate in its conception of the problem as well as in its response. For one thing, homelessness is an ongoing problem that demands permanent, not tem-porary, housing. Also, homelessness and unemployment (and to some extent mental illness) are related problems that should be addressed simultaneous-ly. Finally, Maureen suggested that some attention should be directed to the "about-to-be-homeless." These are people on the verge of being evicted, either by landlords or by others with whom they have been living temporarily. They are doubling or tripling up with friends or relatives, or paying over 70 percent of their budgets for rent so that they are on a precarious, month-to-month foot-ing with their landlords.

Maureen believes that rather than waiting for people to become home-less, "we should be anticipating and preventing the problem." The earlier the problem is addressed, the easier it is to deal with and the better are the results for people. If homelessness can be anticipated, then many people will not end up living in the streets. Consistent with Maureen's idea is the recommenda-tion by the 1987 Report of the Manhattan Borough President's Task Force on Housing for Homeless Families (Dumpson, 1987, pp. 80–81) to create an early-warning system of outreach to families in imminent danger of homelessness. Such an early-warning system would be staffed by New York City's Human Resources Administration, Housing Court, and specially trained caseworkers.

For Maureen, homelessness means "the loss of human connection." What the homeless need, in addition to permanent housing, is social connection with other people. On the streets they are often isolated, and this fact alone can result in serious personal and mental problems. Social policy has not even begun to address this problem, for it is focused almost exclusively on temporary shelter, but Maureen's observation about the importance of social connections to homeless people has been confirmed by research. In an ethnographic study in Austin, Texas, Snow and Anderson (1987) found that identity-related concerns were salient among homeless people and coexisted with their concerns for basic material needs.

SOCIAL POLICY AND THE FUTURE OF THE CITY

As Maureen Howard's comments indicate, there is no coherence to U.S. urban policy; what we have are many disparate policies, all of which fluctuate in response to economic conditions and political protest. In addition to being highly cyclical, these policies are neither planned nor coordinated. Federal, state, and local policies are fragmented and financing is unpredictable.

Current social policies for the city accept and even strengthen the major source of urban problems: capital mobility. Cities and regions (and nations) vie with one another to offer the most extravagant incentives for capital investment. The Reagan administration's encouragement of local competition and its stinginess in social programs only reinforced capital mobility. Local and state government are no match for the economic power and mobility of transnational corporations (Friedland, 1983b).

In the heightened economic competition some Snowbelt cities lose and sink further into decline and fiscal crisis and some Sunbelt cities win and gain a reprieve. However, even the cities that win eventually lose. The development of the Sunbelt and its corporate cities is already riddled with problems. The service sector that has led Sunbelt economic expansion has produced a large mass of low-wage workers whose social needs for roads, schools, and hospitals are putting sharp new pressures on urban infrastructures. In addition, the rapid and unrestrained private development of Sunbelt cities has caused large and growing problems with transportation and environmental pollution. Sunbelt cities, notably Los Angeles, Denver, and Phoenix, now have the most polluted air of American cities. Moreover, alas, capital will eventually extract all the advantages it can and then move on, perhaps to the Third World.

Effective social policy, then, must recognize and deal with the source of the problem—capital mobility. This means focusing on the regulation of major corporate investment decisions by decentralized public bodies, as utilities are presently regulated. Capital is a social resource that has immense social potential; it should not be entirely in the hands of private, self-aggrandizing individuals. As Smith (1979, pp. 282–283) pointed out, public control of corporate locational decisions is needed at the national level as well, in order to ensure regional balance, ecological protection, and needed investment in central cities.

Socialist societies have demonstrated the efficacy of public control of some of the negative effects of uneven development. In socialist Cuba (Barkin, 1978), the U.S.S.R., and the People's Republic of China (Sawers, 1978), measures were taken to avoid the worst excesses of uneven development of the city and the countryside. The construction of greenbelts, comprised of parks, gardens, and forests, around cities and the siting of new industry in the countryside and in small cities were specific mechanisms used to limit the growth of large cities and to promote the development of rural areas. Although these socialist policies did not prevent urban growth, they slowed it and resulted in better management of the problems created by uneven development.

The single most important current social policy bearing on the city is public housing, which we consider next. This part of the chapter focuses on two other issues of import for social policy: (1) measures of the quality of city life and (2) mismatch problems involving city versus suburb and skills of city residents versus the nature of available jobs.

Public Housing

In 1987 there were about 1.3 million families living in public housing in the United States and nearly a million other families on waiting lists to get into public housing. Public housing was inaugurated with the 1930s New Deal and effectively interred under the Reagan administration. New units of federal public housing declined from 68,509 in 1978 to the following figures for Reagan years: 23,730 units in 1981; 5,670 in 1982; –6,651 in 1983 (more units were dropped than added); –93 in 1984; and 1,426 in 1985 (Herbers, 1987). In 1978 authorizations for housing were 7 percent of the federal budget; in 1987 they were down to one-tenth of that, or only 0.7 percent.

The housing problem increased sharply in the 1970s and 1980s. Between 1970 and 1983 rents rose twice as fast as incomes. Lower-income citizens were hit hardest by the spiralling cost of housing. In 1970, 48 percent of households earning less than $10,000 paid more than 25 percent of their income for housing. By 1983, 83 percent of such households were paying more than 25 percent of their income for housing. The shortage of housing has driven up its price. Vacancy rates for low-rent apartments are in the range of 1 to 2 percent in major cities; in some, such as Boston, the vacancy rate is effectively zero (Shields, 1988).

U.S. public housing policy has been characterized by sporadic expansion, mandated by widespread social needs, as in the 1930s, or by general social unrest, as in the 1960s. The New Deal administration of Franklin Delano Roosevelt produced the 1934 National Housing Act, which established the FHA, and the 1938 Housing Act, which inaugurated public housing and urban renewal. The Great Society of the Kennedy-Johnson administration produced the 1965 Housing and Urban Development Act, which created the Department of Housing and Urban Development, and the 1966 Demonstration Cities Act, which created the Model Cities Program. Interspersed between these periods of expansion were stretches of neglect, retrenchment, and negative policies for cities. In 1956 the National Interstate and Defense Highway Act of the Eisenhower administration, along with the earlier 1949 expansion of urban renewal, laid the basis for the wholesale devastation of many inner cities. The 1974 Housing and Community Development Act of the Nixon-Ford administration created the "new federalism" of the community development block grant, which effectively transferred the control of aid to cities from city government to state and federal governments.

Marcuse's (1982) comparative study of West Germany and the United States demonstrates the extent to which private economic interests, especially in construction and real estate, rather than social needs or grassroots demand, dominate housing policy under capitalism. State policy buttresses private interests in many ways, including favoring home ownership (e.g., through its tax policies) and stigmatizing public housing. Current housing policies in the United States strongly favor the well-to-do and disfavor the poor. Although Marcuse's data show that West Germany is more egalitarian than the United States in distributing housing benefits, they also demonstrate that substantial inequality still exists in West Germany.

Largely because of governmental neglect, some public housing developments have physically deteriorated and some are plagued with social problems. Although not a panacea for the internal problems of public housing, tenant management can help. Of fifteen tests of tenant management conducted in the mid-1980s, five failed, eight were still in process, and two were effective: Cochran Gardens in St. Louis and Kenilworth-Parkside in Washington, D.C. (Muwakkil, 1987). Three factors seem to be crucial to the success of tenant-managed public housing: (1) a strong sense of community among residents, (2) a sympathetic housing authority, and (3) strong tenant leadership. Cochran Gardens was built in the 1930s and has about 4,000 residents. Its tenant organization got the capital to carry out needed renovations through an Urban Development Action Grant. As a condition for participating in the redevelopment of its downtown area, the tenant organization received $5.5 million. It then hired tenants so that youths who formerly vandalized the complex were put to work reconstructing it. Since the work was supervised by skilled workers, some of the youths gained enough experience to become apprentices in the building trades (Lehman, 1988).

A study (Gulati, 1982) of tenant participation (which is a level below tenant management) in the administration of 750 public housing developments found that it, too, can improve the quality of life for residents—for example, by increasing services. However, there was no evidence that tenant participation enhanced the administrative process; for instance, it did not reduce rent collection losses. The findings also suggested that tenant participation was more prevalent in highly adverse circumstances, such as severely deteriorated housing, making whatever success tenants achieved that much more remarkable.

While the shortage of public housing is acute, it is only part of a more general housing problem in the United States. More and more Americans are finding it impossible to secure decent, affordable housing. The very term *affordable housing* illustrates the fact that much housing is not affordable. One creative local solution to this problem was a partnership between the Massachusetts Housing Finance Agency and the Bricklayers and Laborers Union, which was formed to build subsidized mixed-income housing in Boston. With the state as financial backer, the union developed property through the formation of a nonprofit corporation. As of early in 1989, the nonprofit corporation had built 230 housing units, which sold for about 40 percent below market prices (Duke and Kluver, 1989). One of the complexes that was built, Tent City in the South End, took its name from the occupation of that site in the late 1960s by community activists who were protesting gentrification of their neighborhood. Because the housing was built without the need for profit, more attention was paid to quality construction and to aesthetics. The result was that this affordable housing for the working class received rave reviews from architecture critics (Goldberger, 1988).

Assessing the Quality of City Life

One technique to improve the quality of life in cities is the use of local indicators (Lyon, 1987), an elaboration of social indicators, which are discussed in Chapter 10. Local indicators are objective measures of various aspects of city life, including education (educational attainment is one measure), health (communicable disease index), housing (crowding, as measured by square feet per person), racism and sexism (unemployment ratios), political activity (percentage of citizens voting), and environment (concentration of particulate matter in the air). The U.S. Census is the major source of these and other relevant measures, especially in its *County and City Data Book.*

Local indicators can be quite helpful in assessing, comparing, and changing the quality of life in cities. The data can be used to make cross-sectional (different cities at the same time) and longitudinal (over-time) comparisons. Local indicators have some major limitations, however. Data on a whole city can conceal important internal variations. Thus, while a city's average educational attainment is high, it may be very low for specific subgroups or areas of the city. To be useful, local indicators should include social characteristics such as race, sex, and age, as well as residence. The smaller the basic unit of analysis, the more flexible the use of the data; in this way, local indicators can be used to make assessments and comparisons of areas within a city. Another limitation of local indicators is their purely objective nature. Educational attainment does not reveal quality of education, for instance, and other objective measures do not reveal the attitudes and feelings of citizens. One way to overcome this shortcoming is to use a community survey in which citizens are interviewed, face-to-face, if possible. The periodic surveys of Chicago reported in the University of Chicago's *Community Fact Book* are a leading example of such a methodology. Needless to say, the information generated by local indicators is worthwhile only if it results in actual improvements in the quality of city life. For this to happen, social support and the political will to make necessary social changes are required.

For a more thorough understanding of city life, local indicators and community surveys should be supplemented by more qualitative methods, including ethnographic study and participant observation. These methods enable an outsider to get closer to the actual conditions of life, material and social psychological, than do quantitative methods. Ultimately, there is no more fruitful way to understand the quality of a city's or a neighborhood's life than to actually become a part of it—meeting its residents, seeing its sights, walking its streets, savoring its tastes, and smelling its aromas.

The Mismatch Problems

One underlying factor that has had a strongly negative impact on the quality of city life is what social scientists refer to as *mismatch problems*. There are two debilitating geoeconomic mismatches in U.S. urban areas. The first is the restriction (through discrimination and zoning) of the poor, especially minorities, to the city, while many jobs are located in the suburbs and exurbs. This is a mismatch between the location of unemployed and underemployed workers and the location of available jobs. The second mismatch is internal to the city: the lack of correspondence between the low educational levels of inner-city poor people, especially younger African Americans, and the high-education job opportunities available to them (Wilson, 1987, p. 102). (This subject was also discussed in Chapter 5.) Changes in the labor market are exacerbating the effect of education on employment. In U.S. cities, having less than twelve years of education increased the chances of being underemployed by a factor of 1.574 in 1970; by 1982, the factor was up to 1.865 (Lichter, 1988, p. 788). Unskilled and low-skill jobs, and jobs requiring little or no formal education, have largely disappeared from American cities. They have moved to outlying areas, including Third World countries, or they have been filled by machines (consider the virtual disappearance of elevator operators). Many of the remaining low-skill, low-education jobs, such as those in fast-food restaurants, are so low-paying that they cannot lift a worker out of poverty.

Transnational corporations have put the city at serious risk by closing down and relocating production facilities. Some cities have managed to replace their old industrial base with information exchange and service functions. However, the substitution of white-collar, knowledge-intensive jobs and low-paying service jobs for blue-collar, labor-intensive jobs has created a major unemployment and underemployment problem for the city's poorest and newest residents, especially African Americans and Hispanics. New York City, capitalizing on its position as a financial, publishing, and media center, experienced overall job increases in the 1970s and 1980s (Kasarda, 1983), but almost all the expansion was in white-collar occupations, resulting in rising unemployment for minority group members. Most of the new jobs went to white middle-class workers, who frequently lived outside the city. Thus non-residents held about one-fifth of all jobs in New York City in 1979, but more than three-fifths of the jobs that paid $50,000 or more per year (Tyler, 1987, p. 466).

What is to be done about these mismatches? The following social policy initiatives are ways to create decent-paying jobs in the city and to increase the mobility of poor minorities to the suburbs: (1) public works programs for needed urban projects, such as new schools and mass transit, which would include substantial job-training and skill-upgrading components; (2) migration regulation of business, including mandatory payment of relocation or retraining expenses for workers; and (3) breaking down suburban class and race barriers through the strong enforcement of civil rights laws and the creation of more public housing in the suburbs.

A major ironic contradiction of so many of our cities is the contiguity of a decrepit public physical infrastructure and millions of unemployed and underemployed workers. One obvious resolution of this contradiction is a massive public works program to provide decent jobs (jobs that lift people out of poverty) for the unemployed to rebuild cities. There are plenty of precedents for such a policy in the United States, going back to the Work Progress Administration, Public Works Administration, and Civilian Conservation Corps (CCC) of the New Deal. The three million young men who worked in the CCC in 1933–1942 built 46,854 bridges, 800 state parks, and many other facilities and structures. These men were fed and housed and paid $30 per month, of which $22 was sent home to their parents.

In 1986 the Joint Economic Committee of Congress estimated that the national public works gap was over $400 billion, the bulk of which was needed to replace city streets, water lines, bridges, sewers, schools, libraries, public housing, and other structures. Cities crumbled as government investment in physical infrastructure fell from 4.1 percent of GNP in 1965 to 2.5 percent in 1985. Since the 1930s, government has resorted to public works only on a cyclical basis. What is needed is an ongoing public works policy with a backlog of needed construction projects that can be automatically implemented whenever unemployment rates cross a given threshold. Sweden uses such a policy, and it contributes substantially to keeping that nation's unemployment rates consistently below 2 percent, a rate not seen in the United States since World War II (Cooper, 1987).

A successful public works policy will not only have to be ongoing but will also have to provide job training for its participants, most of whom should be recruited from the ranks of the poor and unskilled. This will require a substantial investment of resources and the projects must be worthy of the investment. They should be needed projects rather than make-work ones, they should add to the cityscape rather than detract from it, and they should be built to last.

Plant closings and migrations—manifestations of uneven development—are a serious problem for many of our cities. Between 1981 and 1985 about eleven million workers lost their jobs because of plant closings or indefinite layoffs (Tarpinian, 1987). Two-thirds of the job losses occurred in large corporations. A year later, only about one-fourth of the displaced workers were reemployed at jobs that paid at least as much as their previous ones. Corporations have no legal liability or responsibility to a community they leave, even though their departure, often precipitous, leaves thousands of unemployed workers behind and seriously harms the community's social fabric. The siting of new facilities is driven by powerfully rationalized decision making. One version of this rationalization is location theory, which optimizes three major functional necessities of corporations in choosing sites: minimize input (production) costs, maximize revenues (markets), and minimize intermediate costs such as transport (Walker, 1981, p. 387). Nowhere in such a highly quantified and calculated scheme is there room for consideration of humanistic, quality-of-life factors, including the impact of siting (and relocation) on local communities.

A social policy on plant closing could ameliorate this situation. Such a policy would not be aimed at preventing corporations from moving but would require them to give adequate notice of their intentions and to leave something of value behind, such as money for retraining or relocation expenses of displaced workers. Much as this social policy would improve the current situation, however, it would still be inadequate. Experience with plant-closing policies in Western Europe demonstrates that, in addition, comprehensive and ongoing cooperation is needed among government, corporations, and unions. Such cooperation is necessary to sustain a policy that not only notifies but anticipates well in advance likely plant closings and resultant social needs, and that stipulates which parties will provide what resources (Giloth and Rosenblum, 1987).

THE CITY AND SOCIAL CHANGE

The city is the locus of the most intense contradictions of modern capitalist society, as well as the stage for social change. The tensions or dilemmas of the capitalist city have been analyzed by Saunders (1981, p. 267) as threefold: the contradictions between (1) private profits and social needs, (2) strategic planning and democratic accountability, and (3) centralization and local autonomy. Because of the contradiction between private profits and social needs, collective consumption goods are increasingly necessary to support the city's population. Since it is unprofitable for capitalists to produce collective consumption goods, the state must either supply or subsidize them. Castells

(1978, pp. 42–43) documented how state support of collective consumption increased by fourteenfold (as a share of all state expenditure) over the course of a century in modern France. Collective consumption includes shelter, education, transportation, recreation, and health and cultural facilities and services. The state's supply of these necessities composes the basal organization of the city: its physical and social infrastructure of schools, housing, streets, hospitals, libraries, parks, and state offices and bureaucracies. Because the state is universal and a political institution, its role in collective consumption politicizes the city and generalizes its conflicts.

The existing public provision of necessary collective consumption rests on a fragile underpinning. For example, the cheap maintenance of housing, education, and child care rests on the subordination and exploitation of women, who do a great deal of unpaid work in these areas. Without this free labor, the social fabric of the city built around present levels of collective consumption might well collapse. (Here is precisely a most critical political potential of the feminist movement.)

There is a direct connection between collective consumption and the quality of city life. The auto is a prime example. Built as a big-ticket profit item by capitalists, the auto created a number of major collective consumption items, including freeways and environmental pollution controls. The auto disenfranchises many people in society—those who cannot drive or who cannot afford a car, including the poor, children, and the disabled. Thus the auto drives society—to the extent that it shapes and limits human activity. Gridlock is the ironic result to which the auto has brought the city: auto-ized and atomized immobility. In southern California, where the auto reigns as the supreme mode of transport, the average speed is no higher than 33 mph. By 2000, the average speed is expected to drop to 15 mph (Renner, 1988, p. 47).

The auto is more than a means of transport. As Williams (1973, p. 296) pointed out, it also represents a distinct form of consciousness and of social relations: "Private, enclosed, an individual vehicle in a pressing and merely aggregated common flow; certain underlying conventions of external control but within them the passing of rapid signals of warning, avoidance, concession, invitation, as we pursue our ultimately separate ways but in a common mode." Auto travel is experienced as personal choice and as the pursuit of private interest. However, looked at from the outside, traffic flows in a highly regulated manner, controlled by streets and signals. In auto travel, then, as Thompson (1988, p. 311) noted, "the illusion of self-motivated freedom disempowers people from confronting the determinism of the larger social process." Thus the fact that our lives are being determined by our mode of transportation is kept from our consciousness; we assume that the auto maximizes our personal power when, in reality, it diminishes it.

In addition to its distortions of personal and social life, the auto is complicit in a large loss of human life. In 1985 more than 200,000 people in the world died in traffic accidents. Also, research indicates that air pollution from autos exacts a high death toll. For example, the use of gasoline and diesel fuel may cause as many as 30,000 deaths a year in the United States alone. Moreover, the auto consumes a large and growing share of our landscape. In 1987 over 60,000 square miles of U.S. land were paved; this represented about 2 percent of the nation's area and about 10 percent of its arable land. Worldwide, at least one-third of city land is devoted to roads, parking lots, and other auto uses (Renner, 1988, pp. 35, 46).

Collective resistance to the destruction produced by the capitalist transformation of cities centers on a defense of placeness against the disruptions of rapid dislocation (Smith and Judd, 1984, p. 190). *Placeness* (Relph, 1976) is a social psychological and ecological category; it represents community rather than an abstract location. A community is relatively stable over time, is livable and lived in, and has ready access to work sites. Placeness is an increasing human necessity as uneven capitalist development accelerates depredation and dislocation. Home or a home place is a central aspect of self-identity and is necessary for social life.

A sense of placeness requires that urban amenities be improved. Collectively consumed services have to be worthy of the large majority of the population that uses them and they must contribute to community rather than detract from it. Instead of sidewalks (a peripheral, secondary appendage to the street) and pedestrian zones (circumscribed and unnatural), the city needs walking paths that meander naturally and yet connect one place to another, that are comfortable and replenish human energy rather than deplete it, as battling sidewalk traffic does (Castells, 1984, p. 252). One way to use such paths is to connect parks and other public facilities, such as bus and train stations.

The city can humanize its sidewalks and make them safer through modal separations such as bikeways and pedways and through channel prototypes such as pedestrian promenades and arcades (Lynch, 1981, pp. 426–431). Promenades are public spaces in which people can stroll, can see others, and can be seen by others. Good promenades are part of a path through the most active parts of a community, such as Las Ramblas in Barcelona (Alexander, Ishikawa, and Silverstein, 1977, pp. 169–173). They foster social interaction and a sense of place. The city also needs more widespread public accommodations, including comfortable rest areas and clean toilets. Such facilities should be made accessible to all members of society, including those with disabilities. All these amenities and many more could be projects for the needed public works construction in cities. Finally, it should be recognized that these are more than just amenities, a word that trivializes their value. They are vital for facilitating social interaction and for jobs (construction and maintenance), as well as for making the city livable for all its citizens. In Hayden's (1983, p. 69) words, "Built space provides a concrete, physical statement about how a society organizes itself at the scale of everyday life. And its design accounts for a good deal of pleasure or pain, social connectedness or social isolation."

In addition to increased public resources and new social policy initiatives, U.S. cities require expanded grass-roots political input. We already have a social base for grass-roots democratic and progressive social change in the some twenty million Americans who are active in various neighborhood groups (Boyte, 1980). Because of the uniquely American separation of work and residential identities (Katznelson, 1981) and of the high rate of home ownership among Americans, social change in the United States is more dependent on local movements based on issues of consumption than on class conflicts over production—in other words, on demands to the state for services rather than on demands to capitalists for control of production. Thus it is the provider of the social wage (discussed in Chapter 5), the urban social welfare structure (city government and public services, including education, health, and housing), that is the principal target of urban protest.

The strength of local activism was demonstrated in the grass-roots protests of the 1960s and 1970s against the progrowth coalition (Mollenkopf, 1983, p. 210). These protests were successful in four ways. They helped (1) to end large-scale clearance (as in urban renewal), (2) to revise planning input by creating citizen review and participation, (3) to develop a new focus on building rehabilitation and preservation, and (4) to sensitize the public to the defects of growth. Conflict over growth remains a basis for political mobilization in cities. Logan and Molotch (1987) analyzed the city as a "growth machine" and saw city development in terms of conflicts among three principal social actors: (1) the larger, corporate system with its economic imperatives; (2) local elites (especially real estate developers and financiers) interested in profits from development; and (3) ordinary citizens, whose interest in making local communities a resource for everyday life makes them generally opposed to development.

The ordinary citizens of San Francisco have been at the forefront of the contemporary antigrowth movement. After years of political conflict over Manhattanization, San Franciscans in 1983 passed a plan to sharply limit high-rise office construction and to control its design in the city's central business district. In 1986 voters adopted an even stronger measure that reduced by 50 percent the amount of office construction allowed. Even in Manhattan, where progrowth policies have thrived, resistance to real estate development stiffened in the late 1980s. Donald J. Trump's proposed Television City for Manhattan's West Side, featuring a 150-story tower (to succeed Chicago's Sears Building as the world's tallest), encountered strong neighborhood and boroughwide opposition (Gross, 1987). This massive 76-acre project became a lightning rod for community resistance to the developers' excesses. After years of enduring go-go development of high-rise buildings that overcrowded streets, shut out sunlight, and displaced neighborhood housing and merchants, many Manhattanites became antigrowth. Elsewhere, new policies to foster even development have been initiated. In Boston Mayor Raymond L. Flynn inaugurated in 1987 a policy requiring developers who want to build on prime CBD land to simultaneously construct needed housing in outer neighborhoods (Meislin, 1987).

Another vehicle for local protest against overdevelopment and failed urban social policies is the tenants' movement, which pressures local and state government for rent control, eviction regulation, and enforcement of housing codes (Dreier, 1984). This movement has experienced a revival because of the housing shortage, condominium conversions, and gentrification. The tenants' organizations that have had the greatest success in the 1980s, in California, Massachusetts, and New Jersey, have moved beyond renter-specific issues such as rent control to issues of general housing policy, including zoning and tax reform.

The new grass-roots urban social movements in all capitalist societies often function outside parties and other traditional political organizations, and outside class-based organizations such as unions as well. They focus on issues and structures of reproduction, such as schools and housing, rather than structures of production, such as factories and corporations. These movements are highly decentralized and heterogeneous, with a strongly populist aspect (Hirsch, 1981). Their limitations lie in their diffuseness, ambiguous goals, and provincialism. Their potential is best realized when they align themselves with class and party organizations, which provide connections to the larger social structure of society.

After studying major urban social movements—Madrid's Citizen Movement, Paris's Grands Ensembles, San Francisco's gay community, and Latin American squatter movements—Castells (1983) concluded that they can overcome their limitations and achieve social transformation if they mobilize effectively in three areas: (1) improved collective consumption of necessities like housing (as opposed to the current distribution by income); (2) heightened community cultural identity and autonomy through face-to-face interaction (as opposed to current atomization and domination by elite outsiders); and (3) increased power for local areas through neighborhood decentralization and self-management (as opposed to the current centralized, bureaucratized corporations and state).

Successful mobilization of urban social movements also depends on a sense of placeness for a collective identity, for the siting of alternative culture and institutions, and for the creation of a defensible territory. The historical importance of placeness is illustrated by the value of the ghetto to the civil rights and black liberation movements, of People's Park in Berkeley to the 1960s counterculture, and of the factory and working-class district to the labor movement.

Ultimately, city space will have to be liberated from its condition as a private commodity. The concept of a right to the city for all citizens—le droit à la ville (Lefebvre, 1968)—that existed in feudal times must be reasserted. To do this, the dual power of capitalism and the state, both of which are hierarchically exercised in the form of bureaucracy, must be challenged. The roots for such challenge are in the populist protests of neighborhood and environmental groups. But such movements will not make a real dent in capitalist power unless they are articulated through class-based political organization. Thus grass-roots protest must be allied with national and international progressive political organizations, such as the Green Party. In addition to challenging capitalism, the populist and ecological focus of such groups can serve as a humanizing antidote to the technocratic and economistic approaches of the more traditional varieties of Marxism. The potential for progressive social change is apparent; the need for it is great.

REFERENCES

Addams, Jane. 1961 [1910]. *Twenty Years at Hull House*. New York: Signet.
Alexander, Christopher, Sara Ishikawa, and Murray Silverstein. 1977. *A Pattern Language: Towns/Buildings/Construction*. New York: Oxford University Press.
Barbanel, Josh. 1987. "Societies and Their Homeless." *The New York Times*, November 29.
Barkin, David. 1978. "Confronting the Separation of Town and Country in Cuba." Pp. 317–337 in *Marxism and the Metropolis: New Perspectives in Urban Political Economy*, eds. William K. Tabb and Larry Sawers. New York: Oxford University Press.
Bassuk, Ellen L., and Samuel Gerson. 1985. "Deinstitutionalization and Mental Health Services." Pp. 127–144 in *Mental Health Care and Social Policy*, ed. Phil Brown. London: Routledge & Kegan Paul.
Bean, Gerald J., Jr., Mary E. Stefl, and Steven R. Howe. 1987. "Mental Health and Homelessness: Issues and Findings." *Social Work* 32:411–416.
Beauregard, Robert A. 1984. "Structure, Agency, and Urban Redevelopment." Pp. 51–72 in *Cities in Transformation: Class, Capital, and the State*, ed. Michael Peter Smith. Beverly Hills, CA: Sage Publications.
Bendick, Mark, Jr., and David W. Rasmussen. 1986. "Enterprise Zones and Inner-City Economic Revitalization." Pp. 97–129 in *Reagan and the Cities*, eds. George E. Peterson and Carol W. Lewis. Washington, DC: The Urban Institute Press.
Berman, Marshall. 1987. "Ruins and Reforms." *Dissent*, Fall, pp. 421–428.
Borgos, Seth. 1984. "The ACORN Squatters' Campaign." *Social Policy* 15:17–26.
Boyte, Harry C. 1980. *The Backyard Revolution: Understanding the New Citizen Movement*. Philadelphia: Temple University Press.
Brown, Phil. 1985. "The Mental Patients' Rights Movement and Mental Health Institutional Change." Pp. 187–212 in *Mental Health Care and Social Policy*, ed. Phil Brown. London: Routledge & Kegan Paul.
Burt, Martha R., and Karen J. Pittman. 1985. *Testing the Social Safety Net: The Impact of Changes in Support Programs During the Reagan Administration*. Washington, DC: The Urban Institute Press.
Campbell, John L. 1987. "The State and the Nuclear Waste Crisis: An Institutional Analysis of Policy Constraints." *Social Problems* 34:18–33.
Castells, Manuel. 1977 [1972]. *The Urban Question: A Marxist Approach*, trans. Alan Sheridan. Cambridge, MA: MIT Press.
———. 1978. *City, Class and Power*, trans. Elizabeth Lebas. New York: St. Martin's Press.
———. 1983. *The City and the Grassroots: A Cross-Cultural Theory of Urban Social Movements*. Berkeley: University of California Press.
———. 1984. "Space and Society: Managing the New Historical Relationships." Pp. 235–260 in *Cities in Transformation: Class, Capital, and the State*, ed. Michael Peter Smith. Beverly Hills, CA: Sage Publications.
Clarke, Susan E. 1982. "Enterprise Zones: Seeking the Neighborhood Nexus." *Urban Affairs Quarterly* 18:53–71.
Cohen, R. B. 1981. "The New International Division of Labor, Multinational Corporations and Urban Hierarchy." Pp. 287–315 in *Urbanization and Urban Planning in Capitalist Society*, eds. Michael Dear and Allen J. Scott. New York: Methuen.
Cooper, Scott. 1987. "The Next Public Works Program." *Social Policy* 17:14–19.
Daley, Suzanne. 1987. " 'Couch People': Hidden Homeless Grow." *The New York Times*, June 17.
DePalma, Anthony. 1987. "Are Rent Vouchers a Boon or a Bust?" *The New York Times*, November 1.
Deutsche, Rosalyn. 1988. "Uneven Development: Public Art in New York City." *October* 47:3–52.

Dreier, Peter. 1984. "The Tenants' Movement." Pp. 174–201 in *Marxism and the Metropolis: New Perspectives in Urban Political Economy*, eds. William K. Tabb and Larry Sawers. 2nd ed. New York: Oxford University Press.

Drew, Joseph. 1984. "The Dynamics of Human Services Subcontracting: Service Delivery in Chicago, Detroit, and Philadelphia." *Policy Studies Journal 13*:67–89.

Duke, Annette, and Jean Kluver. 1989. "Putting Housing on the Table." *Dollars & Sense*, April.

Dumpson, James R. 1987. *A Shelter is Not a Home*. Report of the Manhattan Borough President's Task Force on Housing and Homeless Families. New York City, March.

Edgerton, Robert B. 1982. "Deinstitutionalizing the Mentally Retarded: Values in Conflict." Pp. 221–235 in *Contemporary Health Services: Social Science Perspectives*, eds. Allen W. Johnson, Oscar Grusky, and Bertram H. Raven. Boston: Auburn House.

Engels, Frederick. 1979 [1872]. *The Housing Question*. Moscow: Progress Publishers.

Fabricant, Michael. 1988. "Empowering the Homeless." *Social Policy 18*:49–55.

Fabricant, Michael, and Michael Kelly. 1987. "No Haven for Homeless in a Heartless Economy." *Radical America 20*: 22–34.

Fainstein, Norman I., and Susan S. Fainstein. 1982. "Restructuring the American City: A Comparative Perspective." Pp. 161–189 in *Urban Policy Under Capitalism*, eds. Norman I. Fainstein and Susan S. Fainstein. Beverly Hills, CA: Sage Publications.

Fainstein, Susan S., et al. 1983. *Restructuring the City: The Political Economy of Urban Redevelopment*. New York: Longman.

Fogelson, Robert M. 1967. *The Fragmented Metropolis*. Cambridge, MA: Harvard University Press.

Friedland, Roger. 1983a. *Power and Crisis in the City: Corporations, Unions and Urban Policy*. New York: Schocken Books.

———. 1983b. "The Politics of Profit and the Geography of Growth." *Urban Affairs Quarterly 19*: 41–54.

Gans, Herbert J. 1962. *The Urban Villagers*. New York: Free Press.

———. 1967. *The Levittowners: Ways of Life and Politics in a New Suburban Community*. New York: Random House/Pantheon.

Gendrot, Sophie N. 1982. "Governmental Responses to Popular Movements: France and the United States." Pp. 277–299 in *Urban Policy Under Capitalism*, eds. Norman I. Fainstein and Susan S. Fainstein. Beverly Hills, CA: Sage Publications.

Giloth, Robert, and Susan Rosenblum. 1987. "How to Fight Plant Closing." *Social Policy 17*: 20–26.

Goldberger, Paul. 1988. "High Marks for Low-Cost Housing in Boston." *The New York Times*, November 6.

Gordon, David M. 1984. "Capitalist Development and the History of American Cities." Pp. 21–53 in *Marxism and the Metropolis: New Perspectives in Urban Political Economy*, eds. William K. Tabb and Larry Sawers. 2nd ed. New York: Oxford University Press.

Gottdiener, M. 1985. *The Social Production of Urban Space*. Austin: University of Texas Press.

Gross, Jane. 1987. "2 Big West Side Projects Fuel Anti-Development Sentiment." *The New York Times*, November 29.

Gudeman, Jon E., and Miles F. Shore. 1984. "Beyond Deinstitutionalization: A New Class of Facilities for the Mentally Ill." *New England Journal of Medicine 311*:832–836.

Gulati, Padi. 1982. "Consumer Participation in Administrative Decision Making." *Social Service Review 56*:72–84.

Gurr, Ted Robert, and Desmond S. King. 1987. *The State and the City*. Chicago: University of Chicago Press.

Harvey, David. 1973. *Social Justice and the City*. London: Edward Arnold.

Hayden, Delores. 1983. "Capitalism, Socialism, and the Built Environment." Pp. 59–81 in *Socialist Visions*, ed. Stephen Rosskamm Shalom. Boston: South End Press.

Herbers, John. 1987. "Outlook for Sheltering the Poor Growing Even Bleaker." *The New York Times*, March 8.

Hill, Richard Child. 1983. "Market, State, and Community: National Urban Policy in the 1980s." *Urban Affairs Quarterly 19*: 5–20.

———. 1984. "Urban Political Economy: Emergence, Consolidation, and Development." Pp. 123–137 in *Cities in Transformation: Class, Capital, and the State*, ed. Michael Peter Smith. Beverly Hills, CA: Sage Publications.

Hirsch, Joachim. 1981. "The Apparatus of the State, the Reproduction of Capital and Urban Conflicts." Pp. 595–607 in *Urbanization and Urban Planning in Capitalist Society*, eds. Michael Dear and Allen J. Scott. New York: Methuen.

Howard, Ebenezer. 1965 [1898]. *Garden Cities of To-Morrow*, ed. F. J. Osborn. Cambridge, MA: MIT Press.

Jacobs, Jane. 1961. *The Death and Life of Great American Cities*. New York: Random House.

Kain, John F. 1970. "The Distribution and Movement of Jobs and Industry." Pp. 1–43 in *The Metropolitan Enigma: Inquiries into the Nature and Dimensions of America's "Urban Crisis,"* ed. James Q. Wilson. Garden City, NY: Doubleday/Anchor.

Kasarda, John D. 1983. "Entry-Level Jobs, Mobility, and Urban Minority Unemployment." *Urban Affairs Quarterly* 19:21–40.

Katznelson, Ira. 1981. *City Trenches: Urban Politics and the Patterning of Class in the United States*. Chicago: University of Chicago Press.

Kennedy, Michael D. 1984. "The Fiscal Crisis of the City." Pp. 91–110 in *Cities in Transformation: Class, Capital, and the State*, ed. Michael Peter Smith. Beverly Hills, CA: Sage Publications.

Kiesler, Charles A. 1985. "Mental Hospitals and Alternative Care: Noninstitutionalization as Potential Public Policy." Pp. 292–315 in *Mental Health Care and Social Policy*, ed. Phil Brown. London: Routledge & Kegan Paul.

Kleniewski, Nancy. 1987. "Urban Renewal and Housing Reform: The Case of North Philadelphia." Pp. 83–108 in *Research in Social Policy: Historical and Contemporary Perspectives*. Volume 1. Greenwich, CT: JAI Press.

Lebas, Elizabeth. 1982. "Urban and Regional Sociology in Advanced Industrial Societies: A Decade of Marxist and Critical Perspectives." *Current Sociology* 30:7–130.

Le Corbusier. 1971 [1929]. *The City of To-Morrow and Its Planning*, trans. Frederick Etchells. Cambridge, MA: MIT Press.

Lefebvre, Henri. 1968. *Le Droit à La Ville*. Paris: Anthropos.

———. 1969. *The Sociology of Marx*, trans. Norbert Guterman. New York: Random House.

———. 1971. *Everyday Life in the Modern World*, trans. Sacha Rabinovitch. New York: Harper & Row.

LeGates, Richard T., and Chester Hartman. 1986. "The Anatomy of Displacement in the United States." Pp. 178–200 in *Gentrification of the City*, eds. Neil Smith and Peter Williams. Boston: Allen & Unwin.

LeGates, Richard T., and Karen Murphy. 1984. "Austerity, Shelter, and Social Conflict in the United States." Pp. 123–151 in *Marxism and the Metropolis: New Perspectives in Urban Political Economy*, eds. William K. Tabb and Larry Sawers. 2nd ed. New York: Oxford University Press.

Lehman, Karen. 1988. "Beyond Oz: The Path to Regeneration." *Social Policy* 18:56–58.

Lerman, Paul, 1982. *Deinstitutionalization and the Welfare State*. New Brunswick, NJ: Rutgers University Press.

Lichter, Daniel T. 1988. "Racial Differences in Underemployment in American Cities." *American Journal of Sociology* 93:771–792.

Logan, John R. 1983. "The Disappearance of Communities from National Urban Policy." *Urban Affairs Quarterly* 19:75–90.

Logan, John R., and Harvey L. Molotch. 1987. *Urban Fortunes: The Political Economy of Place*. Berkeley: University of California Press.

Lynch, Kevin. 1981. *A Theory of Good City Form*. Cambridge, MA: MIT Press.

Lyon, Larry. 1987. *The Community in Urban Society*. Chicago: Dorsey Press.

Marcuse, Peter. 1982. "Determinants of State Housing Policies: West Germany and the United States." Pp. 83–115 in *Urban Policy Under Capitalism*, eds. Norman I. Fainstein and Susan S. Fainstein. Beverly Hills, CA: Sage Publications.

———. 1986. "Abandonment, Gentrification, and Displacement: The Linkages in New York City." Pp. 153–177 in *Gentrification of the City*, eds. Neil Smith and Peter Williams. Boston: Allen & Unwin.

———. 1987. "Why Are They Homeless?" *The Nation*, April 4, pp. 426–429.

———. 1988. "Neutralizing Homelessness." *Socialist Review* 18:69–96.

Marlowe, Julia. 1985. "Private versus Public Provision of Refuse Removal Service: Measures of Citizen Satisfaction." *Urban Affairs Quarterly* 20:355–363.

Marx, Karl. 1967 [1867]. *Capital*, ed. Frederick Engels, trans. Samuel Moore and Edward Aveling. Volume 1: *A Critical Analysis of Capitalist Production*. New York: International Publishers.

Marx, Karl, and Frederick Engels. 1975 [1848]. *Manifesto of the Communist Party*, ed. Frederick Engels, trans. Samuel Moore. Peking: Foreign Languages Press.

Mechanic, David. 1989. *Mental Health and Social Policy*. 3rd ed. Englewood Cliffs, NJ: Prentice Hall.

Meislin, Richard J. 1987. "Boston's Flynn Breaks Rules and Wins Hearts." *The New York Times*, October 31.

Mingione, Enzo. 1981. *Social Conflict and the City*. Oxford: Basil Blackwell.

Mollenkopf, John H. 1983. *The Contested City*. Princeton, NJ: Princeton University Press.

Mumford, Lewis. 1938. *The Culture of Cities*. London: Secker & Warburg.

Muwakkil, Salim. 1987. "Up from the Ashes: Rebuilding Community, Rehabbing the 'Jets.' " *In These Times*, January 21—27, p. 8.

O'Connor, James. 1973. *The Fiscal Crisis of the State*. New York: St. Martin's Press.

Palen, J. John. 1987. *The Urban World*. 3rd ed. New York: McGraw-Hill.

Park, Robert E., and Ernest W. Burgess. 1967 [1916]. *The City*. Chicago: University of Chicago Press.

Parker, R. Andrew. 1985. "Matching Federal Spending to Need: An Urban Policy Scorecard, 1977–1983." *Policy Studies Journal* 13:625–633.

Pear, Robert. 1986. "The Need of the Nation's Homeless Is Becoming Their Right." *The New York Times*, July 20.

Polner, Robert, and Paul Schwartzman. 1988. "The Tragedy of Downward Mobility: Homelessness Hits the Middle Class." *In These Times*, September 28–October 4, pp. 8–9.

Rapp, Charles A., and Ronna Chamberlain. 1985. "Case Management Services for the Chronically Mentally Ill." *Social Work* 30:417–422.

Relph, E. 1976. *Place and Placelessness*. London: Pion.

Renner, Michael. 1988. "Rethinking the Role of the Automobile." Washington, DC: Worldwatch Institute, Paper 84, June.

Riordan, Teresa. 1987. "Housekeeping at HUD." *Common Cause Magazine*, March/April, pp. 26–31.

Rivlin, Leanne G. 1986. "A New Look at the Homeless." *Social Policy* 16:3–10.

Rodgers, Robert C., and Jeffrey D. Straussman. 1986. "Militancy, Union Penetration, and Fiscal Stress: Are They Really Connected?" Pp. 23–45 in *Urban Policy Problems: Federal Policy and Institutional Change*, ed. Mark S. Rosentraub. New York: Praeger.

Saunders, Peter. 1981. *Social Theory and the Urban Question*. New York: Holmes & Meier.

Sawers, Larry. 1978. "Cities and Countryside in the Soviet Union and China." Pp. 338–364 in *Marxism and the Metropolis: New Perspectives in Urban Political Economy*, eds. William K. Tabb and Larry Sawers. New York: Oxford University Press.

Scheff, Thomas J. 1985. "Medical Dominance: Psychoactive Drugs and Mental Health Policy." Pp. 255–271 in *Mental Health Care and Social Policy*, ed. Phil Brown. London: Routledge & Kegan Paul.

Schmitt, Eric. 1987. "Suburbs, Too, Struggle to Shelter Homeless." *The New York Times*, September 8.

Schneider, Mark, and John R. Logan. 1981. "Fiscal Implications of Class Segregation: Inequalities in the Distribution of Public Goods and Services in Suburban Municipalities." *Urban Affairs Quarterly* 17:23–36.

Schwartz, Nathan H. 1984. "Reagan's Housing Policies." Pp. 149–164 in *The Attack on the Welfare State*, eds. Anthony Champagne and Edward J. Harpham. Prospect Heights, IL: Waveland Press.

Scull, Andrew. 1982. "Community Care of the Mentally Ill: Current Realities in the Context of Past Developments." Pp. 237–251 in *Contemporary Health Services: Social Science Perspectives*, eds. Allen W. Johnson, Oscar Grusky, and Bertram H. Raven. Boston: Auburn House.

———. 1984. *Decarceration: Community Treatment and the Deviant—A Radical View*. 2nd ed. New Brunswick, NJ: Rutgers University Press.

Shields, Lynn. 1988. "Endangered Species: The Uncertain Future of Low-Income Housing." *Dollars & Sense*, November, pp. 9–11.

Simmel, Georg. 1964 [1905]. "The Metropolis and Mental Life." Pp. 409–424 in *The Sociology of Georg Simmel*, trans. and ed. Kurt H. Wolff. New York: Free Press.

Smith, Michael P. 1979. *The City and Social Theory*. New York: St. Martin's Press.

Smith, Michael P., and Dennis R. Judd. 1984. "American Cities: The Production of Ideology." Pp. 173–196 in *Cities in Transformation: Class, Capital, and the State*, ed. Michael P. Smith. Beverly Hills, CA: Sage Publications.

Snow, David A., and Leon Anderson. 1987. "Identity Work Among the Homeless: The Verbal Construction and Avowal of Personal Identities." *American Journal of Sociology* 92:1336–1371.

Stern, Mark J. 1984. "The Emergence of the Homeless as a Public Problem." *Social Service Review* 58:291–301.

Suttles, Gerald D. 1968. *The Social Order of the Slum*. Chicago: University of Chicago Press.

Tarpinian, Greg. 1987. "Restructuring and Job Security—Collision Course Bargaining." *Economic Notes* 55:1–6.

Thompson, E. P. 1988. "Last Dispatches from the Border Country." *The Nation*, March 5, pp. 310–312.

Tyler, Gus. 1987. "A Tale of Three Cities." *Dissent*, Fall, pp. 463–470.

Van Weesep, Jan. 1984. "Intervention in the Netherlands: Urban Housing Policy and Market Response." *Urban Affairs Quarterly* 19:329–353.

Walker, Richard A. 1981. "A Theory of Suburbanization: Capitalism and the Construction of Urban Space in the United States." Pp. 383–429 in *Urbanization and Urban Planning in Capitalist Society*, eds. Michael Dear and Allen J. Scott. New York: Methuen.

Walton, John. 1982. "Cities and Jobs and Politics." *Urban Affairs Quarterly* 18: 5–17.

Williams, Peter, and Neil Smith. 1986. "From 'Renaissance' to Restructuring: The Dynamics of Contemporary Urban Development." Pp. 204–224 in *Gentrification of the City*, eds. Neil Smith and Peter Williams. Boston: Allen & Unwin.

Williams, Raymond. 1973. *The Country and the City*. New York: Oxford University Press.

Wilson, William Julius. 1987. *The Truly Disadvantaged: The Inner City, the Underclass, and Public Policy*. Chicago: University of Chicago Press.

Winerip, Michael. 1988. "Group Homes: A Law Works Ever So Quietly." *The New York Times*, November 4.

Wirth, Louis. 1938. "Urbanism as a Way of Life." *American Journal of Sociology* 44:1–24.

Wright, James D., and Julie A. Lam. 1987. "Homelessness and the Low-Income Housing Supply." *Social Policy* 17:48–53.

10

Social Research and Social Policy

Fresh necessities have led continually to fresh researches.
John Yeats, *The Natural History of Commerce*, 1870

Social policy research is a major industry that employs thousands of academics, entrepreneurs, and analysts in universities, government, institutes, and think tanks. Much of the growth in social policy research has been linked to the expansion, especially in the late 1960s and early 1970s, of the Welfare State. Between 1969 and 1974 federal expenditure on nondefense policy research increased by 500 percent. The government contracts out about one-half of this research. The other one-half is performed by the government itself; two of its agencies are engaged in ongoing policy and program evaluation—the General Accounting Office of the legislative branch and the Office of Management and Budget of the executive branch (Rein, 1983, pp. 195–196). Much of the research is done by social scientists. Between 1964 and 1980 federal expenditure for social science research increased from $150 million to $1 billion (Haveman, 1986, p. 74). A similarly explosive growth in social policy research has taken place in other Welfare States, including the U.K. (Cherns, 1986, p. 189). Lehman (1980) has suggested that policy research is now the largest industry in Washington, D.C., and that it will continue to grow because the state, an insatiable consumer of data, will continue to expand and to be more active in society. There are social movement aspects to this phenomenal growth of social policy research: charismatic policy entrepreneurs command expertise in specific issue areas and generate large followings (Kingdon, 1984, pp. 188–193). Perhaps the best example is Ralph Nader's consumer movement, which originally focused on auto safety.

Because of its relative newness, social policy research still lacks a professional identity. To what extent policy research can fully professionalize is problematic (Jennings, 1987). The principal reason is that the professional is only one of four competing varieties of policy analyst. The other three are the scientist, whose interests are methodological and theoretical; the politician, whose interest is advocacy; and the administrator, whose interest is managerial application (Bardes and Dubnick, 1980, p. 123). The field resembles the proverbial elephant assembled by committee.

Social policy is traditionally viewed as problem-reactive: a social problem is identified, existing social policy (or the lack thereof) is critiqued, and new or reformed policies are proposed. In fact, social policy research is also problem discovery and specification. For example, research of social insurance policy does not resolve income maintenance problems so much as it specifies gaps in service, identifies unmet social needs, and unearths the unintended consequences (often problems) of policy. Thus analysis is a process, not a product. We can become enlightened as a result of analysis even if we do not resolve a problem.

Whereas in the preceding chapters our focus was on social policy in various areas of society, in this chapter we are concerned with an analysis of social policy itself. We focus on the social policy research process—the identification of social need, followed by the formulation, implementation, delivery, and evaluation of social policy. Also, we examine the context of social policy research—its conditions, ends, and means. In our view social policy exists within a specific historical period, responds to distinct social needs, operates through particular organizational forms, is provided by social practitioners, and creates identifiable results. We begin with an analysis of social policy research from the perspective of applied sociology, focusing on the identification of social need, organizational influences, and methods of evaluation. Then we discuss new directions for applied sociology. This is followed by an examination of delivery settings for social policy, concentrating on social practice at the personal, organizational, and collective levels. Included in our examination of practice is a look at the work of a survey researcher.

APPLIED SOCIOLOGY

Applied sociology is what it sounds like—the practical application of sociological research findings and insights. Its counterpart is theoretical sociology, in which research is oriented toward theory and is concerned with knowledge for its own sake. The division between applied and theoretical is not as distinct in the social sciences as it is in the physical sciences, where pure (science) and applied (engineering) realms are more clearly demarcated. Applied sociology can be distinguished from the rest of sociology by its orientation to utilization of knowledge for the purpose of making decisions (Lazarsfeld and Reitz, 1975, pp. 35–36). Within applied sociology there are specializations, such as evaluation research. Another example is the recent popularization of clinical sociology, a sociological practice that is directed to the social diagnosis and treatment of groups and individuals in groups (Straus, 1985). In summary, theoretical sociology pursues knowledge for its own sake, applied sociology pursues knowledge for its use, and clinical sociology uses knowledge to pursue therapeutic change.

Applied sociology has grown along with the development of the Welfare State. The progenitor of applied sociology was the Chicago School of the early twentieth century. Sociology was first established as an academic field at the University of Chicago in an effort to understand the empirical relationships between urbanization and the intensification of social problems such as crime and poverty. Chicago's Louis Wirth (1964) proposed in 1942 that politically detached social scientists develop policy ideas for social problems. These planners would use a rational and comprehensive method such as metropolitan planning to anticipate and to moderate urban social problems. (Social planning is further discussed in Chapter 11.) Since they were beholden to no group, Wirth believed, the planners would have the freedom to oppose special interests in order to promote the collective good. In reality, however, planning commissions have proved more ready to give their allegiance to the parochial financial interests of real estate owners and developers, downtown businesspersons, and the construction industry than to local citizens (see Chapter 9). In addition, the rational comprehensive approach to social policy has been criticized as too centralized and too ambitious. Lindblom's (1959) argument for a "muddling through" approach to social policy is the classic example of this criticism. Muddling through consists of trial and error; it is incremental policy that adapts gradually to changes in the environment.

Social policy, contrary to Wirth's hopes, is not a matter of scientifically discovering the solution to a problem and then implementing it. Social policy involves choices; it is bound by contradictions and dilemmas. The solution for one problem will often create another, sometimes unanticipated, problem. For example, Fry and Miller (1981) found that a major interdisciplinary effort to treat skid row alcoholics had the negative and unintended result of creating intensely competitive factions among staff members, which led to an expansion of the local alcoholic population as each faction tried to best the other in recruiting clients. Thus the innovative use of a multidisciplinary team approach to reducing alcoholism had the result of increasing it in a given area.

The new problem created may be anticipated—because social policy does involve trade-offs. The better interest of one group may be sacrificed for that of another group. Thus Social Security rewards retired workers with relatively generous benefits, the costs of which add to the tax burden of current workers. This is not nearly as controversial an example as others because Social Security has deep and widespread public support. A more contentious trade-off is affirmative action for disadvantaged minorities and women at the expense of advantaged white males. These contradictory aspects of social policy are consistent with the nature of social reality and do have at least two virtues, as Nove (1983, p. 141) wryly noted: "A world without contradictions would be an intolerably dull place, and social scientists would be threatened with unemployment."

We begin our discussion of the relevance of applied sociology to social policy research by looking at the ways in which social needs are identified. This is followed by comments on the effects of organizational behavior and the methods of social policy evaluation. The discussion concludes with a critique of applied sociology.

Identification of Social Need

Sociology has traditionally studied social problems. At least since the Chicago School, the tendency has been to analyze social problems in the context of social disorganization. In this tradition social problems like poverty are deviances in society. In fact, both social disorganization and social organization are problem producing. Some of the more serious social problems produced by the way in which societies are organized include degradation of the environment, socioeconomic inequality, and institutional racism and sexism. The concept *institutional racism* means that racism is not a deviance but a structural normalcy of society. The study of social problems as aspects of social structure, combined with the technology for applying sociology, has produced empirical connections between social problems and social needs, including demographic projections, social indicators, and needs assessment.

Demography, a specialization in sociology, is the statistical study of human populations. Demographic projection, or social forecasting, is akin to prediction. The best-known use of applied sociology in prediction is for election outcomes. Pollsters predict election outcomes with great accuracy, at least in the short term. The Gallup Poll accurately predicts presidential elections, including the margin of difference. Although it is also predictive, demographic projection differs from polling in important respects, including the fact that polling's accuracy is based on data from a relatively small, randomly chosen sample of a population, while demographic projection more commonly uses aggregate data on a whole population.

Demographic projection can be quite reliable in the near term because the behavior of masses of people is not likely to change quickly—except, of course, under extreme provocation, as in war. Because of this accuracy, demographic projection is used in a wide range of social policy arenas—for example, to predict the school-age population in order to plan educational facilities.

Forecasting can also be used to predict new social needs. An example is long-term health care in New York State, which is forecast to increase markedly in the near future. Current long-term care facilities and services, which are largely for the aged, include nursing homes, adult homes, family homes, home care, hospices, and adult day care. It has been estimated that the long-term care population will rise from about 400,000 in 1980 to about 640,000 in 2010, a 60 percent increase (Mumpower and Ilchman, 1988, p. 470). It is important to note that this large increase will occur *before* the post–World War II baby boom generation enters old age.

There is a natural link between demographic projection and social indicators, which are measures of social trends. Demographic projection often consists of extrapolating current social trends into the near future. One example of a social indicator that has critical bearing on social policy analysis in the Welfare State is the social dependency ratio (SDR), defined as the number of persons 65 years old and older per 100 persons 18–64 years old. (The SDR was also discussed in Chapter 5.) The SDR is projected to rise 30 percent (from 20 to 26) between 1986 and 2020, largely because the post–World War II baby boom cohort will reach age 65 by the end of that period. Such projections are an important ingredient of social policy analysis. The SDR has crucial implications for Social Security and may be a basis for changing it—for example, by raising the retirement age. This would reduce the growing ratio of retired to active workers and alleviate the tax burden of the latter. The SDR and other demographic measures tend to change at a ponderously slow rate, but the policy implications of their changes can be immense.

Social indicators and the more formal social accounts are systematic aggregate indicators of society's health. Russett's (1964) *World Handbook of Political and Social Indicators* was among the first contemporary uses, but the methodology goes back at least as far as Ogburn's *Recent Social Changes* (1929), which was commissioned by the Hoover administration. Social indicators blossomed in the 1960s in response to the shortcomings of economic indicators such as the GNP (Miles, 1985, pp. 35–36). Key social indicators include income distribution, caloric consumption, infant mortality rate, and school enrollment. The prototype for the collection of social indicators is the decennial Census of the United States. Since its beginning in 1790, the Census has expanded to include many social statistics in the areas of education, employment, family, health, housing, income, social welfare, and population. Each area contains specific indicators such as the SDR. Like the Census, social indicators are collected over time and provide a baseline for measuring social trends.

One application of social indicators that provides a longitudinal index of the health of society is Miringoff's (Goleman, 1988). Miringoff, of the Fordham Institute for Innovation in Social Policy (Tarrytown, New York), created an index of societal health based on such social indicators as infant mortality, teenage drug use, poverty, teenage suicide, high school dropout rate, and income gap between rich and poor. The index for the U.S. stood at 68 in 1970, the first year for which it was calculated. By 1976 it rose to its peak— 72—which indicated a gradual improvement in societal health. However, the index has declined since 1976, indicating deterioration in societal health.

During Reagan's tenure, the decline accelerated: the index stood at 51 in 1980 and it dropped to 35 in 1986, its lowest level ever.

The final variation of the identification of social need is needs assessment, a numerical measure of the extent of a social problem and the type and level of social services that will address it. Needs assessment is based on various kinds of data, including demographic—for example, the number of persons in a given group living below the poverty line and the gap between their income and the poverty line. Such demographic measures accurately assess objective social needs such as income. Needs assessment is also based on structured interviews and visits with people. This approach is more likely to reveal subjective social needs and measures of the quality of life, such as feelings of insecurity.

Despite the growing use of these empirical measures of social needs, there are reservations about their value. Two problems that are slowly being alleviated are methodological: data collection and data on whole societies. It is difficult to collect accurate data, especially for comparing different societies or the same society at different times. The production of valid and reliable social indicators is a sophisticated and costly methodological enterprise that demands a relatively high level of resources; this limits their use. However, national accounting data are improving markedly. International organizations, including the United Nations and the World Bank, have promoted accurate systematic data collection. Regrettably, serious gaps remain, particularly in data from Third World societies where resources are severely limited. A second problem is that these empirical measures are aggregated. They are for whole societies and need to be separated in order to compare social groups within the same society; social scientists refer to this as *disaggregation*. It is precisely these subgroups that are often critical to social policy research. Without disaggregation, African Americans and whites, men and women, rich and poor, and old and young, cannot be compared.

A more serious problem with the identification of social needs is conceptual. Consider life expectancy, the social indicator consensually valued because of the widespread assumption that a longer life span is desirable. But can we assume that a longer life span—an objective measure (years)—is desirable without considering the quality of this longer life—a subjective measure (satisfaction)? In fact, longer life span has become something of a social problem itself, giving rise to competing legal, medical, and social definitions of death. The resultant social need for "quality of death" produced demands for hospices, euthanasia, and living wills, which certify in advance how a person would like to be treated if terminally ill.

This same social problem has emerged at the younger end of the age range, again produced by improved medical technology and clinical services (discussed in Chapter 8). The decision whether or not to prolong a "defective" infant's life has become a public issue that involves the competing interests of the infant, parents, social workers, doctors and hospital administrators, lawyers, the state, and concerned outside groups. This problem also raises the question of interactions among various social indicators. For example, as Anderson (1972) pointed out in comparing health care in the U.K., Sweden, and the U.S., declines in infant mortality (a good thing) can lead to increases in childhood mortality (a bad thing). This is because efforts and technologies that save infants born with serious health problems may only delay mortality from infancy until childhood.

Thus the main question about social indicators is not how accurate their measurement is but exactly what they mean and how they can be used. Mathematical rigor without a framework of social meaning is useless. Indeed, it may be dangerous, as Culyer (1980, p. 194) noted: "One must be ever-conscious that blind quantification—quantophrenia—may be dangerous—and is probably more dangerous—than no formal quantification at all."

Thus the most serious barrier to the use of empirical measures of social needs is the specification of their connection to social policies. Not all measures have the same meaning for different actors in the social policy arena. The demographic changes in recent decades in the American family (discussed in Chapter 6), including the entry of mothers/wives into the paid labor force, smaller family size, and increased family dissolution rates, are undisputed. Despite agreement as to the facts, however, there is considerable conflict as to their implications. Facts must be interpreted and given meaning according to basic values. This produces conflict because values often are not consensual. Thus a progressive analysis of these facts would focus on the modern democratization and diversification of family structure and resultant new social needs, including national child care and parental leave policies. A reactionary analysis of the same facts would emphasize the destruction of the traditional family and the decline of religious values, and would argue for the need to reassert the primacy of the patriarchal family through such policies as the elimination of reproductive freedom of choice and the reintroduction of prayer into public schools.

Organizational Behavior

Organizational behavior is an important parameter for social policy research. Beginning with Weber (1946), sociologists have stressed the independent effects of organizations, especially bureaucracies. They are the principal vehicles through which social policy is implemented. In implementation organizations shape and distort social policy. The principal reason is that they have their own imperatives, which include organizational enhancement. The effects of organizational behavior on social policy occur at two levels: institutional and societal. The effects at the institutional level concern the organization-as-organization and its role in social policy implementation. The effects at the societal level focus on the organization-in-society and its role in the formulation of social policy.

The sociological distinction between manifest (acknowledged) and latent (unacknowledged) functions (Merton, 1957) is fundamental in analyzing organizational behavior at the institutional level. A classic empirical illustration is Scott's (1969) work on sheltered workshops for the blind. While the manifest function of these workshops was the integration of sight-impaired workers into the competitive labor force, the latent function was the survival of the workshops. Survival depended on keeping many sight-impaired workers in the workshops in order to maintain profitability. Thus, although the workshops advertised the goal of outside employment for the blind, they were actually preventing the blind from leaving. The lesson for social policy analysis is clear: it must always consider whether or not a Welfare State organization is placing its interest above the interests of its clients.

The acknowledged goals of an organization are intended to gain public legitimacy and not to describe what the organization actually does. The manifest goals focus attention on valued but remote objectives. Edelman (1983) referred to this as the *symbolic function* of organizations as opposed to their real activities, which yield tangible benefits. The unacknowledged activities of an organization are hidden from public discourse. Consider the case of free public education (discussed in Chapter 7). The manifest goals of schools ooze with platitudes: education of the young, expansion of their horizons and opportunities. But what does the school actually do? It inculcates patriotism and conformity; it allocates social positions to various social classes; it delays the entry of young people into the labor force (helping the unemployment problem); it provides free daytime child care; and it serves as a mating ground for the young. This is how the allocative role of social policy is mystified as it is implemented through large organizations.

Another example of the difference between latent and manifest goals concerns health-care policy (discussed in Chapter 8). Society's consensual goal is improved health, and this is the manifest goal of health organizations. However, implementation of health policy commonly avoids the difficult task of improving health, or even health care, for much of what that requires is beyond the control of the health organization. Instead, administrators typically opt for the achievable goal of equalizing organizational outputs. Thus equality of access to health care becomes the latent goal that displaces the manifest goals of improving health and health care and curing or healing illness. (This process is referred to as *goal displacement* by social scientists.) It is understandable behavior on the part of health organizations. They are evaluated on the basis of their performance, so they strive to gain control over performance criteria. Equalizing services is a goal they can attain, as was pointed out by Chambers (1986, p. 189) with regard to community mental health centers (CMHCs):

Equalitarianism is strongly pursued in program and policy features, which provide mandatory services to all people within particular geographic areas, non-English language capability among staff in relevant geographic areas, and special funding for poverty areas. On those equity standards, the CMHC policy and program operations rate high.

However, Chambers found that the CMHCs were not successful with regard to the social policy goal of prevention of mental health problems.

The results of goal displacement are not all negative. Focusing on equality has had the desirable outcome of improving access to health-care services across age, racial, and social class lines. For example, doctor visits have been nearly equalized nationally across class and race groups (Wildavsky, 1979, p. 54). However, the health gains have been only marginal. The more intractable problems remain, including iatrogenic disorders, illiteracy, poverty, hazardous work sites, a polluted and carcinogenic environment, lack of effective public health and educational efforts, and inadequate or bad individual habits (lack of regular exercise, poor nutrition, and smoking). Such problems lie beyond the immediate control of health organizations. Nonetheless, health organizations are seen as the cause of the failure of the health system because they are the first, and often only, contact that the public has with the health system.

The organizational factor is a consideration in social policy research for another reason: the role of organizations, especially bureaucracies and professions, in formulating and shaping policy. Bureaucrats and professionals have extraordinary influence in the formulation of social policy, perhaps as much as politicians and policymakers and certainly more than client consumers. Note, for example, the considerable influence of the American Medical Association (doctors) and the American Hospital Association (owners and administrators) on the formulation of health policy. Their influence is exerted through lobbying and contributions to political campaigns, as well as through their control of hospitals, medical schools, and other health organizations.

The behavior of professional organizations has particular relevance for the analysis of social policy because they are powerful actors in the main arenas of social policy, especially in education and health. Professionals are committed to an individual service model and are driven by self-interest as well as by altruism. The individual service model, which stresses one-on-one service and professional control, mitigates against the use of appropriate collective approaches. The AMA was strongly opposed to Medicaid and Medicare and delayed their adoption by years. Self-interest leads to a parochial approach. Each profession defines a social need as within its purview and advocates a policy of hiring more of its members. Thus the community mental health center policy fostered development of community mental health psychiatrists and social workers. Not to be outdone, psychology cloned community psychology.

Rather than complementing and complimenting each other, professionals often engage in sibling rivalry (Street, 1967) that leads to mutual discreditation. The disdain that one profession holds for another is picked up by the public and serves to discredit both professions. As Street, Martin, and Gordon (1979) noted, the outcome is strikingly capitalist in character. Professional organizations are proprietary with regard to social problems, social policies, and clients. Gusfield (1981) referred to this as professional competition over the ownership of a public problem. As with capitalists, competition and ownership produce an overriding concern for economic self-interest among professionals. This self-interest translates into the aggrandizement of professional monopoly, status, and control, and the creation of more jobs and higher salaries for professionals. Thus professional self-interest is promoted at the expense of client consumer interests, such as participation in decision making, and convenient and quality service at relatively low cost.

Evaluation

Evaluation is the empirical measurement of result or projected result used in social policy analysis. Typically, evaluation is an assessment relevant to specific outcome criteria and it has three principal modes: experiments, systems analysis, and survey research.

Experimentation is used because few new policies can be tested on an entire population. That would be too costly, even if technically possible. Experimentation enables analysts to assay alternative policies as well as the relative efficiency of one or another approach, and to connect probable causes with desirable effects.

Experimentation is used to evaluate policies that are being considered. A prominent example is the negative income tax experiments conducted in the 1970s. The typical experimental procedure is as follows: From a target group, a random sample is drawn. Those in the sample are then randomly placed in a control group or an experimental group. The new program is given to the experimental group, while nothing is administered to the control group. Both groups are followed over time, beginning with a baseline measure before the experimental program is administered. After time, changes in both control and experimental groups are measured and compared. Any statistically significant differences between the two groups can then, with some scientific credibility, be attributed to the experiment. In the case of the negative income tax experiments, the treatment was the provision of money and the outcome of interest was the effect this money had on work behavior.

The experimental treatment produces a positive, negative, or neutral effect. In the case of the negative income tax experiments, the overall effect was neutral, in that only an insignificant proportion of subjects worked less as a result of receiving money. Although this result contradicted the principal objection to the negative income tax, it was ignored because of political opposition.

The experimental method is a laboratory model and can produce a relatively high level of scientific reliability. Its usefulness for social policy analysis is limited, however, because social groups cannot be strictly controlled and the effects on them isolated. Researchers are strictly limited, and rightly so, in the kind of experiments they can conduct on human beings. Ethical considerations must be paramount in order to prevent subjects from being coerced, manipulated, or physically or psychically harmed (Kelman and Warwick,

1978). The negative income tax experiments were relatively benign, involving the allocation of money. However, in all experimental researches care must be taken to ensure the safety and confidentiality of the treatment. Moreover, the informed consent of the subjects is necessary. Finally, experimentation cannot prove or disprove a social policy. All it can provide is evidence one way or the other.

Systems analysis is a management model with a built-in evaluation capacity or feedback mechanism. Its conceptual roots go back to the promulgation of "scientific management" principles by Frederick Taylor (1911) and it shares the bureaucratic imperatives of hierarchal control and standardization. Hence its proliferation was tied to the growth of the modern bureaucratic corporation and state after World War II. The military-industrial complex—especially aerospace, where bureaucratic corporations (the defense industry) and the state (Department of Defense) cohabit—was the principal spawning ground for systems analysis. Its prototypical setting is the Rand (for Research and Development) Corporation, which was established in 1947.

Systems analysis is the evaluation of the performance of a given policy as part of a quantified, interrelated administrative unit. It depends on mathematical methods drawn from economics, engineering, and statistics. It is based on a simple model: input—throughput—output—feedback, surrounded by a system boundary. The boundary is closed to outside influences, which are referred to as *externalities*. For social policy research, its principal use is in cost-benefit analysis (CBA). CBA is a modern information system that is used to make decisions. It is extremely rational and quantitative in specifying the most cost efficient of alternative means to reach policy objectives. Simple in conception, the system is highly complex in operation and depends on sophisticated data-processing capacity. Therefore it is relevant primarily to large institutions. The Program Planning and Budgeting System (PPBS), which incorporates CBA, was borrowed from the Department of Defense and mandated by presidential order for all branches of the federal government in 1965.

There are a number of serious technical and substantive limitations to the use of systems analysis in social policy analysis. The technical limitations have to do with the quantification necessary in systems approaches. CBA translates costs and benefits into dollar amounts, but the assignment of value is imprecise, even impossible. For example, how can a human life be monetarized? What of the different monetary values assigned to human lives? Thus a white male's life has higher value than an African American female's because of the discrepancy in the potential earning power of each in contemporary racist and sexist society. Accepting such market values of costs and benefits is morally repugnant and politically explosive, even if it is rational.

Other technical problems with systems analysis include the necessity for arbitrary and judgmental choices of the time scale for measurement. For example, is a program that reduces child abuse more cost efficient than one that reduces wife abuse because children can be expected to live longer? Or is the program that reduces wife abuse more cost effective because wives/mothers produce children, whose improved situation will redound to the benefit of future generations? Another technical problem with CBA is distinguishing between costs and benefits. For example, while a new school is a cost, it is also a benefit because its construction and operation provide jobs. Even if accurately distinguished from cost, benefit is difficult to measure. Rossi (1972, p. 25) cited analyses of the Jobs Corps program in the 1960s by three different government agencies. The cost-benefit ratios arrived at were 1.5 to 1, 4 to 1, and 0.3 to 1. These wide discrepancies were produced by different estimates of the expected benefits of the program.

A major substantive problem with systems analysis is the displacement of attention from the goals of social policy to the means for achieving them. Systems analysis is a method in which form determines content. One way this occurs is that the reliance on numerical criteria results in distortion of policy. If, for example, the only quantifiable criterion for evaluation of a given policy is the number of clients served, the content of interaction with clients may be neglected, since that is not quantifiable. The result is evaluation on the basis of how many clients the policy serves rather than how well it serves clients. Another example of how systems analysis drives policy to emphasize form to the detriment of content comes from a study of interagency coordination. In assessing the impact of PPBS on the U.S. Department of Health and Human Services, Morris (1985) found that while PPBS promoted coordination of various agencies, the coordination did not result in goal achievement.

The boundary maintenance aspect of systems analysis turns intrinsic aspects of social policy into externalities. In fact, the underlying premise of Welfare State social policy and social practice—mutual caring among human beings—is itself an externality in a capitalist society. This was pointed out by Culyer (1980, pp. 57–58):

> The nature of the externality that would appear to underlie the Welfare State is not the sort that suggests that a *private* property right/market exchange solution is likely to be satisfactory. The reason for this is that an important foundation for analysis of social policy lies in the proposition that individuals *care about one another.*

Commenting on this externalization of relevant information, Hoos (1983, p. 17) remarked that, in systems analysis, public welfare "is approached as if it were an independent entity, apart from the economic condition, unrelated to the state of the job market, unaffected by cost and distribution of medical services, and divorced from history, geography, culture, and prevailing politics." Systems approaches create narrow boundaries for social policy issues and disregard the organic connections between issues and society. This results in an abundance of sophisticated data about what is contained in the system, but produces little or no understanding of political and social realities.

Despite their methodological weaknesses and the fact that they are only descriptive, empirical measures are often made into fetishes and put to political use. There are political consequences that flow from using a social indicator to define a situation. Block and Burns (1986) demonstrated how one indicator, aggregate productivity, was created and used by the left in the 1930s and 1940s to push for wage increases, and then was coopted by the right in the 1970s to depress wages. These political uses of the indicator occurred even though, from the beginning, it was widely criticized as empirically tenuous. Apparently the demand for scientific measures is so strong that it overwhelms criticism that many of these measures bear little relation to the social reality they purport to describe. Thus such measures meet the definition of a fetish: they are objects that command irrational devotion.

As another example of the politicization of supposedly objective approaches, consider how the Reagan administration used systems analysis as a rationalization for cutbacks in Welfare State programs (Buxbaum, 1981). The Reagan administration actively promoted the application of cost-benefit analysis to social policy, especially with regard to the regulation of working conditions by the Occupational Safety and Health Administration (OSHA). A 1981 executive order by Reagan required all executive agencies to satisfy CBA tests (Noble, 1987). However, for such purposes, CBA is unworkable on its own terms because the universe of costs and benefits cannot be calculated. After a thorough review of the Reagan administration efforts to quantify costs and benefits, Bequele (1984, p. 14) concluded:

> Therefore, the argument that the setting of standards and other policies intended to provide a safe and healthy environment should be predicated solely on whether benefits justify their cost is not sustainable. There is no way that cost accounting, however sophisticated, can capture the many unrecorded costs of accidents, especially those of pain and suffering that befall disabled or deceased workers and their families, and hence the benefits that accrue from a reduction in risks and accidents.

The U.S. Supreme Court ruled in 1981 that OSHA health standards could not be rejected because of their costs (Byrne, 1987, p. 78). Justice Rehnquist's dissenting opinion in that decision, supporting the American Textile Manufacturers Association, epitomized the Reagan policy position: the OSHA health standard (in this case, for airborne cotton dust in textile factories) should represent a balance between the statistical possibility of death or illness and the economic costs of avoiding death or illness.

Even after the setback dealt it by the Supreme Court, the Reagan administration continued to apply CBA to nonhealth standards. In fact, though, its use of CBA was a thinly veiled rationalization for cutbacks in regulatory policies. Whenever CBA did not support Reagan's policy goal, it was tabled or squelched (Fischer, 1987, p. 119). The ease with which CBA was manipulated for conservative political purposes is no surprise because systems analysis has an inherent bias to stability as opposed to change. Two important reasons for this are that boundary rigidity prohibits consideration of exogenous and unplanned change, and that systems tend to gravitate to stasis.

Ultimately, social policy analysis is as much an art as a science, as much politics as economics, as much moral as rational. In its narrow quantification of social reality, systems analysis distorts the social policy process. The social needs addressed by social policy cannot be reduced to merely quantifiable problems; they must be interpreted, and their resolutions are not so much true or false as good or bad (Dery, 1984).

That social policy research does not produce unequivocal solutions does not negate its usefulness. Accumulated social policy research may lead to a general improvement in the level of understanding about given social needs and social problems. Weiss (1983) referred to this diffuse process as *enlightenment*, meaning that social policy research serves as societal learning. It shapes the discussion and the definitions of social policy rather than pointing to specific choices.

New Directions for Applied Sociology

Applied sociology's use in social policy analysis is limited because of its reliance on quantitative methodology and its refusal to get involved with the moral and political issues that dominate social policy. Offe (1984) referred to this stance as the *scientization* of social policy and argued that it was a technocratic misconception because social policy outcomes are ultimately decided by the political relations of social groups. Because of its abstract scientization, social policy research is often ignored. For example, research on 12 social program evaluations found no relationship between the quality of the methodology and the use of the evaluation. The researchers, Berg and Theado (1981, p. 191), concluded that administrators ignored evaluations as meaningless exercises in the application of research methods or regarded them only as an administrative requirement for financial support. Also, in a study of 120 policy research projects, Van de Vall (1986, p. 209) found that "the amount of the researcher's time devoted to methodological problems does not correlate positively with utilization."

Applied sociology was not always mired in valueless abstract scientization. It comes out of a tradition committed both to studying and to resolving social problems. While study is a scientific endeavor, resolution is a political and moral undertaking. It is this latter aspect of applied sociology that has atrophied as major advances have been made in computerization and statistical analysis. MacRae (1985, p. xv) has suggested that one way to restore the valuative aspect to social indicators would be to use policy indicators that "provide actual measures of notions of the public interest, in the form of end-value indicator statistics." This approach would take into account subjective well-being. For example, where life expectancy is a social indicator, the policy indicator might become "quality-adjusted life years," a measure from Weinstein and Stason (1977) that combines length and quality of lifespan. Using policy indicators would require interviewing people in order to assess their life circumstances. The technology for doing this is well developed in applied sociology—in research facilities such as the University of Chicago's National Opinion Research Center (NORC) and the University of Michigan's Institute for Survey Research (ISR). Since 1972, NORC's General Social Survey has done in-depth interviews with a national sample of 1,500 people to monitor changes in a number of areas relevant to social policy analysis.

MacRae has also proposed a field of practical social research that would be independent of academic disciplines. In this way, applied sociology and other applied social sciences would no longer be ad hoc appendages of their disciplines. Technical communities could replace disciplines in policy analysis; they would be the basis for monitoring policy's relevance as well as its scientific credentials. While scientific communities address peers only and aspire to value-free research, technical communities would accept input from the lay public and experts, and would aim for end-value research. This is an important consideration because, as Heclo (1978) found in his analysis of federal policy development, issue networks and clusters of "technopols" (policy analysts and lobbyists) increasingly dominate social policy. These issue networks, as Edelman (1983, p. 145) noted, tend to reinforce existing inequalities in social policy since they have a vested interest (including holding on to their own jobs) in maintaining the status quo. MacRae's technical communities may be an illustration of Gusfield's (1981) observation that science is rhetoric as well as rationale. Gusfield made this comment in a study of the transformation of drunken driving into a public problem. Although it was couched in scientific terms, this transformation reflected ethical and political considerations.

It is important to emphasize that this proposed new direction for applied sociology would retain the scientific model. In contrast, another proposal to improve applied sociology's relevance to social policy—forensic social science—would abdicate the scientific method in favor of the legal approach. Rivlin (1973, p. 61) defined forensic social science as follows:

> Scholars or teams of scholars take on the task of writing briefs for or against particular policy positions. They state what the position is and bring together all the evidence that supports their side of the argument, leaving to the brief writer on the other side the job of picking apart the case that had been presented and detailing the counter evidence.

However, as Bermant and Warwick (1978) have shown, forensic social science is a contradiction in terms because the law is based on an adversarial system with winners and losers, while science promotes collaboration that produces findings. The legal approach is inappropriate for social policy analysis in another way: whereas the law entitles all parties to rights, in social policy analysis not all ideas are equal, and some are downright bad. Social policy should not be required to give equal time to unscientific and discredited proposals such as creationism, racism, and sexism.

The major limitations of quantitative methodology are lack of natural contact with subjects, limited access because of technical elaboration (most people cannot even comprehend its results), and its tendency to become an end in itself. While they are useful, the quantitative methods that dominate applied sociology should be balanced by use of qualitative methods. Whereas quantitative methodology relies on objective measurement of quantities through controlled statistical studies that involve large numbers, qualitative research takes place in a natural setting for subjects (the "field") and involves direct social contact with them over a period of time. The best-known qualitative method is ethnographic participant observation, in which the researcher collects data while participating in the daily lives of subjects. Thus qualitative research is more likely to reveal the nature of social needs, while quantitative research is more likely to demonstrate the extent of those needs (Rossi and Berk, 1983, p. 187). Qualitative research should precede quantitative research because of its utility for selecting categories, variables, and hypotheses for quantitative research. Unfortunately, qualitative research receives little attention (Karapin, 1986, p. 259); the result is research that is mathematically precise but conceptually ambiguous.

Another approach available to moderate the quantitative dominance in applied sociology is multiplism (Cook, 1985). This model uses multiple research methods, qualitative and quantitative, and tests across multiple populations, settings, and times. It promises greater flexibility for discovering, explaining, and communicating findings. Related to multiplism is the research method of successive trials that combines qualitative and quantitative methods. The central procedure is the randomized field experiment. Over time and in a natural treatment setting, successive innovative interventions are tried and tested. A prominent successful example of this natural experiment approach was a program fostering self-help among chronic mental patients (Fairweather, 1980).

A common factor of policy indicators, qualitative methods, multiplism, and natural experiments is that they aspire to ongoing personal contact with the people who have social needs. To this end, Byrd (1980) proposed a "humanized policy model" that incorporates the subjective intuition and judgments of individuals. In this approach, mathematical precision is sacrificed for utility, as insights replace numbers. This is a much needed antidote to the current failure to respect the knowledge of those who actually experience social needs. One reason that technical manipulation of data has displaced human sensitivity is that the expertise required to use quantitative methodology often results in a trained incapacity to deal effectively on the personal level. This same problem has been noted in the performance of physicians—sophisticated clinical skills coupled with insensitive personal treatment of patients.

SOCIAL PRACTICE

Research and social policy can be articulated with social practice from two perspectives. First, applied research is itself a social practice. Since applied research investigates questions of social practice and social policy, intellectual curiosity and a desire to resolve social problems often characterize the personalities of applied researchers. Ellen Duane, whose social practice is discussed below, is a worthy example. Second, research, policy, and practice articulate with one another. The traditional view of this articulation is that research informs, policy guides, and practice effectuates. However, the relationships among research, policy, and practice are more complex and variegated than this simple view would lead us to believe. One variation consists of the ways in which practice both guides and informs research and policy, a subject that we address after we discuss Ellen Duane's practice of social research.

Social Practitioner at Work: Ellen Duane

Ellen Duane is associate research scientist at a university-based research center in the New York metropolitan area. The center specializes in family planning and family health issues and receives much of its funding from the federal government. Ellen directs research projects. Her work includes the design of questionnaires, the training of interviewers, the overseeing of data collection, and some data analysis.

Ellen first got interested in social research when she was an undergraduate student. After receiving a Bachelor of Arts degree, she went on to obtain a doctorate in sociology. She became involved in her current work at the center while doing her Ph.D dissertation on the sterilization intentions of poor women, and she has been on its staff ever since.

Ellen's area of expertise is survey research. Survey research consists of interviews with large numbers of respondents, the results of which are generalizable to even larger populations. (The Gallup Poll is a well-known example of survey research.) A major focus of the center's survey research is the evaluation of user satisfaction with new approaches to family health and family planning service delivery.

In Ellen's view, survey research is very useful so long as it is well done and its limitations are understood. Compared to many other kinds of empirical research, such as complex experimental studies and ethnographies, a centralized survey research project is inexpensive. It also has the advantage of being able to reach large numbers of people who are representative (through random sampling) of even larger populations. Finally, survey research data are readily quantified and relatively easy to manipulate statistically. The drawback of survey research is that it does not usually provide in-depth information. Thus it can give us relatively superficial information about a lot of people, but it does not give us rich data about them or about the contexts of their lives. For such intensive data qualitative research, such as ethnography, is necessary. Survey research works best when discrete responses are the norm—for example, definite yes/no answers, as in "I will vote for X or Y." Survey research is less useful for diffuse responses, which must be interpreted and which depend on the natural context in which they are used—

for example, general answers about the status of one's health. The use of specific research techniques depends on the problem to be addressed, on the resources available, and on the kind of information one desires.

The field of social research was long split between those who advocated qualitative research and those who espoused quantitative research. Although this difference still exists, it has become somewhat muted. Both camps are now more willing to recognize the value of the other and to acknowledge that the best research is usually located on a continuum between qualitative and quantitative, rather than being wholly one or the other. Increasingly then social research incorporates both qualitative and quantitative techniques. For example, in a study of the effects of land redistribution and other reforms in an Indian province, a sociologist (Chasin, 1988) and an anthropologist (Franke, 1988) combined survey research interviews and reinterviews with a year of field work in an Indian village. Their combination of research techniques promises to provide data that are both in-depth and generalizable, and that will be useful for planning socioeconomic development strategies in the Third World.

Some of the research projects Ellen works on have immediate and direct implications for social practice; in this sense, she is doing applied social research. A study of sterilization decision making secured data that will be useful to social practitioners in family health and family planning facilities, including social workers and nurse midwives (discussed in Chapter 8). One goal of this research was an applied one—to reduce poststerilization regret. The research consisted of interviews with 1,814 low-income mothers who said that they were certain they wanted no more children. The mothers were outpatients at clinics in public hospitals in Atlanta, New York City, and Pittsburgh. Of the women, 1,213 were planning on having themselves sterilized and 601 were not. Of the total sample of 1,814, the average age was 28.4 years and the average number of children 2.3.

The value of this research to family planning and family health practitioners lies in its identification of unrealistic and inaccurate beliefs and expectations that low-income women may have about sterilization. The premise of the research was that if social practitioners are aware of the false or unrealistic beliefs of their patients, they will be better able to serve their patients' needs and to prevent or to reduce poststerilization regret. For example, 30 percent of the women who were planning on sterilization did not believe that it would make them absolutely incapable of having a child in the future. In fact, reversal of sterilization is possible in only a very small minority of cases. Also, 21 percent of the women who were not planning on sterilization believed that sterilization caused long-term health problems when, in fact, there is no empirical evidence supporting this belief. Thus there are two forms of regret that may be preventable in the work that social practitioners do with patients. One is the regret of those who want to have children after sterilization; the other is the regret of those who rejected sterilization on the basis of inaccurate beliefs about its negative effects and wished afterward that they had not. Thus if all women who contemplate sterilization are made aware of the facts that it is not reversible and that it does not cause health problems, the level of regret both among women who choose sterilization and among those who do not can be reduced (Cushman et al., 1988).

Ellen gets a lot of satisfaction from the challenge of data collection—creating a questionnaire so that she can obtain the information she wants from the respondents she wants it from, and then testing, revising, and using the questionnaire. The next stage of her career will involve data analysis as well as data collection. She is learning a lot from her colleagues about data analysis. Ellen's work is satisfying also because she and her colleagues teach and learn from one another. Additionally, the flexible hours afford her colleagues who are parents more time to be with their young children.

Although Ellen regards her work as challenging and creative, she would like to do more writing and teaching. For this a faculty position is necessary, and that may be the direction Ellen takes in her career. Her work conditions provide Ellen with a great deal of autonomy with regard to how to conduct research. In the future she hopes to have more autonomy in the choice of research questions and issues as well.

The most frustrating aspect of Ellen's work is her distance from actually resolving social problems. While her research is palpably related to social practice, the connection to social policy is far more remote and abstract. Even when she does her work well—conducting research that provides new, revealing findings—she can have only a very small impact on the resolution of the social problem or social issue she has investigated. For example, research alone cannot reduce the poverty that underlies the reproductive and family problems of many of the women who are the subjects of her research. Yet Ellen does realize a direct connection to the amelioration of social problems at the local level, since the findings of the research on which she works are often shared with social practitioners.

Practice, Research, and Policy

Although social policy is commonly viewed as controlled by distant and powerful actors, it is actually influenced considerably by the social practice of those who provide it at the grass-roots level. Within the general limits set by national, professional, and organizational policies, practitioners have varying degrees of individual discretion—this despite the conventional wisdom that social policy is ordained by those at the top of hierarchal structures, and then passed down to be automatically implemented by lower-level workers.

Schorr (1985) has argued that the distinction between policy and practice is a false one and that practitioners are policymakers in important clinical and organizational respects, including devising individualized therapeutic strategies for clients and manipulating agency routines on behalf of these strategies. The provision level, where social policy meets clients through the mediation of social service workers, is critical for the analysis of social policy.

We will analyze the relationship of the social practice of providers to social policy in three areas: personal, organizational, and collective.

Personal practice At the level of personal policies, social service workers often have considerable discretion in carrying out social policy. For example, public welfare caseworkers, despite their rigidly bureaucratic work structure, demonstrate a high level of individual discretion in the most important decision made by their agency—to accept or to reject an applicant for public aid (Street, Martin, and Gordon, 1979). In 31 percent of decisions in one large public welfare department, the applicant could legitimately have been either accepted, deferred, or rejected by the caseworker. In even more cases—39 percent—the caseworker could have made one of two of the three possible dispositions.

Ironically, this individual discretion flows from the very bureaucratism of the agency. Rules are so vague, complex, and contradictory that the worker cannot possibly carry them all out, but must choose which to execute. In public welfare especially, rules are both encyclopedic and ever-changing, and because caseloads are extremely large, close supervision is impossible. Additionally, caseworker compliance with rules cannot be consistently observed because the hierarchal levels of large organizations prevent eyes-on enforcement by central authorities (Ham and Hill, 1986, pp. 172–173). To some extent, this is also true of bureaucratic organizations in other social policy arenas, including hospitals and schools. Thus social practitioners who are also bureaucrats can maximize their personal satisfaction and their aid to clients by gaining a thorough knowledge of their organization's rules and structure. This gives them greater potential for managing and for negotiating the organizational environment of their social practice (Pruger, 1982).

Individual discretion also results from the special character of the social practice of Welfare State workers who deal directly with clients. According to Lipsky (1980), these street-level bureaucrats have discretion because their jobs are too complex and demand too much flexibility for bureaucracies to want to prevent it, even if they could. Thus teachers are expected to individualize instruction and to create personal relationships with students, even though bureaucratic imperatives mandate standardization of instruction and impartiality in treatment. Not surprisingly, then, research demonstrates the autonomy of teachers in the privacy of their classrooms (McLaughlin, 1985).

The discretion of Welfare State workers does not stem from professionalization. Professional autonomy is a different matter, and it increases as one rises in Welfare State hierarchies. The point is that, because of the effects of bureaucratism, even nonprofessional social service providers have some discretion. Professionalization also increases practitioner control of social practice but, because of the relatively narrow self-interest of professionals, it does not necessarily produce a better social practice from the perspective of client consumers. For this reason, professionalism has been challenged by a radical social practice. Cloward and Piven (1981) have argued that professional social work education should be radically revised to recognize the conflict of interest that exists between client consumers, on the one hand, and agencies and professions, on the other.

Furthermore, the presence of discretion does not automatically lead to more satisfying social practice for clients and workers. Despite the considerable discretion of public welfare caseworkers, there is a great deal of homogenization or uniformity in their treatment of clients. The discretion is largely negative rather than positive, in that caseworkers can more easily prevent bad things from happening to clients than make good things happen for them. It is, in other words, a discretion that can veto but cannot create.

Finally, caseworkers use their discretion to withdraw and to protect themselves in a harsh organizational environment (Ham and Hill, 1986, pp. 139–140). Caseworker retreat is a survival mechanism in the face of the exigencies of the work: large caseloads, lack of resources and support, and low pay and status (Street, Martin, and Gordon, 1979, p. 61). There is another important reason for the withdrawal of social service workers: their terrible isolation (Withorn, 1984, p. 26).

Only when material conditions improve to the point where the job is no longer considered temporary or dead-end, and when social conditions improve to the point where isolation and alienation no longer dominate, will social service practitioners be able to exercise fully satisfying discretionary personal policies. These policies would include influencing others—clients, colleagues, and supervisors—through persuasion, and modifying social policy through judicious implementation (Pierce, 1984, pp. 200–206).

Organizational practice   The majority of social service practitioners work in organizations, usually large bureaucracies. Many of these workers are also members of other policy-relevant organizations: professions and unions. The classical Weberian view of bureaucracy is that it is a hierarchal, top-down structure that allows no maneuverability for lower-level workers, who are mere cogs in the organizational machine. However, beginning in the 1930s (Roethlisberger and Dickson, 1939), sociologists modified this view by demonstrating that bureaucracies do not live up to Weber's ideal type. Bureaucracies do not exhibit full rationality of means to ends, but bounded rationality (Perrow, 1986), in which shifting and unclear ends and imperfect knowledge of ends-means connections produce a source of power for employees. Bureaucrats are not the passive instruments of a rigid and hierarchal administration of rules.

Bureaucracies have both formal and informal systems. The formal system corresponds to the classical view; it is hierarchal and governed by written rules. The informal system is the shadow of the formal system; it is relatively egalitarian and includes procedures to circumvent written rules. The informal system is maintained through word of mouth—the grapevine.

This informal system makes it possible for workers and clients in even the largest and most rigid bureaucracy, including the military, to have access to influence within the organization. Even in a rigidly bureaucratic and coercive organization such as a prison, inmates establish informal systems to gain a measure of control over their lives, through the manipulation of privileges and supplies. Goffman's (1961) pioneering study of a mental institution demonstrated how even inmates in total institutions are able to carve out relatively autonomous personal and social spaces. In a more typical bureaucracy, the hospital, Blumberg (1987, p. 144) documented how nurses and patients circumvent rules and doctors in order to help themselves. Use of the informal system is a socially learned skill that is part of what can be referred to as *bureaucratic competence* (Gordon, 1974). This social learning requires time and experience. Thus on university campuses, the staff, clerical as well as professional, have more knowledge of the informal system than students, and the more senior students have greater knowledge of the system than the other students.

The informal system is a context and a resource for the use of individual discretion. Discretion can be used in at least two vital ways: in getting things done for clients and workers that are prohibited by rules and in controlling the pace of work. Both require that the client and worker have knowledge of their organization and social connections with other clients and workers. Thus, although it is exercised by individuals, bureaucratic competence is a social skill.

The challenges to the pathologies of the Welfare State bureaucracy fall under the rubric of *debureaucratization*, and they take the form of structural reform, including decentralization and deconcentration of social services from large centrally located organizations to small locally dispersed ones (Grunow, 1986). One generally unacknowledged and potentially pathological activity of large organizations is the collection of personal information on their clients. Advanced information-processing technologies that use computers have greatly increased the capacity of organizations to gather information from a wide range of sources and to share it. Thus social welfare organizations such as hospitals and schools commonly collect and store a vast amount of highly personal data on their clients. The mere presence of such an accessible storehouse of information represents some danger to the privacy rights of clients (Laudon, 1986). For this reason, the amount of data collected must be strictly limited to the need of the organization to fulfill its mission, access to the information must be strictly limited to those who need to know it, and the information must be destroyed when its use is over.

Debureaucratization would provide the conditions necessary for greater worker discretion, more flexible forms of work, and more personalized services. Reform is opposed or ignored by bureaucracies because it is perceived as a threat to organizational maintenance and power. Thus debureaucratized models of social service are usually developed outside Welfare State bureaucracies. The contemporary holistic health and self-help movements (discussed in Chapter 8) are examples. While some of their methods have been incorporated into Welfare State bureaucracies—for example, natural childbirth in hospitals—the major agenda of change remains: structural rearrangement of the bureaucracies themselves.

Collective practice In addition to the use of discretion and the informal system, there is another vehicle by which social practice can shape social policy: collective action. Long recognized for its power to improve the material conditions of work (pay and working environment), collective action also has an important bearing on social practice and policy issues. Grossman (1985) documented how one local union of direct-care workers in the Massachusetts Department of Mental Health influenced clinical decisions. The union was able to get the administration to reduce admissions in the face of overcrowding and to transfer a patient who had no psychiatric problems.

Unions afford another opportunity to enhance social practice and to influence social policy: internal social service departments that provide services to members and jobs to practitioners. The United Farm Workers (UFW) was an early advocate of including social practice within unions, both as an organizing tool and as an expression of moral and political vision. The basic model for the UFW social practice is "reciprocity," which defines the relationship between client and worker as mutual aid (Withorn, 1984, p. 67). The client is not a powerless supplicant but an active participant in a complementary social relationship. This reciprocity comes from two sources: the traditional solidarity within unions (the sense of "we-ness") and the equity that members have because they are dues payers and the service providers are hired staff. Thus the typical dominance of clients by professionals that occurs in bureaucratic settings is moderated in the union context. This has important implications for the analysis of social policy. Reciprocity may be a viable model for the provision of social services in other settings.

Although these union social services have proved successful, they are concentrated in only a small number of national and international unions (Martin, 1985) with a tradition of social unionism and with large numbers and proportions of female and state workers. Unions that have developed an internal direct social practice include the Amalgamated Clothing and Textile Workers Union; the American Federation of State, County, and Municipal Employees; the International Ladies' Garment Workers Union; and the United Auto Workers. Other unions have developed social services to a lesser extent: the American Federation of Teachers; Communications Workers of America; the International Association of Machinists; the National Maritime Union; and the Service Employees International Union. These are also the unions that represent large numbers of social practitioners, many of them women. Feminism was an important factor in the emergence of union social services.

Feminism also played a role in the expansion of another vehicle for social practitioners to influence social policy: self-help (discussed in Chapter 8). Despite its limitations, including its tendency to reinforce a blaming-the-victim mentality, self-help offers an alternative means for social practice that is outside the control of bureaucracies and professions. In fact, self-help is both antibureaucratic (democratic) and antiprofessional (lay). Although self-help has been around for a long time, it mushroomed in the 1960s and has continued to grow, largely as a result of the feminist movement. Feminism spawned successful self-help policies for reproductive and medical rights, family violence, rape, and child care. A number of these were copied or coopted by local and state governments, especially in the areas of family violence and rape.

Traditionally, self-help has centered on personal problems such as alcoholism. Alcoholics Anonymous (AA) is the best-known example. However, self-help is gaining currency as a means to deal with social, especially work-related, problems as well. An example is the role that self-help groups play in dealing with work stress and burnout (Maslach, 1982, pp. 111–118). Like the use of discretion and informal systems within bureaucracies, self-help requires knowledge and social contact. It is antithetical to an individualistic approach.

Finally, if social policy analysis is to be influenced by social practice, practitioners must be self-conscious, knowledgeable about their social environments, and concerned for their clients. The exercise of influence on policy depends on motivation, capacity, and opportunity—all of which depend on workers and clients joining together to develop power over their social practice. The latent power possessed by social practitioners and their clients, if joined and activated, has the potential for transforming the major institutions of the Welfare State from conveyor belts for the transmission of capitalist social control into cultural and political battlegrounds. Welfare State institutions are a weak link in the infrastructure of capitalist dominance because they are noncapitalist, sometimes even anticapitalist. Under the right social conditions, they can be transformed into zones of resistance to capitalist political power and cultural domination.

REFERENCES

Anderson, Odin W. 1972. *Health Care: Can There Be Equity?* New York: John Wiley & Sons.

Bardes, Barbara A., and Melvin J. Dubnick. 1980. "Motives and Methods in Policy Analysis." Pp. 101–127 in *Improving Policy Analysis*, ed. Stuart S. Nagel. Beverly Hills, CA: Sage Publications.

Bequele, Assefa. 1984. "The Costs and Benefits of Protecting and Saving Lives at Work: Some Issues." *International Labour Review* 123:1–16.

Berg, William E., and Richard Theado. 1981. "The Utilization of Evaluative Research in Social Welfare Programs." *Social Service Review* 55:183–192.

Bermant, Gordon, and Donald P. Warwick. 1978. "The Ethics of Social Intervention: Power, Freedom, and Accountability." Pp. 377–418 in *The Ethics of Social Intervention*, eds. Gordon Bermant, Herbert C. Kelman, and Donald P. Warwick. New York: John Wiley & Sons.

Block, Fred, and Gene A. Burns. 1986. "Productivity as a Social Problem: The Uses and Misuses of Social Indicators." *American Sociological Review* 51:767–780.

Blumberg, Rhoda Lois. 1987. *Organizations in Contemporary Society.* Englewood Cliffs, NJ: Prentice Hall.

Buxbaum, Carl B. 1981. "Cost-Benefit Analysis: The Mystique versus the Reality." *Social Service Review* 55:454–471.

Byrd, Jack, Jr. 1980. "The Humanization of Policy Models." Pp. 73–89 in *Improving Policy Analysis*, ed. Stuart S. Nagel. Beverly Hills, CA: Sage Publications.

Byrne, John. 1987. "Policy Science and the Administrative State: The Political Economy of Cost-Benefit Analysis." Pp. 70–93 in *Confronting Values in Policy Analysis: The Politics of Criteria*, eds. Frank Fischer and John Forester. Beverly Hills, CA: Sage Publications.

Chambers, Donald E. 1986. *Social Policy and Social Programs: A Method for the Practical Public Policy Analyst*. New York: Macmillan.

Chasin, Barbara H. 1988. "Land Reform and Women's Work in a Kerala Village." Paper presented at Annual Meeting, American Anthropological Association, Phoenix.

Cherns, Albert. 1986. "Policy Research Under Scrutiny." Pp. 185–198 in *The Use and Abuse of Social Science*, ed. Frank Heller. Beverly Hills, CA: Sage Publications.

Cloward, Richard A., and Frances Fox Piven. 1981. "Notes Toward a Radical Social Work." Pp. 445–473 in *Social Welfare in Society*, eds. George T. Martin, Jr., and Mayer N. Zald. New York: Columbia University Press.

Cook, Thomas D. 1985. "Postpositivist Critical Multiplism." Pp. 21–62 in *Social Science and Social Policy*, eds. R. Lance Shotland and Melvin M. Mark. Beverly Hills, CA: Sage Publications.

Culyer, A. J. 1980. *The Political Economy of Social Policy*. New York: St. Martin's Press.

Cushman, Linda F., et al. 1988. "Beliefs About Contraceptive Sterilization Among Low-Income Urban Women." *Family Planning Perspectives* 20:218–221, 233.

Dery, David. 1984. *Problem Definition in Policy Analysis*. Lawrence: University Press of Kansas.

Edelman, Murray. 1983. "Systematic Confusions in the Evaluation of Implementing Decisions." Pp. 131–147 in *Evaluating the Welfare State: Social and Political Perspectives*, eds. Shimon E. Spiro and Ephraim Yuchtman-Yaar. New York: Academic Press.

Fairweather, George W., ed. 1980. *The Fairweather Lodge: A Twenty-five Year Retrospective*. San Francisco: Jossey-Bass.

Fischer, Frank. 1987. "Policy Expertise and the 'New Class': A Critique of the Neoconservative Thesis." Pp. 94–126 in *Confronting Values in Policy Analysis: The Politics of Criteria*, eds. Frank Fischer and John Forester. Beverly Hills, CA: Sage Publications.

Franke, Richard W. 1988. "Redistribution as a Development Strategy: Preliminary Results from a Kerala Village." Paper presented at Annual Meeting, American Anthropological Association, Phoenix.

Fry, Lincoln J., and Jon Miller. 1981. "Responding to Skid Row Alcoholism." Pp. 395–411 in *Social Welfare in Society*, eds. George T. Martin, Jr., and Mayer N. Zald. New York: Columbia University Press.

Goffman, Erving. 1961. *Asylums: Essays on the Social Situation of Mental Patients and Other Inmates*. Garden City, NY: Anchor Books/Doubleday.

Goleman, Daniel. 1988. "How Is America? Social Science Plots Numerical Answers." *The New York Times*, December 25.

Gordon, Laura Kramer. 1974. "Bureaucratic Competence and Success in Dealing with Public Bureaucracies." *Social Problems* 23:197–208.

Grossman, Jon. 1985. "Can a Human Service Union Affect Clinical Issues?" *Catalyst: A Socialist Journal of the Social Services* 5:57–65.

Grunow, Dieter. 1986. "Debureaucratization and the Self-Help Movement: Towards a Restructuring of the Welfare State in the Federal Republic of Germany?" Pp. 192–204 in *Comparing Welfare States and Their Futures*, ed. Else Oyen. Aldershot, UK: Gower.

Gusfield, Joseph R. 1981. *The Culture of Public Problems: Drinking-Driving and the Symbolic Order*. Chicago: University of Chicago Press.

Ham, Christopher, and Michael Hill. 1986. *The Policy Process in the Modern Capitalist State*. Brighton: Wheatsheaf Books.

Haveman, Robert H. 1986. "Social Science and Social Policy: Who Uses Whom?" Pp. 74–84 in *The Use and Abuse of Social Science*, ed. Frank Heller. Beverly Hills, CA: Sage Publications.

Heclo, Hugh. 1978. "Issue Networks and the Executive Establishment." Pp. 87–124 in *The New American Political System*, ed. Anthony King. Washington, DC: American Enterprise Institute for Public Policy Research.

Hoos, Ida R. 1983. *Systems Analysis in Public Policy: A Critique*. Rev. ed. Berkeley: University of California Press.

Jennings, Bruce. 1987. "Interpretation and the Practice of Policy Analysis." Pp. 128–152 in *Confronting Values in Policy Analysis: The Politics of Criteria*, eds. Frank Fischer and John Forester. Beverly Hills, CA; Sage Publications.

Karapin, Roger S. 1986. "What's the Use of Social Science? A Review of the Literature." Pp. 236–265 in *The Use and Abuse of Social Science*, ed. Frank Heller. Beverly Hills, CA: Sage Publications.

Kelman, Herbert C., and Donald P. Warwick. 1978. "The Ethics of Social Intervention: Goals, Means, and Consequences." Pp. 3–33 in *The Ethics of Social Intervention*, eds. Gordon Bermant, Herbert C. Kelman, and Donald P. Warwick. New York: John Wiley & Sons/Halsted Press.

Kingdon, John W. 1984. *Agendas, Alternatives, and Public Policies*. Boston: Little, Brown.

Laudon, Kenneth C. 1986. *Dossier Society: Value Choices in the Design of National Information Systems*. New York: Columbia University Press.

Lazarsfeld, Paul F., and Jeffrey G. Reitz. 1975. *An Introduction to Applied Sociology*. New York: Elsevier.

Lehman, Edward W. 1980. "Policy Research: Industry or Social Movement?" Pp. 201–218 in *Improving Policy Analysis*, ed. Stuart S. Nagel. Beverly Hills, CA: Sage Publications.

Lindblom, Charles E. 1959. "The Science of 'Muddling Through.' " *Public Administration Review* 19:79–88.

Lipsky, Michael. 1980. *Street-Level Bureaucracy: Dilemmas of the Individual in Public Services*. New York: Russell Sage Foundation.

MacRae, Duncan, Jr. 1985. *Policy Indicators: Links Between Social Science and Public Debate*. Chapel Hill: University of North Carolina Press.

Martin, George T., Jr. 1985. "Union Social Services and Women's Work." *Social Service Review* 59:62–74.

Maslach, Christina. 1982. *Burnout—The Cost of Caring*. Englewood Cliffs, NJ: Prentice Hall.

McLaughlin, Milbrey Wallin. 1985. "Implementation Realities and Evaluation Design." Pp. 96–120 in *Social Science and Social Policy*, eds. R. Lance Shotland and Melvin M. Mark. Beverly Hills, CA: Sage Publications.

Merton, Robert K. 1957. *Social Theory and Social Structure*. New York: Free Press.

Miles, Ian. 1985. *Social Indicators for Human Development*. New York: St. Martin's Press.

Morris, Robert. 1985. *Social Policy of the American Welfare State: An Introduction to Policy Analysis*. 2nd ed. New York: Longman.

Mumpower, Jeryl L., and Warren F. Ilchman. 1988. *New York State in the Year 2000*. Albany: State University of New York Press.

Noble, Charles. 1987. "Economic Theory in Practice: White House Oversight of OSHA Health Standards." Pp. 266–284 in *Confronting Values in Policy Analysis: The Politics of Criteria*, eds. Frank Fischer and John Forester. Beverly Hills, CA: Sage Publications.

Nove, Alec. 1983. *The Economics of Feasible Socialism*. London: George Allen & Unwin.

Offe, Claus. 1984. "Social Policy and the Theory of the State." Pp. 88–118 in Claus Offe, *Contradictions of the Welfare State*, ed. John Keane. Cambridge, MA: MIT Press.

Ogburn, William F., ed. 1929. *Recent Social Changes in the United States Since the War and Particularly in 1927*. Chicago: University of Chicago Press.

Perrow, Charles. 1986. *Complex Organizations: A Critical Essay*. 3rd ed. New York: Random House.

Pierce, Dean. 1984. *Policy for the Social Work Practitioner*. New York: Longman.

Pruger, Robert. 1982. "The Good Bureaucrat." Pp. 385–392 in *Things That Matter: Influences on Helping Relationships*, eds. Hiasura Rubenstein and Mary Henry Bloch. New York: Macmillan.

Rein, Martin. 1983. *From Policy to Practice*. Armonk, NY: M. E. Sharpe.

Rivlin, A. M. 1973. "Forensic Social Science." *Harvard Educational Review* 43:61–75.

Roethlisberger, Fritz J., and William J. Dickson. 1939. *Management and the Worker*. Cambridge, MA: Harvard University Press.

Rossi, Peter H. 1972. "Testing for Success and Failure in Social Action." Pp. 11–49 in *Evaluating Social Programs: Theory, Practice, and Politics*, eds. Peter H. Rossi and Walter Williams. New York: Seminar Press.

Rossi, Peter H., and Richard A. Berk. 1983. "The Scope of Evaluation Activities in the United States." Pp. 179–203 in *Evaluating the Welfare State: Social and Political Perspectives*, eds. Shimon E. Spiro and Ephraim Yuchtman-Yaar. New York: Academic Press.

Russett, Bruce M. 1964. *World Handbook of Political and Social Indicators*. New Haven, CT: Yale University Press.

Schorr, Alvin L. 1985. "Professional Practice as Policy." *Social Service Review* 59:178–196.

Scott, Robert A. 1969. *The Making of Blind Men*. New York: Russell Sage Foundation.

Straus, Roger A. 1985. *Using Sociology: An Introduction from the Clinical Perspective*. Bayside, NY: General Hall.

Street, David. 1967. "Educators and Social Workers: Sibling Rivalry in the Inner City." *Social Service Review* 41:152–165.

Street, David, George T. Martin, Jr., and Laura Kramer Gordon. 1979. *The Welfare Industry: Functionaries and Recipients in Public Aid*. Beverly Hills, CA: Sage Publications.

Taylor, Frederick Winslow. 1911. *The Principles of Scientific Management*. New York: Harper.

Van de Vall, Mark. 1986. "Policy Research: An Analysis of Function and Structure." Pp. 199–213 in *The Use and Abuse of Social Science*, ed. Frank Heller. Beverly Hills, CA: Sage Publications.

Weber, Max. 1946. *From Max Weber: Essays in Sociology*, trans. and eds. H. H. Gerth and C. Wright Mills. New York: Oxford University Press.

Weinstein, Milton C., and William B. Stason. 1977. "Foundations of Cost-Effectiveness Analysis for Health and Medical Practices." *New England Journal of Medicine* 296:716–721.

Weiss, Carol H. 1983. "Policy Evaluation as Societal Learning." Pp. 361–374 in *Evaluating the Welfare State: Social and Political Perspectives*, eds. Shimon E. Spiro and Ephraim Yuchtman-Yaar. New York: Academic Press.

Wildavsky, Aaron. 1979. *Speaking Truth to Power: The Art and Craft of Policy Analysis*. Boston: Little, Brown.

Wirth, Louis. 1964. "The Metropolitan Region as a Planning Unit." Pp. 304–318 in Louis Wirth, *On Cities and Social Life*, ed. Albert J. Reiss. Chicago: University of Chicago Press.

Withorn, Ann. 1984. *Serving the People: Social Services and Social Change*. New York: Columbia University Press.

11

Social Change
and Social Policy

So times are chaunged to and fro, and chaunging times have chaunged us too.
Babington, *A Very Fruitfull Exposition of the Commandments*, 1583

As we have noted in the course of our analysis, Welfare State social policy is both the object and the subject of change. For example, Welfare State social policy is the object of change when interest groups aim to direct it in a certain course or when sociohistorical changes shape it, as capitalist wage labor led to Social Security. Alternatively, Welfare State social policy is the subject of change when its programs reshape society, as public education did, or when its constituents and functionaries act as major interest groups in society. Such social change is the focus of this, our last, chapter. After an examination of social change and Welfare State social policy and of the question of where to get the resources for its expansion, we turn to a discussion of social planning. We conclude with some musings on the future of Welfare State social policy.

SOCIAL CHANGE AND SOCIAL POLICY
IN THE WELFARE STATE

Our analysis indicates that social change in Welfare State social policy is over-determined. We can identify two major sources of change: those that are at least conceptually external to the Welfare State, including the economy; and those that result from the Welfare State itself—for example, from the actions of its functionaries.

We note four external sources of change in Welfare State social policy: economic, demographic, social, and political. First, the general state and direction of the economy help to determine Welfare State activity, as can be seen in the effects of the Great Depression of the 1930s and of the relative stagnation since the early 1970s. On a societal and historical level, the development of industrialization is a necessary precondition for the emergence of the Welfare State. Economic changes can both create greater demand for Welfare State activity and straiten resources for that activity. Thus economic stagnation produces greater social needs, such as increased poverty, at the same time that it constrains state action by exerting downward pressure on state resources. Second, the demographic composition of society exerts pressure on Welfare State social policy. Thus the current aging of the population leads to Welfare State expansion of benefits and services for the elderly. Third, social changes bear on Welfare State social policy. Two current changes exerting pressure for the expansion of Welfare State social policy are noteworthy: (1) the mobilization of constituent groups into interest groups and social movements; and (2) the continuing entry of middle-class women, especially those with young children, into the paid labor force. Both developments encourage Welfare State expansion into new areas, such as child care, and the formation of new interest groups such as the disabled. The fourth and final external determinant of Welfare State social policy is political leadership. This influence varies considerably, from the highly expansionist policies of Franklin Delano Roosevelt's New Deal and the Kennedy-Johnson administration's War on Poverty to the restrictive policies of the Reagan administration.

As we said, the Welfare State itself plays a role in shaping social policy. Once in place, Welfare State programs and policies create their own pressure on the direction of the Welfare State. This phenomenon has two aspects. There are the beneficiaries of the Welfare State (the welfare side of the Welfare State), who have vested interests in the benefits and services they receive or will receive at a future date. The growth of the Welfare State demonstrates how difficult it is to rescind benefits once they are in place. Furthermore, there is a sociopolitical momentum to extend benefits in two ways: (1) to give greater benefits to current recipients and (2) to extend benefits to new groups. Thus Social Security has over time both increased its benefits and expanded its coverage. Originally, Social Security was a retirement program with relatively modest benefits. Those benefits have been increased to a substantial level over the past half century, and coverage has been expanded to include the disabled and the health-care needs of the elderly. The second aspect of the Welfare State that exerts influence on its direction is the group that runs it. These are the functionaries or officials (the state side of the Welfare State) who have vested interests in the income, status, and authority of their jobs with the Welfare State.

Thus both beneficiaries and functionaries constitute interest groups that argue for continued Welfare State expansion. No wonder even popular and powerful conservative leaders such as Reagan can only marginally restrain Welfare State growth. Aligned against them are Welfare State interest groups, irreversible demographic and social changes, and the instability of the capitalist economy.

Social change requires both necessary conditions and certain actors. In the grand picture of the historical emergence and expansion of Welfare State social policy, we can identify at least one necessary condition: economic development. To this we can add the emergence of the socialist alternative in the nineteenth century, which served as a goad to capitalism. With regard to the social actors whose leadership is vital for the emergence and expansion of Welfare State social policy, the most important have been the mobilized working class (Korpi, 1983) and the state itself (Orloff and Skocpol, 1984).

Looking forward to the twenty-first century, what developments can we expect in Welfare State social policy? It appears that the overall trend will be further growth in Welfare State activity. The magnitude of that growth—whether or not it reaches the levels that it did in the 1930s and 1960s—will depend on various social forces, some of which remain hidden from our view. However, known factors argue for another period of punctuated growth, perhaps sometime in the 1990s.

First, there is already considerable reaction against the negative, anti-Welfare State social policies of the Reagan administration; one senses here a major shift in public sentiment. There is also some evidence of support for actual expansion of the Welfare State. It can be discerned in rising applications to social work schools, in the growing public desire to reduce the military budget, and in public disenchantment with the philosophy of personal greed that was popularized by Reagan. However, the cyclical ebb and flow of sentiments in society (Zald and Ash, 1965) are difficult to predict, and sentiment is just one factor among many that produces social change.

The second factor that suggests a renewal of Welfare State growth is the relentlessness of certain demographic pressures. These include the aging of the population, which will accelerate in 2010–2020 when the large baby boom generation born in 1945–1955 reaches retirement age.

The third factor arguing for renewed Welfare State growth is the capitalist economy's penchant for producing newly (or newly visible) victimized social groups—today the homeless and female-headed families. These groups may well become the basis for expansion of Welfare State social policy into new areas such as child care.

One critical missing ingredient today for the expansion of Welfare State social policy is a mass base to serve as the mobilizing agency, as labor did in the 1930s and as African Americans did in the 1960s. A likely candidate is women—because of their growing social needs and their expanding political presence, especially within the Democratic Party (joining their predecessors, workers and African Americans). The electoral gender gap is a reflection of this potential for women to lead the next lurch forward in Welfare State activity.

The Issue of Resources

Where will the resources come from to underwrite an expansion of Welfare State social policy and social practice—especially in light of the current constraints on state spending imposed by the fiscal crisis? There are at least three possibilities: (1) tax increases, (2) redirection of military expenditure to social uses, and (3) the mobilization of resources in the nonpublic sector. (Note that none of these is predicated on major economic growth.)

There are two tax increases that about three-fourths of Americans favored in 1987. The first is higher taxes on the wealthy, whose tax rate was reduced by more than one-half, from 70 percent to 28 or 33 percent, by the Reagan administration. Applying the 33 percent rate to all incomes above $75,000 could raise $2 to $3 billion, and only about 600,000 taxpayers would be affected (Kilborn, 1988). We could easily go further and raise the rate above 33 percent on those who earn at least $100,000. This would be progressive, fair, and popular. The second kind of tax increase favored by a majority of Americans is in consumption taxes. However, consumption taxes are generally unfair (regressive) because the poor and working classes spend a greater share of their incomes on the consumption items that are taxed than do the higher social classes. Nevertheless, some consumption taxes, known as "sin taxes," are popular because they cost only those who engage in the sin. Thus increased tobacco and alcohol taxes raise revenue and constitute preventive social policy as well because they discourage personally and socially destructive activities—smoking and drinking. In 1988 tobacco and alcohol taxes were less than one-half of what they were, in real terms, in 1953 (Rhoads, 1988). A third consumption tax increase is far less popular, even though it, too, would serve the social good. This is an increase in gasoline taxes, which would encourage needed conservation and use of public transport as well as raise revenue.

Another source of additional funds for the expansion of Welfare State social policy is monies currently devoted to military expenditure. Military expenditure accelerated dramatically under Reagan. For example, at the onset of the Reagan administration, the military got $7 for each $1 of the federal budget spent on housing. At the end of the Reagan administration, this ratio had increased more than sixfold: $44 for the military for each $1 for housing (Shields, 1988, p. 9). In 1980 the military consumed 26 percent of the federal budget, while social programs (excluding self-financing Social Security) consumed 35 percent. By 1987 the military share of the federal budget was up to 30 percent, while the social share had declined to 28 percent (Riddell, 1987, p. 9). As noted in Chapter 4, Japan, a principal economic competitor of the United States, spends considerably less on its military; this allows it to finance its more developed Welfare State. In the 1980s Japan's military expenditure amounted to only 1 percent of its GDP, or only $163 per person, while military expenditure in the United States was 6.8 percent of GDP or $1,164 per person.

A third source of additional funds for social policy purposes lies outside the public control of the Welfare State. This is the growing capital investment monies of nonprofit organizations such as religious groups, professional associations, universities, foundations, unions, and pension funds. To get an idea of the magnitude of this social sector of the capitalist economy, consider that pension funds alone controlled over $1 trillion in the mid-1980s; this was expected to grow to over $4 trillion in the 1990s (Bruyn, 1987, p. vii). The investment of the resources of these institutions in social policies and social needs has grown dramatically since the 1960s. A prominent example of the potential of social investment's use for social policy ends is the redirection of corporate investment away from South Africa in the 1980s. An illustration of the use of these private funds for social investment is the financing of the construction of affordable housing in central cities (discussed in Chapter 9).

Despite the availability of resources, some analysts argue that the economic cost of the Welfare State has increased beyond its economic capacity (Pusic, 1987, pp. 169–170). Social welfare pluralism, which we now discuss, is one model that accepts this argument and that seeks to adapt Welfare State social policy to the reduced capacity to fund it.

Social welfare pluralism While conservatives advocate for-profit privatization of the Welfare State (discussed in Chapters 6 and 9), liberals expound the virtues of their version of privatization: pluralism. Pluralism advocates a social policy environment in which state, nonprofit, and for-profit agencies, as well as the family, exist as co-equals (Friedmann, 1987, pp. 288–289; Judge, 1987, pp. 27–32). While social welfare pluralism seems well suited to American society, it is, at least as a grand strategy, unworkable, inefficient, and ineffective. It is an unworkable strategy for much of what the Welfare State accomplishes—that is, the provision of benefits, both monetary and in-kind. Although families and nonprofit and for-profit agencies may be suitable for the delivery of social services, they are not appropriate for the distribution of public benefits. Welfare pluralism is inefficient because of the duplication and competition that it engenders—among agencies as well as between the public and private sectors. Welfare pluralism is ineffective because any reduction of the public role in Welfare State activity is likely to lead to greater inequality, not less, and to less accountability (to constituents of Welfare State activities), not more (Johnson, 1988).

The private sector by itself is not a reliable and just instrument of social policy. Families, for-profits, and nonprofits are limited in their capacities by certain structural features. For example, family provision of social welfare services discriminates against women, while commercial provision is distorted by the need for profit. Also, families, for-profits, and nonprofits are all limited by their localism. Localism means adaptation to provincial conditions. Consider the social policies of racial nondiscrimination and integration. Local agencies, especially in the South, often were not helpful in furthering these necessary and just social policies. Indeed, frequently their opposition had to be overcome by the state, sometimes with legal orders and by force of arms. While local self-determination is valuable, it is no guarantee of democracy or justice.

The underlying reason for the fiscal difficulty of the Welfare State is the fact that it operates within the constraints of a capitalist economy. The present fiscal problems of Welfare States demonstrate an intensification of the contradiction between social needs and private profit. Efforts to cut back on the Welfare State—to privatize or to pluralize it—are responses to this contradiction that will only strengthen the hand of private capital and weaken the interest of social justice.

SOCIAL PLANNING

Our analysis of Welfare State social policy and social change leads us to a consideration of social planning. Social planning consists of social policies to meet anticipated social needs or to guide society in a projected direction. Our discussion of social planning focuses on Welfare States, in which capitalist economies (devoted to the maximization of private profit) ensure that social planning is both necessary and underdeveloped. Social planning is necessary in Welfare States because capitalism is unable to resolve the social problems that it creates. Social planning is underdeveloped in capitalist societies because it violates the priority of private capital accumulation. Thus social planning is ideologically and materially marginalized; it is relegated to mop-up and back-up roles in the private capitalist economy.

Social planning does exist in capitalism—it is not merely a utopian idea. In many capitalist nations the public, principally through the state, is actively involved in assessing policies designed to meet future social needs. However, social planning is a fledgling art—undernourished, riven with contradictions, and confronted with powerful opposition. In fact, in the United States, where capitalism remains more uncompromised than in other Welfare States, social planning hardly exists at all. What passes for it here is really social policy of an ameliorative and remedial nature. Ideally, social planning is an anticipatory and preventive undertaking, not a reactive one. Perhaps the only effective social planning that exists in the United States is the land-use control exercised by public bodies—through zoning—in some local areas (Gottdiener, 1985, p. 106).

What, then, is the nature of the uneasy relationship between social planning and capitalism? In the words of Dear and Scott (1981, p. 13), planning is the "socially-necessary response to the self-disorganizing tendencies of *privatized* capitalist social and property relations." Because it is socially indispensable, planning is grudgingly accepted as a necessary evil in capitalism.

The result is a severely limited social planning that does not resolve social needs—indeed, that often compounds them.

An example of the contradictory relationship between capitalist profit imperatives and social planning is slum clearance through urban planning (discussed in Chapter 9). Urban slums are the result of the workings of the private capitalist economy, in which the destitution of marginal workers serves the dual interests of reducing wages and of raising profits, and in which uneven development (in this case, between areas of cities) results from private investment for profit. Because urban slums are unhygienic and unsightly, and because their residents are a considerable embarrassment and a political threat (even if only potentially) to the stability of capitalist rule, slum clearance projects have been a hallmark of capitalism since the nineteenth century. The U.S. urban renewal program was one manifestation of this phenomenon. But because it is controlled by the profit interest of capitalists (private property owners, developers, builders, and speculators), slum clearance only compounds the essential problem. The slums that are cleared are replaced by profitable housing for the nonpoor and by structures, such as parking lots and expressways for commuting corporate employees, that support capitalist interests. Slum residents are forced out and must look for housing in other areas of the city. This produces homelessness and new slums. The overall problem is compounded because the affordable housing stock is reduced, the poor and the working classes are more segregated from the rest of the population, and uneven development is intensified, which results in a highly overdeveloped central business district that is polluted, congested, and inhospitable.

Modern social planning emerged in the nineteenth century as an effort to neutralize social problems, including widespread and highly visible poverty, created or exacerbated by the development of industrial capitalism. A prominent example was the transformation of Paris by Napoleon III's assistant, Baron Georges-Eugène Haussmann, between 1852 and 1870. His project was so large and influential in scope that the term *Haussmannization* came to refer generally to urban redevelopment. The social class interests of this planning effort were clear: Haussmann's plan "reflected the aspirations of a new business-minded upper middle class, and for these entrepreneurs it opened up the old city to the demands of modern commerce and transportation" (Collins, 1971, p. 6).

The Haussmann plan resulted in the wholesale destruction of old Paris and of housing for the poor and working classes and their replacement by wide boulevards, public buildings, and spacious parks. Large real estate developers, especially the Crédit Mobilier, bought much of the property alongside the new boulevards and parks and realized enormous profits as these properties became prime sites for upper-middle-class housing (Saalman, 1971, pp. 22–23). Haussmann's changes also served a political purpose: to defend against mass mobilization by the working class. The wide boulevards were difficult to barricade and they facilitated the rapid transport of troops into the heart of the city, where working-class districts were sited.

In the twentieth-century Welfare State social planning expanded to include the more ambitious goal of ameliorating poverty through such Welfare State measures as income security (Pusic, 1981). A vital third step in this progression in social planning remains to be developed; that is, social planning to eliminate the structural causes of poverty, which include the inequality and injustice of capitalism. The progressive goal for social planning's next development is expansion from an ameliorative and incremental role to a transformative and structural one (Walker, 1984).

With regard to the social practice of social planning—meaning the actual work of social planning that is conducted by trained practitioners—the strongest need is for a broadening of the present narrow technical focus to include a socioeconomic perspective (Kelman et al., 1981). The technical bias of social planning is a legacy of the rational comprehensive model of Louis Wirth and the Chicago School, which is the basis for contemporary urban planning (Smith, 1979, pp. 26–44). Urban planning is also limited by its emphasis on the physical environment to the neglect of the social environment. In addition to their technical skills, such as data collection and analysis, planners need to develop political and organizational skills, including the ability to combine technical analysis with the democratic participation of citizens affected by planning decisions.

Social planning should embrace the idea that social problems and social policies are socially constructed, not simply manifestations of an objective empirical reality amenable to technical assessment and manipulation (Hibbard, 1981). To this end, social planning needs to be reclaimed as a discipline for social practitioners. Social work has a responsibility to develop creative social planning. As Street (1965) noted, "among the responsibilities of social work as a profession and as a set of professional schools are to think imaginatively and develop a knowledge base that deals with social trends and addresses itself to massive social change."

If social planning in the Welfare State is truncated by capitalism, what about social planning in the socialist societies? As discussed in Chapter 4 and elsewhere, socialist societies are generally superior to Welfare States in comprehensive social policy, especially considering the greater material resources of the Welfare States. In contrast to capitalism's hostility to social planning, socialism requires and promotes active social planning. Some of the specific features of socialist social planning are universal health care and education, full employment, and the extension of social resources to peripheral regions to prevent or to mitigate uneven development.

The greater development of social planning under socialism is illustrated in the Third World. As noted in Chapter 4, socialist Third World nations, including Cuba and the People's Republic of China, have made major advances in social planning as compared to capitalist Third World nations. One example concerns a major social problem in the Third World: the increasing concentration of population in major capital cities. This population concentration creates an inordinate demand in the core city for social consumption items such as housing, sanitation, and transport, and it fosters environmental degradation. Research (Vining, 1985) on forty-six Third World nations found that socialist countries were successful in controlling the growth of their core cities. Consider socialist North Korea versus capitalist South Korea. Seoul, South Korea's capital city, has grown in an uncontrolled way since World War II; its population was nearly 14 million in 1985. The main streets of the city are so crowded during rush hours that streetcar transportation has been impossible since 1969. Because of its overpopulation, Seoul faces housing, water, electricity, and sanitation facility shortages. By contrast, Pyongyang, North Korea's capital city, has a population only about one-eighth that of Seoul because its growth has been effectively controlled. Therefore it has escaped the major social problems found in Seoul. Socialist Third World societies such as North Korea have been successful in preventing overurbanization and its attendant problems through two social policies: restriction of migration to cities and development of peripheral areas.

What are the deficiencies of social planning in existing socialist nations? Nove's (1983) analysis of a feasible socialism provides some useful answers. While socialist nations are not limited by the profit demands and bureaucratism of private corporations, they still confront the problems of state bureaucratism. The principal task of social planning under socialism is to develop a workable compromise between centralization and self-management. Centralization can be the rule where the interests of the entire society are paramount, as in regulations to protect the environment, subsidies to sustain public transport, and policies (including investment) to prevent and to correct regional imbalances. Where central direction is not necessary, then local initiative and self-management can be the rule. Thus planning for the type and location of educational and health-care facilities can be done locally and the facilities can be managed by local people. Constituents and groups of constituents (as well as social practitioners) can have an influential role in the planning of individual service units. This constituent and practitioner input can parallel social planning bodies from the local, micro level up to the central, societal level.

Another way in which centralization and self-management can be balanced is through a division in the scope of social planning. Thus, while central planning can mandate and subsidize a general public works policy, local initiative can develop specific public works projects. Additionally, democratic control of such decisions can be accomplished through referenda. At the national level votes can be taken to decide between broad priorities for investment, such as between public and private transport. Local referenda can produce decisions as to how to prioritize investments. By referenda we do not mean mechanical rote processes in which local functionaries mobilize an apathetic and unknowledgeable electorate to ratify whatever policy comes down from the central planning body. Effective policy requires participation and information and the right to choose between alternatives—in other words, real democracy.

CONCLUDING COMMENTS

One of the themes that has emerged from our analysis of social policy and social planning is the existence of an inherent conflict in Welfare States between the resolution of social needs and capitalist economic imperatives. Thus in the United States, capitalist demands for profit cripple social policy and make the nation an obvious social welfare laggard among the developed countries. However, even in more advanced Welfare States—Sweden being a prominent example—the conflict between private profit making and social control of the economy in order to meet social needs is a cause of ongoing tension (Himmelstrand, 1982). Even in socialist nations, which have the most advanced social policy, economic imperatives, such as for technological and industrial development, have set limits on the satisfaction of social needs. This has been the case even though socialist economies are socially controlled.

One major cause of this universal tension between economic imperatives and social needs is a scarcity of resources. In nations where scarcity is not the overriding issue, unequal distribution of resources prevents the resolution of social needs. Thus in the United States, where resources are relatively plentiful, unequal distribution means that the rich get richer while social needs go unmet. However, the conditions of scarcity and of unequal distribution do not account for all the tension between economic imperatives and social needs. How can we understand the presence of such a tension in nations where scarcity and unequal capitalist distribution are not major problems—that is, socialist nations such as the U.S.S.R.? Comparative analysis gives socialist nations high marks for the adequacy and public control of their social policy. However, the same analysts evaluate social policy in socialist nations (in this case, the U.S.S.R.) as lacking when measured against two criteria: (1) allocation of resources according to need and (2) democratic participation of beneficiaries (George and Manning, 1980).

There are several explanations for the shortcomings of social policy in developed socialist nations. One is that socialist societies utilize orthodox Marxist-Leninist models in which the primacy of central planning is assumed. Central planning, in turn, has led to domination by top-heavy state and party bureaucracies, which tend to perpetuate themselves. This overbureaucratization results in bureaucratic pathologies, including inefficiencies maintained by the continuation of outdated or ineffective programs. In this sense, a great strength of bureaucracy—continuity—can turn into a debilitating weakness. Another related bureaucratic pathology, which was discussed in Chapter 10, is goal displacement, in which social policy goals are displaced by the goal of organizational maintenance.

Bureaucratism is a problem in both Welfare States and socialist nations. In capitalist societies large transnational corporations (arguably the world's most autonomous organizations) epitomize the domination of society by centralized bureaucratic interests. In socialist societies party and state bureaucracies are, at least in theory, public institutions. This fact gives purchase to those in socialist societies who mobilize for democratic reform. Private corporations are subject to neither democratic control nor democratic ideals.

Another major limitation of contemporary social policy, whether it be in capitalist or in socialist nations, is that it is limited to the boundaries of the nation-state. Social needs are increasingly international in scope and in causation; they do not recognize national boundaries. AIDS (discussed in Chapter 8) is a dramatic example. Other examples are less obvious but even more serious or widespread in their consequences. Thus international capital mobility and the political and economic power of transnational corporations create widespread social problems in local areas around the world—mass unemployment, underemployment, and environmental ruin being prominent examples. A critical question for the near future is whether or not public transnational institutions such as the UN can expand their activities to counterbalance the power of private transnational corporations. Such transnational public bodies would not necessarily supersede nation-states. However, their development could eventually relegate the nation-state to a secondary, integrating vehicle for meeting social needs (Pusic, 1987, pp. 172–173).

Socialist nations too are negatively affected by the national limits to social policy. Although socialist nations are able to control internal investment decisions, they cannot prevent the international capitalist economy from creating problems for their societies. Historically, the narrow economism and bureaucratism of some socialist nations developed in reaction to the economic imperatives of the world economy, which remains capitalist. Thus Chase-Dunn (1980) has argued that the reason for some shortcomings of socialist nations is external: they have been dominated externally and shaped by the forces of the capitalist world economy. This occurred in two ways. First, capitalist nations are unrelentingly hostile to the emergence and development of socialist nations, to the extent of invading them militarily and of freezing them out of participation in the world economy. Second, the economic power of capitalist nations is used to inhibit socialist development. In response, socialist nations, beginning with the U.S.S.R. in the 1920s, stressed economic development to defend themselves against the capitalist world. As a consequence, after nearly seventy years of industrial development, the U.S.S.R. is an economic giant (while as a capitalist nation it was an economic weakling), but it falls short in the advancement of socialist social goals.

To the extent that the limitations and problems of contemporary social policy transcend political and tribal boundaries, they are problems of human civilization. The crisis for contemporary civilization centers on three primary social tasks: (1) integrating economic imperatives (to produce) and the resolution of social needs (to consume); (2) resolving international social issues within the limitations of nationalist parameters; and (3) maintaining the efficient and just administration of a large-scale and complex human society through bureaucracies, while at the same time assuring the participation of citizens through democratic processes.

The current state of our civilization also involves a crisis of human sentiment. There has been a general shift (perhaps especially in the Welfare States) to an emphasis on subjective experiences instead of (or in addition to) objective, material status. This shift seems to be particularly strong in Sweden, probably the most accomplished Welfare State. It may be an indication of the success of the Welfare State in responding to the material needs of citizens, and its failure to satisfy emotional and communal needs (Allardt, 1986). The cultures of Welfare States do not adequately meet the communal needs of citizens. As Slater (1970, p. 5) noted, U.S. culture frustrates the human desires for community, engagement, and dependence.

Late-twentieth-century humanity stands at a point where traditional religion and nationalism, decadent capitalism, and fledgling, imperfect socialism offer little emotional and spiritual fulfillment. In order to resolve the current malaise of civilization, we need inspiration, hope, and human solidarity. The reemergence of the religious right in all its forms—from the Moral Majority in the United States to Islamic and Jewish fundamentalism in the Middle East—demonstrates a strong need and desire for spiritual fulfillment. The religious right is not the answer, however, for it reinforces narrow patriarchy and tribalism rather than human solidarity, and it fosters traditional social injustices. Human solidarity and social justice are the most noble of our aspirations.

Social justice, exemplified by the concept of human rights, has become a more visible goal since the mid-twentieth century. The dramatic emergence after World War II of national liberation movements, originally in the Third World and subsequently in Welfare States such as the United States (among African Americans and other groups), popularized the concept of human rights. The debuts of socialist societies and Welfare State societies in the twentieth century reflected and reinforced this general drift in human civilization toward greater social justice. Following on the heels of these developments was the founding of the UN, which promulgated perhaps our most important statement of human rights. This document, the Universal Declaration of Human Rights, adopted by the General Assembly of the UN in 1948 (Laves and Thomson, 1957, pp. 432–436) outlined the following necessary components of social justice:

> Article 2. (1) Everyone is entitled to all the rights and freedoms set forth in this Declaration, without distinction of any kind, such as race, colour, sex, language, religion, political or other opinion, national or social origin, property, birth or other status.

> Article 22. Everyone, as a member of society, has the right to social security and is entitled to realisation, through national effort and international co-operation and in accordance with the organisations and resources of each State, of the economic, social and cultural rights indispensable for his dignity and the free development of his personality.

Article 23. (1) Everyone has the right to work, to free choice of employment, to just and favourable conditions of work and to protection against unemployment.

Article 25. (1) Everyone has the right to a standard of living adequate for the health and well-being of himself and of his family, including food, clothing, housing and medical care and necessary social services, and the right to security in the event of unemployment, sickness, disability, widowhood, old age or other lack of livelihood in circumstances beyond his control.

Article 26. (1) Everyone has the right to education.

In addition to the founding of the UN, there are two other manifestations of a sociohistorical drift to human solidarity and social justice: the successes of social policy and the emergence of new social movements. Modern social policy has shown that the material needs of human life (for adequate food, clothing, and shelter) can be met. Urban social movements for better housing and for local control of neighborhoods (discussed in Chapter 9) have raised the expectation that we can move beyond the satisfaction of material needs to address the full range of human needs, including those for political participation and for personal fulfillment. In Pachter's (1982, p. 70) words:

> The new possibilities of the welfare state have brought to the fore problems that previously had been hidden by the need for fighting first for material satisfactions. Socialism has become (again, as in Marx's own time) a cultural movement striving not only for the improvement of material conditions but for the emancipation of the individual personality. It certainly is not a movement of technocrats for a more efficient organization of society.

Local and international struggles for active participation in social and political life are necessary in order to challenge centralized power in both Welfare States and socialist societies. One model for such democratic struggles is that of popular power, illustrated by worker control of industry and by community (neighborhood) control of housing and social services (Hammond, 1988). Other terms for popular power are *self-management, empowerment,* and *insurgency.* Walzer (1982, p. 154) noted the following about the need for socialist insurgency in and against the Welfare State:

> Socialism then requires insurgency, that is, self-government within the welfare state and against it whenever necessary. And it is the great paradox of socialist politics that the state toward which we must always remain tense, watchful, and resistant is or will almost certainly become the most legitimate, rationally purposive, and powerful state that has ever existed.

Whatever concept is used for this phenomenon, the meaning is essentially the same: the creation of social processes that enable all people to believe they can change themselves and the world (Fabricant, 1988). Such social processes aim for a revolutionary transformation of current bureaucratic and capitalist practices in order to restore to the constituents and practitioners of social programs an active and creative role (Preteceille and Terrail, 1985).

Although the prospect may seem remote at times, human beings do change themselves and their societies. Human nature and human society are not fixed and immutable. Consider how recently in history slavery was practiced as a natural feature of human society. It is our ability to consciously modify ourselves as well as our environment that makes us humans singular. As Marx (1964, p. 112) noted, "Man is a species being, not only because in practice and in theory he adopts the species as his object (his own as well as those of other things), but—and this is only another way of expressing it—also because he treats himself as the actual, living species; because he treats himself as a *universal* and therefore a free being."

The route to social justice and human solidarity lies in democratic struggles for self-determination against centralized bureaucratic power and in socialist struggles against capitalist economic exploitation and individualism. It is through the process of these struggles that humankind can create a viable daily life that is both personally and communally satisfying. The successes of social policies in socialism and the Welfare State have created a new plateau for human potential. We are living in a time of promise.

REFERENCES

Allardt, Erik. 1986. "The Civil Conception of the Welfare State in Scandinavia." Pp. 107–125 in *The Welfare State East and West*, eds. Richard Rose and Rei Shiratori. New York: Oxford University Press.

Bruyn, Severyn T. 1987. *The Field of Social Investment*. Cambridge: Cambridge University Press.

Chase-Dunn, Christopher K. 1980. "Socialist States in the Capitalist World-Economy." *Social Problems* 27:505–525.

Collins, George R. 1971. Preface to Howard Saalman, *Haussmann: Paris Transformed*. New York: George Braziller.

Dear, Michael, and Allen J. Scott. 1981. "Towards a Framework for Analysis." Pp. 3–16 in *Urbanization and Urban Planning in Capitalist Society*, eds. Michael Dear and Allen J. Scott. London: Methuen.

Fabricant, Michael. 1988. "Empowering the Homeless." *Social Policy* 18:49–55.

Friedmann, Robert R. 1987. "Welfare States: A Summary of Trends." Pp. 282–289 in *Modern Welfare States: A Comparative View of Trends and Prospects*, eds. Robert R. Friedmann, Neil Gilbert, and Moshe Sherer. New York: New York University Press.

George, Vic, and Nick Manning. 1980. *Socialism, Social Welfare and the Soviet Union*. London: Routledge & Kegan Paul.

Gottdiener, M. 1985. *The Social Production of Urban Space*. Austin: University of Texas Press.

Hammond, John L. 1988. *Building Popular Power: Workers' and Neighborhood Movements in the Portuguese Revolution*. New York: Monthly Review Press.

Hibbard, Michael. 1981. "The Crisis in Social Policy Planning." *Social Service Review* 55:557–567.

Himmelstrand, Ulf. 1982. "Sweden: Paradise in Trouble." Pp. 218–237 in *Beyond the Welfare State*, ed. Irving Howe. New York: Schocken Books.

Johnson, Norman. 1988. *The Welfare State in Transition: The Theory and Practice of Welfare Pluralism*. Amherst: The University of Massachusetts Press.

Judge, Ken. 1987. "The British Welfare State in Transition." Pp. 1–43 in *Modern Welfare States: A Comparative View of Trends and Prospects*, eds. Robert R. Friedmann, Neil Gilbert, and Moshe Sherer. New York: New York University Press.

Kelman, Sander, et al. 1981. "Planning the Planners." *Social Policy* 11:46–51.

Kilborn, Peter T. 1988. "Bringing Down Budget Deficit: Some Big Targets Are in Sight." *The New York Times*, December 29.

Korpi, Walter. 1983. *The Democratic Class Struggle*. London: Routledge & Kegan Paul.

Laves, Walter H. C., and Charles A. Thomson. 1957. *UNESCO: Purpose, Progress, Prospects*. Bloomington: Indiana University Press.

Marx, Karl. 1964 [1932]. *Economic and Philosophic Manuscripts of 1844*, ed. Dirk J. Struik. New York: International Publishers.

Nove, Alec. 1983. *The Economics of Feasible Socialism*. London: George Allen & Unwin.

Orloff, Ann Shola, and Theda Skocpol. 1984. "Why Not Equal Protection? Explaining the Politics of Public Social Spending in Britain, 1900–1911, and the United States, 1880s–1920." *American Sociological Review* 49:726–750.

Pachter, Henry. 1982. "Freedom, Authority, Participation." Pp. 42–70 in *Beyond the Welfare State*, ed. Irving Howe. New York: Schocken Books.

Preteceille, Edmond, and Jean-Pierre Terrail. 1985. *Capitalism, Consumption and Needs*, trans. Sarah Matthews. Oxford: Basil Blackwell.

Pusic, Eugen. 1981. "Social Planning, Social Policy, and Political Change." *Social Service Review* 55:411–418.

———. 1987. "The Development of the Welfare State in Yugoslavia." Pp. 151–173 in *Modern Welfare States: A Comparative View of Trends and Prospects*, eds. Robert R. Friedmann, Neil Gilbert, and Moshe Sherer. New York: New York University Press.

Rhoads, Steven E. 1988. "How to Sin Away the Deficit." *The New York Times*, December 10.

Riddell, Tom. 1987. "Military Buildup, Economic Decline? The Economy's Trillion-Dollar Habit." *Dollars & Sense*, September, pp. 6–9.

Saalman, Howard. 1971. *Haussmann: Paris Transformed*. New York: George Braziller.

Shields, Lynn. 1988. "Endangered Species: The Uncertain Future of Low-Income Housing." *Dollars & Sense*, November, pp. 9–11.

Slater, Philip. 1970. *The Pursuit of Loneliness: American Culture at the Breaking Point*. Boston: Beacon Press.

Smith, Michael P. 1979. *The City and Social Theory*. New York: St. Martin's Press.

Street, David. 1965. "Models of Society and Social Work." Unpublished.

Vining, Daniel R., Jr. 1985. "The Growth of Core Regions in the Third World." *Scientific American* 252:42–49.

Walker, Alan. 1984. *Social Planning: A Strategy for Socialist Welfare*. Oxford: Basil Blackwell.

Walzer, Michael. 1982. "Politics in the Welfare State: Concerning the Role of American Radicals." Pp. 129–154 in *Beyond the Welfare State*, ed. Irving Howe. New York: Schocken Books.

Zald, Mayer N., and Roberta Ash. 1965. "Social Movement Organizations: Growth, Decay and Change." *Social Forces* 44:327–341.

Name Index

Aberg, Rune, **36, 41**
Abramovitz, Mimi, 67, 77, 84, 103, 129, 158
Ackerman, Frank, 94, 103
Adams, Paul, 11, 19, 72, 77
Addams, Jane, 27, 30, 165, 197
Aiken, Linda H., 158–60, 162
Alexander, Christopher, 194, 197
Alexander, Leslie B., 72, 77
Allardt, Erik, 240, 242
Altbach, Philip G., 111, 121, 122
Altman, Drew E., 129, 141, 158
Amenta, Edwin, 24, 30
Amott, Teresa, 63, 77
Anderson, Charles W., 9, 19
Anderson, Leon, 186, 201
Anderson, Odin W., 208, 225
Andrain, Charles F., 35, 36, 41, 144, 158
Arches, Joan, 70, 77
Arendell, Teresa, 125, 158
Aronowitz, Stanley, 111, 114, 121
Arriagada, Ana Maria, 110, 122
Aschbacher, Pamela R., 92, 104
Ash, Roberta, 231, 242
Aveling, Edward, 30, 161, 200
Axinn, June, 69, 77

Babington, Gervase, **229**
Baca Zinn, Maxine, 60, 77
Bane, Mary Jo, 58, 60, 77, 78, 88, 103
Barbanel, Josh, 174, 197
Bardes, Barbara A., 203, 225
Barkin, David, 187, 197
Barron, James, 102, 104
Bart, Pauline, 152, 162
Bassuk, Ellen L., 178, 197
Bastian, Ann, 110, 121
Batra, Ravi, 54, 77
Bean, Gerald J., Jr., 176, 197
Bean, Philip, 6
Beauregard, Robert A., 175, 197
Beeghley, Leonard, 47, 58, 77
Bell, Winifred, 66, 77
Bellah, Robert N., 15, 19
Belous, Richard S., 92, 104
Belsky, Jay, 92, 104
Bendick, Mark, Jr., 183, 197
Bennett, Jon, 44, 77
Bequele, Assefa, 214, 225
Berg, William E., 215, 225
Berger, Joseph, 113, 121
Berk, Richard A., 217, 227
Berkman, Lisa F., 124, 163
Berman, Marshall, 169, 197
Bermant, Gordon, 216, 225, 227
Bismarck, Otto von, 23, 140
Blackwell, James E., 55, 77
Blair, William G., 72, 77
Blakeslee, Sandra, 126, 158
Blendon, Robert J., 141, 158
Bliss, Shepherd, 150, 158
Bloch, Mary Henry, 227
Block, Fred, 4, 6, 65, 77, 79, 214, 225
Bloom, Allan, 110, 121
Bloom, David E., 92, 105
Blumberg, Paul, 9, 19, 54, 77
Blumberg, Rhoda Lois, 223, 225

Boffey, Philip M., 137, 158
Booth, Charles, 26, 30
Borgos, Seth, 180, 197
Botstein, Leon, 110, 121
Boulding, Kenneth E., 45, 77
Bowles, Samuel, 13, 19, 109, 121
Boyte, Harry C., 195, 197
Braverman, Harry, 70, 77, 156, 158
Bremner, Robert H., 122
Bricker-Jenkins, Mary, 94, 104
Brody, Jane E., 136, 158
Brook, Robert H., 130, 162
Brown, Phil, 177, 197, 199, 200
Browning, Robert X., 49, 77
Brozan, Nadine, 89, 104
Brunn, Dennis, 72, 77
Bruyn, Severyn T., 233, 242
Budrys, Grace, 130, 158
Burden, Diane, 98, 104
Burgess, Ernest W., 166, 200
Burns, Gene A., 214, 225
Burt, Martha R., 179, 197
Burtless, Gary, 36, 41, 55, 77
Burud, Sandra L., 92, 104
Busch, Georg, 91, 104
Buxbaum, Carl B., 214, 225
Byrd, Jack, Jr., 217, 225
Byrne, John, 214, 225

Cahill, Kevin M., **159, 160**
Calavita, Kitty, 155, 158
Camasso, Anne E., 44, 77
Camasso, Michael J., 44, 77
Campbell, John L., 181, 197
Canak, William, 53, 78
Caputo, Larry, 138, 158
Carballo, Manuel, 77, 78
Carfagno, Vincent R., 162
Carlson, Dennis, 114, 121
Carruthers, Bruce G., 24, 30
Carsrud, Karen Banks, 113, 121
Castells, Manuel, 166, 192, 194, 196, 197
Cereseto, Shirley, 40, 41
Chalmers, Thomas, 26, 30
Chaloner, W. H., 159
Chamberlain, Ronna, 179, 200
Chambers, Donald E., 63, 77, 96, 104, 209, 210, 226
Champagne, Anthony, 19, 80, 200
Chase-Dunn, Christopher K., 239, 242
Chasin, Barbara H., 219, 226
Cherns, Albert, 202, 226
Chodorow, Nancy, 97, 104
Churchill, Larry R., 127, 130, 158
Clarke, Susan E., 182, 197
Cloward, Richard A., 15, 19, 28, 30, 49, 60, 79, 221, 226
Cohen, R. B., 166, 197
Coleman, James S., 109, 121
Collins, George R., 235, 242
Collins, Glenn, 93, 104
Collins, Randall, 107, 110, 121
Collins, Sheila, 114, 121
Colman, Penny, 44, 77
Colton, Theodore, 149, 161

Conrad, Peter, 134, 139, 143, 158, 159, 161–63
Cook, Thomas D., 217, 226
Coombs, Philip H., 116, 121
Cooper, Scott, 191, 197
Corcoran, Mary, 65, 78
Corrigan, Paul, 71, 78
Cottington, Eric M., 156, 160
Cowen, Emory L., 144, 158
Crain, Robert L., 113, 121
Crawford, Robert, 149, 158
Culyer, A. J., 141, 158, 208, 213, 226
Curran, James W., 137, 138, 158, 160
Cushman, Linda F., 220, 226
Cutright, Phillips, 34, 41

Dail, Paula W., **44, 78**
Dale, Jennifer, 12, 19
Daley, Suzanne, 173, 197
Danziger, Sheldon H., 41, 54–57, 77, 78, 80, 162
Davidson, Laurie, 98, 104
Day, Phyllis J., 29, 30
Deacon, Bob, 40, 41
Dear, Michael, 197, 199, 201, 234, 242
DeFriese, Gordon H., 155, 158
De Kervasdoue, Jean, 133, 158, 161, 163
DePalma, Anthony, 181, 197
De Paul, Saint Vincent, 25
Derber, Charles, 135, 158
Dery, David, 215, 226
De Schweinitz, Karl, 22, 30
Deutsche, Rosalyn, 167, 197
Devine, Joel A., 53, 78
Dickinson, James, 23, 24, 30, 83, 104
Dickson, William J., 222, 227
DiMatteo, M. Robin, 151, 159
Dreier, Peter, 196, 198
Dressel, Paula, 117, 121
Drew, Joseph, 181, 198
Duane, Ellen, 218–20
Dubnick, Melvin J., 203, 225
Duke, Annette, 189, 198
Dumont, J. P., 3, 6
Dumpson, James R., 174, 185, 198
Duncan, Cynthia M., 56, 78
Duncan, Greg J., 58, 64, 78
Durkheim, Emile, 106, 122
Dutton, Diana B., 125, 159
Dworkin, Anthony Gary, 118, 122

Eastaugh, Steven R., **130, 135, 159**
Eckholm, Erik, 86, 104
Edelman, Murray, 209, 216, 226
Edgerton, Robert B., 177, 198
Edmonds, Ronald, 5, 6
Ehrenreich, Barbara, 97, 104, 128, 159
Ehrenreich, John H., 27, 30, 128, 159
Elizabeth I, 10
Ellerin, Milton, 9, 19
Elling, Ray H., 157, 159
Ellwood, David T., 46, 57, 78
Engel, Hannah, 147–49
Engels, Frederick, 30, 156, 159, 161, 166, 198, 200
Erikson, Kai, 156, 159

Erikson, Robert, 36, 41
Etchells, Frederick, 199
Euzeby, Chantal, 76, 78
Evans, Patricia M., 65, 78
Eyer, Joseph, 145, 156, 159

Fabricant, Michael, 70, 78, 178, 198, 241, 242
Fainstein, Norman I., 168, 198, 199
Fainstein, Susan S., 168, 171, 198, 199
Fairweather, George W., 217, 226
Faludi, Susan, 92, 104
Feder, Judith, 140, 159
Feierabend, Ivo K., 36, 41
Feierabend, Rosalind L., 36, 41
Fein, Rashi, 140, 159
Feldstein, Paul J., 132, 159
Fineberg, Harvey V., 139, 159
Finestone, Albert J., 160
Fischer, Frank, 19, 214, 225–27
Flynn, Raymond L., 195
Foege, William, 138, 159
Fogelson, Robert M., 169, 198
Folbre, Nancy, 90, 104
Forester, John, 14, 19, 225–27
Fossett, Mark A., 53, 78
Fox, Kenneth, 2, 6, 79, 81
Fox, Renee C., 149, 159
Fox, Sherwood D., 122
Franke, Richard W., 219, 226
Frankenhaeuser, Marianne, 156, 160
Freeman, Gary, 72, 77
Freidson, Eliot, 135, 159
Freire, Paulo, 111, 114, 122
Freud, Sigmund, 27–29, 150
Freudenberg, Nicholas, 149, 159
Freudenberger, Herbert J., 118, 122
Freudenheim, Milt, 135, 159
Freund, Peter E. S., 151, 156, 159
Fried, Mindy, 95, 104
Friedland, Roger, 169, 186, 198
Friedmann, Robert R., 233, 242, 243
Frohmann, Alicia, 91, 104
Fry, Lincoln J., 204, 226
Fuchs, Victor R., 140, 141, 159

Galle, Omer R., 53, 78
Gans, Herbert J., 75, 78, 166, 198
Gardell, Bertil, 156, 160
Garfinkel, Irwin, 58, 62, 78, 79
Garrett, Patricia, 91, 104, 114, 122
Gartner, Audrey, 153, 159
Gaylin, Willard, 25, 30
Gendrot, Sophie N., 180, 198
Genovese, Rosalie G., 104, 105
George, Rosemary, 112, 122
George, Vic, 39–41, 238, 242
Gerson, Samuel, 178, 197
Gerth, H. H., 228
Gifford, Sandra M., 159
Gilbert, Neil, 242, 243
Gilchrist, Lewayne D., 102, 104, 115, 122
Gill, Derek, 141, 159
Gilligan, Carol, 97, 104
Giloth, Robert, 192, 198
Gintis, Herbert, 13, 19, 109, 121
Ginzberg, Eli, 160, 162
Giroux, Henry A., 111, 121
Glaab, Charles N., 139, 159
Glanz, Milton P., 1, 6, 49, 79
Glennerster, H., 35, 41
Glucksberg, Harold, 131, 159
Goffman, Erving, 223, 226

Goldberg, Gertrude S., 61, 78
Goldberger, Paul, 189, 198
Goleman, Daniel, 101, 104, 151, 159, 206, 226
Goodban, Nancy, 47, 78
Goodin, Robert E., 24, 30
Goodwin, Leonard, 64, 78
Googins, Bradley, 98, 104
Gordon, David M., 169, 198
Gordon, Edmund W., 105
Gordon, Laura Kramer, 71, 80, 98, 104, 210, 221–23, 226, 228
Gordon, Linda, 155, 159
Gorman, E. Michael, 137, 139, 159
Gottdiener, M., 167, 198, 234, 242
Gottschalk, Peter, 54, 56, 78
Gough, Ian, 3, 6
Graham, Hilary, 57, 78
Gray, Alastair McIntosh, 142, 160
Gray, J. A. Muir, 142, 160
Greenley, James R., 16, 19
Greer, Ann Lennarson, 161
Greer, Scott, 161
Gross, Bertram, 65, 78
Gross, Jane, 195, 198
Grossman, Jon, 224, 226
Gruber, Murray L., 127, 160
Grunow, Dieter, 223, 226
Grusky, Oscar, 159, 161, 163, 198, 200
Gudeman, Jon E., 177, 198
Gueron, Judith M., 64, 78
Guillemin, Jeanne Harley, 123, 160
Gulati, Padi, 188, 198
Gurr, Ted Robert, 173, 198
Gusfield, Joseph R., 210, 216, 226
Guterman, Norbert, 199
Gutmann, Amy, 111, 113, 122

Habermas, Jurgen, 12, 19
Hadley, Jack, 124, 160
Ham, Christopher, 221, 222, 226
Hammond, John L., 241, 242
Hammonds, Evelynn, 138, 160
Hansen, Fay, 51, 78
Harkess, Shirley, 105
Harpham, Edward J., 10, 19, 80, 200
Harrington, Michael, 26, 30
Hart, Julian Tudor, 126, 160
Hart, Nicky, 136, 160
Hart, Philip, 55, 77
Hartman, Chester, 175, 199
Harvey, David, 166, 167, 198
Haskins, Ron, 96, 105
Haubert, Maxime, 116, 122
Haussmann, Georges-Eugene, 235
Haveman, Robert H., 54, 55, 78, 202, 226
Hayden, Delores, 194, 198
Heagy, Thomas C., 141, 161
Heclo, Hugh, 5, 6, 62, 78, 216, 226
Hedin, Diane, 118, 122
Hedstrom, Peter, 36, 37, 41
Heller, Frank, 226, 228
Henderson, W. O., 159
Henry VIII, 21
Herbers, John, 187, 198
Heyward, William L., 138, 160
Hiatt, Howard H., 130, 131, 141, 160
Hibbard, Michael, 236, 242
Hicks, Alexander, 37, 41
Hill, Martha S., 65, 78
Hill, Michael, 221, 222, 226
Hill, Richard Child, 168, 182, 198
Hills, Stuart L., 155, 160
Himmelstrand, Ulf, 238, 242

Hingson, Ralph W., 143, 163
Hirsch, Joachim, 196, 199
Hochschild, Arlie Russell, 97, 104
Hoffman, Wayne L., 141, 161
Hogwood, Brian W., 9, 19, 111, 122
Holahan, John, 140, 159
Hollingshead, August B., 124, 160
Holmstrom, Lynda Lytle, 123, 160
Hoos, Ida R., 56, 78, 213, 226
Hopkins, Harry, 27
Hopkins, Richard J., 122
House, James S., 156, 160
Howard, Ebenezer, 166, 199
Howard, Maureen, 183–86
Howe, Irving, 104, 242, 243
Howe, Steven R., 176, 197
Hufbauer, Karl, 134, 160
Hughes, Everett C., 70, 78

Ilchman, Warren F., 206, 227
Illich, Ivan, 135, 160
Ishikawa, Sara, 194, 197
Ismael, Jacqueline S., 31, 78

Jacobs, Jane, 166, 199
Jahoda, Marie, 44, 79
Janes, Craig R., 159
Jencks, Christopher, 109, 122
Jennings, Bruce, 203, 226
Jodice, David A., 39, 42
Joe, Tom, 56, 79
Johnson, Allen W., 159, 161, 163, 198, 200
Johnson, Dale L., 70, 79
Johnson, Janet, 73–77
Johnson, Michael P., 134, 160
Johnson, Norman, 35, 42, 154, 160, 233, 242
Johnson, Virginia E., 134, 161
Jones, Chris, 71, 79
Judd, Dennis R., 194, 201
Judge, Ken, 233, 242
Jung, Carl G., 150, 160

Kahn, Alfred J., 61, 79, 89, 94, 104, 116, 122
Kain, John F., 170, 199
Kamerman, Sheila B., 61, 79, 89, 94, 96, 104, 116, 122
Karapin, Roger S., 217, 226
Kasarda, John D., 191, 199
Katznelson, Ira, 111, 122, 195, 199
Keane, John, 6, 19, 227
Kelly, Gail P., 110, 121, 122
Kelly, Michael, 178, 198
Kelly, William R., 53, 78
Kelman, Herbert C., 211, 225, 227
Kelman, Sander, 236, 243
Kennedy, Michael D., 182, 199
Kern, Rochelle, 143, 157–59, 161–63
Kerns, Wilmer L., 1, 6, 49, 79
Kesten, Alisa H., 9, 19
Keynes, John Maynard, 10
Keyserling, Mary Dublin, 93, 104
Kiesler, Charles A., 177, 199
Kilborn, Peter T., 232, 243
Kimberly, John R., 133, 158, 161, 163
King, Anthony, 226
King, Desmond S., 173, 198
King, Martin Luther, Jr., 82, 183, 184
Kingdon, John W., 203, 227
Kingsley, Charles, 106
Kingston, Tim, 137, 160

Kirk, Stuart A., 16, 19
Kirp, David L., 109, 112, 122
Kleniewski, Nancy, 169, 199
Klerman, Gerald L., 143, 160
Klinkmuller, Erich, 127, 160
Kloby, Gerald S., 54, 79
Kluver, Jean, 189, 198
Korpi, Walter, 231, 243
Kotelchuck, David, 155, 160
Kozol, Jonathan, 113, 122
Kremen, Eleanor, 61, 78
Kurian, George Thomas, 113, 122

Lack, Dorothea Z., 152, 160
Lacronique, Jean-Francois, 133, 158
Lam, Julie A., 174, 201
Lampman, Robert J., 49, 51, 79
Landesman, Sheldon H., 138, 160
Lasch, Christopher, 86, 104
Laudon, Kenneth C., 223, 227
Laves, Walter H. C., 240, 243
Lazarsfeld, Paul F., 204, 227
Lebas, Elizabeth, 167, 197, 199
Lebeaux, Charles N., 8, 19, 37, 42
Le Corbusier, 166, 199
Ledingham, J. G. G., 143, 160
Lefebvre, Henri, 166, 167, 196, 199
LeGates, Richard T., 175, 199
Leggett, John C., 22, 30
LeGrand, Julian, 24, 30
Lehman, Edward W., 202, 227
Lehman, Karen, 188, 199
Lenin, V. I., 238
Leonard, Peter, 5, 6, 71, 78
Lerman, Paul, 178, 199
Levi, Lennart, 156, 160
Levine, David, 66, 79
Levine, Murray, 153, 160
Levine, Rhonda F., 23, 30
Levine, Sol, 156, 160, 161, 163
Levitan, Sar A., 56, 79, 92, 104
Lewin, Tamar, 146, 160
Lewis, Carol W., 197
Lewis, Paul, 44, 79
Lichtenberg, Philip, 72, 77
Lichter, Daniel T., 60, 65, 79, 190, 199
Light, Donald W., 127, 160
Lightman, Ernie S., 72, 79
Lilienfeld, Abraham M., 156, 160, 161, 163
Lindblom, Charles E., 204, 227
Lipsky, Michael, 71, 79, 128, 160, 221, 227
Litman, Theodor J., 128, 159, 160
Lofland, John, 27, 30
Logan, John R., 171, 172, 195, 199, 200
Lohr, Steve, 102, 104
Lora, Ronald, 108, 122
Lubeck, Sally, 91, 104, 114, 122
Lubove, Roy, 26, 30
Luther, Martin, 25
Lynch, Kevin, 194, 199
Lyon, Larry, 189, 199

MacPherson, Stewart, 6
MacRae, Duncan, Jr., 9, 19, 215, 216, 227
Maher, Thomas F., 87, 104
Mann, Jonathan M., 137, 161
Manning, Nick, 39–41, 238, 242
Marcuse, Peter, 174, 176, 188, 199
Mark, Melvin M., 104, 121, 226, 227
Marlowe, Julia, 181, 199

Marmor, Theodore R., 129, 141, 159, 161, 162
Marshall, T. H., 11, 19
Martin, George T., Jr., 17, 19, 21, 25, 28, 30, 48, 49, 71, 79, 80, 210, 221, 222, 224, 226–28
Marx, Karl, 3, 6, 11, 20, 23, 27–30, 83, 156, 161, 166, 167, 169, 197, 200, 238, 241–43
Maslach, Christina, 156, 161, 225, 227
Masters, William H., 134, 161
Matthews, Sarah, 243
McCarthy, Joseph, 29
McCarthy, Thomas, 19
McCroskey, Jacquelyn, 92, 104
McGuire, Meredith B., 150, 161
McIntyre, Eilene L., 65, 78
McKinlay, John B., 126, 129, 144, 158, 159, 161, 162
McLanahan, Sara, 58, 78, 88, 105
McLaughlin, Milbrey Wallin, 221, 227
McMullen, Martha, 127, 161
McNett, Ian, 118, 122
Mechanic, David, 127, 158–62, 178, 200
Meislin, Richard J., 195, 200
Merriam, Ida C., 2, 6
Merton, Robert K., 208, 227
Miles, Ian, 206, 227
Miller, C. Arden, 142, 144, 161
Miller, Dorothy C., 98, 104
Miller, Jon, 204, 226
Millman, Marcia, 153, 161
Mills, C. Wright, 14, 19, 228
Milton, John, 7
Mingione, Enzo, 167, 170, 200
Miringoff, Marc L., 206
Moberg, David, 145, 161
Moffitt, Robert, 56, 79
Mollenkopf, John H., 168, 195, 200
Molotch, Harvey L., 195, 199
Monboddo, James, 32
Monfort, Franklin, 112, 122
Moore, Samuel, 30, 161, 200
Morell, Carolyn, 98, 105, 118, 122
Morris, Michael, 64, 79
Morris, Robert, 40, 42, 213, 227
Moynihan, Daniel Patrick, 4, 6
Mumford, Lewis, 166, 200
Mumpower, Jeryl L., 206, 227
Murphy, Karen, 175, 199
Murphy, Terry, 119–21
Murray, Charles, 4, 6
Mutiso, Roberta M., 33, 42
Muwakkil, Salim, 188, 200
Myles, John, 37, 42
Myrdal, Gunnar, 60, 79

Nader, Ralph, 203
Nagel, Stuart S., 19, 225, 227
Napoleon III, 235
Nathanson, Constance A., 135, 152, 162
Navarro, Vicente, 133, 161
Naylor, Audrey, 92, 105
Neckerman, Kathryn M., 58, 59, 80
Nelson, John R., Jr., 94, 105
Nelson, Margaret K., 154, 162
Nesvold, Betty, 36, 41
Nichols-Casebolt, Ann, 47, 79
Noakes, John, 65, 77
Noble, Charles, 214, 227
Nove, Alec, 205, 227, 237, 243

O'Connell, Martin, 92, 105
O'Connor, James, 3, 6, 172, 200
O'Donnell, Christine, 70, 79
Oellerich, Donald T., 62, 79
Offe, Claus, 3, 5, 6, 8, 19, 215, 227
Ogburn, William F., 206, 227
O'Hare, William P., 52, 54, 79
Ohlin, Lloyd E., 15, 19
Orfield, Gary, 112, 122
Orloff, Ann Shola, 24, 30, 231, 243
Orshansky, Mollie, 46, 79
Osborn, F. J., 199
Ostrander, Susan A., 8, 19
Oyen, Else, 42, 104, 226

Pachter, Henry, 241, 243
Page, Benjamin I., 39, 42
Palen, J. John, 164, 200
Palmer, John L., 6
Pampel, Fred C., 34, 42
Panem, Sandra, 139, 161
Parelius, Robert J., 109, 122
Park, Robert E., 166, 200
Parker, R. Andrew, 172, 200
Pascall, Gillian, 85, 105
Patry, Bill, 70, 79
Pear, Robert, 140, 161, 173, 200
Pearce, Diana, 57, 79
Perkins, Frances, 27
Perrow, Charles, 222, 227
Petchey, Roland, 129, 161
Peters, B. Guy, 9, 10, 19, 35, 42, 111, 122
Peterson, George E., 197
Petrakis, Peter, 153, 161
Pickard, Myrna R., 148, 161
Pierce, Dean, 222, 227
Pittman, Karen J., 179, 197
Piven, Frances Fox, 28, 30, 49, 60, 79, 97, 104, 221, 226
Pizer, Hank, 151, 161
Plotnick, Robert D., 54, 55, 57, 78
Polner, Robert, 173, 200
Pomfret, John, 123
Pontusson, Jonas, 37, 42
Powell, Thomas J., 153, 161
Preteceille, Edmond, 242, 243
Primus, Wendell, 52, 79
Prout, Marianne N., 149, 161
Provence, Sally, 92, 105
Pruger, Robert, 221, 227
Psacharopoulos, George, 110, 122
Pusic, Eugen, 233, 236, 239, 243

Quadagno, Jill S., 11, 19

Rabinovitch, Sacha, 199
Rainwater, Lee, 35, 42
Rajapatirana, Sarath, 34, 42
Ramos, Myra Bergman, 122
Rank, Mark R., 47, 58, 79–80
Rapp, Charles A., 179, 200
Rasmussen, David W., 183, 197
Ratcliffe, John, 142, 161
Raven, Bertram H., 159, 161, 163, 198, 200
Ravitch, Diane, 110, 122
Ravussin, Eric, 153, 162
Record, Frank, 86, 104
Redlich, Frederick C., 124, 160
Rehnquist, William, 214
Reich, Wilhelm, 150, 162
Reichard, Gary W., 122

Rein, Martin, 35, 42, 202, 227
Rein, Mildred, 64, 80
Reischauer, Robert D., 60, 80
Reiss, Albert J., 228
Reitz, Jeffrey G., 204, 227
Relman, Arnold C., 131, 162
Relph, E., 194, 200
Renaud, Marc, 145, 162
Renner, Michael, 193, 194, 200
Rescorla, Leslie A., 92, 105
Reynolds, Bertha Capen, 21, 28–30, 70, 80
Rhoads, Steven E., 232, 243
Richmond, Mary, 27, 30
Riddell, Tom, 232, 243
Riessman, Catherine Kohler, 135, 152, 154, 162
Riessman, Frank, 119, 122
Riley, Matilda White, 136, 163
Ringen, Stein, 36, 37, 41
Riordan, Teresa, 181, 200
Ritzer, George, 155, 162
Rivlin, A. M., 216, 227
Rivlin, Leanne G., 173, 200
Rizzo, Frank, 180
Rodgers, Harrell R., Jr., 37, 42, 57, 59, 78, 80, 96, 105, 115, 122, 147, 162
Rodgers, Robert C., 172, 200
Rodwin, Victor G., 158, 161, 163
Roethlisberger, Fritz J., 222, 227
Rogers, Cheryl, 56, 79
Rose, Richard, 8, 10, 19, 31, 35, 42, 242
Rosenblum, Susan, 192, 198
Rosentraub, Mark S., 161, 200
Rossi, Peter H., 213, 217, 227
Roth, Julius A., 18, 19
Rothman, Barbara Katz, 152, 162
Rowntree, B. S., 46, 80
Rubenstein, Hiasura, 227
Rubins, Leonard S., 159, 160
Ruge, Arnold, 6
Russell, Bob, 83, 104
Russell, Carol Crill, 125, 162
Russett, Bruce M., 206, 227
Rutter, Michael, 93, 105
Ruzek, Sheryl K., 153, 162

Saalman, Howard, 235, 242, 243
Salkind, Neil J., 96, 105
Salmon, J. Warren, 135, 162
Sarri, Rosemary C., 57, 80, 125, 162
Satran, Pamela Redmond, 91, 105
Saunders, Peter, 192, 200
Savo, Cynthia, 154, 162
Sawers, Larry, 187, 197–200
Schaurer, Herman, 122
Scheff, Thomas J., 177, 200
Schiff, Robert L., 131, 162
Schinke, Steven Paul, 102, 104, 115, 122
Schmitt, Eric, 174, 200
Schnall, Peter C., 157, 162
Schneider, Joseph W., 134, 158
Schneider, Mark, 172, 200
Schorr, Alvin L., 67, 80, 220, 227
Schuller, Alexander, 160
Schutt, Russell K., 72, 80
Schwartz, Nathan H., 181, 200
Schwartz, William, 28, 30
Schwartzman, Paul, 173, 200
Scicchitano, Michael J., 155, 163
Scott, Allen J., 197, 199, 201, 234, 242
Scott, Robert A., 209, 227

Scull, Andrew, 177, 178, 200
Scully, Diana, 152, 162
Shakespeare, William, 1, 164
Shalev, Michael, 23, 30
Shalom, Stephen Rosskamm, 198
Shanker, Renee, 155, 162
Shapiro, Isaac, 56, 79
Shaw, George Bernard, 43
Shaw, Nancy Stoller, 140, 162
Sherer, Moshe, 242, 243
Sheridan, Alan, 197
Sherraden, Michael W., 59, 80
Shields, Lynn, 187, 200, 232, 243
Shiratori, Rei, 19, 31, 242
Shore, Miles F., 177, 198
Shotland, R. Lance, 104, 121, 226, 227
Sidel, Ruth, 90, 105, 146, 162
Sidel, Victor W., 146, 162
Silverstein, Murray, 194, 197
Simmel, Georg, 166, 200
Sinclair, Upton, 26, 31
Sindos, Louise, 94, 104
Singer, Jack, 131, 159
Siu, Albert L., 130, 162
Skocpol, Theda, 231, 243
Slater, Philip, 240, 243
Smith, James D., 52, 80
Smith, Michael P., 186, 194, 197–201, 236, 243
Smith, Neil, 168, 176, 199, 201
Smith, Robert A., 149, 161
Smolensky, Eugene, 54, 56, 78
Snow, David A., 186, 201
Somoza, Anastasio, 113
Sorensen, Annemette, 88, 105
Spiro, Shimon E., 30, 42, 226–28
Spock, Dr. Benjamin, 134, 162
Stall, Ron, 159
Stark, Evan, 145, 162
Stark, Rodney, 27, 30
Starr, Paul, 125, 129–31, 162, 163
Stason, William B., 215, 228
Stefl, Mary E., 176, 197
Steinbeck, John, 26, 31
Stern, Mark J., 69, 77, 180, 201
Stinchcombe, Arthur L., 24, 31
Stone, Deborah A., 134, 163
Stout, Hilary, 67, 80, 120, 122
Straus, Roger A., 204, 227
Strauss, Anselm L., 136, 163
Straussman, Jeffrey D., 172, 200
Street, David, 71, 80, 210, 221, 222, 228, 236, 243
Stromberg, Ann H., 105
Struik, Dirk J., 243
Struthers, James, 24, 31
Stuart, Archibald, 63, 80
Sudnow, David, 18, 19
Sullivan, Michael, 11, 19
Sullivan, Ronald, 139, 163
Summers, Lawrence H., 46, 78
Suttles, Gerald D., 166, 201
Suzman, Richard, 136, 163
Swank, Duane H., 37, 41
Syme, S. Leonard, 124, 163
Szasz, Andrew, 156, 163

Tabb, William K., 197–200
Tarpinian, Greg, 38, 42, 89, 105, 147, 163, 192, 201
Taylor, Charles Lewis, 39, 42
Taylor, Frederick Winslow, 69, 70, 146, 212, 228
Taylor, Rosemary C. R., 145, 163
Taylor, Shelley E., 151, 163

Taylor-Gooby, Peter, 12, 19
Teare, Robert J., 70, 80
Teltsch, Kathleen, 115, 122
Terrail, Jean-Pierre, 242, 243
Terrell, Paul, 68, 80
Thatcher, Margaret, 3
Theado, Richard, 215, 225
Therborn, Goran, 11, 19, 35, 37, 42, 51, 66, 80
Thompson, E. P., 193, 201
Thompson, Frank J., 155, 163
Thomson, Charles A., 240, 243
Thurow, Lester C., 9, 19
Tickamyer, Ann R., 56, 78
Titmuss, Richard M., 10, 12, 19
Tolchin, Martin, 67, 80, 125, 130, 163
Tomaskovic-Devey, Donald, 65, 78, 80, 158, 162
Tonak, E. Ahmet, 51, 80
Trattner, Walter I., 27, 31
Trickett, Penelope K., 92, 105
Tropman, John E., 38, 42
Trump, Donald J., 195
Tucker, Robert C., 6
Tyler, Gus, 191, 201
Tynes, Sheryl R., 24, 31

Ullman, Dana, 150, 163
Ungerson, Clare, 97, 105

Van der Veen, Romke, 9, 19
Van de Vall, Mark, 215, 228
Van Weesep, Jan, 180, 201
Vanzetti, Michael, 98–103
Velimirovic, B., 136, 163
Vining, Daniel R., Jr., 237, 243

Waitzkin, Howard, 40, 41, 130, 163
Walczak, David, 155, 162
Walker, Alan, 236, 243
Walker, Richard A., 192, 201
Walsh, Diana Chapman, 143, 163
Walsh, Joan, 64, 80, 115, 116, 122
Walton, John, 182, 201
Walzer, Michael, 241, 243
Warner, Richard, 34, 42
Warwick, Donald P., 211, 216, 225, 227
Weatherford, Bernadyne, 50, 80
Weaver, Mary, 50, 80
Webb, Beatrice, 25, 31
Webb, Sidney, 25, 31
Weber, Max, 208, 222, 228
Weinberg, Daniel H., 41, 77, 78, 80, 162
Weinraub, Bernard, 5, 6
Weinstein, Milton C., 215, 228
Weir, Margaret, 111, 122
Weis, Lois, 121, 122
Weiss, Carol H., 215, 228
Weller, Geoffrey, 126, 163
Wildavsky, Aaron, 49, 80, 141, 163, 210, 228
Wilensky, Harold L., 8, 19, 34, 37, 42
Wilkie, Jane Riblett, 89, 105
Williams, Peter, 168, 176, 199, 201
Williams, Raymond, 193, 201
Williams, Walter, 227
Williamson, John B., 34, 42, 64, 79
Willim, Horst, 157, 163
Wilson, Elizabeth, 117, 122
Wilson, Everett K., 122
Wilson, James Q., 199

Wilson, William Julius, 58–60, 62, 80, 190, 201
Winerip, Michael, 179, 201
Wirth, Louis, 166, 201, 204, 228, 236
Withorn, Ann, 71, 81, 153, 163, 222, 224, 228
Wolf, Douglas A., 56, 79
Wolf, Stewart, 160

Wolff, Craig, 146, 163
Wolff, Kurt H., 200
Woomert, Alison, 155, 158
Wright, James D., 174, 201

Yanowitch, Murray, 40, 42
Yates, Michael D., 72, 81
Yeats, John, 202

Yuchtman-Yaar, Ephraim, 30, 42, 226–28

Zald, Mayer N., 19, 30, 79, 226, 231, 243
Zapf, Wolfgang, 23, 31
Zaretsky, Eli, 86, 105
Zigler, Edward F., 105

Subject Index

Abortion, 9, 83, 152
Accountability, 94, 114, 140–41, 151, 192, 233
ACORN, 180
Activism. See Collective action
Administration, 7–10, 62, 140, 141, 144, 203, 215, 237. See also Bureaucrats
Adoption, 99–100
Adult Basic Education, 113, 184
Adult day care, 206
Adult homes, 206
Advocacy, 71, 99, 139, 153, 157, 180, 184, 203
AFDC, 46–50; cuts in, 56–57; and family dissolution, 58–59; fraud in, 47; myths about, 47, 64; payments for, 38, 47, 67; and poverty, 56–59; and pregnancy, 47; and psychological well-being, 47; recipients of, 47–48; reform of, 67–69; stigma of, 13, 46–47; and workfare, 63–65. See also Public aid
Affirmative action, 9, 74, 205
Africa, 33, 44. See also Third World
African Americans, 55, 183, 207, 212, 240; and AIDS, 138; and CETA, 55; as clients, 18; and the Democratic Party, 49, 231; discrimination against, 60, 74; education of, 109, 111–12; health and health care of, 124–26, 128, 147; labor force problems of, 13, 53, 59–61, 65, 146, 190–91; marriage of, 59, 88; migration of, 49, 60; poverty of, 57–61, 75, 115; as practitioners, 74, 102–3, 146–47; segregation of, 112, 170–71; and social change, 71, 231, 240. See also Minority groups; Race
Aged persons, 23, 34, 49–50, 67; and demographic change, 3, 10, 24, 136, 230, 231; economic redundancy of, 11, 23, 34; educational needs of, 116; health care needs of, 136; and income redistribution, 53; and income security, 45–50, 58, 69, 73, 75; influence of, 13; institutions for, 127–28, 206; poverty of, 55, 58; services for, 146, 206, 230; social isolation of, 10–11; work with, 99

AIDS, 2, 14, 119–21, 124, 136–40, 146, 148–49, 239
Alabama, 67, 70, 74
Alcoholics Anonymous, 225
Alcoholism, 73, 134, 143, 204, 225
Alienation, 15, 86–87, 118, 146, 156, 193, 196, 222
Altruism, 18, 25–26, 45, 131, 210
Amalgamated Clothing and Textile Workers Union, 17, 224
American Federation of State, County, and Municipal Employees, 16, 71, 224
American Federation of Teachers, 224
Amsterdam, 168, 180
Architecture, 189
Arkansas, 64, 67
Asia, 33. See also Third World
Asian Americans, 124
Australia, 33, 35–37, 39, 61, 66, 113, 126, 165
Austria, 35, 66, 91, 113
Autos, 167, 169–70, 193–94, 203, 235

Baltimore, 64, 173
Barcelona, 194
Beijing, 165
Belgium, 35, 36, 62, 66, 165
Bikeways, 194
Birth centers, 154
Birth control, 101–2, 115
Birth rates, 10–11, 50, 87–88, 101–2, 135
Blaming the victim, 153, 176, 224
Boston, 139, 152, 168, 187, 189, 195
Bricklayers and Laborers Union, 189
Britain. See United Kingdom
Buddhism, 150
Bulgaria, 39
Bureaucracy, 4, 24, 208–11; in capitalism, 196, 237–39; discretion in, 221–23, 225; disentitlement by, 128; in health care, 128–35, 154; impersonality of, 17–18; informal system of, 222–23, 225; pathology of, 223, 238; and privacy rights, 223; reform of, 223, 224, 242; and self-help, 224; in socialism, 237–39; and social practice, 15–16, 18, 28, 221–23; of the state, 21, 24–25, 196, 237–39;

strengths of, 22, 129, 238, 239; and Taylorism, 69–70. See also Hierarchy
Bureaucratization, 4, 17, 111, 120, 145, 166, 192, 196, 204, 237–39
Bureaucrats, 10, 17–18, 71, 210, 221–23, 230
Burnout, 16, 70, 103, 118, 156, 225

California, 38, 67, 112, 177, 193, 196
Canada: education in, 110; health care in, 126, 140, 141, 144; income distribution in, 36; income redistribution in, 37; inequality in, 39; poverty in, 37; single mothers in, 61; social wage in, 51; social welfare expenditure of, 35; teen pregnancy and birth in, 102; unemployment policies of, 35, 66; workfare in, 65
Canada Assistance Plan, 24
Cancer, 134, 136, 138–39, 145, 149, 155, 157
Capitalism, 33, 233, 240; and aids, 137; alienation in, 156; and autos, 193; bureaucracy in, 196, 237–39; and caring, 213; changes in, 49; checks on, 22; and cities, 164–73, 194, 235; class structure of, 12; and collective consumption, 192, 195; contradictions in, 192, 238; diswelfares of, 12; and education, 110; failures of, 61; the family in, 85–87; and the fiscal crisis of the state, 234; gentrification in, 175–76; health care in, 129, 145, 151; history of, 21–25; housing in, 188; hunger in, 44; income security in, 76; injustice of, 236, 242; instability of, 231, 234, 235; internationalization of, 168, 239; needs of, 65, 234; occupational safety and health in, 156; poverty in, 44, 236; rationing in, 126–28; and revolution, 241–42; and social dependency, 46; and socialism, 32, 39–41, 53, 236, 238, 239, 242; social isolation in, 15, 86–87; social movements in, 196–97, 241; and social planning, 204, 234–37; social problems of, 25–26, 65, 164–

66, 231, 239; social reproduction of, 83; and social work, 25–26; surplus labor in, 22–23, 65; and the Third World, 32–34; and traditional institutions, 8, 85–86; and the Welfare State, 1, 3, 5, 11–13, 18, 23–25, 39–41, 225, 229; workers in, 13, 22, 23, 45, 65, 156, 166, 235. *See also* Corporations

Caring, 25, 86–87, 89–90, 97–98, 117–19, 151, 177, 213

Carter administration, 155

Case management services, 73–77, 179, 184

Caseworkers, 86, 102–3, 185, 221–22

Catholic Family Services, 98–99

CBD, 166, 168, 169, 172, 195, 235. *See also* Cities

Central planning, 237–39

Charisma, 202–3

Charity, 8, 14, 21, 25–28, 180

Chicago, 27, 72, 115, 131, 157, 165, 168, 173, 181

Chicago School, 166, 204, 205, 236

Child abuse, 92, 99–102, 212–13

Child birth, 132, 135, 142, 144, 147–49, 152–54, 223

Child care: arrangements for, 89–90, 93; and children, 92–93; expenditure for, 89; and the family, 84, 87–88, 91, 97–99; and feminism, 224–25; and flextime, 94–95; medicalization of, 134; need for, 89–92, 114–15, 208, 230, 231; privatization of, 93–94; as a public issue, 14; public support for, 91; in schools, 114–16, 209; staffing of, 63, 89–90, 92, 93, 97; standards for, 92–93; in unions, 17; as women's work, 93, 97–98, 193; at work, 92; and workfare, 63, 68–69, 94; in World War II, 91

Children: and child care, 92–93; child support for, 62–63, 68; and education, 111; and a family policy, 91, 95–96; health of, 144–45; homelessness of, 174; hunger of, 44; hyperactive, 134; mental health needs of, 99; mortality of, 208; and parents, 87–88; poverty of, 23, 55, 57–61; and public aid, 46, 47, 68–69; services for, 115; and Social Security, 50

Children's allowance. *See* Family allowance

China, People's Republic of, 40, 132, 137, 187

CIO, 71–72

Cities, 164–97; African Americans in, 60; amenities of, 194; and the auto, 194; and capital mobility, 186–87; child-care needs in, 90; classification of, 167–70; conflict in, 28, 193; contradictions in, 179–80, 191, 192; crisis of, 167; deindustrialization of, 60; employees of, 183; enterprise zones in, 182–83; fiscal crisis of, 165, 170, 172–73; growth control in, 187, 195; homelessness in, 173–83; and industrial capitalism, 22, 24, 49, 165–66, 235; infrastructure of, 191–92; and migration, 49, 60; mismatch problems of, 190–91; polarization in, 176; public works for, 191–92, 194; quality of life in,

193–94; schools in, 112; and social change, 192–97; social indicators for, 189–90; social movements in, 195–97, 241; social welfare in, 195; and the spatial division of labor, 168; and suburbs, 165, 170–72, 182, 190–91; in the Third World, 236–37; transformation of, 167–73, 194, 195, 235. *See also* Gentrification

City planning, 166, 195, 204, 235, 236. *See also* Social planning

Civilization, 86, 135–36, 239–42

Civil rights, 11, 28, 36, 49, 108, 177, 191, 196

Civil servants. *See* Public employees

Clients: devalued, 70; distinctions between, 198; and feminism, 153; in health care, 123–28, 130–36, 151; in holistic health care, 151; interests of, 209, 211; in mental health, 177–78; and practitioners, 17, 71, 210–11, 221–22, 224, 225; in public aid, 71, 73–77; rights of, 74, 148, 177, 223; screening of, 16; in self-help, 153–54; and social policy, 210, 230; and social practice, 15–18, 71, 220–25; and Taylorism, 70; terms for, 5; and the Welfare State, 4, 5

Collective action, 10, 13, 14, 16–17, 22, 116, 149, 189, 194–97, 224–25. *See also* Social movements

Collective consumption, 86, 166–67, 175, 192–96, 236–37

Collectivism, 3, 8, 11–13, 38, 111, 196, 210

Columbia University, 27, 147

Commodification, 15, 83, 85–87, 111–12, 156, 167, 178, 184, 196

Communications Workers of America, 103, 224

Community: activism in, 189, 241; and AIDS, 138, 140; and capitalism, 8, 15, 192; decline of, 17; disruption in, 156; and enterprise zones, 182; and environmentalism, 149; and family, 85–86; health indicators for, 144; as an ideal, 61; and mental health, 143–44, 177–79; natural helpers in, 154; need for, 240; and placeness, 194; and poor relief, 25, 70; in public housing, 188; redevelopment of, 195; and social movements, 196; study of, 166

Community mental health centers, 209–10

Community organization, 15, 27, 140, 180–82

Confidentiality, 139, 212. *See also* Privacy rights

Conservatism: and cost-benefit analysis, 214; and education, 110–11, 121; and the family, 84–85, 90, 208; and homelessness, 180–83; and self-help, 154; and social policy, 3–5, 231, 233; and the Welfare State, 35–36, 46

Contradictions, 83, 170, 179–80, 191–92, 204–5, 216, 234–35

Convergence theory, 41

Cooperatives, 181

Cooptation, 154

Corporate city, 165, 167–70, 175, 182, 186

Corporations, 53–54, 70; bureaucracy in, 212, 237–39; and cities, 167–71, 195; and deindustrialization, 192; and education, 110–11; and enterprise zones, 182; and the family, 85; in health care, 126, 128–32, 135–37, 142, 146; and location theory, 192; regulation of, 186–87, 192; and social movements, 196; and uneven development, 192. *See also* Capitalism

Correctional institutions, 127–28, 223

Cosmopolitanism, 166

Cost-benefit analysis, 15–16, 212–14

Counseling: and AIDS, 137, 139; for child abuse, 99; for families, 115; and health care, 143, 157; for the homeless, 185; job, 89; by nurses, 147–49; in public aid, 68, 73

Counterculture, 150, 196

Creationism, 9, 111, 216

Crime, 45, 92, 100, 101, 113, 138, 172, 204

Critical analysis, 6, 114

Cuba, 33, 145, 187

Culture, 106, 110, 150, 165–67, 193, 196, 225

Czechoslovakia, 39, 110

Data: aggregate, **205, 207**; collection problems with, 207; cross- sectional, 189; disaggregation of, 207; as fetish, 213–14, 217; interpretation of, 208, 215, 218–20; longitudinal, 189, 206–7; for planning, 236; and privacy rights, 212, 223; qualitative, 217–19; quantitative, 217–19; sample, 205, 211, 216, 218–20; for social indicators, 206–7; use of, 189–90, 202. *See also* Research

Day treatment, 179

Death, 123, 124, 137, 138, 143, 155, 156, 193–94, 207, 208

Debureaucratization, 223

Decentralization, 8, 37–38, 107, 140–41, 168–72, 196–97, 223

Degradation ritual, 46–47

Deindustrialization, 60, 190–92

Deinstitutionalization, 14, 165, 173, 175–79

Delhi, 165

Democracy, 8, 18, 40, 110–13, 192, 208, 224, 234, 236–39, 242

Democratic Party, 10, 23, 27–28, 49, 231

Demography, 3, 24, 48–50, 87–88, 116, 138, 205–7, 230, 231

Denmark, 35–37, 66, 165

Denver, 95–96, 171, 186

Depersonalization. *See* Impersonality

Deregulation, 9, 214

Desegregation, 107–9, 112, 113

Detroit, 22, 167–68, 171, 173, 181

Deviance, 134, 205

Diagnosis, 128–30, 133, 134, 144, 149, 157, 204

Diet, 86, 143, 150, 157

Dirty work, 70, 146

Disabled persons: and capitalism, 12; disenfranchisement of, 193; and income security, 45–50, 69; mobilization of, 14, 230; poverty of, 23, 55; and public amenities, 194; and the Reagan administra-

tion, 9, 50; services for, 146; and the social wage, 13; and the Welfare State, 3, 134
Discrimination, 45, 60, 67, 74, 111, 142, 190, 233
Disease, 86, 115, 128, 134–40, 142–45, 149–50, 155–57, 165–66, 189
Diseases of civilization, 86
Displaced homemakers, 88–89
Divorce, 57–59, 84, 87–89, 144
Doctors. *See* Medical doctors
Dossiers, 134
DRGs, 129–30
Drug abuse. *See* Substance abuse
Drunken driving, 216

Earned income tax credit, 68, 96
East Germany, 39, 110, 127, 157. *See also* Germany
Ecology, 45, 142–45, 166, 167, 186–87, 194, 196–97. *See also* Environment
Economic indicators, 206
Economics, 7, 9–11, 32–41, 45, 55, 85–87, 166–67, 212, 230
Economic stagnation, 9, 16–17, 39, 53, 54, 66, 171, 174, 230
Economism, 196–97, 238–39
Economy of scale, 22, 129
Education, 106–21, 189–90; adult, 89, 113, 116; for AIDS, 137–40, 149; for alcoholism, 143; comparative, 40–41; curricula in, 107, 110, 118, 120; democratization of, 107, 110–11; dialogic, 111, 114; egalitarian and elitist, 110–11; equal opportunity in, 109–10; expenditure for, 108; federalization of, 107–8; formal and informal, 106, 107; growth of, 108; and health, 141–42, 147–48; and human capital, 55–56; and industrialism, 60; and literacy, 113–14; manifest and latent functions of, 209; as necessity, 43–44; and poverty, 64; preschool, 115–16; privatization of, 111; professionalization in, 72; public, 107–8, 111; remedial, 63–64, 113, 118; and social change, 229; and social class, 108–12; as socialization, 8; socialization of, 46, 84; and social reproduction, 106–7; as social right, 11, 241; unionization in, 72; for workers, 12, 107–9, 111, 157; and work success, 88, 108–9, 190. *See also* Schools
Efficiency, 35–36, 55, 62, 127, 129, 144–45, 233, 238, 239
Egalitarianism, 110–12, 188, 222
Eisenhower administration, 188
Elderly. *See* Aged persons
Eligibility, 18, 46–47, 56, 67, 140
Elitism, 110–11
Embarassment, 83
Empathy, 25, 97
Empowerment, 5, 153, 241
England. *See* United Kingdom
Enterprise zones, 181–83
Entitlement, 8, 11, 14, 46, 65
Environment, 189, 237; the city as, 164, 166–67, 173; degradation of, 123, 169, 170, 205, 210, 236–37, 239; and environmentalism, 149, 196; fears for, 138; and health, 141–45; modification of, 242; physical

and social, 235. *See also* Ecology; Pollution
Epidemics, 137–40
Epidemiology, 143–44, 149, 156–57
Equalitarianism, 209–10
Ethnography, 186, 190, 217
Europe, 24, 26, 27, 35, 38, 192
Euthanasia, 207
Expertise, 15–16, 28, 202–3
Exurbs, 171, 190

Factory system, 22, 49, 196
Families, 47, 82–103; and birth, 132; and caring work, 86–87, 96–98, 136; changes in, 10–11, 17, 84–88, 208; child abuse in, 99–102; composition of, 87–88; consumption in, 86–87; dissolution of, 58–59, 87–88, 208; education in, 106, 107, 111; and health, 218–20; homelessness of, 174, 184–85; income of, 52, 53, 61; and mental health, 143; poverty of, 54, 56–61, 63, 67; and public aid, 46, 47; recreation in, 85–86; sanctuary function of, 86–87; services for, 115; size of, 86–87; social isolation of, 15, 85–87; social needs of, 88–96; and social production, 85–86; and social reproduction, 82–98; social work with, 29; stresses in, 85–87, 99–102; surrogate, 179; and taxes, 68; and the underclass, 60; and unemployment, 44; variations of, 84–85; violence in, 153, 212–13, 224–25; and Welfare State pluralism, 233–34; and women's subordination, 98, 233. *See also* Female-headed families; Patriarchy
Family allowance, 13, 35, 38, 61–62, 66, 69, 91, 95–96
Family planning, 102, 115, 142, 144, 147, 218–20
Family policy, 90–96
Family Support Act, 61, 68–69
Fear, 133, 138, 139
Federal government, 38, 188; and AIDS, 137, 139, 140; and child care, 91, 94; and education, 107–8; expenditure of, 21, 28, 126, 232; and deinstitutionalization, 178; and health care, 140–42; and housing, 174, 180–81; and illiteracy, 113–14; and income security, 46, 48–49; and policy development in, 216; and policy research, 202, 218; and systems analysis, 212; and urban social problems, 154–66, 172–73
Federalization, 48–49, 63, 107–8
Female-headed families, 2, 55, 57–65, 87–88, 94, 96, 101–2, 116, 174, 231
Feminism, 17, 90, 117, 118, 143, 146, 148–55, 193
Feminization of poverty, 57–61
Fetish, 213–14
Feudalism, 21–23, 25, 37, 45, 196
Finland, 35–37, 66, 96, 113, 157
First World, 33–41. *See also* Capitalism
Fiscal crisis of the state, 2–5, 69, 170–73, 182, 230, 234
Fiscal welfare, 10, 52
Flextime, 94–95

Food Stamps, 28, 48–50, 55, 67
Ford administration, 188
Foster care, 99–101
Foundations, 8, 233
France: collective consumption in, 193; education in, 110, 116; family policy of, 91, 96; health care in, 144; income distribution in, 36; income redistribution in, 37; inequality in, 39; life expectancy in, 33; minimum income policy of, 62; nuclear waste industry of, 181; poverty in, 37; single mothers in, 61; social wage in, 51; social welfare expenditure of, 35; teen pregnancy and birth in, 102; unemployment policies of, 35, 66
Frankfurt, 168
Freudianism, 27–29, 150
Full employment, 9, 11, 37, 40, 65–66, 69, 76
Functionalism, 11–13, 24, 75, 85–87, 208–9

Gallup Poll, 138, 205, 218
Gatekeeping, 16
Gays, 9, 136–40, 196. *See also* Homosexuality
Gender, 45, 58, 97, 98, 102, 117–20, 146, 152. *See also* Sex
Gender gap, 231–32
General Assistance, 46–50
Gentrification, 60, 165, 175–76, 189, 196
Germany, 23–25, 140. *See also* East Germany; West Germany
Ghetto, 60, 167, 176, 196
Glasgow, 168
Goal displacement, 209–10, 213, 238
Grass roots, 180, 183, 184, 188, 194–97, 220
Great Depression, 10, 28, 49, 230
Greenbelts, 187
Green Party, 196
Group homes, 178–79
Groups, 82–83, 109, 118–19, 150, 167, 204. *See also* Self-help
Guinea, 33

Haitian Americans, 138
Halfway houses, 14
Harris Poll, 116
Haussmannization, 235
Headstart, 28, 93, 94, 115–16
Health, 123–57, 189; and capitalism, 86–87; comparative, 40–41; determinants of, 141; expenditure for, 126; and family, 218–20; and health care, 141, 209–10; and hunger, 44; indicators of, 126, 144; and race, 124; right to, 11, 241; and social class, 124; and sterilization, 219–20; and work, 155–57
Health care, 35, 46–48, 123–57, 193; access to, 209–10; for AIDS, 137, 139, 140; alternative, 150–55; for chronic disease, 86, 135–36; comparative, 126–27, 144–45; corporatization of, 70, 126, 128–32, 135–37, 142, 146; costs of, 141–42; and deinstitutionalization, 178; demedicalization of, 143, 149–57; distortions in, 123–24, 135–36;

and health, 141, 209–10; for the homeless, 184; maternal, 95, 147; medicalization of, 132–37, 142, 143, 149, 152; as a necessity, 43–44; needs for, 40, 63, 135–45; neonatal and prenatal, 91, 115, 123–24, 132, 135, 147–49, 154; and physical fitness, 86; practitioners in, 145–49; preventive, 127, 141–45; rationing of, 124–28; remedial, 86, 132–35, 149–50; in schools, 114–16; and self-help, 153–55; and social class, 124–28; socialization of, 128–29, 140–45, 157; technology in, 123–24, 127, 129; for women, 151–55; for workers, 157

Health insurance, 4, 9, 38, 66, 125–27, 130–31, 136, 140–42, 148, 178

Hierarchy, 17–18, 103, 108, 117, 146, 150–52, 156, 196, 212, 220–22

Hispanics, 75, 103, 111–12, 124, 138, 147, 170–71, 190–91. *See also* Mexican Americans; Minority groups; Puerto Ricans

HMOs, 129

Holistic health, 148–51, 157, 223

Home, 83, 86–87, 171, 183–86, 188, 194, 195

Home care, 139, 146–47, 206

Homelessness, 173–86; causes of, 174–78, 183, 231, 235; and conservatism, 183; as deprivation, 44, 164; estimates of, 173–74; and health care, 131; hidden, 173, 185; practitioners with, 183–86; programs for, 184–85; and public aid, 73; and the Reagan administration, 5; shelters for, 173, 174, 176, 178–80, 184; and social isolation, 186; as a social problem, 2, 14, 165, 231

Homemaker services, 99, 181

Homophobia, 139

Homosexuality, 134, 138, 139, 149. *See also* Gays

Hong Kong, 168

Hoover administration, 206

Hospices, 139, 206, 207

Hospitals, 18, 127–35, 136, 145–49, 152, 154, 176–79, 219, 223

Housework, 88, 97–98

Housing, 34, 189, 193, 196, 233; bias in, 183; and child abuse, 101; and cities, 166–67, 172, 235; conversion of, 180, 184–85; cost of, 187; and deinstitutionalization, 178, 179; destruction of, 169, 171, 235; expenditure for, 232; gentrification of, 175–76; and health care, 127, 141–42; and homelessness, 14, 173–86; permanent, 184–86; and the Reagan administration, 180–83, 232; shortage of, 174–75, 178, 181, 187, 189, 196; as social need, 40; as a social right, 11; and suburbs, 171–72; temporary, 184, 185; and the tenants' movement, 195–96; transitional, 184; vouchers for, 181. *See also* Public housing; Squatting

Houston, 118, 168, 172, 173

Hull House, 27, 165

Humanism, 3, 136, 143–44, 192, 194, 196–97, 217, 240–42

Human needs, 16, 70, 240–42

Human rights, 11, 40, 140, 240–42

Hungary, 39, 95

Hunger, 44

Hunter College, 146–47

Hypertension, 151, 156–57

Iatrogenic disorders, 124, 134–35, 149, 210

Iceland, 36

Ideology, 12–13, 25, 41, 98, 133, 145, 153–54

Illinois, 112, 115

Illiteracy, 14, 113–14, 184, 210

Immigration, 26–27, 107

Immunization, 135, 145

Impersonality, 4, 17–18, 136, 149, 151–52, 154, 156, 221

Income distribution, 8, 36–37, 40, 51–54, 141, 206

Income maintenance. *See* Income security

Income redistribution, 4, 10, 23, 36–37, 51–54, 109, 142

Income security, 8, 96, 113, 236; changes in, 48–50; definition of, 45; federalization of, 48–49; and the feminization of poverty, 57–61; and full employment, 65–66; growth of, 48–49; and income redistribution, 51–54; and inequality, 52–54; and a minimum income, 45–46, 61–62; and the minimum wage, 66–67; and poverty, 43–45, 54–61; practitioners in, 69–77; programs for, 46–48, 68–69; and socialized child support, 62–63; and social policy, 45–51; and the social wage, 50–51; and unemployment insurance, 67–68; and universalism, 45; and workfare, 63–65; and the working poor, 56–57

India, 219

Individualism, 12, 38, 85–86, 133, 151, 153, 166, 225, 242

Industrialism, 12, 21, 32–33; and alienation, 156; changes in, 60; convergence theory of, 41; dispersal of, 49, 60; and literacy, 22; and social dependency, 46; in socialism, 145; social problems of, 25–26, 235; and social work, 25–26; and Taylorism, 69–70; and urbanization, 164–65, 169; and the Welfare State, 24, 34, 230, 231

Industrial social work, 28–29

Inequality: within cities, 172; city and suburban, 171–73; comparative, 36–37, 39–41, 188; and education, 108–12; in health care, 124–32, 141–42; in housing, 188; and income redistribution, 51–54; minimizing, 75; and poverty, 54; racial-occupational, 53; and social needs, 238; as a social problem, 205; within suburbs, 172; and the Welfare State, 233–34

Infancy, 25, 44, 82, 93, 115, 123–24, 134, 147–49, 152, 207–8

Infant mortality, 124, 126, 144, 147, 206, 208

Inflation, 49, 53, 66, 67

Informed consent, 212

In-kind benefits, 8, 47–48, 64, 91

Innovation, 118, 120

Institutionalization, 23, 136, 176–78, 223

Institutional racism, 205

Intake, 99, 128

Interest groups, 11, 13, 15, 128, 204, 216, 229–31

International Association of Machinists, 224

International Ladies' Garment Workers Union, 224

Interstate highways, 60, 169, 171, 188

Inverse care law, 126

Ireland, 35–37

Irish Americans, 119

Islam, 240

Isolation. *See* Alienation

Israel, 36, 37, 61, 62, 165

Italian Americans, 98

Italy, 35–37, 51, 66, 116

Jakarta, 165

Jane Addams School of Social Work, 27

Japan, 33; economic growth of, 36, 53; education in, 110; full employment policy of, 66; income distribution in, 36; income redistribution in, 37; inequality in, 39; military expenditure of, 38–39, 232–33; social expenditure of, 36; social wage in, 51; unemployment in, 76; unemployment policies of, 35, 66

Judaism, 240

Juvenile delinquency, 15

Kennedy-Johnson administration, 27, 49, 188, 230

Kenya, 33

Keynesianism, 10

Kidcare, 141

Kuwait, 165

Labeling, 134

Labor: in capitalism, 12, 33–34, 43, 168; cheap, 168, 173, 182; family, 85; in hospitals, 130; and mental health, 33–34; movement, 196, 231; nonunion, 173; offshore, 11; paid and unpaid, 87, 193; productivity of, 36, 92, 214; and social dependency, 46, 60; social reproduction of, 83; surplus, 11, 170; in the Third World, 33, 168; and the Welfare State, 13, 23, 37, 40–41, 231. *See also* Workers

Labor force, 108; and African Americans, 59–61, 65; and capitalism, 22, 26, 65; changes in, 190; corporate demands on, 110–11, 169; in health care, 145–46; as human capital, 55–56; problems of, 65–68; schooling of, 110, 114, 190; unemployment in, 14, 22, 49; and women, 10–11, 67, 87–88, 97, 117

Labour Party, 23

Lagos, 165

Laissez faire, 38

Language, 106, 240

Latin America, 33, 116, 196. *See also* Third World

Law, 7–9, 216

Learning, 82–84, 92–93, 113, 223. *See also* Education

Legitimation, 12, 72, 133, 209

251

Leisure. *See* Recreation
Lesbians, 140
Liberalism, 4, 5, 28, 45, 49, 233–34
Life chances, 94, 144, 171
Life cycle, 53, 58
Life expectancy, 207, 215; and the aged, 10–11, 136; and AIDS, 138; comparative, 33, 126; and economic development, 34; and medicalization, 134–35; and race, 124; and social dependency, 49; as a social problem, 136, 207; and Social Security, 67; of women, 88
Lifestyle, 86, 141–45, 150, 153
Literacy, 22, 34, 40, 107, 113–14
Liverpool, 168
Lobbying, 128, 132, 140, 210, 216
Local government, 38, 165–66, 181, 186, 225; and child care, 91; employees of, 71, 117, 183; and enterprise zones, 182; and federalism, 188; fiscal crisis of, 172–73; and health care, 126, 157; and income security, 46, 49, 69; and transnational corporations, 186; and zoning, 234
Location theory, 192
London, 26, 165, 168, 174
Los Angeles, 137–38, 165, 168–70, 172, 173, 186
Luxembourg, 36, 62, 113

Machines, 22, 133, 151–52, 156, 190. *See also* Technology
Madrid, 196
Manhattanization, 176, 195
Manifest and latent functions, 208–9
Market place, 39; and child care, 90; and education, 111–12; and enterprise zones, 182–83; and the family, 85–87; and gentrification, 175–76; and health care, 125–28, 144–45; and holistic health care, 151; and labor discipline, 13; and liberalism, 4; and the medical model, 133; and poverty, 56; and privatization, 181–82; problems of, 8, 12, 33–34, 44, 65, 212, 213; and social dependency, 46; and social isolation, 15; and social welfare expenditure, 2; and suburbanization, 171; and surplus labor, 22; and the Welfare State, 18; and workfare, 65
Marriage, 59, 84, 87–88, 98, 125
Marxism, 3, 11, 27–29, 83, 166–67, 196–97, 238
Maryland, 102, 112
Massachusetts, 177, 189, 196, 224
Mass media, 34
Maternity benefits, 35, 91, 95, 144
McCarthyism, 28
Means test, 25, 46
Medicaid, 47–48, 68–69, 100, 125, 130–31, 147–48; and the AMA, 210; applicants for, 67; and deinstitutionalization, 178; payments, 48; and policy expansion, 21, 28, 135, 141
Medical doctors, 15–16, 27, 47, 126–35, 146, 149, 150, 154, 210, 217
Medicalization, 132–35, 152, 155
Medical model, 132–35, 142, 151, 179

Medicare, 21, 28, 47–48, 55, 129–32, 140, 141, 178, 210
Medication, 124–25, 132–35, 152, 177, 179
Mental health, 33–34, 99, 124–25, 143–44, 176–79, 209–10
Mental illness: of children, 99; and family, 87; and homelessness, 14, 131, 176–79, 185, 186; needs of, 16; and poverty, 44–45; prevention of, 143–44; and reinstitutionalization, 178; and research, 217; and Social Security, 50; treatment of, 177–79
Mental institutions, 100, 127–28, 143, 177–78, 223, 224
Mental retardation, 99, 178
Meta-policy, 8–9, 11
Mexican Americans, 183
Mexico, 168
Michigan, 57, 112
Middle class: African American, 60; as beneficiaries, 24; and child abuse, 99; economic problems of, 16–17, 176; and education, 107–9, 111, 121; and gentrification, 175–76; health and health care of, 124–28, 151; homelessness of, 173; housing of, 180, 183; as practitioners, 26, 75; and psychotherapy, 27; and self- help, 154; and suburbs, 172; and uneven development, 171; and urban policy, 167, 235
Middle East, 240
Midwives, 132, 133, 147–49, 152–54, 219
Migration, 49, 60, 156, 167, 173, 191, 237
Militarization, 38–39, 231–33
Military-industrial complex, 212
Minimum income, 62, 69, 76
Minimum wage, 9, 26, 56, 63, 65–67
Minnesota, 63, 67, 95
Minority groups, 183; affirmative action for, 205; and AIDS, 139; and education, 109, 112–13; in health care, 146; and public employment, 71; and the Reagan administration, 9; segregation of, 171, 176, 190; and social change, 71; and unemployment, 190–91; in Welfare State work, 17, 146
Mismatch problems, 190–92
Mississippi, 38, 67
Mobility, 11, 16–17, 108–9, 128, 156, 171, 173, 186–87, 191, 193
Monopoly, 128–35, 150, 211
Morality: and alcoholism, 143; and deviance, 134; and education, 109–11; and homelessness, 180; learning of, 83–84; and the mentally ill, 178; and quantification, 212; and rationing, 127; and research, 215; and social practice, 25, 224
Morbidity, 124, 143, 156
Moscow, 165
Multifamily, 88
Multiplism, 217

National Education Association, 120
National health insurance, 4, 9, 38, 66, 140–42, 148, 178
National Health Service, 127, 141–42
Nationalism, 239, 240
Nationalization, 38, 181
National liberation movements, 240

National Literacy Crusade, 114
National Maritime Union, 28–29, 224
National Welfare Rights Organization, 49
Native Americans, 75, 124, 150, 183
Natural helpers, 154
Nature, 148–52, 217, 242
Needs assessment, 207
Negative income tax, 95–96, 211–12
Neighborhoods, 175; African American, 60; and enterprise zones, 182; group homes in, 178–79; middle class, 172; self-help in, 154; services in, 128; and social movements, 194–96, 241; study of, 166, 167, 189–90. *See also* Community
Netherlands: family policy of, 91; health in, 126; income distribution in, 36; income redistribution in, 37; inequality in, 39; literacy in, 113; minimum income policy of, 62, 76; social wage in, 51; social welfare expenditure of, 35; squatting in, 180; teen pregnancy and birth in, 102; unemployment policies of, 35, 66; urbanization of, 154
Newark, New Jersey, 119, 137, 172
New Deal, 10, 11, 21, 27–28, 48, 187, 191, 230
New England, 44, 154
New Guinea, 90
New Haven, 47, 157, 171
New Jersey, 44, 95–96, 98–103, 112, 119–21, 196
New Right, 9, 111
New York City, 15, 92, 148, 165, 195; AIDS in, 137–39; as a converting city, 168; deindustrialization of, 60; gentrification in, 176; hardship ratio of, 172; home-care workers in, 146–47; homelessness in, 173, 174, 179–80, 185; housing vouchers in, 181; public aid in, 63, 64; redevelopment in, 169; in social work history, 26; white-collar jobs in, 191; workers' clinic in, 157
New York State, 67, 90, 93, 112, 139, 178, 205–6
New Zealand, 36, 110
Nicaragua, 113–14
Nixon administration, 188
Nonprofits, 1–2, 8, 93, 178–79, 181, 183, 189, 233
North Korea, 237
Norway, 35–37, 39, 66, 126
Nuclear war, 138
Nuclear waste, 181
Nurses, 15–16, 73, 86, 115, 145–46, 223
Nursing homes, 119, 128–30, 145, 178, 206
Nutrition, 40, 44, 86, 96, 115, 124, 142, 147–48, 150, 181

Occupational segregation, 53, 98
Oedipal conflict, 97
Old Age, Survivors, and Disability Insurance. *See* Social Security
Old old, 67, 136
Ombudspersons, 136
Organisation for Economic Cooperation, 35, 37
Organizations, 128, 208–11, 222–23, 238–39. *See also* Bureaucracy
Out-of-wedlock births, 58–59, 101–2

Outreach, 179, 184, 185

Pain, 134–35, 152
Paraprofessionals, 70
Parental Benefit Insurance, 95
Parenting, 87, 91, 92, 101, 111, 115–16, 120, 134, 147, 207
Paris, 165, 196, 235
Participant observation, 190, 217
Paternity benefits, 90–91, 95
Patients. See Clients
Patriarchy, 84–85, 90, 98, 142, 152, 208, 240
Patriotism, 209
Peace studies, 120
Peasantry, 22, 45, 49
Pedestrians, 194
Pensions, 25, 34, 35, 45. See also Social Security
People's Park, 196
Personal troubles and public issues, 14–15, 28–29
Philadelphia, 165, 169, 180, 181
Philanthropy, 21
Placeness, 194, 196
Poland, 39, 116
Policy feedback, 24
Polish Americans, 22
Political parties, 23, 37, 196, 238–39
Pollution, 141, 145, 186, 189, 193, 210, 235
Poor laws, 10, 21–22, 25, 43
Poor persons. See Poverty
Popular power, 241
Populism, 196
Poverty, 3, 29–30, 47, 54–61, 108, 188, 206–7; and AIDS, 140; in capitalism, 26, 44, 235; categories of, 13, 23, 46; characteristics of, 58, 74–76; and child abuse, 99; and child care, 92–95; and child support, 62–63; in cities, 165–67, 170–71, 204, 235; city and suburban, 172; comparative, 36–37; as a crime, 21; determinants of, 55; and economic stagnation, 230; and education, 109, 111, 115–16; and family planning, 218–20; and full employment, 65–66; functions of, 75; and health/health care, 124–28, 141–42, 154, 210; and homelessness, 173–83; incidence of, 2, 54–55, 57–58; and income redistribution, 52–54; and income security, 45–50, 53, 75, 96, 236; and inequality, 54; means test for, 25; and mental health, 143; of peasants, 22; as a public issue, 14; and public works, 191–92; and the Reagan administration, 5, 9; relative and absolute, 54; rural, 56; social deficit of, 44–45, 73, 76; and social planning, 236; and social work, 25–27; as a state concern, 21; stigma of, 44–45; and taxation, 232; and uneven development, 171; and urban renewal, 169; and work, 56–57, 96, 190. See also Female-headed families; Poverty line; Underclass; War on Poverty; Working poor
Poverty line, 46, 54–57, 63, 68, 69, 125, 210
Power, 83, 164, 225

Practitioners, 179; and administrators, 15–16; and AIDS, 138–40, 148–49; and burnout, 16, 70, 103, 118, 156, 225; and clients, 71–72, 225; devaluation of, 16, 70–71; discretion of, 16, 70, 221–23, 225; factions among, 204; in family planning, 219–20; feminist, 151–55; gender relationships of, 102; in health care, 132–35, 145–49; in holistic health care, 150–51; with homelessness, 183–86; and impersonality, 17–18; isolation of, 222; latent power of, 71, 225; in mental health, 179; pay of, 72; and political struggle, 4–5, 13, 16; professionalization of, 17, 25–28, 71–72; in public aid, 69–77, 221–22; radical, 71, 221–22; and research, 220–25; in research, 217–20; in schools, 116–21; in social planning, 236; and social policy, 4, 220–25; tasks of, 16; and Taylorism, 69–70; and unions, 17–18, 71–72, 224–25; women as, 86, 96–98, 117–21. See also Caseworkers; Medical doctors; Midwives; Nurses; Social workers; Teachers
Pregnancy, 47, 68, 90–92, 101–2, 115, 124, 142, 144, 154
Prevention, 101–2, 137–45, 153, 157, 210, 232, 234
Primal model of social dependency, 25
Privacy rights, 139, 178, 223
Private practice, 17, 18, 76, 124–25
Private sector, 70; and AIDS, 137; and child care, 92, 93; and education, 111; and health care, 126, 128–35, 141, 145; and housing, 183, 188; pay in, 72; and privatization, 8, 111, 180–83; and public sector, 8, 49, 70, 98, 111, 117, 126, 141, 233–34; and social policy, 1, 2, 40; and social welfare expenditure, 35, 45; and the Welfare State, 35–36, 188, 233–34
Privatization, 4, 8, 93–94, 111, 181–83, 233
Professionalization, 17, 21, 25–28, 71–77, 154, 203, 221–22
Professionals, 10, 15–18, 179, 210–11, 221–22, 224
Professions, 4, 13, 118, 132, 148–50, 154, 222–25, 233
Proletarianization, 17, 21–23, 135, 156
Proletarians. See Workers
Promenades, 194
Provincialism, 196, 233–34
Psychiatric social work, 28, 210
Psychiatry, 210
Psychotherapy, 18, 27, 99, 124–25, 143–44, 179
Public aid, 115, 164; bureaucratism of, 221; categorical nature of, 46, 61–62; fraud in, 47; and homelessness, 176, 184; and income redistribution, 53; introduction of, 28; and the mentally ill, 177; payments of, 47, 59, 63, 67; and poverty, 55–57, 75; recipients of, 47–48, 56, 58, 73–77; reform of, 67, 76–77; and social class, 34, 60; stigma of, 13; and the Welfare state, 23–24; and work effort, 46,

64; workers in, 17, 69–77, 221–22; and workfare, 12, 63–65. See also AFDC; General Assistance; Supplemental Security Income
Public assistance. See Public aid
Public employees, 24, 35, 69–77, 172, 183, 224
Public health, 40, 123, 128, 142–45, 149, 210
Public housing, 8, 115, 164, 172, 181–82, 185, 187–89, 191
Public transportation, 169, 232, 237
Public works, 10, 191–92, 194, 237
Puerto Ricans, 147
Punctuated growth, 20–21, 48, 231
Pyongyang, 237

Quality of life, 40, 146–47, 177, 188–90, 192–94, 207, 215

Race, 82, 103, 109; desegregation of, 107, 108, 233–34; and discrimination, 45, 111; and health, 124; and health care, 127, 210; and health-care jobs, 146; heterogeneity of, 37, 120; and human rights, 240; and poverty, 58, 62; and rationing, 127; segregation of, 166, 170, 171; and social indicators, 189. See also Minority groups
Racism, 13, 60, 74, 139, 142, 143, 189, 205, 212, 216
Rape, 153, 224–25
Rationality, 192, 204, 212, 214, 222, 236
Rationing, 124–28
Reagan administration, 9; and AFDC, 56–57; and AIDS, 137; and CETA, 55; and child care, 93–94; and cities, 172, 186; and cost-benefit analysis, 214; and decline in societal health, 206–7; and education, 108, 110–12; and female-headed families, 57, 125; and greed, 231; and health care, 130; and homelessness, 174–75, 180–83; illegality in, 9, 214; and income redistribution, 52; and inequality, 53–54; legacy of, 5; militarization in, 232; and occupational safety/health, 155–56, 214; and poverty, 55; and public employees, 69; and public housing, 187; reaction to, 231; and taxes, 232; and unemployment insurance, 68; and Welfare State cutbacks, 4, 16, 21, 50, 55–57, 68, 108, 125, 186, 214, 230; and the working poor, 56–57
Reciprocity, 29, 83, 224
Recreation, 85–86, 134, 193
Referral, 128, 152, 181
Reform, 8, 24, 26, 165–66, 223, 238–39
Rehabilitation, 153, 178–80, 184–85, 195
Relationships: and the auto, 193; conflict in, 44; gender, 97, 118; impersonality in, 17–18; of parents and children, 87; of practitioners and clients, 17–18, 29, 73–77, 153, 221, 224; reciprocity in, 29, 76; and social reproduction, 82–83; stress in, 44; subordination in, 118

Religion, 129; and capitalism, 8; in the corporate city, 169–70; decline of, 21, 133, 240; and homelessness, 180, 183; and public schools, 111, 120; resources of, 233; and social practice, 25, 27
Rent control, 195–96
Reproduction, 9, 83, 88, 155, 208, 218–20, 224–25. See also Sex
Research, 202–25; action, 116; on alienation, 156; applied, 203–20; ethics of, 211–12; evaluation, 204, 211–15; expenditure for, 202; experimental, 63, 95–96, 153, 177, 211–12, 217; and informed consent, 212; limitations of, 215; limitations on, 211–213; multiplism, 217; natural experiment, 217; policy indicators in, 215–17; qualitative, 190, 217–19; quantitative, 190, 208, 212–13, 215–19; social indicators in, 188–89, 215–16; and social policy, 218, 220–25; and social practice, 217, 218, 220–25; and societal learning, 215; survey, 190, 218–20; and technical communities, 216. See also Data
Residential treatment centers, 143, 178
Revolution, 12, 21, 22, 241–42
Right-to-know, 157
Rizzo administration, 180
Role, 108, 153
Roosevelt administration, 27, 187–88, 230
Rotterdam, 168
Ruling class, 11

St. Louis, 167–68, 172, 188
San Diego, 64, 172
Sandinistas, 113–14
San Francisco, 119, 137–40, 157, 165, 168, 171, 172, 195, 196
Sanitation, 135, 142, 178, 236–37
Schizophrenia, 33, 177
School of Social Service Administration, 27
Schools: achievement in, 94, 96, 110, 113, 118; as child-care facilities, 94, 114–16, 120; and citizenship, 110–12; criticism of, 110–11; desegregation of, 109, 112; dropouts from, 68, 206; have and have-not, 112; as health-care facilities, 114–16, 127, 144; medical, 136, 149, 153; and the New Right, 111; nursing, 145–46; planning for, 205; and privacy rights, 223; private and public, 120; public, 84, 107–8; residential, 100; segregation of, 112; sex education in, 102; and social control, 84; and socialization, 84, 106, 111; and social policy, 107, 111, 208; social practice in, 117–21; and social reproduction, 83–84, 106–7; and social stratification, 108–12; staffing of, 63; student tutors in, 118–19; tracking of, 108, 112. See also Education
Science, 133, 203–4, 211–12, 214–17
Scientific charity, 25–26
Scientific management. See Taylorism

Second World, 33–34, 39–41. See also Socialism
Segregation, 108, 112–13, 166, 170–72, 177, 235
Self-activity, 5, 196, 237. See also Empowerment
Self-care. See Self-help
Self-help, 118–19, 138, 152–55, 217, 223–25
Self-identity, 44, 186, 194–96
Self-management. See Self-activity
Seoul, 237
Service Employees International Union, 224
Settlement houses, 26–27, 165
Sex, 82, 115, 134, 138–40, 149, 152–54, 189, 209, 240. See also Gender
Sex education, 9, 102, 115, 119, 139, 149
Sexism, 74, 142, 151–52, 189, 205, 212, 216
Sheltered workshops, 209
Sierra Leone, 33
Singapore, 165, 168
Slavery, 242
Smith College, 28–29
Smoking, 141, 144, 145, 210, 232
Snowbelt, 13, 60, 170–72, 186. See also Sunbelt
Social casework, 27, 29. See also Social workers
Social change, 229–42; and the city, 192–97; and class struggle, 83; cycles of, 21; and the family, 84–90; grass-roots, 194–95; and income security, 48–50; radical, 71; and schools, 111–12; and self-help, 153; and social indicators, 190, 206–8; and social movements, 196–97; and social policy, 1, 21, 229–34; and unions, 71–72
Social class, 10, 60, 62, 103, 119; in capitalism, 12, 22, 39–41; and the city, 166–67, 170–71, 235; and class consciousness, 22; and class struggle, 23, 24, 37, 83, 166–67, 195; and education, 108–12, 114–16, 120, 209; and gentrification, 175–76; and health, 124; and health care, 124–28, 136, 210; and ideology, 133; and inequality, 54; and mental health, 124–25; polarization of, 54, 176; and public aid, 34; segregation by, 170–72; and social change, 231; and social movements, 196–97; and social reproduction, 82–84; and Social Security, 24; and the social wage, 51; and the state, 11, 37; and taxation, 232; and uneven development, 171
Social control, 14, 84, 154, 156, 225
Social democracy, 23, 37–38, 181
Social dependency, 34, 49–50, 85–86, 96–97, 172
Social dependency ratio, 49–50, 206
Social diagnosis, 26, 27
Social forecasting, 205–6
Social indicators, 189–90, 206–8, 214–16
Social insurance, 23–24, 34, 46–51, 203. See also Social Security
Social investment, 233
Socialism: agenda for, 241–42; as alternative to capitalism, 21, 23, 231; bureaucratism in, 237–39;

and capitalism, 32, 39–41, 53, 236, 238, 239, 242; economic development of, 239; economism of, 238, 239; failures of, 61, 238, 239; and full employment, 40, 236; health and health care in, 127, 145, 236; and insurgency, 241; and literacy, 40; paradox of, 241; potential of, 241–42; practitioners and clients in, 237; problems of, 145, 239, 240; and revolution, 22; social needs in, 238; social planning in, 236–39; social welfare in, 39–41; strengths of, 145, 187; successes of, 242; and uneven development, 189, 236–37; in the United States, 5, 26; and the Welfare State, 4, 37–41; and workers, 22
Socialization, 8, 12, 51, 83–84, 95, 97–98, 106–8
Social movements, 14, 16, 28, 49, 165–67, 194–97, 202–3, 230, 240–42
Social needs: of the aged, 3, 136; characteristics of, 8; comparative, 33–34, 39–41; of deindustrialization, 192; and economic stagnation, 230; of the family, 90–91; and health care, 125–26; for housing, 174–75, 187–88; identification of, 203, 205–8, 217; of immigrant workers, 26–27; internationalization of, 239; and militarization, 39; versus private profits, 192, 234, 238; and social planning, 234; and social policy, 8, 28; of the Third World, 33–34; of women, 89, 231
Social planning, 192, 204, 234–39. See also City planning
Social problems: and the city, 164–66; comparative, 33–34; in industrial capitalism, 25–26; internationalization of, 239; and medicalization, 124–35; of the mentally ill, 179; and professions, 210–11; and public housing, 188–89; as public issues, 14; and schools, 112–16; social construction of, 236; and research, 203–5, 217–20
Social reproduction, 82–98, 106–7, 196
Social science, 7, 14–15, 26, 74, 156, 165–67, 202–25
Social Security, 39, 46–51, 62, 68, 232, 240; and demographic change, 50; growth of, 11, 23–24, 34, 230; and homelessness, 184; and influence of the aged, 13; and the New Right, 9; payments for, 47, 67; and poverty, 55; and the Reagan administration, 9, 10; recipients of, 47–48; reforms for, 67; and social class, 24; and social dependency, 206; support for, 205; trade-offs of, 204–5
Social services, 68, 193–94; for the aged, 181; for AIDS, 139–40; case management, 73–77, 179, 184; for child abuse, 99–102; consolidation of, 128; debureaucratization of, 223; eligibility for, 18; for the homeless, 184–85; privatization of, 181; in public aid, 71, 73–77; retrenchment of, 181; state provision of, 8, 154; of unions, 17; and

Welfare State pluralism, 233–34; and workfare, 64
Social status, 9, 17–18, 44, 75, 108, 109, 134, 175, 211, 222
Social stratification, 108–12, 124–28, 146–47
Social wage, 13, 50–51, 166–67, 195
Social welfare expenditure, 1–3, 8, 10, 21, 28, 34–36, 39–41
Social work, 15, 20, 25–30, 73–77, 98–103, 221–22, 231, 236
Social workers, 4, 14–18, 28, 70–77, 102, 115, 147, 179, 219–20
Society, 205; alienation in, 156; and the auto, 193–94; capitalist, 12, 15, 156, 164, 196; and caring work, 117; change in, 83, 107, 196–97, 230, 241–42; comparative study of, 32–41, 207; contradictions in, 29–30, 192; and deinstitutionaliza-tion, 178; ebb and flow of senti-ments in, 231; health problems of, 135–40, 142–45; and income distri-bution, 52–54; and income secu-rity, 45–46; integration of, 107, 108, 111; interests of, 237; medicalization of, 134–35; per-sonal troubles and public issues in, 14–15; and poverty, 44–45; re-production of, 82–98, 106–7; scale and complexity of, 4, 8, 46; social control in, 14; and social depen-dency, 46; and social indicators, 206–7; socialist, 187, 237; and so-cial policy, 1, 7; and social work, 27; stability of, 12, 45; traditional, 18
Sociological imagination, 14
Sociology. See Social science
Solidarity, 15, 17, 18, 45, 71, 85–87, 224, 240–42
South Africa, 90, 95, 233
South Korea, 90, 237
Spain, 36, 39, 126
Speculation, 60, 171, 175–76, 180, 235
Spirituality, 150, 240
Squatting, 180, 196
Standard of living, 22, 33, 36, 45–46, 53–54, 70, 75, 176, 241
State: and bureaucracy, 21, 154, 212, 238–39; and class struggle, 23; and collective consumption, 192–93, 195; as data consumer, 202; and ed-ucation, 107–9; and enterprise zones, 183; and health care, 128–32, 135, 136, 144; and housing, 188; and income security, 45; legitimacy of, 12, 72; limited boundaries of, 239; and poverty, 44; and racial in-tegration, 234; rise of, 21, 24–25, 231; and social dependency, 46; in socialism, 40, 238; and social move-ments, 195–96; and social plan-ning, 234; structure of, 38; and the wealthy, 54; and Welfare State plu-ralism, 233–34; and women, 155; and workers, 166–67
State government: and child care, 91, 94; and cities, 172, 188; and deinstitutionalization, 177; em-ployees of, 71, 117; and health care, 126, 140; and income secu-rity, 46, 48–49; and reformers, 165–66; and self-help, 225; and social policy, 24–25, 38; and transna-tional corporations, 186

Stereotypes, 119, 152, 172
Sterilization, 218–20
Stigma, 13, 18, 44–47, 63, 70–71, 134, 136, 139, 143, 188
Stress, 44, 85–87, 100–101, 103, 144, 156–57, 225
Subemployment, 65
Substance abuse, 68, 99, 138, 206. See also Alcoholism
Suburbanization, 107, 111–12, 170, 171
Suburbs, 60, 111–12, 119–21, 165, 167, 169–72, 174, 182, 190–91
Sudan, 90
Sudden infant death syndrome, 134
Suicide, 68, 73, 138, 206
Sunbelt, 170, 172, 186. See also Snow-belt
Supplemental Security Income, 46–50, 55
Surplus labor, 22–23. See also Unem-ployment
Survey research, 47, 190, 216, 218–20
Sweden: change in, 240; civil rights in, 36; economic performance of, 66; family allowance of, 96; full employment policy of, 66, 76; health and health care in, 126, 144–45, 208; inequality in, 36–37, 39; influence of labor in, 23, 37; labor productivity in, 36, 66; mili-tarization in, 38; nationalization in, 38; occupational safety and health in, 157; parental leave pol-icy of, 95; politics in, 37–38; pov-erty in, 37; public works in, 191; sex education in, 102; sex role de-bate in, 98; single mothers in, 61; social wage in, 51; social welfare expenditure of, 35, 66; teen preg-nancy and birth in, 102; tension in, 238; unemployment policies of, 35; unemployment rates in, 191; unionization in, 37; urbaniza-tion of, 165; as Welfare State leader, 35, 37–39, 240
Switzerland, 35, 36, 66, 113
Sydney, 168
Systems analysis, 212–15

Tacoma, 179, 183–86
Taxation, 141; and cities, 172, 173, 182; and corporations, 171; and en-terprise zones, 182; and the fiscal crisis of the state, 2, 172; and fiscal welfare, 10, 52; and housing, 188; and income redistribution, 36–37, 51, 53; and income security, 46; progressive, 10, 36; reform of, 68, 196, 232; and subsidies, 8, 171
Taylorism, 69–70, 146, 168, 212
Teachers, 15–18, 83, 93, 106–7, 110, 111, 114–21, 134, 221
Team approach, 204
Technology: and AIDS education, 139; in applied research, 203–4, 215–17; and capital mobility, 173; and economic development, 34; in health care, 123–24, 127–36, 145, 148–52, 207–8; and the internation-alization of capitalism, 168; and political mobilization, 34; and pri-vacy rights, 223; and social prob-lems, 207–8; and suburbanization, 170; and unemployment, 13, 60

Teenagers, 68, 89–90, 101–2, 115, 116, 144, 147, 206
Tenants, 154, 182, 188–89, 195–96
Territoriality, 166–67, 196
Texas, 67, 70, 112
Third World, 41; capitalist and so-cialist nations in, 33, 145, 236–37; data collection in, 207, 219; defini-tion of, 33; and enterprise zones, 182; exploitation of, 33, 131–32; health care in, 131–32; hunger in, 44; life expectancy in, 33; national liberation movements in, 240; poverty of, 33; social welfare ex-penditure in, 34; and uneven de-velopment, 171, 186; urbanization in, 236–37; and the world econ-omy, 33, 131–32, 168, 171, 182, 190
Tokyo, 165, 168, 174
Toronto, 72, 168
Total institutions, 223
Toynbee Hall, 26
Training, 8, 12, 55–56, 63–64, 68–69, 72, 177, 191–92, 217
Transnational corporations, 131–32, 171, 173, 186, 190, 238–39
Transportation, 40, 46, 63, 181, 186, 193, 232, 235–37
Triage, 127
Tutoring, 118

Ukrainian Americans, 22
Underclass, 60, 62
Underemployment, 3, 22, 33–34, 56, 57, 65, 190, 239
Undernutrition, 44
Unemployment, 189; and African Americans, 59–61; in capitalism, 22, 26, 33–34, 65, 76, 239; and child care, 92; and child support, 62–63; chronic, 59; city and subur-ban, 172, 190–91; comparative policies for, 35, 66; and deindustri-alization, 191, 192; in the Great De-pression, 10, 49; and health, 141–42, 156; and homelessness, 173–74, 179, 185; and income secu-rity, 45–50; and the market, 12, 56, 65; and mental health, 33–34; as a public issue, 13, 124; and public works, 191–92; social deficit of, 44–45; and social stability, 12; and the social wage, 13; structural, 13, 14; and uneven development, 192; and urbanization, 165–66; and the Welfare State, 3, 13, 35
Unemployment insurance, 24–25, 28, 35, 46–50, 67–68
Uneven development, 65, 167, 171, 175, 187, 192, 194, 235–37
Unions: basis of, 22; benefits of, 121; and collective action, 196, 224–25; decline of, 71–72; and the fiscal crisis of the city, 172; growth of, 26–27; industrial, 23; influence of, 28, 37, 72; and occupational safety/health, 157; and plant clos-ings, 192; and practitioners, 17, 28, 71–72, 103; public employee, 71–72, 103, 120–21; and the public school, 107; resources of, 233; and the rise of the Welfare State, 23, 37; and social change, 71–72, 107; and social policy, 13, 16, 222–25; social services of, 17, 224; and

urban redevelopment, 168–69; and workers' pay, 72
United Auto Workers, 224
United Farm Workers, 224
United Kingdom: cities in, 168; conservative retrenchment in, 3; education in, 110; the family in, 84–85; health care in, 127, 140–42, 144–45, 208; inequality in, 36–37, 39; minimum income policy of, 62; occupational safety and health in, 157; policy research in, 202; poverty in, 10, 21–22, 25, 43, 45–46, 57; and the rise of the Welfare State, 23, 24; single mothers in, 57, 61; social wage in, 51; social welfare expenditure of, 35, 39; social work in, 26, 71; teen pregnancy and birth in, 102; unemployment policies of, 35, 66
United Nations, 44, 114, 137, 207, 239–41
United States: aging population of, 3, 10–11, 116, 136; AIDS in, 137–38; the auto in, 193–94; census of, 52, 54, 57, 88, 189, 206; child-care needs of, 88–95; cities of, 165, 167–73; conservative retrenchment in, 3; economic problems of, 9, 16–17, 39, 53, 54, 66, 156, 174; education in, 9, 107–13; environmentalism in, 149; the family in, 85–88; fiscal crisis in, 69; health and health care in, 50, 123–57, 177, 208; heterogeneity of, 37, 61; homelessness in, 173–83; housing problems in, 189; hunger in, 44; illiteracy in, 113–14; income redistribution in, 52; individualism in, 38; inequality in, 36–37, 39, 40, 52–54, 75, 238; labor productivity in, 36, 66; migration in, 49; militarization of, 38–39, 232–33; nationalization in, 38; occupational safety and health in, 9, 149, 155–57, 214; origins of Welfare State in, 101–2; physical fitness in, 86; political decentralization of, 37, 140–41; poverty in, 37, 54–61, 75; privatization in, 181–83; public housing in, 187–89; religion in, 240; research in, 202; social change in, 11, 16, 85, 195; social movements in, 240–42; social welfare expenditure of, 1, 3, 8, 35, 39, 45; social work in, 26–28; squatting in, 180; suburbanization in, 170–72; taxation in, 232; unemployment policies of, 35; urban policy of, 186, 188, 235; as Welfare State laggard, 35–39, 41, 46, 51, 53, 61, 90–91, 95, 96, 102, 113, 140, 157, 234, 238; as Welfare State leader, 110; workers in, 13, 37, 40, 41, 71, 155–57
United Way, 1, 183
Universal Declaration of Human Rights, 240–42

University of Chicago, 27, 115, 190, 204, 216
University of Michigan, 47, 216
Urbanization, 26, 85, 164–67, 204. See also Cities
Urban renewal, 60, 168–69, 171, 175, 188, 195, 235
USSR, 108, 110; AIDS in, 137; bureaucratism in, 238–39; economic development of, 239; health care in, 140, 141; inequality in, 40; literacy in, 113; social policy of, 40–41, 238; social welfare expenditure of, 39; uneven development in, 187; workers' pay in, 40

Values, 12, 38, 45, 60, 82–84, 109, 110, 208, 215–16
Veterans' benefits, 35
Volunteers, 115, 119, 180
Voucher programs, 48, 111, 181, 185

War, 29–30, 38–39, 138, 205
Warfare/welfare expenditure, 2, 3, 5, 232–33
War on Poverty, 4, 15, 21, 28, 55–56, 115, 188, 213, 230
Washington, DC, 68, 176, 188, 202
Wealth, 4, 5, 9, 52–54, 83, 164, 232
Welfare. See Public aid
Welfare hotels, 174, 179–80
Welfare State pluralism, 233–34
West Germany, 53, 110; health care in, 127, 144; housing benefits in, 188; income redistribution in, 37; inequality in, 36, 39; minimum income policy of, 62; occupational safety and health in, 157; single mothers in, 61; social wage in, 51; social welfare expenditure of, 35; unemployment policies of, 35; urbanization of, 165. See also Germany
White Anglo-Saxon Protestants, 107, 109
Wisconsin, 63, 67
Women: and AFDC, 47; affirmative action for, 205; African American, 74; bodies of, 152, 155; and capitalism, 61, 86–87; caring work of, 86–87, 96–98, 102, 146; and CETA, 55; child-care responsibilities of, 88–89, 91–93, 97–98, 114–16; as clients, 18; and the Democratic Party, 231–32; double burden of, 87; economic independence of, 88; and entry into paid labor force, 10–11, 88–89, 208, 230; and the family, 84–88, 233; and family planning, 217–20; health care of, 151–55, 157; in health care, 146–49; longevity of, 88–89; mental health of, 143; oppression of, 86–87, 98, 155, 193; and poverty, 23, 55, 57–61, 75; and socialism, 61; and social policy, 9; and Social Security, 67; as teachers, 117–20; in

unions, 17, 224; unpaid work of, 193, 223; violence against, 153, 212–13; and Welfare State work, 17, 74, 117, 146
Work, 46; burnout in, 70, 156; controlling the pace of, 223; deskilling of, 70; flextime for, 94–95; and health care, 127, 142, 149, 155–57; and home, 83, 86, 195; and a minimum income, 96; overload in, 120, 155; and parental leave, 95; and poverty, 46, 56–57, 96; and public aid, 63–65; safety and health of, 155–57, 210; satisfaction with, 70, 96, 146; skilled and unskilled, 190–91; and social benefits, 40, 46, 91; underload in, 156; white collar, 190–91
Workers, 3; active versus retired, 204–6; in bureaucracies, 220–25; child-care needs of, 90–92; class consciousness of, 22; clinics for, 157; and the Democratic Party, 10; deprivations of, 43–44; deskilling of, 70; discipline of, 12, 22–23, 65; divisions among, 23; economic problems of, 16–17, 176, 235; education of, 107–9, 111, 157; and gentrification, 175–76; health and health care of, 124–28, 157, 214; and holistic health care, 151; housing for, 183, 189; as human capital, 55–56; income of, 2, 53–54, 61; income security of, 45–51, 56, 58, 67–68; influence of, 23, 26, 37, 41; interests of, 166; job problems of, 65–66, 155–57; and the minimum wage, 56, 66–67; poverty of, 22–23, 235; and the Reagan administration, 5, 9, 53, 155–56; relocation and retraining of, 191–92; and revolution, 22, 235; and self- help, 154; as social class, 12; social needs of, 26–27, 43–45; social rights of, 66, 240–42; social wage of, 13, 50–51; and social work, 26, 27; and taxation, 51, 232; as threat to capitalism, 22, 23, 45, 235; and unions, 22, 71–72; and the Welfare State, 11, 24, 231. See also Practitioners
Workers' Compensation, 26, 35
Workfare, 4, 12, 63–65, 68–69, 94
Working class. See Workers
Working poor, 56–57, 69, 148, 174, 176
World Bank, 33, 36, 38, 44, 126, 207
World War II, 49, 60, 91, 168, 170–71, 191, 206, 212, 237, 240

Yale University, 154, 157
Yuppies, 175–76

Zaire, 131–32
Zoning, 168–69, 171, 178, 190, 196, 234